HOWL
LIKE THE
WOLVES

HOWL
LIKE THE WOLVES
GROWING UP IN NAZI GERMANY
BY MAX VON DER GRÜN

TRANSLATION FROM THE GERMAN BY JAN VAN HEURCK
DOCUMENTATION BY CHRISTEL SCHULTZ
PREFACE BY MALTE DAHRENDORF

WILLIAM MORROW AND COMPANY
NEW YORK   1980

Translation copyright © 1980 by William Morrow and Company, Inc.

Original copyright © 1979 by Hermann Luchterhand Verlag GmbH & Co KG, Darmstadt and Neuwied, West Germany

First published in German under the title *Wie war das eigentlich?*

Printed in the United States of America.

1 2 3 4 5 6 7 8 9 10

Library of Congress Cataloging in Publication Data

Grün, Max von der.
  Howl like the wolves.

  Translation of Wie war das eigentlich?
  Bibliography: p.
  Includes index.
  Summary: The author intersperses his account of his youth in Nazi Germany with numerous documents and photographs from that period.
    1. Grün, Max von der—Biography. 2. Authors, German—20th century—Biography.
[1. Grün, Max von der. 2. Authors, German. 3. Germany—History—20th century.
4. World War, 1939-1945—Germany] I. Title.
PT2667.R83Z52413   838'.91409 [B] [92]   80-19144
ISBN 0-688-22252-8   ISBN 0-688-32252-2 (lib. bdg.)

TABLE OF CONTENTS

"Hitler wanted Communism"; "Without him I believe that Germany would not have been built up again." We find these and similar statements in Dieter Bossmann's collection of essays written by German schoolchildren, a book entitled *Was ich über Adolf Hitler gehört habe* [What I have heard about Adolf Hitler]. This collection was published in 1977, but it was clear long before then how little German young people know about National Socialism. Bossmann's book merely exposes a chronic defect in the German educational system that has existed since the earliest days of the Federal Republic, resulting from a multiplicity of causes. Certainly the defect is not the fault of the young people themselves but instead makes clear a failure on the part of the older generation, among whom it has never really become popular to take a clear-cut stand against Fascism. Ultimately each generation derives its entire knowledge of history from the generation that immediately precedes it: Young people cannot know what their elders fail to teach them.

The problem began immediately after the famous and infamous twelve years of the Third Reich came to an end (and as we all know, it was not the Germans themselves who ended them), when Germans repressed the shocking events in which they themselves had actively or passively participated, or altered those events in their minds in such a way that they could live with what had happened and could turn their attention to rebuilding their shattered country with an easy conscience. The onslaught of anti-Fascism was swiftly eliminated, above all by "de-Nazification" and the widespread integration of former Nazis into the new state. Reports and literary depictions designed to clarify the experiences of recent German history went largely unnoticed and had no effect on political thinking. The existence of a new democratic order and the abundance of present-day problems that clamored for immediate attention provided many people with a ready excuse for leaving the past in the past. A cosmetic job was performed on the National Socialist era until it began to look no more serious than a traffic accident. No open discussion took place between the generations about this period.

Ever since around 1960, the authors of literature for German children and young adults have been attempting to initiate such a discussion, and although some of their efforts certainly merit our attention, most of the works that they produced represent an attempt at self-justification and express a clearly perceptible relief that the German people are finally free of the specter. Their books were incapable of overcoming the "communication gap" between the generations with regard to the Hitler era. Obviously, because of their anxiety, insecurity, and repressed feelings of guilt, Germans had not only neglected to pass on to their children historical information that it was essential for them to know, but they had even failed to awaken in them a readiness to listen and to discuss what had occurred.

Nor must we forget that under the stress of German reconstruction and the development of a society based on the principle of conspicuous consumption, literature lost status and developed into a mere source of entertainment to which people no longer turned in order to gain knowledge, insight, and awareness of problems. The general lack of information and perception about the National Socialist era reflects a general decline of interest in history, which, once again, is something that the younger generation acquires from its elders. The increasing tempo of a consumer economy contributed to the tendency to gloss over the facts of history, and especially the facts of recent history.

In my opinion, Max von der Grün's book not only bears out what I have been saying but is a major contribution toward solving the problem. In this book the author has struck off on a new course: He interweaves his autobiography with the tale of historical events. Because he was born in 1926, the years of his developing consciousness were all spent during the twelve years of the Hitler era—for in fact he had no other choice. By interweaving the story of his personal life with the events of a universal, collective history, he lends to the depiction of this history a depth and penetration that could not have been achieved by means of a mere autobiographical account, a mere factual recitation of historical events, or a mere assemblage of historical documents. To be sure, a purely autobiographical account can reveal how a single person reacted to the events of the National Socialist era, but such a treatment cannot describe what "actually" happened. (We have seen many examples of such books.) The abstract objectivity of a factual historical account may leave readers cold—especially young readers—and fail to really engage their emotions. Thus the union of both approaches combines the advantages of both and avoids their disadvantages. Moreover, by employing this method, Max von der Grün is able to show how the individual human being is affected by historical events and also to reveal the interaction between the two. The individual is that "common man" whom traditional historians have always been inclined to forget or overlook. As we all know, in the traditional view it is the great leaders who "make" history, whereas the common man is merely the passive receiver of their actions; thus it does not matter if one simply ignores him. But in reality it is the many little people who make history, who actually enact its events, and who are often forced by the great and powerful to enact them precisely as the latter desire. Max von der Grün's approach represents an innovation, for he consistently views history from a new perspective, that of the man looking up from below, and thus this book clearly constitutes a contribution to the democratization of history: For anyone who is as directly affected by history as the "common man" should play a major role in determining what that history is to be.

The author also shows how it was possible, during the twelve-year sway of the Third Reich, for the individual to exist by treading a thin line between criticism and resistance of the regime on the one hand, and playing along with everyone else on the other. Thus he avoids the cliché of suggesting that during that era people were either 100 percent Nazis or 100 percent anti-Nazis—a false impression, by the way, that is often encouraged by the treatment of the Nazi period in literature written for young adults. In *Howl Like the Wolves* Max von der Grün combines a clear declaration of his anti-Fascist position—a position resulting from his experience of historical events—with insight and the ability to draw fine distinctions. The truths he utters are often uncomfortable for both sides. In 1978 a paperback edition of Horst Burger's story *Vier Fragen an meinen Vater* [Four questions I asked my father], originally published in 1976, was published in Germany under the title *Warum warst du in der Hitler-Jugend?* [Why were you in the Hitler Youth?]. Burger's story solves the problem of how to familiarize young people with the historical experience of National Socialism by describing, in historical perspective, a discussion that takes place in contemporary Germany between a father and his son in response to the son's questions about the National Socialist era. Max von der Grün's account, which follows in the same tradition, represents a novel, well-constructed, and highly informative attempt to reveal "what things were really like," and thus to communicate truth across the passage of time. It is a book that everyone should read.

Malte Dahrendorf
Professor of Education
University of Hamburg

HOWL
LIKE THE
WOLVES

ABBREVIATIONS

ADGB	Allgemeiner Deutscher Gewerkschaftsbund (German Trade-Union Federation)
Afa-Bund	Allgemeiner Freier Angestelltenbund (Employees' Federation)
BDM	Bund Deutscher Mädel (German Girls' League)
BRD	Bundesrepublik Deutschlands (Federal Republic of Germany, or West Germany)
DDR	Deutsche Demokratische Republik (German Democratic Republic, or East Germany)
Gestapo	Geheime Staatspolizei (Secret Police)
HJ	Hitler-Jugend (Hitler Youth)
KPD	Kommunistische Partei Deutschlands (German Communist Party)
NSDAP	Nationalsozialistische Deutsche Arbeiterpartei (National Socialist German Labor Party, known as the Nazi Party for short)
SA	Sturmabteilung (storm troopers or "brownshirts")
SS	Schutzstaffel ("protection squad" better known as "blackshirts")
SD	Sicherheitsdienst (security police)
SPD	Sozialdemokratische Partei Deutschlands (German Social Democratic Party, i.e., the Socialist Party)

1926

Of course you can't choose your parents or the times into which you are born.

I was born in 1926 and have often asked myself what things were really like then, just eight years after World War I, which the Germans had lost. The Kaiser was forced to abdicate and had fled to Holland; in 1919 Germany was proclaimed a republic and came to be known as the Weimar Republic. I was born in Bayreuth, in the district of the city known as St. Georg. From the window of our home we looked down on the prison. My mother was twenty-five years old and was, as they said in those days, a maidservant; my father was twenty-six and a journeyman shoemaker. My mother earned twenty reichsmarks a month [then approximately $4.60], plus free room and board, for which she worked from twelve to fourteen hours a day; at harvesttime during the summer and fall she often worked even longer. She had every other Sunday off, but at harvesttime she even had to give up her free Sundays. My father worked, on days when there was something for him to do, in shoemakers' workshops. With luck he could get three or even four days of work a week, but usually he only worked two days, and the money my parents earned between them was not enough to enable them to rent a place to live.

When I was born, my mother did not want to lose her job, so I grew up in my grandmother's home in the mountain district known as the Fichtelgebirge near the Czechoslovakian border, about sixty kilometers north of Bayreuth, along with all those of my uncles and aunts who still lived at home and were not yet married. They were, if they had jobs at all, employed in the chinaware industry.

Had my parents already heard of Hitler by the time I was born? I doubt it, and if they had, then like most Germans they did not take him seriously. Most people regarded him as a maniac who ranted and raved, who had founded a new political party, and who talked a lot of hot air in order to recruit new members. He used abusive language about other people and, of course, promised the world to anyone who would join his cause.

Adolf Hitler was the son of an Austrian customs officer. He lost his father when he was fourteen. After attending secondary school in Linz for several years, he tried without success to get himself accepted as a student at the Vienna Academy of Fine Arts. When he failed at this attempt he gave up the idea of trying to train himself for any of the usual professions and between 1909 and 1913 he earned his living by doing odd jobs in Vienna while he lived in a hostel for the poor. It was during these years that his political views were formed. Despite his impoverished circumstances he did not identify with the proletariat but dreamed of becoming a famous artist and architect. Under the influence of two nationalistic movements in Vienna, he acquired a hatred of labor unions and Socialists as well as anti-Semitic convictions.

When the war broke out in 1914, he was in Munich. He volunteered for military service. In the Army, for the first time, he found the support and discipline that he had encountered nowhere else. As a messenger on the Western front he was awarded the Iron Cross Second Class and the Iron Cross First Class. At the end of the war, after having been gassed, he was in a military hospital in Pomerania where he 'decided to become a politician.' . . . The Bavarian military high command ordered him to be trained and employed as a political agent (Vertrauensmann) to circulate propaganda both within and outside the army. In the course of these activities he joined the German Labor Party and assumed responsibility for its organization and expansion; the party soon began to acquire many new disciples in Bavaria.

In 1920 he named the movement the National Socialist German Labor Party. The 1920 party program combined nationalistic goals (equality of rights between Germany and other nations, the acquisition of German colonies, the annexation of Austria) with markedly socialistic ideas (the nationalization of industry, land reform, a sharing by workers in the profits, an end to the domination of the economic system by invested capital). Some part of this program appealed to all classes of society. In addition, anti-Semitism was an integral part of the party program (the Jews were to lose their civil rights).

Krautkrämer/Radbruch,
Wandel der Welt

14

My father told me that he first became concerned over Hitler's National Socialist German Labor Party (the NSDAP) when the number of brawls occurring in taverns during party rallies and election campaigns began to increase. During these brawls Nazi party members brutally and unscrupulously clubbed, shouted down, and threw out of the tavern anyone who disagreed with them. The Nazis only too often acted on the promise of their battle cry, "If you won't be my buddy, I'll smash your skull."

At this time the average worker was earning 33.9 reichsmarks [approximately $7.80] a week; but the minimum amount a family of two needed to live on was 45.6 reichsmarks [approximately $10.49]. Since World War I had ended in 1918, the number of hours people had to work every week had not diminished but increased. In 1926, the year I was born, the large labor parties had 940,500 paying members, 134,248 of whom belonged to the KPD, the German Communist Party, and 806,268 to the SPD, the Social Democratic Party [Socialists]. By 1933 the number of paying members in the Communist Party had diminished, whereas there were almost 1,000,000 Social Democrats.

Almost 4,000,000 workers were organized in the independent trade unions, and the Christian trade unions contained more than 600,000 members. In 1926 Joseph Goebbels, who had joined the National Socialists in 1922, became district leader of Berlin. As a rule, someone became a district leader when he had begun to establish and organize a local branch of the NSDAP in a new city. Most of the people who became district leaders had not returned to their professions or continued their studies at the end of World War I, but had become actively involved in various veterans' organizations and volunteer corps. Many had failed in their attempts to find their way back into some kind of profession, almost all of them had broken off their training in their chosen careers, and only a few, such as Joseph Goebbels, had completed their secondary-school education. Hitler wanted Goebbels to recruit people in the working-class districts to join the National Socialists.

In the same year, 1926, a book was published that later fit in precisely with the Nazis' plans: *Volk ohne Raum* [A people without space] by Hans Grimm. In this book Grimm appealed to the working classes to join the nationalist cause and to prepare for

15

Joseph Goebbels, Hitler's minister of propaganda.

the German conquest of new "living space." Along with Hitler's
Mein Kampf, this book became the principal ideological hand-
book of the Nazi movement and, after Hitler had come to power,
was required reading in all the schools.

These, then, were the times into which I was born. I was the
child of poor parents who had only one great concern: How shall
we get enough to eat tomorrow? But what they did not know
was that even the problem of getting enough to eat was in reality
a political problem. Poverty reigned throughout Germany. We
had no electric light; from the ceiling hung an oil lamp, which
we could light only in an emergency, for we had to count every
penny. The four families who lived in the house had only one
primitive toilet among them, and it did not flush. Every day, at
least once, my grandmother or a neighbor used to pour a bucket
of hot water into the waste pipe and sprinkle some lime in to
keep the toilet from stinking too much on hot days. But it stank
all the same.

We ate meat only once every other week. Our main meal every
day consisted of herring pickled in brine. As a child I was given
only the tail, but to make up for it I was given lots of potatoes.
They satisfied the appetite, or at least they filled one's stomach.

16

Later, when I was attending school, I used to raise rabbits, often as many as thirty at a time, which I could either sell, or sometimes we slaughtered one ourselves so that we could occasionally have meat on the table.

Most of the houses in our area had wood-burning stoves. We used to fetch the wood out of the nearby forest in a handcart. The woodpiles in the gardens and the yards revealed whether and how well people had made provision for the winter. Winters in the Fichtelgebirge were long and cold.

At party rallies Adolf Hitler was speaking about the future of the Germans, about the great German people who would be free only when they had freed themselves from the Jews.

One could read his words, whose meaning was perfectly clear, as early as 1926. Hitler's book *Mein Kampf* [My struggle] had been published in 1925, and his party program had been published long before that, in 1920. This program stated: "We demand land and soil (colonies) in order to nourish our people and to provide a place for our surplus population to settle.

"Only a German can be a citizen. Only a person of German blood—regardless of his religious denomination—can be considered a German. Thus no Jew can be a German."

The "Jewish question" was, from the very beginning, an integral component of National Socialist ideology. The persecution and the ultimate annihilation of the Jews did not result from any "degeneration" of National Socialist ideals, but formed an essential part of the Nazi creed.

Adolf Hitler certainly did not invent anti-Semitism, a phenomenon of world history that has existed for many centuries. However, Hitler was the ideologist who gave to anti-Semitism a decidedly biological emphasis that it had never possessed before, and as a politician he was determined to carry on its ultimate conclusions this brand of anti-Semitism interpreted in racial terms. . . .

Hitler's theories presupposed a connection between the task of conquering new living space in the East and the idea of the physical extermination of European Jewry, for after all, the native soil of these Jews lay precisely in those Eastern European territories that Hitler wanted Germany to conquer. Thus, shortly before the outbreak of the war, he once again publicly stated what he had already prophesied in *Mein Kampf*: that if there were a

17

war, it would result not in the destruction of Germany but in the destruction of the European Jews.

Walther Hofer

Hitler also demanded a "German" press. All newspaper personnel were supposed to be Germans (non-Jews), and he paved the way to the later burning of the books when he said: "We demand a legal battle against art and literature that has a demoralizing influence on our national life, and the abolition of organizations that violate this demand."

He alone wanted to decide what constituted art and literature. He demanded the right of the government to exercise absolute censorship.

Hitler had chosen to make the swastika his symbol. An Indo-Germanic sign, it had already turned up on the steel helmets of the various so-called volunteer corps. The Nazi flag consisted of red ground, with a white field on which the black swastika was displayed to striking advantage.

Even before Hitler came to power in 1933, his party, employing the strategy of modern advertisers who exhibit their trademarks to attract buyers, displayed its flag on every possible occasion. At the frequent party meetings and marches, gatherings and election rallies, the flag was always prominently displayed, as were the swastikas on armbands. And the times favored familiarizing the people with the NSDAP program by constantly exposing them to the same insignia. After World War I the victors, in the Versailles Peace Treaty, had obliged Germany to pay large and oppressive war reparations fees. Territories—even territories in which the majority of the people were German— had been separated from the German Reich both in the East and in the West. This fact had wounded the nation's pride.

Gerold Anrich

1927

In 1927 Germany became a full member of the International Court of Justice in The Hague in Holland. This move was important because it represented the German Reich's first step since World War I to regain the respect of the international community, and it had done so by subjecting itself to international law.

But the country was seething internally. The persecution of artists whose creations could not be reconciled with German thought patterns, as the Nazis wrongly understood them, began very early. In every period of history reactionary men who wish to reverse the course of history have taken special vengeance on artists, writers, and journalists. They have always been—and if one thinks of Heinrich Böll, who is now being accused of sympathizing with terrorists, still are—favorite targets of men who sanction artistic creations only if such creations coincide with their own political views. Anything that did not fit into their political theory, the Nazis regarded as "soiling one's own nest," as modern Germans say. During the Nazi era the phrase "to soil one's own nest" was still unknown, but people spoke of the "defamation of the German people"—whereby the right-wing Germans claimed that they alone represented the German people.

To serve their purposes, the National Socialists coined terms like "degenerate art," or even worse, "non-Aryan art."

In every age people have distorted historical truth—and this was as true under the Nazi regime as it is today. Each person interprets history in accordance with his own political views. During the twenties Germans were trying to find explanations for their military defeat in 1918. However, since the old militarists and conservative politicians could not admit that through their policies they had driven millions of people to their deaths for no reason, they invented another explanation for Germany's defeat: The left-wingers at home had attacked "the unvanquished army at the front" from the rear, had in fact stabbed it in the back. The phrase "stabbed in the back" became a political concept. Hitler's favorite slogan was that "their own homeland attacked our soldiers from the rear."

General Erich Ludendorff, who had been one of the worst of the warmongers, was honored as a war hero by the German people because of his relationship with von Hindenburg, the President of the Weimar Republic; from the battle of Tannenberg until the end of the war, the two men had collaborated in conducting military operations against the Russians. In 1923 Ludendorff conspired with Hitler to overthrow the democratic government of Bavaria.

The slogan "the November criminals" [referring to those responsible for German capitulation to the Allies in 1918] was used by the rightists as a political weapon against those who favored compliance with the terms of the Treaty of Versailles and a parliamentary system of government.

In 1926 Ludendorff founded the Tannenberg League to combat "international forces," as he called the Freemasons, Jews, Jesuits, and Marxists. Hitler had accepted Ludendorff's aid as he accepted the aid of anyone who he believed could help to pave his way to power. Ludendorff was very popular among the Conservatives in the Republic, and thus when he made common cause with Hitler, they told themselves that Hitler could not be so bad after all. In 1927, the final version of the "Program of the NSDAP" was published. It was accessible to everyone, and everyone had the opportunity to think about what it said. Thus, it is completely untrue to say that the Nazis ever kept their intentions secret.

People who were not interested in politics, people who maintained that they had enough to do just to manage their own affairs quite certainly did not read the Nazi program. And in those days, just as they do today, they claimed, when political catastrophes occurred, that they did not know or even suspect what was going on.

I know from my mother that the different opinions about Adolf Hitler, whose influence no one could overlook after the year 1927, often cut right across families. Some people supported

Handbill issued by Hitler and General Ludendorff during their
abortive attempt to overthrow the democratic government of
Bavaria and then the Weimar Republic in 1923:

Proclamation
to the German people!
The government of the November criminals
in Berlin is today abolished.
A provisional German national government
has been formed by
General Ludendorff,
Adolf Hitler, General von Lossow,
and Colonel von Seisser.

him because he promised employment and that he would make Germany "great." Others opposed him—not because they knew about his political platform and rejected it, but out of a sort of instinct, without being able to justify or put into words what they had against him. But if one listened carefully to the things Hitler said, one could tell, long before he came to power, what he was really after: absolute dominion not only over Germany, not only over all of Europe—which involved the enslavement of other peoples—but over the entire world.

Like many other people, my grandmother, my mother, and her sisters and brothers did not recognize this fact. Only my grandfather remained skeptical, and I remember very clearly how he sometimes used to say softly, "That man will bring us bad luck."

1928

My grandmother used to say that in those days the ground was being auctioned right out from under the very feet of many farmers because they were no longer able to pay their taxes or the high interest on their mortgages. In 1928, two of my uncles lost their jobs. Sometimes they were lucky and managed to hire themselves out as day laborers for one or two days a week, but then they had to be satisfied with whatever wages they were offered, so that at least they would be able to give my grandmother a couple of marks to help pay for their food. Naturally they, like my parents, did not have the money to rent a room of their own but slept at home in a makeshift garret that had been built just under the roof.

That year Germany achieved a record of a remarkable sort: the highest number of workers ever on strike at the same time— 723,415. Although the workers were aware of the risk they were taking by striking, their fear was outweighed by the bitterness they felt at being refused decent wages while their employers were once again earning large profits.

Nevertheless, the German political situation did not really seem too bad, for when parliamentary elections were held, the two major labor parties, the SPD (Social Democrats) and the KPD (Communists), won 42 percent of all the votes between the two of them, and the Federal Chancellor [Reichskanzler], Hermann Müller, was drawn from the ranks of the Social Democrats, who thus controlled the country's most powerful political office. The Social Democrats were still the strongest party in Germany, with the support of over 9,000,000 voters, whereas only 800,000 people had voted for the National Socialists. Germany had a functioning parliament, the Reichstag, and all indications were that it was developing into a permanent, stable democracy. Once again German intellect was the admiration of the world; German scientists enjoyed international reputations; Germany was foremost in the field of architecture; and the German capital, Berlin, had become a world center of culture.

In August, 1928, Germany signed the Kellogg-Briand Pact, which also contributed to the growth of Germany's reputation in the world. The nations that signed this pact condemned war as a means of solving their problems and resolving conflicts:

> Article I. The High Contracting Parties solemnly declare, in the names of their respective peoples, that they condemn recourse to war for the solution of international controversies and renounce it as an instrument of national policy in their relations with one another.
>
> Article II. The High Contracting Parties agree that the settlement and solution of all disputes or conflicts, of whatever nature or of whatever origin they may be, which may arise among them, shall never be sought except by pacific means.
>
> (Originally signed by the United States, France, Belgium, Germany, Great Britain, the British Dominions and Ireland, Italy, Japan, Poland, and Czechoslovakia. By the end of 1929 fifty-four nations had joined the pact, including the Soviet Union, which signed it on September 6, 1928.)

At the end of the year Alfred Hugenberg (1865-1951) became chairman of the German National People's Party. From then on the nationalistic Opposition parties waged sharp political warfare in the Reichstag. Hugenberg was an extremely rigid nationalist, who from 1909 to 1918—a period including the decisive war years—had been chairman of the board of directors of the Krupp armaments concern. After World War I he founded newspapers and film companies like UfA [Universum-Film-Aktiengesellschaft or Universal Films Corporation], and through these media exercised great influence on public opinion. Moreover, he was the one who ultimately combined all the conservative political parties in Germany and, in conjunction with Hitler, formed the Harzburger Front in 1931. A selection from his newspaper *Der Tag* [The day] will serve to demonstrate its rabble-rousing tone:

> With all our hearts we hate the present structure of the government, its form and its content, its origin and its essence. We hate this structure because it is governed not by the best Germans

24

but by a parliamentary system that makes any responsible leadership impossible. . . . We hate this structure because it blocks our prospects of liberating our subjugated fatherland and purging the German people of a false war guilt, of winning for ourselves the living space we need in the East, of freeing the German people once again, and of protecting German agriculture, industry, trades, and crafts from deadly economic war, and restoring their vigor. We want a strong government led by the best man, not one run by irresponsible braggarts and political favorites.

A traditional German kitchen with a placard on the wall expressing Christian sentiments that would undoubtedly have offended the Nazis: "The path to happiness leads through the lowly gate of repentence."

1929

My mother had found a job as a maidservant at a farm near Bayreuth, and her employer gave her permission to bring me, then three years old, to the farm to live with her. My father was journeying from place to place ("being on the road," they called it) and used to knock on the doors of shoemakers and ask them for work. Sometimes he managed to get work for one, two, or three days, but he was paid very little. Usually he worked only for food, drink, and a place to sleep. The food was fairly scanty, for these shoemakers with their own workshops did not have very much themselves.

In summer and fall things got a little better, for then you could go into the woods to pick berries and sell them to merchants for a few pennies. We could get between three and five pfennigs [about one cent] for a pound of blueberries, between eight and twelve pfennigs [about two to three cents] for a pound of cranberries, and ten to twenty pfennigs [about two to five cents] for a pound of fresh mushrooms. There was an abundance of mushrooms and berries in the woods in our area.

I was raised with the farmer's children, and because I was another mouth to feed, a portion of my mother's wages was deducted. At that time it was still customary for domestic servants to enter into a sort of annual contract, which was sealed by a handshake between the farmer and the servant. A servant could change jobs only at Candlemas, that is on February 2 of each year.

My mother owned only one pair of leather shoes, which were for church on Sunday or for dances at the tavern hall. The rest of the year she walked around in wooden shoes without stockings.

On the farm, work was regulated not by the clock but by the sun and rain, summer and winter. Working sixteen hours a day was not unusual, especially at harvesttime. The farmers owned no tractors yet and, indeed, hardly any machines at all, so that

A railway car being used as a home by a family of eight.

all work in the fields was done with horses. The farmer's children, who were no more than nine years old, had to help out in the fields, the stable, and the house. No one worried about the laws prohibiting child labor. The more children you had, the more free labor you possessed.

In the spring of 1929, the political turmoil increased. In March the Prussian Minister of the Interior banned public assemblies and open-air parades. Despite the enforcement of this ban by Berlin Chief of Police Zörgiebel, a Social Democrat, and even though the Social Democratic Party and the labor unions had appealed to everyone to observe it, on May 1 some 200,000 workers obeyed the summons of the German Communist Party (KPD) to attend a peaceful demonstration. A bloody riot between the police and the demonstrators resulted. The official story was, naturally, that the demonstrators were responsible for the bloodbath and that the police had not participated in the fray. Demonstrators were said to have been fighting each other at the barricades, but eyewitness accounts and newspaper reports told

28

a different story. It has been proven that the police even shot at people who were merely looking out their windows or bending over their balconies, and it has been proven that even housewives who were simply out shopping were shot too. A total of thirty-one people was killed, hundreds were wounded, and more than twelve hundred workers were arrested.

Since 1890, the First of May had been the international workers' holiday. May 1, 1929, was the bloodiest May Day celebration in the history of the German labor movement.

Author Erich Weinert (1890–1953), one of the founders of the periodical *Linkskurve* [Left wing], wrote the following ironical poem entitled *The Miracle of May 1, 1929*:

The police stood, with desperate courage,
In battle with the criminal Reds,
Who in mad fury were shooting from every side,
From every rooftop and peephole.
But the police stood their ground, they did not waver.
It says so in the police report.
Thousands of bullets whistled past,
But the police
Stood there quietly
And politely cleared the streets.

Then spoke the Commandant of Berlin
(you could hear his voice quaver):
"Now we will have to draw our guns
Or no policeman will be left alive.
But please don't shoot at people! You know
A warning shot works just as well."
So then they fired a shot or two.
And the shooting
Was very soon over.
The police were so noble.

And when they inspected the battlefield,
There were many dead to report,
And hundreds of wounded lay there.
Then the police heroes
Counted the rest of their number,
And behold! Not a single policeman was missing!
A hundred workers in a row!

But no police
At all among them.
That was the miracle of the First of May.

In 1929, the world suffered an international economic crisis. It began with the collapse of the stock exchange in New York. The overproduction of consumer goods by manufacturers was not accompanied by an increase in the purchasing power of consumers, so that production had to be cut back, resulting in increased unemployment. The value of stock plummeted. Many people sold their stock in order to salvage at least a little of what they had had; banks failed and were no longer able to pay back to their clients the money they had paid into their savings accounts. The Americans were thus forced to withdraw the capital they had invested in Europe, and this withdrawal in turn caused economic disaster in Europe, especially in Germany, where the Americans had invested most heavily.

In December there were one and a half million unemployed in Germany; one month later there were two and a half million; one month afterward there were three and a half million. And as the numbers of unemployed increased, more and more firms went bankrupt, especially manufacturing and small businesses.

Coffee being burned as fuel in a brewery in Rio de Janeiro.

As a result, it became impossible to sell millions of tons of foodstuffs because people did not have any money to buy food or luxury items. Thus, for example, in Holland potatoes were simply used for fertilizer; in Brazil they loaded ships with coffee beans, took them out to sea, and dumped the beans into the water; and in Canada wheat was burned. And these things went on even though millions of people in the world were starving.

The Ballad of the Sack-Heavers
[Die Ballade von den Säckeschmeissern]

1. Oh, I long to go to a foreign land
   Where the slender palm trees tower,
   In Brazil on the Rio Grande
   They want men to be coffee-sack throwers.
   For the world has much too much coffee,
   And a hundredweight brings too little money,
   So the conscience of the world decrees
   That half the harvest gets dumped in the sea.
   Throw it in, my boy,
   It makes sense, my boy,
   There's something behind it, my boy,
   This'll be some winter, my boy.
   So come all you vacationing families,
   March to Hamburg as fast as you can,
   Get on the first boat to leave,
   So you can sail away to Brazil
   And throw coffee into the sea.

2. And when the human shark on the Rio Grande
   Has profited on his soggy coffee,
   We'll be exported from this wealthy land
   To help on the Canadian prairie.
   For the world has much too much wheat,
   And a ton brings too little money,
   Food might end up cheaper for the buyer,
   So the extra wheat must go into the fire.
   Throw it in, my boy,
   It makes sense, my boy,
   There's something behind it, my boy,
   This'll be some winter, my boy.
   So come all you workers and pack your things.

The good harvest has ruined the prices.
Breadfruit is only a gift of the devil.
So take your bit of bread
And feed it to the hungry flames.

3. They're throwing wheat into the fire,
They're throwing coffee into the water.
Now when will those throwers of sacks
Toss those fat robbers after?
You see, there's something behind it, my boy,
You see, this'll be some winter, my boy,
You'll never see its like again, . . .

> Text: Julian Arendt, Ernst Busch
> Melody: Hans Eisler
> From the proletarian film *Kuhle Wampe*

Another important event that took place in 1929 was the appointment of Heinrich Himmler to the post of Chief of the SS.

The SA and the SS were the private armies of the NSDAP. Hitler founded the SA or Sturmabteilung [storm troopers] in 1921 to serve as a political combat unit. [In 1923, after the failure of his attempted coup d'etat known as the "beerhall putsch," Hitler spent several months in prison. When he was released, he resumed his activities and worked to re-form the National Socialist Party.] After the rebuilding of the NSDAP in 1925, the SA developed into an armed police squad whose members now wore a uniform (a brown shirt and an armband marked with a swastika). As a strike force and an army equipped to fight a civil war, it attracted large numbers of the unemployed and rootless, particularly during the period of the international economic crisis. In 1930, it already had almost 200,000 members. After Hitler had seized power, the SA became more important than ever by using terrorist methods to destroy the labor organizations. Countless members of the SA were guilty of numerous crimes during the Kristallnacht and in connection with the concentration camps. Later the SA was overshadowed by the SS.

The SS [Schutzstaffel or protection squad], the elite organization of the National Socialist Party, came into being in 1925 and was entrusted with ensuring the protection and security of the Party and of its Führer, Hitler. In 1929, the SS had 280 members. Candidates had to be at least six feet tall and had to be able to trace their ancestry back to the year 1750. Later the SS had holiday resorts and its own schools, Napola [*National-Politische Akademien*, national-political academies] and Junker schools [schools that trained young people to become the new Nazi aristocracy designed to replace the Junkers, the aristocracy of Prussia]. Heinrich Himmler decisively shaped the character of the SS.

Heinrich Himmler (1900–1945) had joined the NSDAP in 1923 and had participated in Hitler's beerhall putsch. After Hitler, he shared with Hermann Göring the distinction of being considered the most powerful representative of the National Socialist regime. In the years following the putsch, he expanded the terrorist system of the SS and the Gestapo (Geheime Staatspolizei, or secret police) by combining governmental with Party agencies. Himmler's nationalistic politics climaxed in his radical implementation of the "final solution of the Jewish problem."

1930

The rapid rise in the numbers of unemployed created virtually insuperable problems for the German government. What had formerly been a comparatively minor problem—the financing of unemployment insurance, which in turn involved the whole federal budget—led to the collapse of the Hermann Müller government. When the Cabinet that had served Hermann Müller was removed from office, the result was the collapse not only of the Great Coalition but of the last parliamentary government of the Weimar Republic.

Hitler, who in public speeches expressed strong support for the German worker, had for a long time been engaged in secret negotiations with industrialists in the Rhineland and the Ruhr district. These men knew that once Hitler had come to power, he intended to promote the "national renewal" of Germany, which they expected would favor their interests and enable them to attain their own ends.

Although care should be taken not to overestimate the amount of support Hitler received from German industrialists—for Hitler was by no means, as the Communist Party maintained at the time and still maintains today, a "product" of German heavy industry—nevertheless it should be pointed out that individual industrial magnates made substantial contributions to his cause. Between 1930 and 1933, Kirdorf [1] contributed between six and seven hundred thousand reichsmarks to the NSDAP; Flick [2] and Vögler [3] supported the Party from 1932 on, and Sir Henri

[1] Emil Kirdorf (1847-1938). Mining industrialist, who began to support Hitler even before the great economic crisis.
[2] Friedrich Flick (1883-1972). Steel magnate and armaments manufacturer, who controlled coal and mining industry in all occupied countries during World War II. After imprisonment as a war criminal, he rebuilt empire as head of Flick Industries.
[3] Albert Vögler (1877-1945). Industrialist and politician, who served in Reichstag, and in 1933, with other representatives of steel industry, helped Hitler to power.

Deterding,[4] who controlled the Shell industries, began to support it as early as 1930. Hugenberg annually turned over to Hitler approximately one fifth of the political contributions he received from the giant industrial concerns. Schacht [5] established ties between Hitler and commercial and private banking establishments as well as the German Bank. In the hope that by supporting Hitler they could more easily weather the difficulties of the economic crisis, all these banks helped to finance the [National Socialist] Party's struggle to win votes in the critical elections of 1932. Moreover, Thyssen,[6] who had allied himself with the NSDAP before 1923, enabled Hitler to build his party headquarters in Munich.

A. Hillgruber

In 1930, there were already 4,400,000 unemployed people in Germany. Hence many women were forced to take responsibility for supporting their families. The extent of the poverty in Germany in those days is almost impossible for contemporary young people, who can take their comforts for granted, to comprehend. The following account by a forty-eight-year-old woman may help to make this poverty clear.

My husband is out of work, and so I have been forced to go to work myself. To keep our situation from becoming too desperate, I have to contribute to the support of my family, which consists of my husband, three children ranging in age from three to thirteen, and myself. I live in the Zeitz district and do cleaning work in a wool-combing establishment. Since I have almost an hour's train ride, I get up at 4:30 A.M. The train leaves at 5:10 and arrives at the town where I work at 5:55. Work starts at 6:00, and so I have to run the entire distance from the railroad station

[4] Sir Henri Deterding (1866-1939). Headed Royal Dutch Shell Industries, which he had formed from Royal Dutch Petroleum Company and Shell Companies in 1907.

[5] Hjalmar Schacht (1877-1970). Banker, headed Reichsbank under Weimer Republic and again under Hitler. Later interned in concentration camp for opposing some of Hitler's economic policies.

[6] Fritz Thyssen (1873-1951). A founder of United Steel Works, which was part of Thyssen & Company Conglomerate. One of first major German industrialists to support Nazis, though from 1935 on, because of persecution of Jews, he opposed regime. He emigrated to France and was eventually placed in a concentration camp.—Tr.

to the factory in order to get there on time. There I clean wool-combing machines until 2:15 P.M. The only train I can take to get home does not leave until 5:13. I have to wait at the railroad station until it comes. I'm home at 6:00. Then there are a lot of things I still have to do. I have to cook dinner, get everything ready for the following day, and examine the children's things to see if they are still clean and in one piece. When you are away all day, you have to take a little extra care about the children's things because you have no chance to observe the damage that might have been done to them during the day and catch it in time. In the evening also I am tired and utterly exhausted from having been up and working for so long, and I have to wait until Sundays to mend our clothes, underwear, and stockings. Sometimes I even have to give up some sleep in order to attend party meetings and workers' welfare meetings; as chairman I even have to conduct the latter meetings myself. On Saturdays I get home at the same time as usual. Then the first thing I do is go to the co-op to buy enough groceries to last all week. Every four weeks, all by myself, I have to wash a big pile of laundry for my family. The evening before I get everything ready so that I can get started early Sunday morning. Except for laundry days, Sunday begins at 7:00 A.M. Then I have to clean house and mend our clothes. At the same time I am preparing the midday meal. Sunday actually begins for me at 2:00 P.M. I end the day by attending some event held by the labor organization or by taking a walk. So it goes day in, day out, week after week, the day of the working woman. The lot of the worker.

E.B., L., forty-eight years old

Hitler talked constantly about providing jobs and promised that he would get the unemployed off the streets. This promise was one of the reasons why he and his party nearly won the parliamentary elections of 1930. The elections held on September 14, 1930, resulted in the following shift of power in the Reichstag: Whereas the Social Democrats (SPD) lost almost no seats, the Communist Party went from fifty-four seats to seventy-seven, and the National Socialists climbed from twelve seats to one hundred and six. [The losses were incurred by middle-class conservative parties such as the German National People's Party and the Roman Catholic Center Party.]

The enormous growth of the power of the NSDAP did not mean that millions of voters embraced the National Socialist creed, but that these people had rejected the status quo.

Hitler and his friends exulted over this victory at the polls as a breakthrough. Many middle-class voters who had been members of the conservative parties, especially the National People's Party, had turned to the National Socialists because they were disillusioned with the policies of their own parties. The parliamentary system was shaken to its foundations.

A private telegram sent by the *Frankfurter Zeitung* [The Frankfurt news] after the parliamentary elections had been held describes the political situation at that time: "Insofar as one can judge in the early morning hours, over twelve million German voters have proclaimed their opposition to the governing parliamentary system and to the policies that until now have been pursued by democratic means. More than one third of the deputies elected are totally unsuited to the business of running a government—they are the enemies of any parliamentary government. The situation is grave indeed."

The Nazi members brought into the Parliament an atmosphere it had never possessed before: coarse, obscene, brutal. Speakers for the Opposition and members of the government coalition were shouted down; beatings even took place, and any legislative work was effectively blocked.

But the large numbers of unemployed were not the sole factor that contributed to the shift in voter support to Hitler's party. The Ulm court-martial also helped.

Three officers from the Army garrison at Ulm had appeared before the Supreme Court of Justice in Leipzig, the highest court in Germany, comparable to the Federal Court of Justice that today exists in Karlsruhe, because of their alleged "sowing of National Socialist sedition" in the Army; they were tried for treason and sentenced to eighteen months' confinement in a fortress. [Confinement in a fortress was a punishment for lesser offenses and was considered more honorable than confinement in a regular prison.] Adolf Hitler was summoned to Leipzig to testify as a witness, and in his statement, which was actually a propaganda speech, he declared that he would use only legal means in his efforts to win political power. He would undertake neither a putsch nor a coup d'état, but he left no doubt that, once he had acquired power, he would abolish the Weimar Republic and abrogate all international treaties. "Then"—and these were his very words—"heads will roll." This statement, later known as the "legality oath," was music to the ears of the middle class, who had never come to terms with the young Weimar Republic and were always keeping an eye out for a "strong man."

I have always maintained the view that any attempt to sow sedition among the armed forces would be sheer madness. None of us can derive any advantage from undermining the armed forces. . . .

Where these matters are concerned, nothing whatever can be done except under my orders. The government and all my political opponents are free to examine my speeches and orders. Moreover, all orders I issue are based on this fundamental principle: If an order violates the law, it must not be carried out. When my orders were not obeyed, I have always taken immediate and vigorous action. As a result, many Party members have been expelled from the Party, Otto Strasser among them. Otto Strasser actually toyed with thoughts of revolution. I never expressed approval of his plans. . . .

However, I can assure you that if the National Socialist movement is victorious in its struggle, a National Socialist Supreme Court of Justice will be established, and atonement will be made for November, 1918, and heads will roll! . . .

Presiding Judge: How do you plan to go about establishing the Third Reich?

Hitler: Our system prescribes only the foundation of the struggle, not its goal. We are becoming members of lawful organizations and in this way we will make our Party into a decisive factor. To be sure, once we possess the constitutional rights, we will cast the nation into what we regard as the proper mold.

Presiding Judge: So you will use only constitutional means?

Hitler: Of course.

The spectators in the courtroom applauded Hitler. These words of Hitler's finally alerted other countries to the fact that Germany had lost its internal political stability. International capital was afraid of Hitler and withdrew capital investments from Germany. The result was that unemployment rose still higher, and misery increased.

Kurt Tucholsky, who had been accused of having called German soldiers "swine" in one of his poems, composed a reply that included a precise description of Germany's poisonous political climate:

I admit that I have called these things by their true names. One of my poems, "Give Me Three Minutes of Your Time!", contains the following lines:

You were polished. You were drilled.
Were you still God's image?
In the barracks—in the sentry box
You were lower than the filthiest louse.
The officer was a pearl,
But you were only "louts!"
And even in your mass graves you were the swine;
The officers lay by themselves.

One has to have been hit between the eyes by a check from one of Hitler's big-business contributors not to understand what I am saying here.

"You were the swine"—that is, to those who called you swine!
And who called you swine?
The German officers.

Not just one, but a hundred, a thousand, ten thousand . . . for them it was a mark of good breeding to speak of the "louts," the "swine."

I and those of my friends who share my pacifist views do not regard the phrase "a front-line soldier" as, in itself, a title of honor. The front-line soldiers of all nations did not deliberately seek out this horrible and senseless experience; they were forced into it by a violence that, when it is inflicted by Bolsheviks, makes the whole world cry out in outrage. These front-line soldiers have included genuine heroes, counterfeit heroes, decent chaps, dull-witted clods, criminals, factory-owners in disguise, poor scoundrels—all types.

But Germans who hack away at other Germans in the manner that the Nazis have introduced into German politics (for it is

40

they who have done this and not the Communists)—this type of thing is new in our history.

In Wiesbaden, after the lecture, I drove past the Nazis. They stood there and uttered their odd battle cry, "Huuu—!" and threw stones and old junk and in general acted terribly brave. For I was just one man and they were a crowd. I looked into their eyes: goaded, stupefied, bellowed into submission . . . and without any ideas behind them.

Destroy the reputation of every pacifist; pursue the republicans like wolves; poison political life; combat government ministers with personal slurs; howl through the streets and smash windowpanes; after a failed putsch, know nothing and deny everything; be evasive in court. . . . What does one call such people?

As far as the German front-line soldiers are concerned: *they* were not swine.

Tucholsky (1890–1935, committed suicide in Sweden) was one of the most important left-wing political writers in the Weimar Republic. He wrote under various pseudonyms, primarily for the periodical *Die Weltbühne* [The world arena]. He had assessed the situation clearly: The storm troopers of the SA were brave only in a group; alone they were cowards, for they had no political arguments. Their instrument was violence in tune with their famous motto, "If you won't be my buddy, I'll smash your skull!"

Tucholsky was not the only one who recognized the brownshirted peril and described it and who warned against Hitler because he had long ago perceived his true goals. Many German writers saw the catastrophe impending and wrote openly about it.

The Communist Party had also recognized Hitler as Public Enemy Number One. In 1930 the Politburo of the Central Committee of the German Communist Party published a resolution against Fascism:

IV. The struggle against Fascism, as a political struggle of the masses, must be conducted on the broadest possible base. . . .

V. This struggle must be conducted on ideological grounds through the relentless unmasking of the deceptive phrases used by Fascists concerning their alleged "struggle against the Young Plan," [an Allied plan to help with postwar rehabilitation] their alleged "struggle against capitalism," their alleged "sympathy with the working class." The Party must disclose what lies behind these phrases and reveal the true policies of Fascism. . . .

VI. The demoralization among the working-class adherents of the Fascist movement, a demoralization which is doubtless increasing, makes it necessary that we distinguish between the Fascist leaders and the masses of their misled followers. Thus in the present aggravated stage of the struggle, the systematic application of the watchword, "Strike down the Fascists wherever you find them!" is inappropriate. Given the existing situation, our principal watchword must be the political and militant struggle of the masses and of all working people against Fascism, with the aim being its total annihilation.

> From the Resolution
> of the Politburo of the Central Committee
> of the German Communist Party (KPD),
> June 4, 1930

1931

In the middle of the year I had to return to my grandparents' house in the Fichtelgebirge. My mother had quarrelled with the farmer she worked for because she did not want me, a five-year-old, to rake hay in the meadows or to clean the manure out of the cowshed.

One of my uncles was now wearing an armband marked with a swastika; he could not afford a uniform. He had joined the SA. Another uncle had become a member of the SPD (Social Democrats), whereas my grandmother's sympathies, as always, lay with the German Nationalists.

In the living room hung a large picture of President von Hindenburg. His face, with its big mustache, used to frighten me, and when I was in the same room with it, I always felt that I was being watched.

But both my uncles, the Social Democrat and the National Socialist, were out of work, or as one would say today, did occasional odd jobs.

Our family argued a lot about whether the Nazis or the Sozis [the Socialists, i.e., the Social Democrats] were better Germans. The arguments sometimes took a grotesque form. If there was no meat on Sunday, my Nazi uncle would claim that the Sozis, these men without a fatherland, were responsible; if there *was* meat, he would say that we would have meat every day once Hitler came to power. These same arguments could also be used to prove just the opposite. But my uncles never physically attacked each other, for after all they were brothers, and they only yelled at each other inside their own four walls. Often my grandmother smoothed over the quarrels, and yet each brother clung to the image of Germany propagated by his own party.

As a rule my grandfather did not take part in these altercations. Only when he felt things had gone too far, he would sometimes

43

say ironically, "All I know is that three pounds of beef make a good soup."

My grandfather was a drayman who worked for a building contractor. In those days, at least in rural areas, very few people transported goods by truck. Horse-drawn vehicles still dominated the roads. I was always happy when my grandfather allowed me to accompany him into the stables. Sometimes, when I gazed excitedly after some passing motorcycle, my grandfather would say, "Remember, boy, horses smell, cars stink."

This year the political climate in Germany shifted even farther toward the right. The National Socialists (NSDAP), the German Nationalists, and the German Association of Veterans ("Steel Helmets") formed the Harzburger Front. Hugenberg, its initiator, thus united the conservative forces of Germany against the Republic. Hitler was his most important ally. The Harzburger Front declared: "Determined to protect our country from the chaos of Bolshevism and, through effective self-help, to save our political system from the whirlpool of economic bankruptcy . . . we declare that we are prepared to assume responsibility in Germany and in Prussia, by means of governments led by nationalist forces . . . we demand the restoration of German weapon power and armament levels." Such statements were well received by the people because by that time the number of the unemployed had already risen to 5,660,000. People used to line up in front of factories, employment offices, stores, and other public buildings in the hope of finding work, and they would accept any job, even if they were hired for only a couple of days or even a couple of hours.

The Iron Front was formed in opposition to the Harzburger Front. It was a union of the Social Democrats, members of labor unions and sports clubs for working-class people, and the National Flag, the Black-Red-Gold Veterans' Association—in other words, a union of left-wing forces that did not, however, include the Communists.

The Communists had their own organization, the Red Federation of Combat Veterans, which continued to function illegally after it was banned in May, 1929. In 1930, it had over 100,000 members (50 percent of whom were members of the German Communist Party, the KPD) and was led by Ernst Thälmann. We will

44

never know whether history might have taken a different course if the two left-wing groups had joined forces. At any rate, this left-wing bloc would have had a majority, and thus it might have had a chance to use parliamentary means to prevent Hitler's seizure of power.

Carl von Ossietzsky commented on the formation of the Iron Front, revealing his reservations:

> Now, after the end of the Christmas truce [between the warring parties], we are hearing a new catchword whose power is about to be tested. The Iron Front is being formed by the supporters of the Republic. The SPD, the Black-Red-Gold Veteran's Association, labor unions of varying political orientations, and Republican leagues, are all trying to band together to resist Fascism. The Front is long, there is no doubt of that; but it is not easy to assess yet how deep it goes or what intellectual reserves it possesses. Some segments of the Front—those where the workers are standing—probably truly deserve to be called "iron"; others are made of more pliable stuff, and some are no better than pancake batter. Everything will depend on their powers of endurance and reinforcements. Politics are now in an age of matériel warfare.
>
> It is not easy to adopt a critical posture toward a movement to which one must wish every possible success. One should not discourage the only group determined to actively combat Fascism. . . .
>
> It is an illusion to attempt to "resist" Fascism. One must attack it on its own social terrain. If the parties of the working classes finally grasp this, then and only then will proletarian strength rise again in Germany, strength to make history rather than simply retard it.

Carl von Ossietzsky (1889–1938) was a writer and a dedicated pacifist and humanist. In 1927, he began to manage the periodical *Die Weltbühne* [The world arena]. In 1936, he was awarded the Nobel Peace Prize, but Hitler did not allow him to accept it. Two years later he died of the effects of his confinement in German concentration camps.

Hitler had proclaimed when the Harzburger Front was founded: "No one desires peace more than the nationalist Opposition parties; but if, in the course of harsh competition, the interests of various nations clash, no nation can fail to mobilize its own forces to tip the scales in one direction or the other. No statesman can preserve the peace when his country is defenseless." Until the very end Hitler talked about peace incessantly. In the first sentence he would talk about peace, in the second about rearmament; in the first about reconciliation, in the second about war; in the first about alliances, in the second about betrayal; and nevertheless, almost an entire nation followed him wherever he led.

Most people, including, to a degree, my own family, probably did not understand the consequences that must follow, consequences that Ernst Niekisch prophetically described in 1931 in his book, *Hitler, ein deutsches Verhängnis* [Hitler, a German doom]. They cheered those who promised them work and bread. They did not read Hitler's writings, they turned off the radio when he was making a speech; but many people followed him because he was supported by the "bigwigs," the factory owners and industrialists. For these powerful men Hitler had long ago become acceptable. His politics promised increased industrial production—in other words, profits. In his alliance with the industrial bosses, Hitler ignored the interests of the German working class. Industry and the world of high finance were running on Hitler's course. The best example of this phenomenon is an address by the industrialist Carl Friedrich von Siemens in New York on October 27, 1931, at a dinner held by the General Electric Company. Von Siemens presented Adolf Hitler to the Americans as the only valid alternative for Germany, and said that in the future everyone would have to come to terms with him:

> Communism and the Hitler movement are both growing in strength, but there is the following fundamental difference between them: The former group is prepared to achieve its goals through revolutionary measures, that is barricades in the streets and civil war; if it comes to that, the decision will be made in the streets. The latter group wants to achieve its goals through lawful means, that is, through the ballot. But it will take measures to ensure that there is no repetition of the events of November, 1918, when the revolutionaries encountered no resistance in the streets. The military forces of our nation are too weak to put out

the fires if they should flare up simultaneously in many different areas of Germany. . . .

People do not pay sufficient attention to the fact that it is the selflessness of his movement and the noble national ideals it embodies that are attracting young people of all classes to his banner. . . .

The root of the Hitler movement is the struggle against Socialism, in other words against Marxism. . . . You in the United States . . . will understand better than anyone else that a strong and healthy Germany must necessarily be a united Germany with a regard for its own national interests. . . .

Hitlerism, or—as we call it—National Socialism, is in no way a monarchical movement. I believe that the German monarchy will forever remain a thing of the past. But National Socialism *is* opposed to the unbridled domination of the government by the Parliament, a system that unfortunately has been laid down in our Constitution. The German people . . . are not ready for this form of democracy. . . .

The pact between heavy industry and the NSDAP is the subject of a novel about German industry, *Union der festen Hand* [lit. The union of the firm hand], by Erik Reger (1893–1954). This book, one of the most important literary documents to come out of the Weimar Republic, uses the Krupp Works as an exemplar by which to describe the history of the German labor movement and its industrial antagonists during the period 1918–1929. Although the author dedicated his book "To the German people," and although the book was awarded the distinguished Kleist Prize, it awakened virtually no response in the general reading public of 1931.

A short time ago this book became available once again. It can contribute to our understanding of one aspect of history: the history of the vanquished, in other words of the common people. For the history of a people is written by writers of fiction as well as by historians, since writers are among the vanquished, or at least they are not among the victors. Often they have been persecuted, cast out, outlawed, beaten up.

Perhaps Reger's book might have opened people's eyes if it had found its way to the readers its author desired. I can no longer say exactly what or even whether my family used to read. My father at least used to read the Bible. He had joined a religious group whose members considered themselves serious students of the Bible and who, after World War II, became known as Jehovah's Witnesses. Then, as now, they were conscientious objectors who resolutely refused to serve in the military and thus to serve the cause of war. But in those days anyone who refused to bear arms was considered an enemy of the state.

Later Hitler interned all these people in concentration camps, and my father was not destined to be spared this fate.

My grandfather used to read the Farmer's Almanac. We had hardly any books in our house except, on occasion, a few cheap romantic novels. However, my family devoured the newspapers. They tore them out of each other's hands in the morning at breakfast, but not really in order to keep abreast of the political situation. The only political information my family gleaned from the newspapers was what they read in the headlines. Actually all of them merely wanted to scan the want ads to see if there were any jobs available for them. If they found a job listed that fit their training, my uncles and aunts leaped onto their bicycles to be the first to apply. Often they would travel twenty or thirty kilometers, only to discover that hundreds of people were already waiting at the door or that the job had been filled a long time ago.

Once again they could only wait for the following day, for the next newspaper, and then it began all over again. Year after year.

Only my grandfather had work. He was a calm and prudent man. He was as calm as his two ponderous cart horses, which he fetched out of the stable every morning at seven o'clock.

1932

Actually I ought to have started going to school that year, but in those days school began at Eastertime, and because I had been born at the end of May, I was put off for another year. This mattered very little to me, my parents, and my grandparents. The forest began directly behind the houses, and we children knew our way around the woods. We knew where we were safe and where danger lay in wait for us. We lived in a peaceful children's world; the freedom seemed to us boundless. We knew no care, and we did not yet understand the cares of our parents or grandparents. Even if poverty reigned at home, a piece of bread spread with homemade butter, a jug of milk, or some thin, hot soup was always waiting for us. We would not have asked for more, for we knew nothing else.

When I say "we," I mean that my family was not the only one suffering from poverty; all the families in our neighborhood were in the same situation.

During the summer we boys wore nothing but lederhosen, which did not need to be mended, but because they were never washed or cleaned at all, they soon began to stink. We wore wooden shoes—my father carved mine for me—and in the summer we went around barefoot. According to the wisdom of poor people, a tough, leathery layer of skin on the soles of the feet protects them better than shoes. We no longer felt the stones along the roads or the stubble in the fields when we had to help with the harvest. In return for our work the farmers used to give us children potatoes, milk, or eggs—things that we would otherwise have had to pay for. The houses of the rich people—in our area these were the factory managers, lawyers, and doctors—we saw only from the outside.

My aunt used to work as a maid for the manager of a chinaware factory. When she had some time off and came home, she used to tell us about the life rich people led. To me the things she said seemed miraculous, like something out of a story about the land of milk and honey. She used to talk about the different kinds of wine that were served with different foods; she spoke of pastries, pheasant, quail, white bread, and I always used to imagine myself sitting down at the table on which my aunt was spreading all these precious things. I admired my aunt, I revered her, and I made up my mind to marry her when I was older.

It was all like something in a fairy tale, and whenever I passed the factory manager's villa, which lay hidden in a spacious garden filled with trees and shrubs, I used to think that inside that house was the land of milk and honey, but that you could only get in after you had first eaten your way through a mountain of cake. Which I naturally would gladly have undertaken.

Toward the end of the thirties this factory manager for whom my aunt had worked as a maid died in a concentration camp. He was a Jew.

The peace was deceptive, the freedom was deceptive. To be sure, the lights were not yet going out in far-off Berlin, but more and more dark clouds were gathering and they were growing harder and harder to dispel.

This year the number of unemployed reached an all-time high— 6,128,429. Their lot and their misery were almost indescribable.

Every day millions of people reported to the employment agencies in the attempt, at least temporarily, to earn a couple of marks. Public kitchens opened all over Germany, and the unemployed men, accompanied by their wives and children, would stand outside and wait to receive a bowl of thin soup. Often this was the only hot meal they had all day.

In his 1932 novel *Kämpfende Jugend* [Militant youth], Walter Schönstedt describes the mood of the unemployed:

> An uninterrupted stream of people came and went at the employment bureau for unskilled workers in the Kreuzberg district. Langscheidt, the porter, stood in the vestibule looking fat and self-important. On the fourth floor one got one's card stamped, and on the fifth floor was the employment agency, where one sat down and waited. Everywhere the air was stifling and stale. The windows were only open at the top. . . .
>
> "Probably there won't be any work today; it's already eleven."

50

"Hey, Gustav, did you ever have a job?"

"Me? Not since I got out of school. When I was a big wheel at school, I did. Probably I'll never get another one," he said calmly. And half laughing, half regretfully, he went on, "And when I was ten, my old man said: 'Gustav, someday you're going to be a lawyer!' Nowadays I'm just 'that piece of dung' at home."

Kater was chewing on a match. "That's what we all are," he said casually. "But never mind. Why don't we become criminals? We haven't got a chance in any other line of work. Too bad you aren't a lawyer; then I would have a cheap defense attorney. . . ."

A man wearing black horn-rimmed glasses and a glossy black jacket entered the room. Everyone leaped to his feet. The man took his place on the platform and looked down at the people below him.

"Come on, man! Don't keep us waiting so long!"

"Keep cool, young man, okay?"

The jobless men crowded around him and looked up at him as if at a teacher who has interesting stories to tell.

He began loudly. "Two men to distribute flyers, restaurant on the Friedrichstrasse."

"How much? How many marks an hour?"

"It doesn't say. In any case it's a restaurant, and you'll be sure to get a noon meal."

"Ha! We know all about those noon meals! Unpeeled potatoes and gravy! No one wants to go there!"

"What do you expect? But you can't keep people from working! Come on now, who wants to go? Wages to be arranged after you get there."

Two old men came forward. They handed over their dole cards and left with quiet smiles on their faces. With a look of contempt, Spinne nudged Gustav. "Distributing flyers! So that's the kind of work people like us are supposed to do now! Apprenticeships just aren't available anymore. Crap!"

Someone laughed very loudly. No one turned around to look at him. Sixty jobless men were waiting to get work. But none of them had any hope. The man with the glasses assumed an increasingly momentous air. He rummaged fussily among the papers in his hand and, fumbling, drew out a new job listing. Again the room grew still, and the eyes of the waiting men became tense.

"Two men wanted to beat carpets. Experience required. Eighty pfennigs an hour. Two hours' work apiece."

51

Ten, twelve men pressed forward and waved their cards in the air. "Here!" "Me!" "Me!". . . .

"Hold on, only two men. Who has been out of work for longer than a year and a half?"

Almost all the men in the group fit the bill. The man selected two young people and told them to go at once to Grossbeerenstrasse 58 and ask for Mrs. Schnacke.

"Watch out for the money that falls out of the carpets!" someone called after the two young men.

The circle around the employment clerk was still waiting.

"Will there be anything more today?"

"I don't know. You could wait and see. After all, you have such a lot of free time!"

"You old pen-pusher, that's what you think! Come on, move your ass and look to see whether there's any more work! . . ."

"You think, because you get plenty of rest, that we have a lot of free time too, eh? I still have to go to the welfare office at Cottbus Dam."

Disappointed, every man crept back to his place. They were always disappointed. Always and everywhere. Disappointed and humiliated. They were driven from place to place carrying useless forms, driven from one office to another, from one authority to the next. Often for no other reason than to get some paper stamped. Only a few of them grumbled. They swallowed everything deep down inside them. And it all swelled into a monstrous lump of rage and hate.

The SA and the SS terrorized people in the cities and in the countryside with an ever-increasing brutality. Regular organized raiding parties turned up suddenly, struck down dissenters, and escaped again without being recognized. Usually the police were powerless to do anything about these attacks, and besides there were a number of police officers who secretly, or even quite openly, sympathized with the Nazis. One day my Social Democrat uncle came home with a gaping wound in his forehead. My grandmother dressed the wound and scolded him for being a brawler, for she regarded it as a fixed principle that not the Nazis, but only the Sozis, used to hit other people.

Finally the government made an effort to resist the Brownshirt terrorism. In April, 1932, it banned the SA and SS, which had already become a sort of civilian army. The government enacted the ban through an emergency decree.

Article 48 of the Constitution empowered the government to act upon a decree that had been signed by the president of the Republic without first obtaining the consent of the Reichstag. Heinrich Brüning, who was Federal Chancellor [Reichskanzler] and leader of the Zentrumspartei [Center party] governed largely by means of emergency decrees.

Because of the ban, the Nazis no longer wore brown or black shirts but white ones. But their acts of terrorism continued unabated.

After the banning of the SA and the SS, the former crown prince of Germany wrote to Groener, the defense minister and minister of the interior and a supporter of the Weimar Republic: "I find it incomprehensible that you of all people, the defense minister, are helping to destroy the marvelous manpower material assembled in the SA and the SS, whose members are acquiring valuable training in these organizations."

On that day, if anyone was still in doubt about the matter, it became clear where the powerless scions of the German imperial family stood: squarely on the side of Hitler and the military—and the "marvelous manpower material." For militarists, men have always been manpower material, and still are.

Intrigues toppled Minister Groener, and Chancellor Brüning was forced to leave the government with him. Franz von Papen became chancellor and on June 1 formed a Cabinet containing a "concentration of the nationalist parties." By June 14, the ban on the SA and the SS had already been rescinded, and Nazi terrorism became more brutal than ever.

After the repeal of the ban on the SA and the SS, the Nazis changed their tactics. They now sought to penetrate the working-class districts, the so-called Red strongholds, for in these areas the majority of the people voted a Communist or Social Democratic ticket. The results were street battles that almost amounted to civil war. In Hamburg-Altona alone, the clashes that occurred on July 17 resulted in 19 dead and 285 wounded. This day became known later as the Bloody Sunday of Altona.

The Nazis did not even hesitate to commit murder. The following example is representative of their methods. A police report dated August 8, 1932, states: "During the night between Tuesday and Wednesday, thirty-five-year-old Konrad Pietrzuch, a Communist, was murdered in Potempa. At around 11:30 several uniformed members of the SA, who had come to Potempa in a private motorcar, forced their way into the unlocked room in which Konrad Pietrzuch, his brother Alfons, and his mother were sleeping. Shouting, 'Out of bed, you damned Communists! Hands up!' they dragged Konrad Pietrzuch, who was sleeping in the same bed with his brother Alfons, from his bed and severely abused him. Konrad Pietrzuch fled into a small room adjoining the bedroom. His brother Alfons received a blow on the head, which resulted in a wound that bled profusely. One of the perpetrators pushed open the door of the little room and fired one shot into the room. Thereupon the perpetrators left the house. Then Pietrzuch's mother entered the other room and found her son lying dead in a pool of blood. One of the perpetrators was apprehended immediately after the crime."

And what happened next? On August 22, 1932, a special court in Beuthen sentenced the five Fascist murderers to death. Six weeks later their sentence was commuted to life imprisonment!

After hearing the verdict, Hitler sent the murderers a telegram: "My comrades! In view of this monstrous death sentence I feel myself united to you in boundless loyalty. From this moment on your freedom is a matter of our honor. The battle against a government under which this was possible is our duty."

After Hitler had seized power, all five men were released and received a decoration that, appropriately enough, was called the Order of Blood.

The upper-middle-class newspaper *Hamburger Nachrichten* [The Hamburg news], which was, be it noted, by no means a Nazi newspaper, wrote concerning the verdict in Beuthen: "What was condemned in Beuthen was not an act of violence committed against a fellow-German, but the elimination of a Polish scoundrel, who in addition was also a Communist—in other words, a deficient human being on two scores. . . . Have German judges not yet grasped the fact that a border war is taking place in the East between the noble German race and the subhuman Poles, and that the German people are engaged in a struggle for their very existence?" Let me repeat that this was not written by some Nazi gutter-press sheet, but by a middle-class paper that was considered responsible and reliable. It was only one step from these words to the mass murder of "subhuman" people by the "noble German race." Whether the "subhuman people" were Jews, Russians, Poles, Gypsies, French, Dutch, Hungarians, or Rumanians did not matter, for only a member of the "master race" had a right to live.

This year the seven-year term of President von Hindenburg came to an end. It was necessary to hold new elections, elections in which the members of the government would be chosen directly by the people [for only elected members of the Reichstag could serve in the cabinet]. Hitler wished—indeed was forced—to run for parliament if he wanted to come to power. However, he was not yet a German citizen, but an Austrian.

But the Nazis knew how to handle this problem, too.

The first National Socialist government had come into being in Lower Saxony in 1931. This government appointed Hitler administrative adviser of the province of Braunschweig and thereby made him into a German citizen. The Nazis were never overly sensitive about observing the law. They more or less made up laws as they went along or twisted existing ones to suit their own purposes. To the Nazis, the act of bending the law was neither a crime nor a misdemeanor. Everything was achieved "legally," so the way to supreme power was now paved.

Hitler, who claimed that he would defend law and order, left no one in doubt of his goals, nevertheless: "Our opponents reproach us, and me in particular, with being intolerant and hard to get along with, saying that we do not want to work with other parties. . . . I have one thing to say about this right now: The gentlemen are quite correct, we are intolerant! I have set myself the goal of getting rid of Germany's thirty political parties."

This meant a one-party state, the elimination of all opposition, and ultimately a dictatorship.

In the presidential elections none of the candidates received the absolute majority he needed on the first ballot. In the second ballot, von Hindenburg received 19,400,000 votes and Hitler 13,400,000 votes.

However, the Nazis held 230 seats in the Reichstag and thus

everyone wanted them to have a share in the government. Hitler turned down the suggestion that he serve as Vice-Chancellor. He wanted all the power for himself, not merely to be second-in-command to Chancellor Franz von Papen.

Soon thereafter, von Papen, too, was ousted, and, on December 2, General von Schleicher became Chancellor. When his attempt to forge a new coalition with the National Socialists, the trade unions, and the Social Democrats failed, he resigned.

Eight weeks after von Schleicher took office, Adolf Hitler was Chancellor of Germany.

1933

This year at Easter I began school.

There's a picture that shows me carrying a big schoolbag, which we used to call the "treat bag." My treat bag had been stuffed two thirds full of paper. Only the top third held a little fruit, chocolate, and hard candy.

Naturally, everyone in class wanted to look inside everyone else's treat bag. I refused to let anyone look in mine, and so did a couple of other boys. We were ashamed because you couldn't look deeper than a handsbreadth into our bags without seeing the paper.

My grandmother had accompanied me to school. Neither my father nor my mother had time to do it. My mother could not get her employer to give her any time off, and my father was wandering around somewhere looking for work. This arrangement made me very unhappy. The other children had come to school with their parents or at least with one of their parents. Some of the fathers who accompanied their offspring to school were dressed in the brown uniforms of the SA, for Adolf Hitler had become Chancellor only a few weeks before.

He had seized power. The phrase "seizure of power" became one of the most popular expressions used in the Third Reich. Henceforth, many of Hitler's speeches were introduced by the phrase, "Since my seizure of power. . . ." He actually saw himself as a superhuman being and presented himself to the people as a messiah. The propagandists used to exploit this aura of divinity. Expressions such as "God-sent Adolf Hitler, whose ministers are his Apostles" were not unusual. Hitler's greatest asset was his flair for rhetoric. He had exercised his speaking talents in the bars and beerhalls of Munich early on, and these talents had quite literally formed the basis of his political career. His "solemn seriousness," his seductive, chauvinistic words, combined with the use of sarcasm and mockery and the pontifical air of a political missionary enabled him to exert an extraordinary effect on a broad segment of the population. He said what his audiences were secretly thinking, he knew how to strengthen their prejudices and their longings, and when he had finished speaking, he left them feeling that they had partaken of some new truth.

On the night of January 30, 1933, after President von Hindenburg had appointed Hitler Chancellor, the brown-shirted columns of the SA marched through the streets carrying lighted torches. They sang their songs of victory, but also their marching songs and their songs of hatred. In the windows many people placed small candles, which at that time were known as Hindenburg lights.

I do not know exactly how powerful the SA was in our town. But I do remember that in the evening my uncle who belonged to the SA marched through our town with his Party cohorts like all the others. I stood at the side of the street with the boys from the neighborhood and watched my uncle march by, singing and carrying a torch in his hand. Who knows, I may even have felt proud of him; he was no longer wearing just the armband, but a brown uniform in which I thought he looked very impressive.

I do not know what my family said about all this at home, but probably my grandmother was as proud as my aunt, who was a fanatical Hitler-worshipper. And later my uncle often said to me proudly, "Maxl, now the new age is about to begin." Finally one day my grandfather damped his enthusiasm: "Just make sure that you earn something and stop being a financial drain on your mother; even in your new age people are supposed to work, not sit around doing nothing!"

Hitler told us that January 30, 1933, was the first day of the Thousand-Year Reich. Today we know that this "empire" lasted for only twelve years, and we know how it ended.

In a sense, the beginning was already the end.

Many people had foreseen the end, even if they could not suspect how terrible that end would be. Many people had warned of what was coming, but for the majority of the German people, who were intoxicated by flags, uniforms, march music, and the sound of marching feet, those who warned and admonished were only alarmists, left-wing elements, nest-soilers, radicals, or fellow travelers. On February 1, Hitler proclaimed his new government officially in power. He did not do so before the Reichstag, the elected parliament, but over the radio. The meaning was clear enough. Now everyone knew that Hitler no longer needed a parliament.

Were the people clearly aware of his contempt for the parliament? I doubt it. In any case, my family considered it quite proper that Hitler had ceased to address "that crowd," i.e., the deputies of the Reichstag, and had turned directly to the people. My grandmother regarded this procedure as a great step forward, and I know that from then on she spoke of Hitler as the People's Chancellor and no longer as the Reich Chancellor.

Hitler did not yet possess enough money to rule alone, to rule as a dictator. He needed support from industry and the great financiers.

On February 4, he was already meeting with a group of industrialists in Cologne, at the home of a banker named Schröder. After the war Schröder testified at the war-criminal trials in Nuremberg: "The efforts of men in positions of economic power were generally directed toward bringing a strong leader to power in Germany. . . . When, on November 6, 1932 (the day of the parliamentary elections), the NSDAP suffered its first setback [loss of votes] and thus had passed the zenith of its power, it became particularly urgent that it receive the support of the men who dominated the German economy."

On October 20, 1933, the great industrialist Otto Wolff drew up a list of the contributions from industry to right-wing political parties during the year 1931–1932; Hitler's party alone had received almost 180,000 reichsmarks [approximately $75,000].

The other major political parties had not yet become silent about the shift in power, and the Communists called for a general strike, but the workers failed to respond to the appeal:

> The German Communist Party, addressing all the members of the proletarian public, and appealing simultaneously to the ADGB [the German Trade-Union Federation], the Afa-Bund [the Independent Employees' Federation], the SPD [Social Democratic Party] and the Christian trade unions, calls on you all to join the Communists in a general strike against the Fascist dictatorship of

Hitler, Hugenberg, and von Papen, against the destruction of labor organizations, and for the freedom of the working class.

Die Rote Fahne [The red flag],
January 31, 1933

But the Social Democrats declined to engage in an extraparliamentary struggle. Presumably (and they may have been correct in this assumption), they did so because they feared that it might result in a fearful bloodbath, for no matter what happened, the SA and the SS would take Hitler's side. At that time no one knew exactly how the German armed forces would react. The formation of a Popular Front composed of the left-wing members of the middle class, the Social Democrats, and the Communists might well have represented Germany's last chance to save democracy and the Republic. But the left-wing parties had spent so much time quarreling with each other that they were separated by ideological trenches too broad to permit them to close ranks and form a united front against Hitler:

> In their opposition to the threat of a coup d'état by this government, the Social Democrats and all the members of the Iron Front stand with both feet firmly planted on the ground of legality and the Constitution.
>
> They will not make the first move toward stepping off this ground. Instead they will employ all the constitutional and legal means at their disposal to wage a relentless war against this government. They will leave to their adversaries the sole responsibility for initiating the kind of war that can no longer be waged, by either side, with the conventional weapons of political struggle. . . .
>
> Our situation is extremely dangerous. However, it also contains within itself the potentiality to develop, with amazing speed, in a more favorable direction.

Vorwärts [Forward],
January 30, 1933

Although the SA and the SS had already begun arresting people on January 30, 1933, the real wave of arrests did not begin to sweep across Germany until after the Reichstag fire of February 27. After all, it was not just any old building that had burned, but the forum of democracy.

There was no one for whom this fire—even today it is not entirely clear who set it—came at a more opportune moment than it did for the Nazis. Naturally they blamed the "radicals" for the whole thing. Now they had the pretext they needed to arrest all the Communist leaders and many Social Democrats and deputies of the Reichstag. All left-wing publications, including trade-union papers, were banned. Well-known intellectuals and authors with left-wing sympathies were arrested:

> During the night following the Reichstag fire, using lists of names that had been drawn up beforehand, police began to raid the homes of Communists, Social Democrats, and left-wing intellectuals who were not affiliated with any political party. Among the first of the many writers and artists to be arrested were Carl von Ossietzsky, Ludwig Renn, Egon Erwin Kisch, and Erich Mühsam. Social Democratic deputies to the Reichstag were also arrested, among them men as conservative as Otto Eggerstedt, who up until the time of von Papen's [government] had served as Chief of Police in Kiel, and who was later murdered in a concentration camp. Erich Rossmann and Ludwig Marum, Reichstag deputies from southern Germany, fell victim to this reign of terror. . . . In the spring of 1933, Ludwig Marum was imprisoned in Kieslau Concentration Camp and was murdered there a year later after suffering severe abuse. After his arrest in June, 1933, Erich Rossmann was taken to Heuberg Concentration Camp, where he was subjected to endless interrogation and abuse, as a result of which he almost died. Later he reported that only the aid of his Communist fellow-prisoners enabled him to survive this difficult time. In March, 1933, Stefan Meier, Social Democratic deputy to the Reichstag from Baden, was arrested and taken to Ankenbuck Concentration Camp, where he was confined until March, 1934. During the war he was arrested again and in 1941 was sentenced to three years in prison. After serving out his prison term, he was taken to Mauthausen Concentration Camp, where he was murdered in 1944. In the spring of 1933 Adolf Biedermann, the SPD deputy from Hamburg, was killed by SA troops in a railroad train and his body thrown out onto the tracks. . . .
>
> Max Seydewitz

The Opposition was wiped out overnight. Nazi propagandists

simply claimed that the "Red mob" had set fire to the Reichstag and that therefore it was "legal" to arrest them. It was as easy as that.

I am convinced that everyone in my family believed what the propagandists said, for by that time the propaganda machine was already so powerful that there was almost no way people could escape the daily indoctrination or the loud speeches of the Nazi leaders.

The first "show trial" of the Third Reich, which was destined to be followed by countless others, was instituted against Marinus van der Lubbe, alleged to have been the arsonist who had set fire to the Reichstag.

Van der Lubbe was sentenced to death even though at that time no existing law decreed the death penalty for the crime of arson.

On the day after the Reichstag fire an emergency decree, signed by von Hindenburg and designed to ensure "the protection of the people and the State," was announced to the public. This decree set aside basic, fundamental constitutional rights (for example, the individual's right to liberty and to respect for the sanctity of his person, the ban on mail censorship, and the freedoms of opinion and assembly). This decree was enacted within a period of only a few hours, under the pretext that it was essential to the prosecution of the struggle against the Communists; in reality it represented the basic law underlying the National Socialist system. With this decree of February 28, 1933, Germany ceased for a period of twelve years to be a nation governed by constitutional law.

Before the burning of the Reichstag, Goebbels had written in his diary: "We will produce a masterpiece of political agitation. . . . First an attempted Bolshevist revolution must flare up. Then we will choose our moment to strike."

Fifty thousand SA and SS troops living all over Germany were employed as police so that the mass arrests could be carried out quickly and were sworn in with a simple handshake.

The prisons were so crowded that there was no more room for all the people who had been arrested. Therefore, the Nazis hastily erected so-called preventive detention camps, which later developed into the concentration camps. Some of the concentration camps, above all those in the East, in occupied Poland, later became extermination camps. Now the time had come when you could be arrested on mere suspicion, and the case did not even have to be examined by a magistrate. From now on justice was anything that served the interests of the regime.

In an article in *Der Völkische Beobachter* [The national observer], the newspaper of the NSDAP, the construction of the concentration camp at Dachau was justified on the grounds that one could not simply allow Communists and Social Democrats to run around loose because they would endanger the State (when the Nazis spoke of "the State," they meant themselves) by agitating against National Socialist policies. "This measure was taken in the best interests of the State, without regard to petty scruples."

From the outset Dachau was planned to house 5,000 people; the Nazis were not petty in this respect either.

I do not know whether my SA uncle helped to arrest anyone, but it is possible that he did, for as far as I know he was never at home in those days.

At an election rally Hermann Göring had formulated the goal toward which the Nazis were working when he said, "It is not my responsibility to dispense justice, but only to annihilate and exterminate."

And he was not talking about exterminating conditions, but people.

The theatrical producer and actor Wolfgang Langhoff (1901–1966) was one of the first people to be arrested after the Reichstag fire. Later he was sent to Papenburg Concentration Camp, and after his release wrote a book about his experiences called *Die Moorsoldaten* [published in English as *Rubber Truncheon; being an account of thirteen months spent in a concentration camp* by E. P. Dutton & Co., Inc., New York, 1935]. The following excerpt from this book describes how the SA and SS troops used to treat the so-called prisoners under preventive detention:

"Big shots from the SS and the SA came to the cellar too. Unit Leader Lohbeck and SA Battalion Leader Sporrenberg were often there. They always addressed long speeches to us, especially at night, when they were drunk, and they threatened to shoot us

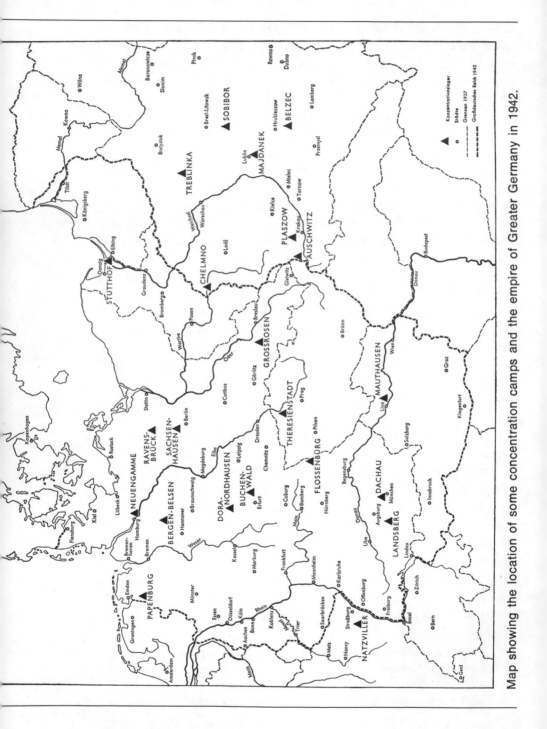

Map showing the location of some concentration camps and the empire of Greater Germany in 1942.

on the spot if any of us ever told anyone anything that went on in the cellar. Lohbeck said, 'Today they fished a guy out of the Rhine. Four holes in his belly. He was another one who couldn't keep his trap shut.' I was down there for seven days and I saw everything! Can you imagine, seven days!"

He threw himself onto his straw mattress sobbing. I put my arm around him and said, "Take it easy now, pal. It'll pass. You don't have to tell us any more."

But nothing could stop him now. The memory had him in its grip, and he spent hours telling us all the details.

"They had also dragged a woman into the cellar: they called her Mathilde and 'the regimental whore.' They made her watch, and afterward she had to wipe up the blood from the floor with a bucket of water.

"The worst time was always curfew, when all the pubs were closed down. Then the tipsy SA and SS guys went into the cellar, and anyone who wanted to could beat up the prisoners."

"And you, did they hit you too, when you were being interrogated?"

He grabbed my arm, looked me in the eye, and said, "I was interrogated too. . . ."

He told us everything, but he did not say a word about what they had done to him in the interrogation room. He only said, "Afterward an SS guy took me to the toilet. I stuck my head in and let the water flow over my head."

Papenburg Concentration Camp was the place that gave birth to the song "Die Moorsoldaten" [lit. The moor soldiers, or the Börgermoor song, named after the camp, Börgermoor, and its marshes], which later became world famous.

On March 5, five weeks after Hitler's seizure of power, parliamentary elections were held once again, for Hitler wanted the people to accord him nationwide approval of his policies. Despite enormous propaganda, the NSDAP did not win the majority of seats it desired.

This election must have been a bitter disappointment to the Nazis; but what he had not been able to achieve legally, Hitler achieved by invalidating the eighty-one parliamentary seats held by members of the Communist Party.

On March 17, Hermann Göring delivered an address at a meeting of the Pomeranian Provincial Federation in which he said about the annihilation of the Marxists: "As the previous speaker stated that the return of Marxism must not be permitted, I want to say just one thing: Not only will Marxism not return, but we will stamp it out! I will rub the noses of these creatures in the dirt until they are done for. Not only will we wipe out this plague, but we will also expunge the word *Marxism* from every book. In fifty years no one in Germany will even be allowed to know what the word means. . . ."

I wonder what Göring's audience were thinking about while they listened to these words. Was it clear to them that he was talking quite openly about murder, about mass murder, or had they already been stirred up to such a frenzy that the extermination and murder of people who disagreed with them did not faze them in the least?

Hitler still tried to maintain the fiction that he was using legal means to govern the country. In 1933, he could not yet afford to violate the now-hollow Constitution openly. President von Hindenburg was still alive; the middle class, the nobility, and the armed forces stood behind the old man; and at that time there was still, at least in theory, a possibility that the armed forces could be made to march against the SA and a civil war might be kindled from above. Therefore, Hitler needed laws that would legalize his terrorist methods. He achieved his aim through the Enabling Act, which was approved by all the parties except the SPD. The Communists were no longer represented in the Reichstag; their deputies had either fled or been arrested. The Enabling Act authorized the Hitler government to enact laws without the consent of the Reichstag:

Article 1. Laws may be enacted by the Government as well as by the procedure provided for in the Constitution. . . .

Article 2. Laws enacted by the Government may deviate from the Constitution as long as these laws do not relate directly to the institutions of the Reichstag and the Reichsrat [Federal Council] as such. [Note: the Federal Council was dissolved on February 14, 1934.] The rights of the President of the Republic remain unimpaired. . . .

Article 5. This law will go into effect on the day it is promulgated. It will become invalid on April 1, 1937. It will also become invalid if the present Government is replaced by another.

While this law was being put to the vote, Hermann Göring, then President of the Reichstag, sat on a platform and observed the reactions of the deputies through a telescope!

Hitler's dictatorial powers were extended with the aid of this law, for with it German provinces that resisted the central government were "brought into line." "Federal representatives" replaced the provincial governments provided for by the Constitution. The terrorist activities of the SA were stepped up, and the first boycott of Jewish businesses began. In Prussia alone the number of people under preventive detention exceeded 25,000.

The first signs that Hitler, through Joseph Goebbels, wanted to be sole arbiter of what constituted German culture, or was supposed to, were already apparent in the earliest years of the National Socialist movement. After 1933, incidents followed each other in rapid succession. In Breslau students with National Socialist sympathies forced their way into lending libraries, reading rooms, and bookstores and removed "un-German" books from the shelves; among them were books by Stefan Zweig,

An SA man standing in front of a Jewish shop in Berlin in April, 1933. The lower sign says, "Germans! Beware! Do not buy at Jewish shops!"

Thomas and Heinrich Mann, and many others. The students had absolutely no legal pretext for taking such action, but Hitler's party backed them up.

Hitler protected murderers, so it was only natural that he should protect a few book thieves.

"Minor incidents" like these were only secondary manifestations. On May 10, funeral pyres were erected in Berlin and other university towns, and the books of writers who were considered offensive went up in flames.

The list of forbidden books was a long one. It was comprised of 12,400 titles and the complete works of 149 authors, almost all of whom were highly respected in Germany and throughout the world:

Johannes R. Becher	Karl Kraus
Vicki Baum	Else Lasker-Schüler
Walter Benjamin	Heinrich Mann
Werner Bergengruen	Klaus Mann
Ernst Bloch	Thomas Mann
Bertolt Brecht	Walter Mehring
Hermann Broch	Erich Mühsam
Alfred Döblin	Carl von Ossietzsky
Lion Feuchtwanger	Erik Reger
Leonhard Frank	Erich Maria Remarque
Oskar Maria Graf	Joseph Roth
Ödön von Horvath	Anna Seghers
Peter Huchel	Ernst Toller
Hermann Kasack	Kurt Tucholsky
Franz Kafka	Armin T. Wegner
Alfred Kerr	Franz Werfel
Erich Kästner	Arnold Zweig
Hermann Kesten	Stefan Zweig
Egon Erwin Kisch	Carl Zuckmayer

Some 25,000 books fell prey to the flames; in Berlin alone around 800 tons of books were confiscated. The students, some of whom were in uniform, uttered pithy pronouncements as they threw the books into the flames:

Against class struggle and materialism (Karl Marx)

Against decadence and moral disintegration (Heinrich Mann and Erich Kästner)

Against turncoats and political treason (F. W. Förster)

Against the soul-destroying overestimation of instinctual drives (Sigmund Freud)

Against the falsification of our history (Emil Ludwig)

Against unpatriotic journalism (Theodor Wolff)

Against the literary betrayal of soldiers of World War I (E. M. Remarque)

Probably Erich Kästner was the only writer who personally witnessed the burning of his own books:

The Day My Books Were Burned

In 1933 my books were burned in Berlin with a grim solemnity and pomp by a certain Herr Goebbels, in the great square next to the State Opera House. Goebbels triumphantly called out the names of twenty-four German writers who were supposed to be symbolically eradicated for all time. I was the only one of the twenty-four who turned up personally to observe this impudent, theatrical spectacle.

I stood in front of the university, wedged in among students wearing SA uniforms, the flowers of our nation, watched our books flying into the quivering flames, and listened to the schmaltzy tirades of the cunning little liar. Funereal weather hung over the city. A head from a broken bust of Magnus Hirschfeld [1] had been stuck on a long pole and was waving back and forth high above the silent crowd. It was loathsome.

Suddenly the shrill voice of a woman shouted, "That's Kästner over there!" A young cabaret performer, who was forcing her way through the crowd with a male colleague, had seen me standing there and expressed her amazement at excessively high volume. I started feeling ill at ease. But nothing happened. (Although in those days a great many things used to "happen.") The books kept flying into the fire. The tirades of the cunning little liar went on unabated. And the faces of the brown-shirted regiment of students, their chin straps fastened beneath their chins,

---

[1] Magnus Hirschfeld (1868-1935) was a German physician and sex researcher who favored tolerance in matters of sexual behavior and defended the rights of homosexuals.—Tr.

stared straight ahead without expression at the flaming pyre and at the gesticulating little demon as he chanted his psalms.

In the dozen years that followed, I only saw books I had written during the few times when I was abroad. In Copenhagen, in Zürich, in London. It is a strange feeling to be a writer whose books are banned and never to see them on the shelves and in the show windows of bookstores. Not to see them in any city in one's native land.

It was twelve years before the Third Reich came to an end. Twelve years was long enough to destroy Germany. And one needn't have been a prophet to predict, in satiric verses, this [book-burning] and other similar events. One was unlikely to err because of one item: the character of the German people. Naturally the satirist must know the object of his criticism. I know mine.

However, the Nazis had forgotten to burn the books of one writer, whose work they had misunderstood. In his famous letter, "Burn Me!" Oskar Maria Graf (1894–1967) placed himself on the list of proscribed authors, and in retaliation the Nazis drove him into exile.

Burn Me!
A protest on the occasion of the German book-burning
of May 10, 1933.

Like almost all left-oriented Socialist intellectuals in Germany, I, too, have experienced some of the blessings of living under the new regime. During a period when I happened to be out of town, the police appeared at my home in Munich to arrest me. They confiscated a vast number of irrecoverable manuscripts, painstakingly assembled research material, all my business papers, and a great many of my books. All these things will probably end up being burned. Thus I have been forced to abandon my home, my work, and—what is perhaps the hardest of all—my native soil, in order to escape imprisonment in a concentration camp.

But I have only just become aware of the most delightful surprise of all: According to the *Berliner Börsencourier* [The Berlin market-courier] I have been placed on the white list of authors in the new Germany, and all my books, with the exception of my most important work, *Wir sind Gefangene* [English translation *Prisoners All*, A.A. Knopf, New York, 1928], are recommended. Thus I have been appointed to serve as one of the exponents of the "new" German mind!

In vain I ask myself: What have I done to deserve this disgrace?

The "Third Reich" has eliminated almost every significant work of German literature, has dissociated itself from all authentic German poetry, has driven the majority of its most important writers into exile, and has made it impossible for their works to appear in Germany. A few pompous, know-nothing hack writers and the irresponsible vandals currently in power are trying to destroy everything in our literature and art that has won the respect of the world and to make the meaning of the word *German* synonymous with narrow-minded nationalism. This is a nationalism that inspires the suppression of even the slightest liberal impulse, a nationalism under whose orders all my honest Socialist friends are being persecuted, imprisoned, tortured, murdered, or driven to suicide out of sheer despair.

And the champions of this barbarous nationalism, which has nothing, *absolutely nothing*, to do with being a German, have dared to claim me as one of their "intellectuals," and to place me on their so-called white list, which when judged by the conscience of the world can only be regarded as a *black* list! I have done nothing to warrant this dishonor!

My whole life and all that I have written gives me the right to demand that my books be surrendered to the pure flame of the funeral pyre and not to the bloody hands and the depraved brains of the gangs of brown-clad murderers.

Burn the works of the German spirit! This spirit will prove as imperishable as your disgrace!

I implore all decent newspapers to print this protest. (This protest was first published in the Vienna *Arbeiterzeitung* [Labor news] on May 12, 1933. The following passage is an excerpt from an unpublished sketch found among Graf's papers after his death: "I immediately sent my protest to as many newspapers as possible and—incredible as it may seem—it appeared in papers all over the world, from Spitsbergen to Cape Town, from Tokyo to New York and San Francisco. It came close to making me famous, except of course in the Third Reich. There people were quite vexed by this piece of obstinacy, and the students and professors of Munich instituted a special book-burning session in the great hall of the university in order to give my books the treatment they deserved.")

The exodus from Germany into exile had begun: Producers, directors, actors, writers, painters, musicians, sculptors, composers, and scientists—almost an entire generation of intellectual and creative people—left the country.

Berlin, which until 1933 had been one of the world's cultural centers, sank into insignificance overnight.

Some artists found a new home in other countries, whereas others kept traveling from country to country, forever in flight from the Nazis. Many committed suicide.

On May 15, 1933, in a letter to Albert Einstein, Thomas Mann wrote about his attitude toward Fascist ideology: "No matter what its supporters may claim, its essence does not (as Hitler says) consist in 'elevation' or 'uplift,' but in hatred, vengeance, a base lust to kill, and a narrow-minded Philistinism." And on May 15, 1933, the Frenchman Romain Rolland wrote an open letter to the editor-in-chief of the *Kölnische Zeitung* [The Cologne news]: "It is true that I love Germany and have always defended it against the injustices and misunderstanding it has

Thomas Mann (1875-1955) emigrated to Switzerland in 1934.

72

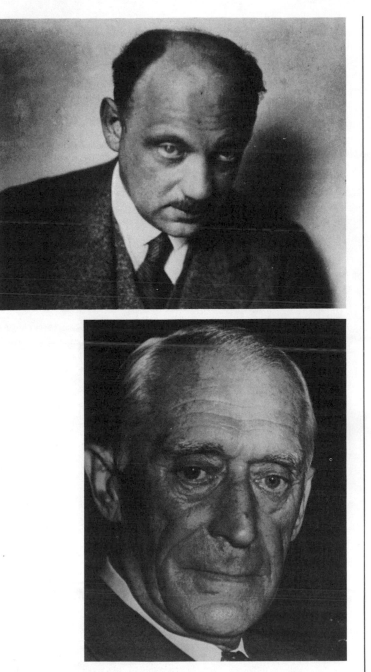

Above: Georg Kaiser (1878-1945) emigrated in 1938.
Below: Leonhard Frank (1882-1961) emigrated in 1933.

Above: Lion Feuchtwanger (1884-1958) emigrated in 1933.
Below: Franz Werfel (1890-1945) emigrated in 1938.

James Franck (1882-1964), a German-American physicist, was "given a leave of absence" from his teaching position in 1933. Many other German professors lost their jobs at the same time.

suffered at the hands of other nations. . . . So don't you see that this nationalistic, Fascist Germany is the worst enemy of that true Germany that is the basis of its unity? Such political policies constitute a crime committed not only against humanity as a whole, but against your own people."

The painter Max Liebermann, who at that time was eighty-four years old, was a Jew and thus, according to Nazi views, not a true German. In every country in the world he was celebrated as one of the greatest of all German artists. The Nazis did, of course, classify his work as "degenerate art," but he was so highly esteemed internationally that they could not simply make him "disappear." In 1933, he declined reelection to the post of President of the Prussian Academy of Fine Arts and until his death in 1935 led a retired life in Berlin. A remark that Liebermann is credited with having coined expresses better than a multitude of words the relationship of artists to the Nazi government: "It is impossible for me to eat as much as I would like to throw up."

For the rest of his life Liebermann was not permitted to paint; the Nazis had forbidden him to practice his art.

Of course, the Nazis' propaganda machine was not without its effect. After all, there was nowhere one could read different accounts of events or where one could hear another opinion. Everything conformed to the party line; no opposition was expressed either in the provincial legislatures or in the press, not to mention on the radio, of which the Nazis had taken firm control on the very first day. Joseph Goebbels alone decided what could appear in print or be broadcast. He issued to the editors-in-chief of all the newspapers orders that specified everything down to the last detail. Goebbels said verbatim: "We make no secret of it. We and we alone control the radio, and we will use radio in the service of our own ideas and ensure that no other ideas are expressed." Censorship was absolute.

All the activities of everyday life were given a military orientation. This military aura extended even into the realm of language. Henceforth one heard only:

instead of "employment office"—"labor mobilization"
instead of "job procurement"—"labor battle"
instead of "worker"—"soldier of labor"
instead of "work"—"service to Führer and folk"
instead of "entrepreneur"—"factory leader"
instead of "staff" (or "personnel")—"subordinates" (or "followers")
instead of "factory meeting"—"factory roll-call"
instead of "industrial agreement"—"the industrial order"
instead of "equal partners in society"—"the labor front"
instead of "production"—"the production battle"

It is easy to understand that if, for whatever reasons, these words are hammered into a person's brain every day, they soon become a part of his language, and he does not necessarily stop

"Soldiers of labor" present arms to Hermann Göring,
reviewing the Reich Labor Service
in Saarbrücken in November, 1935.

and think about where they came from and why they were coined
in the first place.

On October 15, the Chamber of Culture was founded and
placed under the control of Goebbels. This position enabled him
to supervise and direct German literature. However, most of the
members of this Chamber of Culture did not need his "supervision," for they were in any case writing just the kind of thing the
Party wanted them to write—that is, they conformed.

Mediocrity, "kitsch," was now the order of the day. If Karl May
[popular author of boys' adventure novels], who was one of
Hitler's favorite authors, had still been alive, he would certainly
have been chosen president of the Chamber of Culture. However,
I can readily imagine that Karl May would have turned down the
offer.

In 1933, many Germans were still far from willing to join
Hitler's ranks with cheers and loud cries of "Heil!" There was
resistance, not only from intellectuals but also from working-
class people. Resistance groups formed in the Ruhr district, in
the Saar, in Upper Silesia, in Hamburg and Berlin and the large

77

industrial centers. Not only Communists and Social Democrats, but also Catholic priests and Protestant ministers rebelled.

In my home town there were teachers and clergymen, both Protestant and Catholic, who were strongly opposed to Hitler. They used to call the brown shirts of the Nazis "the Devil's dinner jacket." Of course, they could not say it out loud, but they hid their true feelings, as my father did. When someone greeted my father by saying, "Heil Hitler!" he would reply, "Grüss Gott!" If someone said to him, "Grüss Gott!" he would answer, "Heil Hitler!" People could not really tell where he stood.

On Sundays my SA uncle used to sit down at the dinner table wearing his uniform. My grandmother did not like this at all. She simply said: "If you think that because you're wearing a uniform, it means that you're grown up now and that I ought to raise my arm and salute you, then you're sadly mistaken. I can still box your ears if I feel like it. The only people who need a uniform are people who are not dry behind the ears yet. Only young scamps (today we would say "hooligans") have to wear uniforms."

At this age—I was seven or eight years old—the other boys and I used to travel across the nearby Czechoslovakian border to Asch in groups of five or ten at a time. We children did not notice any difference between Czechoslovakia and Germany. Germans, or at least people who spoke German, lived on the other side of the border too, and most of them supported Hitler. They did so even though the Czech government had forbidden people to hang Nazi flags outside their windows.

These were the Sudeten Germans, who later wanted to "return home to the Reich."

There was only one difference between the two countries, a difference to which we had to accustom ourselves all over again every time we went there: In those days people in Czechoslovakia still used to drive on the left-hand side of the road.

But this, too, was destined to change very soon.

Were people in our little town really aware of the political changes that had taken place there? Definitely. The number of Brownshirts was increasing, and many people used the greeting "Heil Hitler!" even though they were not yet officially required to do so; and in offices and homes pictures of Hitler now hung beside the picture of President von Hindenburg.

My SA uncle got a job working on a road-building project that paid thirty-five marks a week. My mother got a job helping out in the chinaware factory three days a week. My father bought a used cobbler's sewing machine and began to repair shoes and boots for our friends and neighbors. He worked in our kitchen, for he could not afford to rent a workshop.

I was allowed to drive to the stone quarries with my grandfather and was proud of my ability to guide the horses with the reins. My school friends used to envy me, but they did not know, any more than I did, that it was not really necessary to guide the horses, for they knew the way all by themselves.

My grandfather was and remained opposed to the Nazis, and sometimes he would say, when I alone could hear him, "Rabble, mob, scum." When he said this, he would place his forefinger on his mouth and give me a conspiratorial wink.

He despised the Brownshirts so much that he used to secretly spit at them when they went by. Once he boxed the ears of my uncle—who after all was twenty-two years old—because he had once again appeared at Sunday dinner dressed in his uniform, for we were a strict Lutheran family and believed that uniforms were inappropriate at a time of prayer. I can still hear, as if it were yesterday, the voice of my grandfather as, trembling with rage, he shouted at my uncle, "Take off that rotten shirt!" I only saw him so angry two or three other times, at the most.

Only much later did I learn that my grandfather had risked his life by saying what he said to my uncle, for at that time children had already begun denouncing their parents, and the parents would end up in concentration camps without knowing why. The time had come when people no longer trusted each other, when parents were afraid of their children and children of their parents. My father did not talk about politics. Sometimes we received visits from people I had never seen before. They talked about things I did not understand, but in any case I was usually sent out of the house while they were there.

Not until later, long after my father had been imprisoned, did I learn that once a week he used to smuggle out of Czechoslovakia and into Germany newspapers and periodicals that were banned in our country. The method was as perilous as it was simple: He used to unscrew the handlebars of his bicycle, roll up the newspapers so tightly that they would fit into the hollow framework of the bicycle, screw the handlebars back on, and calmly pedal back across the border.

On November 12, parliamentary elections were held again. At the same time a referendum was held to determine whether the people approved or disapproved of Hitler's foreign policy. As might have been expected after the reign of terror that had preceded the referendum, 95 percent of the 96 percent of the electorate who turned out voted approval.

For the Nazis, all was right with the world.

But the reality of life in Germany was quite another matter:

April 7, 1933

We in Germany have plunged into a second Middle Ages of which the "Margoniner case" is a representative example. Margoniner is a wholesale cattle dealer. When the boycott [of Jewish businesses] came into effect he fell into the hands of the SA, who subjected the man to the following treatment at Nazi Party headquarters: They beat him with rubber truncheons until the man was disfigured; then they cut off his hair, cut a wound in the shape of a swastika into his back, rubbed salt in the wound, placed the hair they had cut off his head inside it, and sewed up the wound. In this half-dead condition Margoniner was turned over to the Jewish Hospital, and the Chief of Staff, Professor Dr. Gottstein, then brought Chief of Police Heines to see this half-dead man. No one knows what Heines said. But the poor man was photographed in the hospital, and everyone is hoping that they will be able to save his life. But Adolf Hitler is lying when he says, "In Germany no one is harming a single hair on a Jewish head."

Walter Tausk

Not far from my home town was a large estate, for centuries the property of a noble family that had produced many generals. One day an SA squad forced their way across the water and into the castle and raised the Nazi flag, with its swastika, above one of the little towers; up until then the baron had successfully refused to raise this "banner of disgrace," as he called it, on his property. On the following day he was found dead. He had shot himself in the mouth with a hunting rifle.

My grandfather wept. The insignificant drayman Christian von der Grün and the highly respected baron had known each other well. During World War I my grandfather had served as orderly to the baron, who was then a cavalry captain, and later they used to spend hours together talking about horses. For in addition to his grand estate, the baron also owned a stud farm. On many a Sunday he had sent his own coach, decorated with his coat-of-arms, to pick up my grandfather because he needed his advice about a sick horse.

My grandfather never used to ride inside the coach but always sat up in front next to the coachman. I used to stand by the fence and watch them as they drove away.

I was very proud of my grandfather.

1934

One is almost tempted to say that from now on every year began more horribly than the last year had ended. But probably only a few people in the Reich were aware of this fact. Those people who had managed to get work again—no matter how poorly they were paid—were inclined to interpret the new regime in terms of what it appeared to have done for *them*: Hitler had given them work.

Naturally the number of unemployed persons in Germany was decreasing, but this same trend could be observed in all other countries as well, for the international economic crisis had passed its climax.

In Germany highways were being constructed and the armaments industry was increasing production. But tens of thousands of people had been arrested, many were pressed into the Labor Service, and dissenters disappeared behind the barbed-wire fences of the concentration camps.

Blond hair now became the hallmark of the true German. Everywhere one confronted the image of the radiant Teuton—blond, big and tall, powerful, and confident of victory.

Hitler did everything he could to keep the growing younger generation in a state of ignorance and stupidity. On January 24, a law was passed, and a special ministry was immediately created to implement it: the Ministry for the Supervision of the Total Intellectual and Ideological Education and Training of the NSDAP. In the past, schoolchildren had written essays about humanitarianism and the love of one's fellow man; now the dominant themes were the loyalty of the Nibelungs or the valiant Germanic warrior-hero.

At the beginning of my second year in school, several boys in my class appeared dressed in the uniform of the Jungvolk [a branch of the Hitler Youth for boys between ten and fourteen] —a brown shirt and short black corduroy trousers—even though they were not required to wear them in school. But we children knew perfectly well that the fathers of these boys were members of the SA, the SS, or some other Nazi organization. Naturally, the boys liked the way they looked in their uniforms. They believed that they were better than the rest of us, and often they expected their uniforms to make up for the poor grades they made in school.

The fathers of these boys were what in those days were known as "hundred-percenters," who, my mother used to say, even slept with their arm raised in salute and so gradually became left-handed because their right arm was always stretched out. The "authentic German" mode of greeting had become "Heil Hitler!" When you said this you raised your right arm to about the level of your forehead.

Even our school lessons conformed strictly with the attitudes of the National Socialist regime. We learned to read by studying the letters of the alphabet, and naturally the words chosen to illustrate each letter all pointed in the same direction. For example, the word chosen to represent the letter *R* was not *rose* but *Reichswehr* [German Armed Forces]:

> The Army Arrives
> Rum-di-bum! Rum-di-bum! Rat-a-tat-tat-tat!
> "Hurry, Rudi, the Reichswehr! Robert and Reinhold are already on the way. And how the girls are running! Renate and Rosemarie are in the lead. Everyone wants to see the Reichswehr. Look, they're already coming across the bridge. The captain is riding at the head of the column. All the others are following him."
> It's the most fun over by the band. All the boys and girls are running along beside it. Aha, and there is a big fat man in it! He has to blow the big horn. How fat his cheeks are when he blows the horn!
> Renate and Rosemarie stop and laugh and wave, but Robert, Reinhold, and Rudi are running along beside the soldiers.
> Robert says, "I would like to join the Reichswehr today." Rudi and Reinhold would like to join up too. But Rudi would like to be a captain right away.

Another example:

We Help

"Listen, Ursel, there's someone at the door!"

"Who can it be?"

"Heil Hitler, Ursel!"

"Heil Hitler, Uncle Weber!"

"Ulrich and Günter, is it really you? And in uniform? And in such weather?"

"We're collecting things for the Winter Aid. [The Winter Aid was a compulsory Nazi charity. The clothing and money collected were ostensibly used to relieve hardship suffered during the winter.] Don't you have something [for us] too?"

"Of course! Just a minute! Here, Ulrich: an overcoat, a suit, a pair of underpants, and these overshoes."

"Papa! Papa! Ursel wants to give something too! Ursel has some talers [old silver coins worth about three marks, or seventy-one cents]. Here! Four—nine—fourteen talers!"

"Thank you very much, Ursel!"

"Thank you very much, Uncle Weber!"

"Heil Hitler!"

It was easy to inspire young people with enthusiasm. The Nazis traded on their love of adventure and grouped them into leagues and organizations that it was very difficult for them to avoid. It was considered un-German not to be a member of a National Socialist organization, and who wanted to be accused of being un-German?

Basically young Germans were grouped into the following organizations:

Children between the ages of six and ten were cared for by members of the National Socialist women's organization.

Boys between ten and fourteen became members of the Jungvolk, and the girls joined the Jungmädchen or, as it was actually called, the Jungmädel. [*Mädel* is an old-fashioned "folksy" word for *Mädchen* (girl). The group was literally "Young girls."]

Young people between the ages of fifteen and eighteen entered the Hitler Youth (HJ for Hitlerjugend) or the German Girls' League (BDM for Bund Deutscher Mädel).

These organizations were by no means all. Additional ones ensured that until the day he died no German would ever succeed in getting out of uniform. The Labor Service [Reichsarbeits-

Above: A member of the Hitler Youth
at a holiday camp in 1934.
Below: Jungmädchen learning the Nazi salute, May, 1937.

dienst] was for young men as well as for girls and young women. It was followed by service in the armed forces [Wehrmacht] with all its branches, the Army, the Navy, the Air Force, and, later, the reserves—the Army Reserve, the militia, the Home Guard. The women were organized in the German Women's Association [Frauenschaft]. Various branches also existed within the SA and the SS, such as the cavalry corps or the motor corps. The German people were organized down to the last man, woman, and child. Almost no one could escape. In this way, the men in power were able to supervise and control almost every member of the uniformed and organized "masses."

Besides the swastika each organization had its own symbol, a runic character, a pennant, a banner, or a flag. In addition to the regular schools, Nazi Party schools—the Adolf Hitler schools and the so-called Ordensburgen [literally "fortresses for a military or religious order," such as the Knights Templar], which were

SS Reichsführer Heinrich Himmler
inspecting a unit of ordinary SS in June, 1934.

training schools for future political leaders—were established later. Biology, competitive sports, and German folklore were among the principal fields of study.

The SS Junkerschulen trained young men to be SS Youth Leaders. No effort was made in these schools to prepare students for a more demanding type of examination like the *Abitur* [an examination that German students must pass in order to graduate from secondary school and qualify for admission to a university]. Their education concluded with a period of "practical training" in a concentration camp.

In other words, young men were forced to guard and probably torture—perhaps even kill—dissidents in order to receive their diploma from the SS. This example, more than any other, makes it clear how deluded young people can be abused to serve a political goal. Every day it used to be drummed into the heads of these youngsters that the inmates of concentration camps were enemies of the State, Jews, traitors—in short, "worthless human beings."

But what was he like, this new representative of the German "master race" in my own family, who wore his uniform when he sat down at the table on Sundays and stuffed himself with Grandmother's mashed potatoes? My uncle was now earning almost fifty marks a week. However, this was not because wages had risen but because people were now being forced to work longer hours. Every day he and his fellow workers worked at their road-construction jobs for three hours longer than they had done in the past, and of course they had to work on Saturday too.

To be sure, gradually the unemployed were being taken off the streets. But where did they go from there? Into uniform! They either joined the Armed Forces, the Labor Service, or served as auxiliary police in the SA or the SS. Soon there were so many men in uniform that civilian labor was once again in short supply. And because manual labor without the help of machinery was being encouraged, a larger work force was needed.

Every day the people were fed with proverbs from the Führer. The cheapest utility radio set [called a "people's receiver"] sold for thirty reichsmarks, for every German, said the propaganda, was supposed to be able to afford a radio. In truth, a radio in every German family enabled those in power to blare their slogans into the most insignificant corner of the Reich. The voices of Hitler and Goebbels reached even those people who never read a newspaper and did not have the slightest interest in politics. Our rulers had become omnipresent.

Every day one saw, read, and heard them everywhere: in the press, which always conformed to the party line, on the radio, in films, and in the newsreels, which in those days were as popular as the daily television news programs are today. We saw Hitler at banquets and parades, both of which events took place somewhere every day. The Nazis were master practitioners of the ancient Roman formula that all the people needed were bread and circuses.

Hypnotized by flags, banners, speeches, and marching feet, the German people did not awaken from their organized delirium. They were left no time to think about why the whole production was being staged. Like everything else, the music too was simple and easy to understand: hiking songs, folksongs, war songs, songs of the new Germany—and constantly the music of marching bands.

Knowledge and education also took a form that was simple and easy to understand: Between 1931 and 1939 the number of university students decreased by 78,290. Under Hitler there was no demand for academic training; the Führer needed soldiers, not educated people.

During this year, ordinances and decrees rained down on the people until society conformed in the most minute detail to the requirements of the uniformed National Socialist State.

On April 20, Hitler's birthday, Heinrich Himmler was appointed Chief of the Prussian Secret Police (Prussia was the largest and most important province of Germany). On April 24, a law established a People's Tribunal. This tribunal was not required to abide by the existing laws in any respect; its verdicts were based exclusively on National Socialist ideology. Probably we will never know exactly how many people disappeared, were "shot while trying to escape," or committed suicide in those days, but there are survivors who can tell what happened then. And there are official reports like this letter written on June 27 by

Ritter von Epp, the Federal Representative in Bavaria, to President von Hindenburg, which shows how the bestial murder of a Communist worker was hushed up:

I have canceled the criminal proceedings instituted following upon the physical injury, resulting in death, of the mechanic Oskar Pflaumer of Nuremberg, because the actions directly associated with this incident involved culpable participation in, as well as the aiding and abetting of, the crime.

According to the report of the public prosecutor's office of the Superior Court of Nuremberg-Fürth, these proceedings were based on the following facts:

. . . "In the course of this general action,[1] on August 16, 1933, the married, twenty-nine-year-old mechanic Oskar Konrad Pflaumer of Nuremberg, who had been extraordinarily active in Communist activities, was apprehended along with several other people and was secured in the main police guardhouse. At around 11:00 P.M. that same night, under the direct orders of Battalion Leader Korn, several SA men conducted Pflaumer into the aforementioned SA guardhouse for the purpose of interrogating him and bringing him face to face with other Communists. During this night Pflaumer . . . was very severely abused there by a number of SA men, so that on August 17, 1933, at around 5:30 A.M., shortly after he was brought back to the police guardhouse where he had been taken after his arrest, he died of these injuries. In the view of the coroner the results of his dissection suggest [2] that Pflaumer . . . a man of athletic build, was 'laid out' and was also 'bastinadoed,' [3] and that the bleeding beneath the skin caused by these blows . . . brought about . . . his death . . . .

"If . . . the trial . . . were to be conducted, it would prove impossible—even if the trial itself were held in closed session—to prevent the public at large from finding out what occurred. This would severely damage and undermine the reputations of the SA, the Party, the police, and the National Socialist State in general.

"However, the damage to the German Reich would be even greater if—as is bound to happen—other nations were to learn of these events. . . .

"Because the crime did not result from an ignoble motive but instead was designed to achieve a highly patriotic goal and served to promote the National Socialist State, the cancellation of the legal proceedings . . . does not appear incompatible with the orderly practice of criminal law."

The chief public prosecutor of the Provincial Court of Nuremberg is in agreement with these views.

The Minister of Justice [4] also recommends the suppression [of the proceedings]. . . .

I found it impossible not to concur with these arguments.[5]

1 The "general action" referred to here is the terrorist action waged jointly by the police and the SA in Nuremberg, in order to prepare the city for the Fascist Party conference which was to be held there.

2 In reality the physician attached to the superior court had expressed no doubt whatever about the fact that the Communist "was tortured and beaten to death with blunt objects in the cruellest manner."

3 The bastinado was a common method of punishment under despotic, feudal Oriental regimes and involved beating the offender with a stick, especially on the soles of the feet.

4 In Bavaria this man was Hans Frank.

5 Franz Gürtner, the Reich Minister of Justice, whose responsibility it was to act on the contents of this report, also felt no scruples about letting the murderers go free.

The following account of the murder of the writer and pacifist Erich Mühsam (1878–1934) also illustrates the bestial treatment the Nazis dealt out to their opponents. Intellectuals like Mühsam who resisted the Nazis and accused them of being "cutthroats" and warmongers, were condemned to death and often were killed by slow torture:

Erich Mühsam had begun to traverse his Way of the Cross: from the Lehrter Strasse jail, to Sonnenburg Concentration Camp, to Plötzensee Prison, to Brandenburg Concentration Camp, to Oranienburg Concentration Camp.

Later Kreszentia Mühsam described a visit she had made to see her husband: "He was in terrible shape. I found it difficult to conceal my horror. He was sitting on a chair and was not wearing his glasses—someone had broken them; they had knocked out his teeth, and the monsters had trimmed his beard so that he resembled a caricature of a Jew. When he saw me he forced out the words, 'Why have you come into this hell?' And when we parted, he said, 'You can be sure of one thing, Zenzl: I will never behave like a coward!' "

Later one of his fellow prisoners described his impressions of the much-abused Erich Mühsam: "His face was as red as fire and very swollen, and his eyes were bloodshot. He collapsed feebly onto his straw mattress. 'The swine,' he said, 'blew their noses into my mouth.' By the following day his left ear had swollen up like a cauliflower ear, and a pustule could be seen emerging from the auditory canal. They left him in this condition, without helping him at all, for eight days. Erich Mühsam told me, 'You know, I'm not afraid of dying, but this process of being slowly murdered, that's the really awful thing.' "

The SA men pretended that he was going to be shot. Mühsam was forced to dig his own grave in the prison courtyard. Then they stood him up against the wall and aimed their weapons at him. They ordered him to sing the Horst Wessel Song [a Nazi song second only to the German national anthem in importance], and Erich Mühsam sang the Internationale [the Communist rallying song]: "Nations, hear the bugles calling." His tormentors drove him back into the barracks. When he wanted to write to his wife, a camp guard bent back his thumbs until he had dislocated the joints. Then he said, "Now you can write your wife."

To the very end, Erich Mühsam followed the path he had chosen back in 1918: "And even if they kill me, to give in means to lie!" Another fellow sufferer reported later, "On one of the last evenings of his life, Erich Mühsam told me, 'If you hear that I have committed suicide, don't believe it.' " On July 6, 1934, the SS took control of Oranienburg Concentration Camp, which until then had been run by the SA. One hundred and fifty SS men arrived from Württemberg and Bavaria.

The proletarian writer Karl Grünberg recalls: "On the afternoon of July 10, 1934, Erich Mühsam was taken to the guardroom. There, in a tone of courteous scorn, SS Company Commander Ehrat addressed him as follows: 'So you are Herr Mühsam? The Mühsam of the Soviet Republic in Munich? Listen to what I am going to say to you now. By tomorrow morning you are to hang yourself. You understand what I mean, hang yourself by the neck. If you do not carry out this order, we'll do it ourselves!' Greatly agitated, Mühsam returned to his fellow sufferers and told them what had happened. He said that despite all he had already suffered, he would not under any circumstances hang himself now.

"At 8:15 that evening Mühsam was taken to the administration building. He never returned. Later he was seen crossing the yard accompanied by SS Company Commander Werner. Next

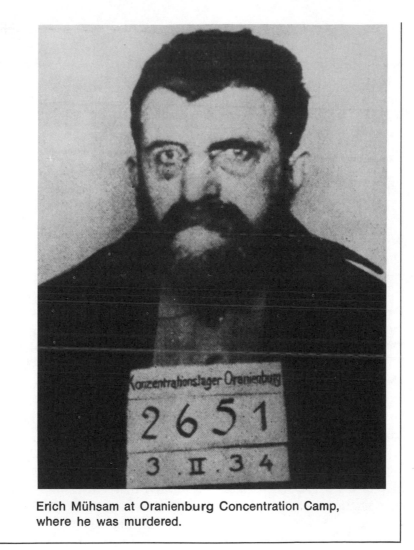

Erich Mühsam at Oranienburg Concentration Camp,
where he was murdered.

morning he was found dangling from a rope in Latrine No. 4;
his feet hung down into the toilet hole. The knot had been tied
with a professional skill of which Mühsam, who was half blind,
would never have been capable."

Jürgen Serke

On June 30, wide-scale assassinations, which had been ordered by Hitler personally, took place all over Germany; this action later became known as the Röhm putsch.

Ernst Röhm (born 1887) wanted to make the SA into a revolutionary army, a people's army. However, Hitler needed the support of the German Armed Forces and their generals [who would not have approved of such a revolutionary force] in order to accomplish his goal—the conquest of Europe. Hitler got rid of Röhm, who had been his intimate friend, and spread the rumor that Röhm had been planning a putsch against him. Under cover of the strictest secrecy, Röhm and all the higher-ranking officers of the SA were arrested and shot.

In this way Hitler succeeded in getting rid of his burdensome rival. From then on the SA ceased to play any political role in the Reich except for providing a brown-shirted backdrop at military parades. Thus Hitler betrayed his Brownshirt movement and openly allied himself with the officers of the German Armed Forces and with the moneyed classes. The mass assassinations caused the German people no little disquiet, for up until then the SA had been considered the mainstay of the Nazi Party. Even today it is not known how many members of the SA were shot. However, we do know that Hitler did away with a few of his old enemies [who were not members of the SA], and caused to "disappear" Conservative and middle-class critics who had taken a stand against him.

On July 12, Hermann Göring delivered an address to the German attorneys-general in which he cynically justified the assassination of the SA men. He openly admitted that Hitler had ordered and sanctioned the murders. Thus Hitler was the sole determinant of legality. The law of the land had been abolished: any murder was legal if the Führer approved it; every crime became a legal necessity if it were committed against someone opposed to the Führer's aims.

As I have stated, the death sentences, which, without recourse to the courts, were passed by the leader responsible for the State in order to defend this State from attack, are legal. They have been sanctioned by the Führer and, in obedience to his absolute authority, by me as well. Thus every man who died during this action, whether he was executed or whether he died by

94

suicide or while resisting the forces of the State, died in accordance with the law. It is not your concern, gentlemen, whether we acted correctly in this matter or whether we happened to kill the right people; your only concern is to determine the identities of the condemned. This must be your sole interest. Thus you have to know: Schmidt-Breslau was shot on legal grounds. But: hands off; do not attempt to obtain any further information. Naturally, it is necessary for you to know this much, for otherwise, from now on, any act of murder or manslaughter could be justified on the grounds that the perpetrator was implementing a legal decree. Thus in each case the Ministry of Justice will supply the attorneys-general and the public prosecutors within whose jurisdiction it falls with the names of the persons in question. Absolutely no further action is to be taken with regard to these persons, and no investigation is to be made. The state police departments have been instructed not to release any information. . . .

Let us assume that, in accordance with orders, Herr Müller has shot Herr Meyer. All the same, someone may know that Herr Müller was not on good terms with Herr Meyer, that the two of them did not get along. It is easy to imagine such cases. But in this case it was not Herr Müller but we, the authorities, who were responsible for pronouncing the sentence of death; Herr Müller merely carried out the sentence. It is possible that in this case rumors might start flying around and people might say that the murder had been committed for personal motives. If Meyer's name is on your list, then you are simply not to investigate the case or concern yourself with it in any way. . . .

I believe that you now have a clear picture of the situation and that in future you will be able to execute the duties of your office in the way the Government demands.

In his address to the Reichstag on July 13, Hitler himself justified the assassination of the SA leaders. He lied to the people, telling them that his personal intervention had preserved them from terrible danger.

But not everyone believed him. Not only people who had grasped the true political situation, but even the rank-and-file members of the SA distrusted his words. My grandmother told me that from then on, my SA uncle never wore his uniform when he sat down to Sunday dinner. He had lost faith in Hitler. He also stopped attending Party meetings and for this reason was expelled from the SA a few months later. He did not try to get the SA to accept him back. As a result of the assassination of the SA leaders, the SS, which had hitherto been only a branch of the SA, became a separate and independent organization on July 20, receiving its orders thereafter directly from Hitler. Only a couple of years later the SS had become a state within a state. Soon their black uniforms began to spread fear and horror among the people. Thousands of people confined in prisons and concentration camps were used by them as a source of cheap labor; their overseers were stupid men who had been goaded into a frenzy, and they did their jobs with great thoroughness. Torture was an everyday occurrence; human beings were slaughtered like animals. The official version for the victim's families was that they had died of heart failure.

Despite the increase in acts of Nazi terrorism, resistance did not cease. Even inside the concentration camps new resistance groups kept forming.

The Jews imprisoned in Sachsenhausen Concentration Camp used to sing an old Yiddish folksong for which one of them had composed new words:

> Ten brothers were we once,
> We used to trade in wine.
> One of us is dead,
> And now we are only nine.
> Oh, Yidl with the fiddle,
> Tevje with the bass,
> Sing me a little ditty,
> We have to go into the gas!
> Oi-yoi, oi-yoi, yo-yoi!
> Sing me a little ditty,
> We have to go into the gas!
>
> And now I'm the only brother,
> With whom shall I mourn?
> The others have been murdered!
> And I grieve for all nine!
> Oh, Yidl with the fiddle,
> Tevje with the bass,

Hear my last little ditty,
I must also go into the gas!
Oi-yoi, oi-yoi, yo-yoi!

(These new words to an old Yiddish folksong were composed in
Sachsenhausen Concentration Camp by Rosebery d'Arguto, the
former choir leader of a workingmen's choir in Berlin-Neukölln.
D'Arguto later died in the gas chamber at Auschwitz.)

On August 2, Hindenburg died and was buried with great
pomp in Tannenberg, East Prussia. Hitler now united in a single
person the offices of president and chancellor, so that from now
on he was the Führer [leader] of the Reich, which was soon to
become the empire of Greater Germany.

The millions of people who cheered him saw the future in
the rosiest hues.

My aunt got a job in the chinaware factory; during the winter
my grandfather transported timber from the woods. This was
dangerous work, in the course of which people repeatedly met
with fatal accidents. But they had work, they drank their beer,
and they did not worry about politics. On those rare occasions
when they did engage in political debate, someone usually closed
the argument by saying, "But the Führer will take care of that."
However, my father no longer kept silent; more and more people
came to see him, and they were never the same people. Listening
to their hushed conversations, I would hear that someone who
had still been around last week had been arrested and sent to a
camp. The visitors arrived secretly, usually at night when I was
already asleep. I was not supposed to know anything about what
was going on, for after all I was just a child and might have
innocently let something slip. Nevertheless, I sometimes used to
listen at the door, for my room was right next to the living room.

1935

This year the writer Ernst Wiechert (1887–1950) delivered an address to students at the University of Munich that was not merely courageous but downright suicidal. This speech included the following statement: "It is quite possible for a people to cease to distinguish between justice and injustice. It is also possible that such a people may for a time win a gladiator's glory. But such a people already stands on the brink of a precipice, and the law decreeing its destruction has already been written."

Ten years later his prophecy was to be fulfilled.

Although Wiechert was not among those authors whose books had been burned or banned, in 1938 the Nazis sent him to Buchenwald Concentration Camp, and he was released only because his imprisonment had triggered international protest. Wiechert describes his life in the concentration camp in his book *Der Totenwald* [The forest of the dead], which naturally could not be published in Germany until after the war was over.

According to the terms of the Treaty of Versailles, Germany was allowed to maintain an army of only 100,000 men. On March 16, Hitler announced the reinstitution of universal conscription, which meant a breach of Germany's international treaty obligations. In reality, Germany had already had more soldiers than it was allowed for a long time now, for members of the SA and the SS had received the rudiments of military training.

Though he was obviously rearming Germany, on May 21, in a speech addressed to the Reichstag, Hitler announced his willingness, in most areas, to observe the terms of international agreements.

The people believed him, for all they wanted was peace, and many foreign statesmen and politicians trusted him too.

Another reason why the Germans wanted to believe Hitler's words was that, after years of unemployment, they were back at work again and did not want to risk losing the little comforts

Hitler just before the Reichstag session of May 21, 1935.

that their hard-earned wages now enabled them to procure. Among other things Hitler said the following in his speech:

4. The German government is prepared at any time to participate in a collective, cooperative effort to guarantee peace in Europe.

5. The German government believes that the reestablishment of cooperative relations among the nations of Europe cannot be achieved through the unilateral imposition of terms on one nation by another.

6. The German government is entirely prepared to enter into nonaggression pacts with its various neighbor-states. . . .

8. The German government has made public the extent of its buildup of the new German Armed Forces. Under no circumstances will it deviate from the changes already outlined. . . . However, with regard to armaments it is prepared at any time to abide by any limitations that are likewise accepted by the other nations. . . .

10. The German government is prepared to consent to any restriction that will lead to the elimination of that heavy weaponry which is particularly suitable for use in an attack. . . .

13. The German government is prepared at any time to consent to an international agreement that would effectively neutralize and prevent any attempt on the part of one nation to interfere in the internal affairs of another nation. . . .

100

We crouched in front of the radio in my grandmother's house and listened to Hitler's speech. Neighbors and friends who did not yet have a radio had been invited too. In those days this practice of listening to the radio in groups was called "communal reception" [Gemeinschaftsempfang]. The streets were empty the way they are today during an international championship soccer match. After the speech, everyone breathed a sigh of relief, and they felt certain that Hitler would not start a war. If we were nevertheless forced to go to war, it would involve, at most, the English and the French, who might start a war because—we were told—they envied the Germans.

In 1935, I used to be given twenty pfennigs as pocket money every Saturday morning. This was enough for a movie. In those days the theaters were already showing Westerns and Dick-and-Doof films [comedy films something like the Laurel and Hardy films], and naturally we did not want to miss those. But also on the corner there was a bakery where you could buy a bag of broken-up pieces of chocolate, which also cost twenty pfennigs. Thus we always suffered a conflict of conscience over what to buy with our twenty pfennigs. So we used to buy the chocolate and then try to get into the movie free. Naturally, if we were caught without a ticket, we got slapped—and not gently! When we got home, we did not tell anyone what had happened, for if we had we would immediately have gotten another thrashing.

The noose around the neck of everyone in Germany was being drawn tighter and tighter. On April 23, the President of the Reich Chamber of Literature announced that Germans could read nothing but Aryan literature—for example, they could no longer read Heinrich Heine because he had been a Jew—nor were they permitted to read the works of any German writers who had emigrated, which included almost all writers of contemporary German literature. Anyone caught reading forbidden books or newspapers was sentenced to a term in prison, if not to a concentration camp.

The regime took advantage of every opportunity to show off its achievements, for example, at the dedication of the first section of highway connecting Frankfurt and Darmstadt. Even today some people are still circulating the myth that Hitler was the one who invented the German expressways. However, the truth is that the

101

plans for the expressways had been drawn up in 1924. To be sure, Hitler realized their possibilities and decided to act on the plans, but he had much more in mind than simply supplying work to the unemployed. Ever since his seizure of power, he had been systematically preparing for war, and thus he needed good roads so that military vehicles could be moved more rapidly during wartime.

Rearmament, the preparations for war, the persecution of dissenters, and the effects of the new "Nazi religion" were also becoming a problem to church organizations. What was their attitude toward Hitler and his regime? We know that many of the faithful—Protestants as well as Catholics—made no secret of their aversion to National Socialism, especially in rural areas, where priests and ministers enjoyed a position of great respect. But the thing that mattered to the ordinary pastors—namely the Word of God—did not always matter to the men who occupied the higher echelons of the Church hierarchy—the Church administrators, the bishops, and the cardinals.

In the summer of 1935, a terrible accident occurred at the Westphalia Explosives Manufacturing Corporation, in which sixty workmen were killed by an explosion. Bishops of both confessions gave funeral orations. The Catholic bishop spoke of the dark powers of fate and prayed for God's mercy. The Protestant bishop, Dr. Peter, said: "Death is swallowed up by victory. This thought liberates us from the uncanny hostility of this occurrence. Therefore, let us pray, along with the Führer, 'Lord, do not let us turn coward.'"

This response was cynically inappropriate considering that the victims were the first claimed by a gigantic armaments race. Even Dr. Peter must have realized that people rarely employ explosives for peaceful purposes.

On March 28, the bishops attending a Catholic bishops' conference in Fulda stated their unequivocal support of Hitler:

> For valid reasons, which have been repeatedly explained, relating to their dutiful concern to maintain the purity of the Catholic faith and to preserve the inviolable exercises and rights of the Catholic Church, the Supreme Shepherds of the Catholic dioceses of Germany have, in recent years, adopted a negative

attitude toward the National Socialist movement and expressed this attitude in prohibitions and admonitions that they intended to remain in force as long as the reasons for this attitude persisted.

We must now acknowledge that the highest representative of the German government, who is also the authorized leader of the aforementioned movement, has made public and solemn declarations acknowledging the inviolability of Catholic doctrine and the immutable exercises and rights of the Church, and that in addition the German government has expressly guaranteed the completely binding nature of agreements made between the Church and the individual provinces of Germany. Thus, without annulling our condemnation, expressed in the measures we have taken in the past, of certain religious and moral errors, the episcopate believes that we can now trust that it is no longer necessary for us to uphold the universal prohibitions and admonitions previously described.

At the present hour, as at any other, Catholic Christians who regard the voice of their Church as holy have no need of any special admonition to encourage them to maintain their loyalty to the lawful authorities and to perform conscientiously all their duties as citizens by remaining fundamentally opposed to illegal or revolutionary conduct of any kind.

Thus the faithful Catholic had been told by the highest dignitaries of his faith that any form of resistance against Hitler violated the commandment of the Church. How was a layman, a man of naive faith, to see through Hitler's machinations or to learn to distrust him, when the bishops of his Church told him that Hitler was acceptable after all, as long as he did not violate the rights of the Church or appropriate its property?

Nevertheless, until the bitter end in 1945, resistance to Hitler in church circles continued—as is proved by the fact that many clergymen, both Protestant and Catholic, were sent to prison or to concentration camps and were tortured or murdered there.

They had not only distrusted Hitler, but also the higher authorities in the church. The Christian faith was more important to them than the observance of virtuous conduct in relation to their criminal government. We have proof that some clergymen preached sermons that openly encouraged the people to engage in active resistance.

Eyewitnesses told me that a minister from our neighboring parish was arrested by two Gestapo men at the entrance to the church after church services were over. It was not unusual for the Gestapo to attend church services, where they just sat and listened. If the minister let fall even one word against Hitler or if his sermon lent itself to an ambiguous interpretation, he would be arrested.

However, there were two laws which, more than any others, shaped the future face of the Third Reich. When many things about those days have long since been forgotten, the Germans and the other peoples of the world—especially the Jews—will still remember these laws.

On September 15, the government passed the Citizenship Law and the Law to Protect German Blood and German Honor. These were the Nuremberg Laws, which derived their name from the fact that they were submitted and approved during a special session of the Reichstag held in Nuremberg:

Article 1

(1). No one can be a citizen unless he belongs to the defensive league of the German Reich and, for this reason, is under particular obligation to it. . . .

Article 2

(1). No one can be a citizen of the Reich unless he is a citizen of German blood or German-related stock, whose conduct proves that he is willing and able to serve faithfully the German people and the German Reich. . . .

Article 3

The Reich Minister of the Interior, with the consent of the Deputy Führer, is enacting the legal and administrative regulations required to implement and supplement this law.

Citizenship Law of September 15, 1935

Article 1

(1). Marriages between Jews and citizens of German blood or German-related stock are forbidden. Any marriages entered into in violation of this law are invalid, even if, in order to evade this law, the couple are married abroad.

(2). Only the Public Prosecutor can take legal action to invalidate such marriages.

Article 2

Extramarital intercourse between Jews and citizens of German blood or German-related stock is forbidden. . . .

Article 5

(1). Anyone who violates the prohibition of Article 1 will be sentenced to prison. . . .

(2). A man who violates the prohibition of Article 2 will be sentenced to jail or prison.

Article 6

The Reich Minister of the Interior, with the consent of the Deputy Führer and the Reich Minister of Justice, is enacting the legal and administrative regulations required to implement and supplement this law.

Law to Protect German Blood and German Honor,
enacted on September 15, 1935

The Nuremberg Laws laid the groundwork for the later extermination of the Jews.

On October 18, 1935, a law was passed "to ensure the continued derivation of the German people from healthy stock." From now on Germans were not permitted to marry unless it had been established beyond a shadow of a doubt that no hereditary diseases existed in their families. The healthy-stock law laid the groundwork for the later practice of euthanasia. Anyone who, according to the National Socialist point of view, was "unworthy to live," was condemned to death.

I have a mentally and physically handicapped son. If he had been born in 1935, he would certainly never have lived to the age of three. Hitler's myrmidons and accomplices—among them a great many physicians who later conducted ghastly experiments on human beings—would have come to take my son away, and a short time later I would have been informed that he had died in the course of a "necessary" operation.

Never at any time in human history, or in any country in the world, had such laws as these existed before—not even in periods of the greatest barbarism, and certainly not among so-called savages or uncivilized races. These laws are an outrage and a disgrace, and clearly it is equally disgraceful that a jurist like Hans Globke, who wrote the commentaries to the Nuremberg

Laws and served as a senior civil servant in the Ministry of the Interior from 1932 to 1945, was allowed to serve as secretary of state in the Chancellery of the Federal Republic of Germany from 1953 to 1963. He was the one who actually conceived the rules of implementaton, the methodological instructions, which facilitated the practical application of the Nuremberg Laws.

The Law for the preservation of racial purity draws a biological distinction between those of Jewish and German blood. The growing decay, during the decade preceding the total reorganization of our country, of people's awareness of the significance of keeping our blood pure, and the dissolution of all our traditional German values that accompanied it, made it particularly urgent that legal measures should be taken. Because the Jews alone represent an acute danger to the German people, the primary purpose of the law is to prevent any further intermingling of Jewish and German blood. . . .

No law enacted since the National Socialist revolution represents such a radical departure from the intellectual attitudes and conception of the State that dominated the last century as does the Citizenship Law. In this law National Socialism rejects the doctrines of the equality of all men and the basically limitless freedom of the individual in relation to the State, in favor of the harsh but necessary recognition of that inequality and diversity of human beings decreed by natural law. The disparity between races, peoples, and human beings necessarily results in distinctions between the rights and duties accorded to various individuals. The Citizenship Law realizes this disparity, which is based on life and the immutable laws of nature, in the fundamental political order of the German people.

From Stuckart and Globke's Commentaries
on the Legislation of the German Racial Laws

Globke's case makes it clear that men who, during the Nazi era, paved the way for the mass extermination of human beings—even if they "only" wrote a legal commentary—were able to rise to the highest position of power in the newly created state, the Federal Republic of Germany.

1936

This was the year of the Olympics. The summer games were held in Berlin, the winter games in Garmisch-Partenkirchen.

Naturally, we children were very interested in the Olympics. After all, I was already ten years old, and sports were one of the principal subjects we were taught in school. Anyone who was good at sports was also considered a good student.

Although it was drummed into our heads every day that anything or anyone non-German was completely worthless, a black man became our idol: the American Jesse Owens, winner of four Olympic medals. In the playing field we used to play at being Jesse Owens; whoever could jump the farthest or run the fastest or throw some object the greatest distance became Jesse Owens.

When our teachers heard us, they forbade us to play such games, but they never replied to our question of how a black man, a member of an "inferior" race, could manage to be such a consummate athlete.

Hitler and his regime regarded the Olympic Games as the most favorable of opportunities to show the world what massive support Hitler was accorded by his people. The eyes of the entire world were turned toward Berlin, and they saw how the people cheered him. Berlin was a sea of flags, and nothing was visible but law, order, cleanliness, and discipline. However, neither athletes nor officials nor anyone in a position of authority was taken to see the concentration camps. They saw only the sugar-coated facade of the Third Reich, and yet countless human beings in Germany were held prisoners behind barbed wire under the most inhumane conditions.

The Saar region had not actually been taken away from Germany by the Treaty of Versailles but had merely been placed under the control of the League of Nations (precursor of the United Nations), whose headquarters were in Geneva, and its economy oriented toward France. The peace treaty had provided that after a period of fifteen years a plebiscite was to be held in the Saar region to determine whether the people themselves wanted the Saar to belong to Germany or France.

In the plebiscite of 1936, 91 percent of the people of the Saar region voted to join the German Reich, and Hitler reckoned this outcome as his own personal triumph. The Saar region was also important to him in another respect, for it contained vast coal mines and steelworks. The area was extremely important to the German armaments industry.

At the celebration held in Saarbrücken in honor of the "liberation" of the Saar, Hitler stated that he would make no further territorial claims on France. He failed to mention, however, that for a long time he had been casting an eye at Alsace-Lorraine, which had been awarded to France in the Treaty of Versailles. He added, "In the end blood is stronger than anything written on paper. What was written with ink will one day be wiped away again by blood. Woe to him who is unwilling to learn from these facts."

For Hitler treaties were always only paper, which he tore up when they ceased to promote his interests or hampered his policies.

In order to guarantee the security of France, the Treaty of Versailles had also provided that no German military forces might be stationed along the strip of land thirty miles wide that extended along the east bank of the Rhine. This area used to be called the "demilitarized zone."

On March 7, German troops marched into this zone and also occupied land on the west bank of the Rhine. Once again Hitler had violated a treaty and declared it invalid with soldiers' boots. But the people of the Rhineland greeted the soldiers of the new German Army with wild enthusiasm.

To be sure, on March 18, the League of Nations issued a condemnation of the German occupation of the Rhineland, but it took no steps beyond this lame protest. This fact strengthened Hitler's conviction that France and Great Britain were weak nations that would collapse under the first attack.

Hitler had always permitted the German people to ratify his "victories." On March 19, after the occupation of the Rhineland, another plebiscite was held in which more than 98 percent of the voters voted in favor of Hitler and his policies.

One is quite justified in questioning the accuracy of this figure, for the Nazis were never very particular about telling the truth. In any case, even if only 40 percent of the people had voted in his favor, Hitler would not have ordered his troops to return from the Rhineland:

> Monday, March 30, 1936
> The German people have surrendered! HE has been elected with ostensibly 98.8 percent of the votes—and therefore some 50,000 votes were worthless. I and many others do not believe these figures and think that they were deliberately manufactured. The results of the plebiscite were falsified! It was announced that 100 percent of the votes cast in Rotsürben, near Breslau, and other villages, endorsed Hitler's policies. But the inhabitants of these villages themselves say that they deliberately wrote *No* on their ballots in order to make misunderstanding impossible.
>
> Walter Tausk

On June 17, Heinrich Himmler, the most unscrupulous member of Hitler's staff, became chief of all the police in Germany. Whenever my grandmother heard Himmler speak on the radio or saw his picture in a newspaper, she would invariably say, "I'm afraid of that man. It's awful that the Führer surrounds himself with people like that."

It must not be forgotten that vast segments of the population worshipped Hitler to the point of idolatry. The subtle propaganda that daily rained down onto every German head strongly encouraged this adoration. If something happened that offended people's sense of justice and morality, they would simply say, "If only the Führer knew. . . ."

The people were so credulous that they actually believed that the Führer knew almost nothing about the acts of injustice taking place in their land. After all, they thought, he's busy with "high-level" political concerns. It seemed impossible that the Führer could have ordered all these atrocities. In this way people succeeded in shifting away from themselves the responsibility for what was going on.

On July 16, just two weeks before the opening of the summer Olympics, the Spanish Civil War began, in the course of which, with German and Italian military aid, the Fascist General Franco succeeded in defeating the Spanish Republican forces and the brigades made up of people from all over the world who had come to fight on their side.

Hitler never concealed the part his troops were playing in the Spanish Civil War. When it ended in 1939, he had the German troops he had sent to Spain—the Condor Legion—parade through the streets of Berlin. Spain had supplied the field for the young German troops and their officers to practice maneuvers.

On September 30, Franco became head of the Spanish government, and by November 18, Germany and Italy had already granted the new government their official recognition. The world saw clearly what was going on. Hitler and Mussolini made it clear that their sympathies and their interests lay with the dictator Franco.

Years before the outbreak of World War II, in which English and American planes bombed the German civilian population, German aircraft were bombing Spanish cities. For example, the town of Guernica was almost totally annihilated.

Pablo Picasso's painting *Guernica* has this crime as its theme. In Hermann Kesten's book *Die Kinder von Gernica* [*The Children of Guernica; a novel*, Longmans, Green & Co., New York, 1939], published in 1939 while Kesten was in exile, a boy who survived the bombing describes the attack:

"Dear sir, these planes flew down so low, as if they were curious, and then I was running, feeling nothing yet, not horror, not despair, not this pain tearing my guts. I simply ran. I saw! These planes shot at the running people who had already left the air-raid shelters. There was a plaza in front of the church, the Sheep Market, where the sheep were penned in; the planes shot at the sheep with machine guns, you understand, and the sheep died bleating helplessly, like children. And the howling dogs fell down and stopped howling. And the planes shot at the lowing livestock at the cattle market; the cows, with their gentle eyes, fell over and stopped mooing. They shot at people as well as animals. None of it mattered to them. They had been paid to do it, and they also shot out of a holy conviction. I ran and saw.

Suddenly a hand grabbed me, pushed me into a hole; in the middle of the marketplace the earth had been torn open; a hole descended into the belly of the earth, but it was only a hole made by exploding shells; I lay in the hole stretched out at full length, and there was noise and smoke. There was no more sky. Finally the noise stopped. The planes had left. Then a hand lifted me out of the shell hole. There were two people standing in the square, myself and someone else. Delirium, like being blind, like being deaf. The stillness after the ear-splitting din, so horribly still, a hundred times more horrible than the noise. And pieces of cars on the roofs, roofs in the gardens, burning trees, broken windows, houses hit by bombs and torn open from the roof to the cellar. And pools of blood, dark puddles of blackish blood. And the dead. Death has no shame. It wipes every face and leaves it bare. If God had human feelings, he would have to look away from the dead. Isn't he ashamed when he sees the dead looking so naked? And this moaning in the burning houses. And everywhere the dead. Dogs, cats, livestock, men, women, children stretched out, crouching, sitting up, all dead. And then the wounded. How they scream! Nothing is capable of shocking human beings.

"Later, in Paris, I read in certain newspapers that not the airplanes but anarchists had set Guernica on fire, torched the houses, shot nuns, slaughtered children. And people read these things, and people believe these things. And people can do evil things and then deny it! And the thieves stand on both sides of the street and point the finger of guilt at innocent people; everyone knows that thieves do this. First they murder; then they lie. Is that allowed? Sir! They lied! They lied!"

Carlos pounded on my knee with both fists.

"Yes, indeed," I said. "Those who murder also lie."

"Victories make people drunk," my grandfather always used to say, "and suddenly even sensible people begin to talk nonsense."

It was true that since 1933 there had been nothing but victories, and many people had actually gotten drunk on the victory fanfares, the victory celebrations, the flags, and the music of marching bands.

Naturally all these victories were victories for the Aryans, that is, for the non-Jews. The Aryan man was idealized until

111

he became a physical and mental "superman." Soon there was a strictly German art, a strictly German literature, and even a strictly German physics.

The German Nobel Prize winner Professor Philipp Lenard went so far as to propose the ridiculous theory that success in the area of scientific endeavor is determined by race, and that only the Aryan is capable of the highest scientific achievement.

The Concept of Race in Science
    a) "German Physics"
[An excerpt from the writings of Nobel-Prize-winning scientist Professor Philipp Lenard]
    "*German* physics?" you will ask. I could just as easily have said "Aryan physics" or "the physics of the Nordic races," the physics of the reality-probers, the physics of the truth-seekers, the physics of those who founded natural science. People will disagree with me and say, "Science is and always will be international!" But this belief springs from a fundamental misapprehension. In reality science, like everything produced by human beings, is determined by race, by the blood. The illusion that science is an international phenomenon can arise if, on the grounds of the universal validity of scientific conclusions, one mistakenly concludes that they were derived from universal sources, or if one overlooks the fact that the people of various countries who have produced scientific results identical with, or closely akin to, those of the Germans, have been able to do so only because, and to the degree that, they too are or were derived primarily from the interbreeding of Nordic races. Peoples of other racial mixtures practice a different kind of science. . . .

In 1933, the year of the book burnings, measures had been taken against literature that did not meet with the Nazis' approval; now the Nazis began to eliminate and ban from the museums works of sculpture, painting, and architecture that they considered "un-German." An exhibition was organized in the House of German Art in Munich, which was designed to introduce the German public to examples of non-German art. The exhibition was entitled "Degenerate Art."

The Nazis regarded as degenerate any artist whose works showed him against war and for humanity, anyone who depicted

Plakat für die Ausstellung „Entartete Kunst", 1936. In der Ausstellung waren u. a. Werke von Klee, Barlach, Marc, Beckmann, Hofer, Kokoschka, Feininger und Nolde zu sehen.

Ausstellung im Weißen Saal der Polizeidirektion, Neuhauserstraße, Eingang Augustinerstraße
Geöffnet: Werktags von 10 bis 21 Uhr, Sonntags 10 bis 18 Uhr
Eintritt: Für Einzelpersonen 20 Pfennig. Bei geschlossenen Betriebe 10 Pfennig.
Anmeldung der Führungen im Gauamt der N.S.-Gem. „Kraft durch Freude" Abt. Propaganda

Poster advertising the exhibition of "Degenerate Art" held in 1936. Works by Klee, Barlach, Beckmann, Hofer, Kokoschka, Feininger, Nolde, and many others were shown at this exhibition. The poster says:

DEGENERATE ART

Exhibition of "cultural documents"
reflecting Bolshevism and Jewish subversion.
March 4-March 31, 1936.

What we see at this interesting exhibition
was once regarded as serious art!!!!!

Exhibition in the White Hall of the Police Directorate,
Neuhauserstrasse, entrance on Augustinerstrasse.
Open workdays from 10:00 to 9:00, Sundays from 10:00 to 6:00
Entrance fee: 20 pfennigs per person.
10 pfennigs per person in employee groups
under direction of a tour guide.
Group tours should report to the Propaganda Division
of the District Office
of the National Socialist Association "Strength through Joy."

Left: Käthe Kollwitz (1867-1945)
Right: George Grosz (1893-1959) emigrated
to New York in 1932.

man in his moments of fear, in his pain and human frailty, who failed to glorify the blond Teuton or strength, power, and victory.

The works the Nazis gathered together in Munich provided a panorama of modern art. One saw names that were known all over the world then as now: Käthe Kollwitz, Lovis Corinth, Oskar Kokoschka, Emil Nolde, Otto Dix, Paul Klee, Franz Marc, George Grosz, to name only a few.

No art critic was allowed to express any criticism of the new Nazi "art." From now on Goebbels demanded "aesthetic contemplation," in other words, extravagant praise of what the Nazis propagated under the guise of art, most of which one can probably dismiss as utter trash.

Nazi art was bombastic, overblown, and gigantic. One of the leading representatives of this art was the sculptor Arno Breker, who today is still busily at work in the Federal Republic of Germany.

But Goebbels knew well enough that the works he had exhibited as examples of degenerate art were the authentic art of the twentieth century. Many Nazi bigwigs had "degenerate" paintings hanging in their own homes. On June 3, 1938—to skip ahead here—all paintings listed as degenerate were confiscated, without compensation to their owners. The Nazis collected 12,890 works of art. In other words, paintings were stolen from artists or from the owners, whether private citizens, museums, or some other kind of public establishment.

Goebbels was also aware, however, that money was to be earned with these paintings. He had more than seven hundred art works transported to Lucerne, Switzerland, and sold at public auction, for Germany needed foreign bills of exchange to purchase the raw materials required by the German armaments industry.

Because of this auction many art works that are now being

Arno Breker's "Always Prepared" (1937)

admired in museums all over the world were preserved for generations to come, if not for the Germans themselves.

To jump ahead in time once again: Eventually the destruction of art works assumed even greater proportions. In March, 1939, some 4,829 works were burned on a funeral pyre in the courtyard of the main firehouse in Berlin. Irreplaceable things were destroyed. The longer the Nazis remained in power, the more "thorough" was their destruction of culture.

On December 1, 1936, a law was passed regarding the Hitler Youth. Article 2 stated: "In addition to the training they receive in their homes and schools, all German young people are to become members of the Hitler Youth in order to receive a physical, mental, and moral education in the spirit of National Socialism that will enable them to serve their people and the nation as a whole."

In this way, all young Germans were to be incorporated into organizations and formal structures. Shortly thereafter, Hitler offered a more extensive definition of his views on the education of youth.

Human swastika formed by members of the Hitler Youth in 1934.

"You too belong to the Führer."

My theory of education is harsh. All weakness must be hammered out. The youth who grow up in my *Ordensburgen* [training schools for future political leaders] will terrify the world. I want a youth that is violent, masterful, intrepid, cruel. Young people must be all these things. They must endure pain. There must be nothing weak and tender about them. The magnificent, free predator must once again flash in their eyes. I want my young people strong and handsome. I will have them taught all types of physical exercise. I want athletic young people. This is first and most important. Thus will I wipe out the thousands of years of human domestication. Thus will I see before me the pure, noble raw material of nature. Thus can I create something new.

I want no intellectual education. Knowledge would ruin my young people for me. Rather I would have them learn only what they acquire voluntarily as they follow their play instincts. But they must learn self-control. They shall learn to conquer the fear of death in the course of the most difficult trials. Then they will

117

Hitler talking to a German child.

have attained the stage of heroic youth. From this will grow the stage of the free being, the human being, the god-man. In my training schools the beautiful, self-governing god-man will be enshrined as an image of worship and will prepare the young for the coming stage of maturity and manhood. . . .

But Hitler did not finally discard his mask until his speech in Reichenberg on December 2, 1938.

These young people will learn nothing else but how to think German and act German. And when, at the age of ten, this boy and this girl enter our organizations and there, frequently for the first time in their lives, breathe and feel a breath of fresh air, then four years later they will leave the Jungvolk to enter the Hitler Youth, and once again we will keep them there for four years; and then, instead of returning them to the hands of those adults who created our old social classes and ranks, we will immediately admit them into the Party or put them in the National Socialist Labor Front, the SA or the SS, in the National Socialist Motor Corps, and so on. And if they remain there for two years or for a year and a half and have not yet become totally dedicated National Socialists, then they will be sent to work in the Labor Service and will be polished there for six or seven

118

months, all by means of a single symbol, the German spade. And if any remnants of class consciousness or the arrogance of rank is left in them after six or seven months there, they will be turned over to the Armed Forces to undergo an additional two years' treatment. And when, after two or three or four years they return home again, then, in order to prevent them from slipping back into the old way, we will immediately put them back in the SA, the SS, and so on. And they will never be free again, not their whole lives long.

It is hardly possible to conceive of a more cynical statement. What Hitler had said, in different words, was: "I need cannon fodder, soldiers for conquering Europe." These young people were not supposed to be educated in how to become human beings; they were to know only what they needed to know in order to be able to enslave other peoples later. This was Hitler's simple "pedagogical" formula.

1937

This year my twenty-pfennig weekly allowance was not increased. The wages my uncles and aunts and my mother were earning had not increased either. Of course, now and then my grandfather would slip me an extra twenty pfennigs on the sly, but even so I never had enough money for my needs, for I had begun to read. I indiscriminately devoured everything in print that I could get my hands on. In those days you had to pay a fee in order to borrow a book from a public library—ten pfennigs for every book. And since I read very fast, I often read through a book in just one day by staying up and reading half the night.

I also used to read parts of my father's big Bible, which was filled with the notes he had recorded in the margins.

In order to earn money for library books, I delivered newspapers. They were not daily papers—for to deliver them I would have had to get up at five o'clock every morning—but weekly newspapers and magazines. I used to load two big heavy pouches onto my bicycle. In return, I received about five reichsmarks from the wholesale dealer, who deposited the bale of papers outside the door of my house every Saturday morning. In the course of my work, I also used to earn a couple of extra marks, for if a paper cost twenty-eight pfennigs, people usually gave me thirty pfennigs and let me keep two pfennigs for myself. Sometimes I even got a five- or seven-pfennig tip, but as my mother always used to say, "Small animals make manure too."

My job was hard because my customers often lived vast distances apart. I had to go to remote and solitary farms, which, heaven knows, was no fun in winter. But every Saturday evening I used to rejoice over the money I had earned by my own efforts. I was able to pay for library books and buy books of my own and sometimes still have something left over.

Hitler had now been in power for four years.

On January 30, he had the Reichstag extend for another four

years the law with which he had inaugurated his term in office, the Enabling Act. But even without this law, he would have been able to continue to carry out his plans, for now he had unlimited powers.

In 1936, one of my uncles had been drafted into military service, and in 1937 he came home on leave for the first time. He was wearing a blue uniform, for he served in the Luftwaffe [air force] as a member of the ground crew. We children worshipped him, but he did not feel nearly as comfortable in his uniform as we imagined he did.

"Let's hope there isn't going to be a war," he used to say over and over. When my grandmother and his brothers and sisters laughed at the whole idea, he would simply say, "If you only knew all the things that go on behind barracks walls." He never told us anything more about it.

"Naturally," my grandmother would reply, "the Führer must be prepared for war in case the French and the English attack us someday."

Technology and modern means of communication had made the world smaller. A regular system of civilian air travel had been established, though in those days it took four hours and forty minutes to fly from Berlin to London, a trip that today takes only fifty minutes. Naturally these civilian planes were also forerunners of those used later by the Luftwaffe and served as test models for new types of planes.

The people appeared to have come to terms with Hitler; even many people who had been opposed to him in the beginning, now that they had jobs again, had decided to put up with the situation.

Before long the labor supply began to run short. The Armed Forces were drafting more and more young, able-bodied men into the barracks, and the armaments industry was operating at full speed and needed labor. More and more women took over factory jobs that in the past had been held only by men.

My father still had his shoemaker's workshop in the kitchen, to the annoyance of my mother, who was never able to get her kitchen properly clean. His customers kept growing more numerous.

Once again people had a little money; they had new shoes

made or had the old ones thoroughly repaired. My father was earning more money, and sometimes he worked until very late at night in order to hold on to all his customers.

That year our district got electricity. My mother was glad, for now she no longer had to start a fire in the stove in the morning simply in order to boil the water for our coffee. Now an electric immersion heater did it in just one minute. Of course, we could not afford an electric range, so we continued to cook on a charcoal range, which was usually heated with wood. To people who had never known anything but poverty and hardship, these changes constituted a modest degree of prosperity.

I was supposed to have joined the Jungvolk a long time before, and now that I was eleven I was already a year late. But by dint of various tricks, my mother had always managed to keep me from joining. Once she got out of it by saying that we did not have enough money to buy me a uniform; another time she said that I could not appear at roll call because I had to help a farmer with his farmwork. Of course, I would have been happy to join the Jungvolk, for all my school friends were members, and I thought of it as a grand adventure. They played war games, built outdoor campfires, staged scouting expeditions, and played at "tracking the enemy" in the woods. To play this last game you had to be very good at sneaking up on people, and I was one of the best "sneakers" in our class. My grandfather had taught me how to move through the woods without making a sound so as not to scare off the grazing deer.

When my mother and I worked for some farmer at harvest time, we used to be paid with potatoes, which we could store in the cellar, or with bread, butter, eggs, and flour, but not with money.

Every other week my father used to disappear for the weekend. He was smuggling newspapers like *Das Goldene Zeitalter* [The golden age] and *Der Wachturm* [The watchtower] into Germany from Czechoslovakia. When he returned home, strange men began to visit him again. They came from Weiden, Hof, Bayreuth, and even from Bamberg and Würzburg. These men then passed on to their fellow-believers the newspapers that my father had smuggled in from abroad.

On July 1, 1937, Pastor Martin Niemöller was arrested and

sent to Sachsenhausen Concentration Camp; in 1941, he was sen to the camp at Dachau; and later he was sent to the Southern Tyrol, where he was freed by Allied troops in 1945.

During World War I, Niemöller had been a U-boat commander and had been awarded what in those days was the highest German military decoration, the Order of Merit. He was one of the most fearless leaders of the Confessing Church, which was combating official Church policy.[1]

After sentence had been passed on Pastor Niemöller, the following text was read from the pulpits of all the Protestant churches:

> The Protestant Christians of Germany have awaited with deep anxiety and profound emotion the outcome of the trial before a special court called to reach a verdict concerning the grave charges brought against Pastor Martin Niemöller. The court sentenced him to seven months' imprisonment in a fortress and imposed a fine of 2,000 reichsmarks; in addition it determined that because of the period of confinement that Pastor Niemöller underwent preceding and during the trial, he might be considered to have already served his seven months' sentence and might also be excused from paying 500 marks of his fine.
>
> According to law a person may be sentenced to confinement in a fortress only 'if the crime was not directed against the welfare of the people and the criminal acted on the basis of strictly honorable motives.' Thus the verdict of the court established that Pastor Niemöller did not transgress against the people's welfare and that he acted out of strictly honorable motives. . . .
>
> Martin Niemöller has *not* been set free. He has been sent to a concentration camp—for an indefinite period. Thus it is insinuated that he is guilty of being an "antisocial parasite." This treatment cannot be reconciled with the verdict of the court. It is written that "the law must always remain the law."

Even today some people claim that no one during the Nazi era knew about the existence of the concentration camps. At least

[1] The Confessing Church was a faction of the German Lutheran Church, composed of lay members and clergy, that opposed National Socialism and thus opposed the dominant faction in the Church. Martin Niemöller organized groups of pastors into a Confessional League in 1933-34, and in 1934 proclaimed his opposition to Hitler in a written declaration.—Tr.

124

those Germans who were sitting in church that Sunday morning and heard that proclamation read from the pulpit or read it in the church news must have known about the camps.

On April 10, the German writer Heinrich Mann gave a speech in Paris. Naturally Heinrich Mann, like his brother Thomas Mann, was called a political agitator, a German-hater, a Jew-lover, and whatever else the Nazis called the German emigrants in order to defame them and make them sound untrustworthy. But the emigrants were the ones who admonished the German people—those who were not indifferent to their people's fate—and who clearly perceived that Hitler's policies would lead to war and thus, inevitably, to disaster.

> Hitler is driving Germany toward a disastrous war. Thus he places before the German people the question of the fate of our homeland. Therefore, the paramount task of the German Popular Front [a coalition of Communists, Socialists, intellectuals—anyone opposed to Hitler] can only be to combat Hitler's warmongering policies, the intolerable burdens of armament manufacture, the compulsory war preparations, and to fight for the preservation of the peace. This fight for peace, which will also save our youth from extermination on the battlefield, will promote the true national interests of the German people. It is possible to maintain peace and spare millions of people the immeasurable suffering of war if Hitler is overthrown before he has the chance to light the torch.
>
> Any delay in the outbreak of war achieved through the strengthening of international peace, any victory won by the Spanish populist army against the interventionist troops, any resistance by the German masses increases the possibility of victory over Hitler, the enemy of the people. . . .
>
> Only the German Popular Front will have the strength to develop all the liberal impulses in the people that have been suppressed and to unite the people in large-scale mass movements. Only the German Popular Front is capable of uniting the people against Hitler. Only the German Popular Front is capable of creating a free and happier future for Germany.

Who was able to hear or read this speech, who in Germany had the opportunity to procure the foreign newspapers in which it was printed? Certainly not my parents.

The German emigrants living abroad were not the only people who were raising the alarm about Hitler's policies; there was also a secret resistance movement within the Reich itself. Thus during the year 1937, more than 900,000 anti-Hitler publications appeared in Germany, 84,000 of which were written in code; there were writings of all kinds that had been copied by hectograph, and 788,000 publications expressing opposition to the National Socialist system. For example, these publications stated, and proved with statistics, that the so-called Four Year Plan for the stimulation of the economy was no economic plan at all, but a plan for war.

Anyone convicted of producing or distributing these publications, or even of happening to have one in his possession, was sentenced by a special court and ended up in a concentration camp or was immediately sentenced to death.

Opposition political parties and resistance groups made repeated attempts to show what really lay behind the slogans and lies of the Nazis. In 1936, the Socialist Action Group, an illegal organ of the SPD [Socialists], tried to put the myth of Job-Provider Hitler in its proper light:

Up with Wages!

Since Hitler's seizure of power there has been a shocking decrease in wages. In part, they have been deliberately lowered; in part, the decrease has resulted from the rise in prices and the reduction in purchasing power. Today one has to pay one mark for what, four years ago, one could buy for seventy-eight pfennigs.

This means that if a worker was earning forty marks a week four years ago, and he is still receiving the same wages today, he is in reality no longer earning forty marks but only thirty.

However, if, in the course of the last four years, the value of his wages has sunk from forty marks to thirty, in reality he is not even earning thirty marks, but only twenty-two and a half.

For certain deductions are subtracted from his thirty marks, legally prescribed deductions as well as the so-called voluntary deductions, which are larger than they have ever been before.

Thus, when the National Socialists say that workers cannot be paid higher wages, this does not mean that these workers are living in the same conditions as before, but that they are actually much worse off than they were in the past!

At one time German workers were among the highest-paid workers in the world. How is their situation now? . . .

The National Socialists say, "An increase in wages is possible only if there is a rise in the production rate!" So, despite the exploitation of workers for all they are worth and despite compulsory labor, is the production rate during the Hitler era not rising but actually sinking? But how can one expect to increase the production rate if one produces nothing but products that are valueless to the economy, such as cannons and factories for the manufacture of substitutes for raw materials that could be purchased abroad for a third of the cost? The National Socialists say, "We have put millions of people back to work!"

Yes, but in the process they have managed the feat of creating billions in debts, and nevertheless, they are not paying formerly unemployed workers much more for their labor than these workers were receiving, in the form of government relief, in the days of the Weimar Republic; and they are paying those workers who *were* employed under the Weimar Republic much less than they received then.

That year one could already see symptoms of war brewing all over the world, for the Sino-Japanese war [1935–1945] had begun on Chinese soil. German warships were bombarding the city of Almería in Spain. Mussolini, the leader of Fascist Italy, visited Germany in order to confer with Hitler regarding their future plans in Spain and Africa.

To be sure, the bombs and shells were exploding far from Germany, but the wars outside her borders were being waged with German military equipment.

The German people thought that they could look forward to a long era of peace, for whenever he appeared in public Hitler never missed an opportunity to speak about his desire for peace and talk of his hand stretched out in friendship, which the other countries and statesmen needed only to grasp.

On September 7, he declared the Treaty of Versailles null and void. He claimed that all those regions that had been taken away from Germany (Alsace-Lorraine and Eupen-Malmédy in the West, Upper Silesia, the Warta district, and the Memel territory in the East) actually belonged to Germany, that they had been stolen by the victorious Allies after World War I, and that they must now be given back to Germany. If this restitution could not be accomplished peaceably, Germany would have to resort to martial methods. This announcement was grist to the mills of those Germans who had always felt that the Treaty of Versailles had humiliated their country.

The world community, including France, Great Britain, and the League of Nations, scarcely protested. In fact, the British Conservative politician Lord Halifax, acting in the name of Prime Minister Chamberlain, even assured Hitler that Britain would permit Germany to expand its borders provided that it did so without causing a war.

Such concessions lent support to Hitler's policy of aggression and strengthened him in his belief that the Western democracies were too weak to risk war. Hitler was convinced that they would all bow to him, but he failed to understand that these men were fighting to preserve the peace. They actually believed that if they met Hitler halfway and maintained friendly relations with him, they could prevent war.

However, Hitler had decided long ago that there would be a war; now all he had to do was to convince his generals of the fact.

On November 5, he invited the Commanders-in-Chief of the three branches of the Armed Forces, as well as the Secretary of State for Foreign Affairs, to a conference, in the course of which he revealed his plans for war. The only objections the generals raised were of a military nature, for they believed that Germany was not well enough prepared for war to defeat enemies like France and England.

The following is an excerpt from the discussion, as recorded by Colonel Hossbach:

Berlin, November 10, 1937
Notes on the conference held in the Chancellery
on November 5, 1937, from 4:15 P.M. to 8:30 P.M.
Persons present:
The Führer and Chancellor of the Reich
The War Minister,
    Field Marshal von Blomberg
The Commander-in-Chief of the Army,
    General Baron von Fritsch

The Commander-in-Chief of the Navy,
  Admiral Dr. Raeder
The Commander-in-Chief of the Air Force,
  General Göring
The Secretary of State for Foreign Affairs,
  Baron von Neurath
Colonel Hossbach

By way of introduction, the Führer states that the subject of today's conference is so important that in countries other than Germany it would probably be considered appropriate to discuss it in the forum of the assembled cabinet ministers, but that precisely because of the importance of the subject he—the Führer—has decided not to allow this matter to be discussed by members of the cabinet. His following statements are the result of exhaustive reflection and of his four and a half years of experience in governing the country. He wishes to explain to the gentlemen present his basic thoughts about the possible and necessary development of our situation with regard to foreign policy, and in the interests of developing a German political policy based on long-term considerations he wishes his remarks to be regarded as his legacy in the event of his death. . . .

Condition 1: Time, 1943–1945.

After this period we must expect the situation to change to our disadvantage. The rearmament of the Army, Navy, and Air Force, as well as the training of the officer's corps, have been almost completed. Their equipment and weaponry are modern, but if we waited much longer we would be running the risk of their becoming outdated. Moreover, we cannot always prevent information about 'special weaponry' from leaking out. The acquisition of reserve troops is limited to the recruitment of young men from each new generation as it comes of age, for we cannot add to our military forces by the recruitment of additional older men who have not received the proper training. In comparison to the rearmament of the rest of the world, we are gaining in strength. If we were to refrain from taking any action until the period 1943–1945, our lack of food reserves might bring us closer each year to a critical food shortage, which we do not possess sufficient foreign bills of exchange to counteract. . . .

Condition 2:

If the social tensions in France should develop into a major internal crisis that would absorb the attention of the French Army and thus prevent it from taking any active military steps against Germany, the time would have come for us to move against the Czechs. . . .

Condition 3:

If France should become so deeply involved in war with another nation that it cannot advance against Germany.

To improve our military and political situation in the event that Germany should become involved in a war, our number-one priority must be the simultaneous overthrow of the Czechs and Austria, so that we will have eliminated the threat of a flank attack in case we are forced to advance our troops toward the West. . . .

The Führer believes that Condition 3 may be imminent because of the possibility that current tensions in the Mediterranean area might create the requisite conditions, in which case he is determined to take advantage of the situation whenever it develops, even if it should do so as early as 1938. . . .

The moment of our attacks on the Czechs and Austria must depend on the course of the war fought by Italy, England, and France and thus ought not, for example, to coincide with the opening of hostilities on the part of these nations. The Führer also states that he does not intend to enter into any military agreements with Italy but wishes to be free to pursue his own course and, by taking advantage of an opportunity that will present itself only once, to initiate and carry out the campaign against the Czechs—a campaign in which the Czechs must be attacked "with the swiftness of lightning. . . ."

I, the undersigned, personally testify to the accuracy of this document.

> Signed:
> Hossbach
> Colonel, General Staff

Naturally the German people knew nothing about this conference, though in the munitions factories people were already working in three shifts around the clock. Many of them did not even find this strange, for they believed that the Führer merely wanted to rearm to catch up with other nations. At least, that was what the propagandists said every day. And the Führer had to know what he was doing, for after all he had a much better view of what was going on than anyone.

130

1938

That year the Volkswagen factory opened in Wolfsburg. Soon, it was claimed, every German would own a car, which would be purchased for around one thousand marks. People used to save up five marks weekly or monthly for it. Until the war started, private citizens could buy cars, but soon the factory stopped producing vehicles for anyone but the Army. After World War II the "beetle" became a kind of symbol of German prosperity.

My school friends, our neighbors, and even my teachers had repeatedly urged my parents to let me join the Jungvolk. Some of them urged this because they considered it my duty to the nation; other, well-intentioned people did so because they believed that if I were in the Jungvolk—and later in the Hitler Youth—it might go a long way toward protecting my father, of whose religious views, and the political views resulting from them, no one in the neighborhood was, of course, unaware. My father was dead set against my joining the Jungvolk, but my mother wavered, for she believed that things would be a lot easier for me if I did not cut myself off from my classmates. Nevertheless, she did as my father wanted and kept on inventing excuses to keep me from joining up.

Naturally, I wanted very much to be a member; all my school friends were members and got to wear a uniform, and I felt like an outsider when the other children at the middle school used to tease me. Many of them called me names because I did not march along with the rest of them.

But secretly I used to accompany them anyhow. I would sneak out of the house and march along in the last row wearing my lederhosen.

Of course, my mother found out what I was doing, but she did not say anything about it and did not tell my father. I was attracted by the adventure of the thing, for the Jungvolk used to march through the woods, pitch tents, bivouac, cook over an open campfire, and play war games in the woods—Blacks against Whites. One group wore a white band around their left arms, and the other wore a black band. If the band was torn off a boy's arm, he was considered dead. He had to lie there on the ground until the game was called off, and then the "corpses" were counted. The group that had captured the larger number of armbands was the winner.

My school friends always found some excuse to get my parents to allow me to come with them, even though I did not wear a uniform. They needed me as a scout because I knew my way around the woods better than anyone else. They accepted the fact that I did not wear a uniform, for poverty was something you did not laugh at; poverty was something taken for granted.

I had begun to notice that my parents were becoming increasingly nervous and that they were frightened whenever there was a knock at our door. Usually the people at the door turned out to be friends or someone who shared my father's faith. We were seldom visited by strangers, except perhaps some stray peddler or salesman.

Many people were experiencing the same feelings as my parents. Their fear of the Gestapo never left them in peace.

People used to disappear suddenly from our neighborhood just as they did from others. As a rule, the Gestapo arrested people at night. When we children asked our parents why this person or that person did not seem to be around anymore, we might be told that these people had gone on a trip. But usually we did not get any answer at all.

The year 1938 was the year of the "peaceful occupations," of the annexation of land that belonged to other countries, of phrases like "Home into the Reich" and "One people, one Reich, one Führer." It was the year of jubilation when almost every German in the country was drunk with victory. Probably the German people have never cheered as much in all their history as they did that year. The special bulletins on the radio came thick and fast.

On July 11, 1936, the German government had signed a formal written agreement that it would not violate the independence of Austria.

Over the years the Austrian Nazis, with the support of the Germans, had become a powerful force in the country's internal politics. The German press incessantly stirred up opposition to all the various Austrian governments, and German propaganda finally convinced the Austrians to consent to Austria's "annexation" by the German Reich.

Schuschnigg, who at that time was the Federal Chancellor of Austria, believed that in order to restore peace in his country, he would have to take violent measures against the Austrian Nazis. He wanted to use military force to combat them. This proposal, in turn, gave the German propagandists a cause to complain and to clamor that in Austria people sympathetic to the Germans were being oppressed. Chancellor Schuschnigg tried to prove them wrong by announcing that a plebiscite would be held on March 13, 1938. Hitler feared this plebiscite because he was not certain that the Austrians might not vote in Schuschnigg's favor after all. If the plebiscite had taken place and the Austrians had voted to preserve their country's independence, Hitler would have had no pretext for annexing Austria to the German Reich.

Schuschnigg had not reckoned with the speed of the Germans and was unaware of the intrigues being carried on behind his back. During the night of March 10, Hitler issued to the German Armed Forces the so-called Order Number One, instructing them to proceed with the Otto Enterprise, the military occupation of Austria.

The strings of the occupation were being pulled by Hermann Göring and Austrian Interior Minister Seyss-Inquart, who for a long time had been negotiating secretly with the Germans.

March 11, 1938

(Otto Enterprise)

1. It is my intention, if I fail to achieve my goal by other means, to move armed forces into Austria, establish law and order, and prevent any further acts of violence against Austrians who feel an allegiance to Germany.

2. I am in command of the entire enterprise. The following officers, under my orders, will be in charge of the following operations:

The Commander-in-Chief of the Army will command land-based operations with the Eighth Army in the combination and strength recommended to me, and in conjunction with what appear to be the recommended distributions of the Air Force, the SS, and the police.

The Commander-in-Chief of the Air Force will command air operations with the forces recommended to me.

3. Assignments:

a) Army: The march into Austria is to proceed in the manner proposed to me. The primary goal of the Army is the occupation of Upper Austria, Salzburg, Lower Austria, and the Tyrol, the swift capture of Vienna, and the securing of the Austrian-Czechoslovakian border.

b) Air Force: It is the task of the Air Force to demonstrate its power and to drop propaganda material; to occupy Austrian airfields in the event that we may wish to fly in additional troops; to support the Army in its appointed sphere of activity; and in addition to furnish combat units capable of carrying out special assignments.

4. Those forces in the Army and Air Force who have been assigned to carry out this enterprise must be prepared to march and attack by no later than twelve o'clock on March 12. 1938. I alone have the right to issue permission to fly or march across the border and to determine the moment when the occupation will begin.

5. The troops must conduct themselves in a way that reflects their awareness that we do not want to wage war against a brother people. It would be to our advantage if the entire enterprise were carried out without the use of force and took the form of a peaceful entry warmly welcomed by the population. Thus all acts of provocation should be avoided. If, however, there should be resistance, it is to be crushed, with the greatest ruthlessness, by force of arms. Austrian military units that switch their allegiance to us are to be immediately placed under German command.

6. For the time being no security measures are to be taken along German borders with nations other than Austria.

Adolf Hitler

On Saturday, March 12, German troops crossed the Austrian border. They were greeted with unprecedented rejoicing by the Austrian people.

It seemed as if all of Austria were delirious with joy.

134.

Once again one of the goals that Hitler had set himself in 1924 in his book *Mein Kampf* had been achieved.

On March 12, on his way to Vienna, Hitler visited his home town, Braunau am Inn. On March 15, standing in the Heldenplatz [Hero Square] in Vienna, he proclaimed: "From now on the oldest province of the German people in the East will serve as the newest bastion of the German nation and thus of the German Reich. As Führer and Chancellor of the German nation and the German Reich, I now announce, in the presence of German history, the entrance of my native land into the German Reich. . . ."

Hitler always loved lofty sentiments, and many Germans listened to them gladly.

A new law passed in the Reich confirmed Hitler's statement once more: "Austria is a province of the German Reich."

The annexation of Austria and its incorporation into Germany fulfilled a dream that the majority of Austrians and Germans had harbored for almost a hundred years.

In 1918, after the dissolution of the Austro-Hungarian Empire, German-speaking Austria, as an "Alpine country," acquired the status of an independent state. Thus it did not prove particularly difficult for Hitler to fetch the Austrians "home into the Reich," for the majority of them had never really grown accustomed to belonging to such a truncated fragment of a state.

But the wild cheering of the Austrians, their frenzied enthusiasm had surprised even Hitler, for up until the very last minute German military leaders feared that the occupation might lead to a military confrontation.

Inevitably the "peaceful" occupation of Austria convinced Hitler that not a single power in Europe could prevent him from achieving his goals. From now on the Reich became known as Greater Germany, and most Germans were delighted by the *Anschluss* [annexation]. A neighbor woman called to my grandfather across the fence, "They won! Without firing a shot!"

My grandfather took hold of my shoulder and led me away, and after we had gone a few steps, he said softly, "Boy, you mustn't believe that. I say only one thing, remember, they will win themselves to death."

Naturally, I did not understand what he meant at the time,

but because I regarded my grandfather as equivalent to God, I nodded.

The great event was duly celebrated in the schools, too. I still remember how our history teacher stood at the head of the class and said, "Our Führer cannot be defeated."

Everyone there believed him. I believed him too.

And for the first time I was very angry at my grandfather because he did not seem happy when I told him what I had heard in class: "Our Führer cannot be defeated."

All he said was, "Everyone has to die."

We boys were enraptured by the marching columns of troops and the cheers of the Austrians, which we saw and heard in the newsreels. To us it seemed logical that the Austrians, who after all spoke German just as we did, should now be members of the German Reich.

But the cheering Austrians soon sobered up. Austrian mineral wealth was stripped away, and the Austrian capital of Vienna was reduced to the status of a mediocre provincial town. The Austrian Army took an oath of allegiance to Hitler, and immediately after the annexation SS Reichsführer Heinrich Himmler went to Vienna in order to extend his regime of violence there. During the first night, in Vienna alone, the SS arrested 67,000 people, including countless Jews, intellectuals, Socialists, and Communists. Thousands of people fled the country.

And once again Hitler allowed the people to ratify his "take-over" in order to prove to other nations that the rape of an entire country in reality conformed to the wishes of its people.

Note that Hitler did not hold his plebiscite until his take-over of Austria was already an accomplished fact.

It is interesting to examine the voting ballots printed for use in the plebiscite: They showed a large circle for *Yes* and a small circle for *No*.

However, anyone in Germany or abroad who believed that the "annexation" of Austria had brought an end to the unrest in Europe had failed to perceive Hitler's true intentions.

Over three million German-speaking people of Czech citizenship were living in Czechoslovakia. Hitler regarded these people as Germans, and he wanted to fetch them "home into the Reich" just as he had done with the Austrians. Naturally there were also

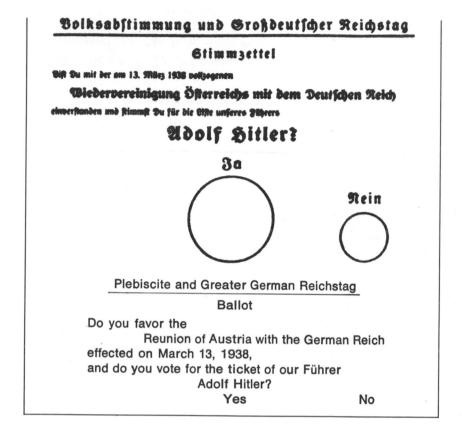

Volksabstimmung und Großdeutscher Reichstag

Stimmzettel

Bist Du mit der am 13. März 1938 vollzogenen

Wiedervereinigung Österreichs mit dem Deutschen Reich

einverstanden und stimmst Du für die Liste unseres Führers

Adolf Hitler?

Ja

Nein

Plebiscite and Greater German Reichstag

Ballot

Do you favor the
Reunion of Austria with the German Reich
effected on March 13, 1938,
and do you vote for the ticket of our Führer
Adolf Hitler?
Yes   No

military considerations involved. Anyone who takes a look at an old map of Europe will immediately be struck by the fact that Czechoslovakia "pierced" German territory like an arrow, or as Hitler put it, "pierced into German flesh."

Hitler wanted to break off or dull the point of this "thorn." By means of an unprecedented propaganda campaign the idea was daily hammered into the heads of the Germans in Czechoslovakia that they were being oppressed by the Czechs. Konrad Henlein became the leader of the Sudeten Germans. Naturally Henlein was a Nazi and received the support of the German government.

On March 28, just a few days after the occupation of Austria, Hitler received a visit from Konrad Henlein and instructed him as to what measures he should take in Czechoslovakia. The Republic of Czechoslovakia was made up of many nationalities, and

137

the nation itself had been formed, after World War I, from one portion of the old Austro-Hungarian Empire. To be sure, the CSR (*Československa republica*) had become a functioning democracy, but it was having problems with its German, Hungarian, Ruthenian, and Polish minorities. Hitler used the desires, demands, and to some degree justifiable claims of the German minority in order to achieve his goal—the breaking up of the Czech nation and the incorporation of areas inhabited by German-speaking Czechs into the German Reich.

At that time, the Republic of Czechoslovakia had already become a modern industrialized nation, and Czech industry—particularly the Skoda Works in Pilsen (Plzeň), one of the largest weapons factories in Europe—was of potentially great importance to the German armaments industry.

Konrad Henlein formed a military unit, the Henlein Volunteer Corps, which was financed by the German Reich.

Hitler wanted to conquer Czechoslovakia as quickly as possible. One year before, on June 24, 1937, he had already issued top-secret orders, designated by the code name Green, to the German Armed Forces.

Command-Level Document

                                        Berlin, April 22, 1938

Fundamentals of the Green Study
Summary of the Conference between the Führer
and General Keitel on April 21
A. Political considerations
    1. Strategic attack straight out of the blue without any cause or justification must be rejected. The effect: world opinion against us, which might lead to serious consequences.
    Such a measure justified only for elimination of the last enemy on the Continent.
    2. Action after a period of diplomatic altercations that gradually reach a crisis and lead to war.
    3. Lightning-fast action on the grounds of some untoward incident (for example, the assassination of the German ambassador in connection with an anti-German demonstration). . . .

C. Propaganda
    1. Handbills for the instruction of Germans in the Green country.

2. Handbills with threats for intimidation of Green citizens.

We children felt very close to the Czech, or the Sudeten German situation, for we lived only a stone's throw from the Czech border. We began to ride our bicycles into Czechoslovakia more often than before, going to Asch and Eger (Cheb). At that time, we still did not have to be checked by the Czech border guards. Children were not subject to border controls. Once I myself saw Henlein's troops on parade in Asch, but I did not find them at all exciting. We already knew all about this sort of thing. The demonstration was no different from one of the SA parades we had seen at home, except that the men were not wearing uniforms.

But even we children were aware that at night many Germans smuggled weapons across the border to Henlein's men.

My father's face became more and more careworn, but I did not suspect that the unrest along the Czech border was making it increasingly dangerous for him to smuggle his newspapers into Germany and that one day he might easily be caught.

Meanwhile, I had learned how to listen carefully to what people said. When they said "Heil Hitler!" I could tell whether they meant it sincerely or were simply saying it in order to avoid getting into trouble. No one in our little town would have dared to criticize Hitler and his policies in public. Even in private circles it was too risky, for you could never be sure that the people you talked to did not associate with someone who might pump them about what you had said.

It was a time in which a person could no longer trust his own brother or his school friends or—incredible as it may seem—even his or her husband or wife. Married people used to accuse each other of being involved in "subversive" plots, and one spouse would denounce the other to the Gestapo simply because this was an easy way to get rid of a burdensome partner. Throughout the Reich the torture and murder continued behind prison walls and barbed-wire fences.

One morning, when I was on my way to school with a couple of neighbor boys, we saw a man being led from his house by two SS men. I paused on the sidewalk to watch what was happening, not knowing that I was actually watching an arrest. An SS man jumped out of his parked car and shoved me in the chest. He shouted at me, "What are you gaping at like an idiot? Scram, go to school! Haven't you ever seen an antisocial parasite before?" The man they were taking away was a friend of my father's, and later I learned that he had been accused of having a love affair with a Jewish woman.

A letter written by Heinrich Himmler to Gürtner, who at that time was the Minister of Justice, sheds some light on the reality hidden behind the flag-draped facade of the German Reich:

Dear Minister:

Around two months ago you expressed to me your opinion that too many people in the concentration camps were being shot while attempting to escape. Although I personally did not share your opinion, since, in all such cases that had occurred up until that time, the shots had invariably been fired from a distance of more than thirty, forty, sixty, or eighty yards, I ordered SS Group Leader Eicke to impress, once again, on the *Totenkopf* [Death's head] units in charge of guarding the concentration camps, that they are not allowed to shoot at anyone except in cases of the direst emergency. The faithfulness with which my orders were obeyed has had what I regard as shocking consequences!

The day before yesterday I was at Buchenwald Concentration Camp, where I was shown the dead body of a fine twenty-four-year-old SS man whose skull two criminals had crushed with a shovel. The two criminals escaped.

I inspected the inmates of the camp again and am deeply troubled by the thought that through the exaggerated clemency that always results when soldiers are curbed in their duty to shoot prisoners attempting to escape one of my fine young men had to lose his life.

I wish to inform you that I have rescinded my order to shoot only in the direst emergency and have reinstated the old order that, strictly in accordance with regulations, escaping prisoners are to be shot after they have three times been called upon to halt, or, in case of a violent assault, without any warning at all first.

Two other criminals who clearly knew about the planned escape attempt, were—after the SS man had already been killed —shot, from a distance of fifty or sixty yards or so, while attempting to escape, on the road leading back to the camp. I am at-

140

tempting by every possible means to track down and capture the two men who actually committed the murder.

I must inform you that when a duly constituted court has sentenced these two murderers to death, I intend to ask the Führer to arrange that the execution be carried out not in the courtyard of any building attached to the court, but in the concentration camp, before the assembled three thousand prisoners, and that if possible the men be hanged with a rope on the gallows.

Heil Hitler!
Signed:
Yours, H. Himmler

What the National Socialists regarded as literature and used to call "writing" was at bottom nothing but an embellishment of Nazi ideology expressed in antiquated or debased language. The themes of this writing centered almost exclusively on the German people and nation. The so-called *Blut-und-Boden* [blood and soil] school of literary composition glorified German rural life and participation in the communal life of the nation; it preached the dissolution of the individual in the group. It paid homage to the concept of the Reich, to the cult of the Führer, loyal obedience to one's superiors, and loyalty to the flag. Literature served to inculcate propaganda and train people for future military service. Sacrifice and comradeship were idealized and falsified. The trashy literature promoted by the Nazis played a particularly important role in the indoctrination of the young. These young people were supposed to be separated from all past cultural and humanistic traditions and to be prepared exclusively for the duties they would be expected to perform in the service of their masters. In the book *Marschtritt Deutschland* [Germany on the march], Alfred Schütze describes the Nazi Party congress of 1938:

Wet and heavy, the flags hang from their staffs beneath the steady drizzle of the rain. Outside in the camps the water stands a foot deep in the tents. The constant rain depresses everyone, and yet it seems as if the entire city of Nuremberg were filled with ceaseless singing and the sound of bells.

Outside in Langwaser, in the tent encampment of the Hitler

141

Youth, everyone is very busy. All the flags they carried as they marched past the Führer during the Adolf Hitler March have been taken back to the camp and installed on the hill of flags. The flags have returned to the community of young people to whom they belong. Before the hill of flags the 50,000 young people who came to Nuremberg in order to attend this youth rally are busily carrying on their activities.

Once again a gray sky filled with fat clouds hangs over the city. The 50,000 young people set off in long, seemingly endless columns and fill the vast sphere of the old Nuremberg Arena. None of the boys and girls allow the dismal weather to dampen their mood. They stand and wait for the Führer, 9,000 candidates for entrance into the Party and 52,000 Hitler Youth and wolf cubs [members of the Jungvolk]. And if, like last year, pouring rain should shroud the colorful scene of this unique youth rally in gray veils, these boys and girls would go on waiting all the same, for there is nothing in the world that could prevent German youth from waiting for the Führer.

The various units have lined up long before the Führer's arrival. Next to the arena, at the zeppelin field, the planes of the Air Force are practicing for Armed Forces' Day. With perilous turns and loops, one squadron after another flies over the arena, over the heads of the thousands of boys and girls, and again and again wild cries of enthusiasm rise toward the heavens, again and again the young people burst into cheers and applause at the sight of the magnificent achievements of the machines and their pilots.

Outside the gates of the arena stand the young flag-bearers, ready to march inside. The sound of distant cheers informs them that the Führer has arrived to see his young people. First the marching bands, then the columns of standard-bearers start to move out, on the left the black flags of the Jungvolk, on the right the red-and-white flags of the Hitler Youth. They march toward each other, they meet before the reviewing stand, the black mingles with the red, and then the columns separate again and march along in front of the flag-decked platform, directly opposite the Führer. The sound of the marching drums accompanies the flags as they move along.

And then the thousands of boys and girls sing the song sung by the soldiers in Austria a few weeks before when they crossed the bridge uniting Braunau with the old Reich—the song "Long was the night. . . ."

The command echoes harshly across the broad field: "Standard-bearers, at ease!" The flagstaffs make a dull thud as they strike the wooden platform. . . . At the head of all the flags stands the Herbert Norkus flag of Berlin, a blood-red flag, old and tattered. This flag is one of many that waved before the Hitler Youth during the years of struggle, and now it stands there looking modest and shabby among the banners of the new German youth. The eyes of the thousands of young people in the Nuremberg Arena must be drawn to this modest flag as the Reich Youth Leader now calls out to them the words of the Führer: "Woe to him who does not believe!"

These words once roused German youth to action, and during the years of struggle the German youth in Austria carried these words in their hearts. The Reich Youth Leader says that if it were possible for any human beings to prove themselves worthy of the Führer, these young people dedicated to struggle would have done so. These young people have had faith in the victory of National Socialism and in the German people. With this faith in his heart fifteen-year-old Herbert Norkus was beaten and stabbed to death by a crowd of bestial people in the gray streets of Berlin far away in the North. Through this faith the struggle of youth for a greater and better future has been fulfilled.

The wind gently stirs the hundreds of flags, the sky becomes more and more overcast, and slowly it begins to rain. Even during the long march of the flags to this rally the sun was not always shining. Often the rain-soaked flags hung hard and heavy on the shoulders of the standard-bearers. They paused in front of the house where the Führer was born in Braunau am Inn, they waved above the St. Johannis Cemetery in Berlin, and they soared in the air before the tomb of Albert Leo Schlageter. These flags stood before the shrines of the [National Socialist] movement in the Royal Square in Munich, and they waved in that hour of celebration before the white tents of the camp in the highlands. Now they stand before the Führer.

The Führer speaks to all the boys and girls who stand before him, and yet his words hold a deeper significance for the standard-bearers of the Adolf Hitler March than they do for any of the others. "I count on you, blindly and confidently . . ." the Führer cries to his young people, and in reply a single cry of affirmation resounds across the field.

Before me stand boys from the East March of Germany [i.e., Austria], who are participating in a Party rally for the first time.

Even at the time of our departure from Braunau, we had already noticed that these boys have a different attitude toward the events of this congress than their comrades from the old Reich. They have experienced the struggle more directly. The longing that has filled them for years is now given vent again and again in enthusiastic cries. The boys have removed their neckerchiefs and are waving them in the air above their heads; they draw their bowie knives out of their sheaths and clash them together. They try by every means and with innovative variations to give expression to their enthusiasm.

Only one small boy dressed in brown, who is standing directly in front of me, seems to have been overwhelmed by the greatness of this hour he is being permitted to experience. He is standing in silence in the midst of his cheering and shouting comrades. . . . Perhaps he is not even aware that great tears are flowing down his face. . . .

The Führer has finished speaking. The boys of the old Reich stand shoulder to shoulder with those from the East March of Germany and Rudolf Hess declares that the young men before him have a right to be proud that they are the first group in the newly created Greater Germany to take an oath of allegiance to the Führer. Slowly and solemnly the words of the oath, which candidates for admission to the Party repeat after the Führer's representative, echo across the arena, and slowly the Party flag is raised to the top of a towering flagpole.

Then the Führer walks through the ranks of his young people, past the bright and colorful national costumes of the girls from his native land. The boys maintain an iron discipline. They would all like to cheer, they would all like to call out to the Führer, expressing their love and gratitude, but they have been ordered to maintain their ranks. Each of them knows that the Führer is looking at him. . . .

Sixty thousand boys and girls are experiencing the greatest moment of their lives. In a few hours they will leave the festive city where the Party congresses are held and return to their home towns, where they will tell everyone about the moment when the Führer walked past them and looked straight at them.

The Führer has completed his walk through the arena. As he climbs into his car, one hears the measureless roar of adulation, no longer restrained by any order, with which the youth of Germany bid farewell to their Führer. Slowly the car moves off to-

144

ward the exit. Once again the Führer lifts his hand to salute the young people and their flags.

Every day the situation in the Republic of Czechoslovakia was becoming more critical, and everyone feared a civil war. The Sudeten Germans became increasingly vehement in their demands that the German Reich be allowed to annex the German-speaking areas of Czechoslovakia [i.e., the Sudetenland]. Armed confrontations occurred along the border, people were deported, and shootings and murders were nothing unusual.

Konrad Henlein proclaimed that everyone had a right to self-defense. Thus, any Sudeten German could use a weapon to defend himself against a Czech.

It was no longer safe for us children to wander around near the border. My mother, seconded by my grandfather, had strictly forbidden me to accompany other children to the border. Naturally, I did not obey them, for I wanted to be with the other boys. We sneaked furtively through the woods, and sometimes we ran straight into a group of Czech soldiers, but they simply laughed at us and did not even bother to send us back.

My father almost never spoke a word anymore.

He soled shoes and read the Bible. Fewer and fewer people came to him to get their shoes repaired, even though he was considered the finest shoemaker in the area. It had become too dangerous for his customers to visit a man who was known to be opposed to the regime and who would probably one day be arrested.

On July 18, Hitler told his generals: "I am determined to take advantage of any favorable opportunity that presents itself after October 1 to realize this goal (the destruction of Czechoslovakia)."

For him the date was already fixed, and he hesitated only because he did not know how the other nations of Europe would react. He was certain that they would not, as they had done in the case of Austria, let the matter rest after making a few lame protests.

On March 28, 1938, the Czech government, led by President Eduard Benes, proposed passage of a new statute on minorities that would legally guarantee special rights to German Czechs.

Henlein, acting under orders from Hitler, refused to approve the new statute. He demanded additional rights. If the Czechs had complied with his demands, they would no longer have been in control of their own country.

On September 25, at the Berlin Sports Palace, which had housed the Reichstag ever since the Reichstag fire, Hitler declared:

> Thus, I have only one thing to say: Two men are now engaged in confrontation; there stands Herr Benes, and here am I! We are two different types of men. When, during the great international struggle [i.e., World War I], Herr Benes was just lounging around the world, I did my duty as a decent German soldier. And today I confront this man as the highest ranking soldier of my country! . . . With regard to the Sudeten German problem, my patience is now at an end. I have made Herr Benes an offer that simply involves the implementation of what he himself has already promised. The choice is now up to him: peace or war. He will either accept this offer and now finally give the Germans their freedom, or we will procure this freedom for them ourselves. Let the world take note: During the four and a half years of the war and the long years of my political career, there is one thing of which no one has ever been able to accuse me—I have never been a coward. I am marching now at the head of my people as its highest ranking soldier, and the world should know that a people march behind me—a different people from those of 1918. We have made up our minds! Now let Herr Benes make the choice!

Some important events had preceded this address to the Reichstag. On May 9, Mussolini, the Italian dictator, had paid a visit to Hitler. Mussolini promised to side with Hitler in his quarrel with Czechoslovakia; in return, since Austria already belonged to the German Reich, Hitler promised to give up his claims on the Southern Tyrol.

After World War I, the Southern Tyrol had been ceded to Italy, but now the Germans living in this region, like those in Czechoslovakia, were insisting on their right to self-determination and demanding that a plebiscite be held. Thus Hitler sold out the Germans in the Southern Tyrol so that he could "lead home" the Germans in Czechoslovakia. For military reasons Czechoslovakia was more important to him than the Southern Tyrol, and besides he did not want to alienate Italy, which was Germany's ally.

The Western powers, especially Great Britain, were extremely uneasy over developments in Central Europe. They feared there would be war, and not without reason. However, they were not prepared for war. They needed to keep the peace at any price. For this reason, on September 15, British Prime Minister Chamberlain flew to Berchtesgaden on the Obersalzberg to see Hitler and try to negotiate a solution to the Czechoslovakian problem. Two days before his visit, martial law had been declared in the area along Germany's border with Czechoslovakia, which meant that people could be shot without a trial.

On September 12, three days before Chamberlain's visit, Hitler had declared at the Nazi Party Congress in Nuremberg: "The Germans in Czechoslovakia are not defenseless, nor have they been abandoned. Mark my words."

Thus Hitler had told the world at large unmistakably that the Sudeten Germans were well-armed and that they could count on the military aid of the German Reich.

The British prime minister knew these facts too. Therefore, he had to intervene if Europe was not to plunge into war. The Sudetenland abounded with murder and arson and more and more people were wounded in the fighting; for a long time the Sudeten Germans had been behaving as if they were the true rulers of the land. Of course, Hitler was delighted, for now once again the hour had come when he could make his entrance as the peacemaker. Once again he could put out the fire that he himself had set.

The Sudeten Germans screamed their battle cry louder and louder: "We want to go home to the Reich!"

Today, when they hold meetings of their so-called Sudeten-German Brotherhood, the Sudeten Germans disclaim all knowledge of these facts; today they describe those days as if they had been terrorized by the Czechs. Historians often misrepresent the facts. Probably Chamberlain actually believed that Hitler was prepared to smooth over the existing conflicts by peaceful means. He was from an old English family in which a promise given still counted for something.

The situation was getting more and more hectic. On September 22, Chamberlain flew to see Hitler for the second time. Hitler negotiated no longer; he issued Chamberlain an ultimatum: If his demand that the Sudetenland be incorporated into the Reich had not been approved by September 28, German troops would march into Czechoslovakia. In reality, German troops had long ago been placed in position at the Czech border and were simply waiting for orders to cross over.

It was now clear to everyone that there was bound to be a war, for the Czech government had rejected Hitler's ultimatum. However, at that time German officers were planning to have Hitler arrested as soon as he gave orders to attack. But the events of the following days frustrated this plan.

The president of the United States took a hand in the matter and reminded everyone that Hitler had signed treaties whose terms even he was obliged to observe. But it was actually the intervention of Mussolini, who did not particularly want a war to break out either, that brought about the conference in Munich.

Present at the conference were Chamberlain, French Premier Daladier, Mussolini, and Hitler. In order to preserve the peace, the representatives of the other nations decided to cede the Czechoslovakian Sudetenland to the German Reich.

The agreement reached at this conference became known as the Munich Pact.

Chamberlain was greeted with great enthusiasm by the citizens of Munich. He rode through the city in an open car and was cheered and celebrated as the bringer of peace. However, Hitler had signed everything in Munich merely to get nearer to his goal.

Chamberlain regarded the treaty as an agreement by whose terms everyone concerned had to abide. Given what we know today, Chamberlain sounds rather naive when, after landing in London, he held out a piece of paper toward the waiting crowd and said, "The peace for our time." The English cheered him just as the Germans had. They believed in the peace. On October 3, Hitler was greeted as a liberator by Konrad Henlein in the town of Eger (Cheb).

On October 1, my father had been arrested.

Two SS men had been lying in wait for him in the neighbor's house opposite our own. When he arrived home on his bicycle, the two men stepped out of the shadow of the house and called to him not to move or they would shoot him. I saw everything that occurred. I just happened to be standing in our neighbor's hayloft, looking out the trapdoor.

My father was very calm. He leaned his bicycle against the wall of the house and looked at the two SS men. At this moment a car turned into our street, and two more men dressed in black leather coats got out. One of the men unscrewed the handlebars from my father's bicycle, extracted the newspapers from inside the frame, and held them out to my father with a triumphant smile. Then my father was shoved into the back seat of the car, the two SS men who had lain in wait for him sat down beside him, one on either side, and the car drove away.

I know that I was holding a bundle of hay in my arms and staring rigidly out the trapdoor. The whole scene had been as unreal as something out of a movie. I did not wake up until the neighbor woman called, "Max, they've taken your father away."

I jumped down from the hayloft into the yard, a distance of four meters, straight onto the manure pile, climbed onto my bicycle, and rode to the farm outside our town where my mother sometimes used to help out after she finished working at the chinaware factory. When she saw me coming, she slowly set down the two milk jugs, and when I finally stood before her gasping for breath, she said very calmly, "I already know. It was bound to happen. Now you must join the Hitler Youth."

Hitler's journey to Eger took him through our little town of Schönwald. He stood in an open car and greeted the cheering crowd with raised arm. People on both sides of the street were behaving like maniacs and kept on shouting, "Sieg Heil!" or simply, "Heil!"

I stood in the forefront of the crowd. Our entire school was here for the occasion. Beside me stood my aunt, who considered Hitler inferior only to God. She had become a so-called hundred-percenter.

I know that it was a beautiful day, and people were either wearing uniforms or their Sunday best. My school friends were in uniform, and I, too, was wearing an armband with a swastika on my arm, just as my aunt had demanded. The girls were standing in a row in their white blouses or brown jackets.

I stood among the cheering people and raised my arm to salute. But I no longer remember whether I too cried "Heil!" Quite possibly I did, for my mother had made it clear to me that in certain situations one had to howl along with the wolves if one were not to be devoured by them.

When he drove past me, Hitler was so close that I could have reached out and touched him. I do not know whether I thought about my father while all this was going on. We did not know where the SS had taken him.

Probably I would have preferred to sneak away rather than to stand there in the lane of people as the "great Führer" drove along the street that we children traveled every day on our way to school. But my mother had sent me to attend the procession and had said, "You are going. You must see this so that you will never forget it."

She herself stayed at home. Probably she could have robbed every place in town, for no one was at home but the sick and infirm.

Naturally my grandfather did not attend the great event either. He had gone to the stone quarries with his horses to fetch a load of granite, just as he did every day. But when I ran into the stable in the evening to help him feed the horses, I found that he was already waiting for me. While he was pouring oats into the horses' feeding troughs, he said, "Well, did you see him?"

I must have started crying, for I remember the large checked handkerchief he handed me. Then he added, "I hope that you got a good look at him. I hope that you will never forget him!"

After my father's arrest, things became more difficult for me at school. Even our neighbors were no longer as friendly toward us as they had been, and every day I became more aware of how they were avoiding me. My school friends did not want me to walk with them when we went home from school. And no matter how much better I did in my schoolwork than the other children, my teachers were never satisfied with me. They ignored

150

me and, even though I always raised my hand, never called on me to answer questions. My report card said that I did not participate in class. The teachers always found fault with something about me, for it was not advisable to praise a pupil whose father had been locked up as an antisocial parasite. They made it clear how they felt about me and, when they bothered to ask me questions at all, always asked trick questions.

In November, Ernst vom Rath, the Secretary of the German Embassy in Paris, was shot and killed there by a Jew named Grynspan. The Nazis welcomed this crime because it gave them a reason to increase the stringency of their racial policies. The papers were full of headlines like "Jews Murder German Diplomat." My family, too, felt indignant, and my aunt said, "The Führer is right; the Jews are our affliction." There are various versions of the story of why Grynspan committed the murder. Probably he wanted to draw world attention to the suffering that was being inflicted on the Jews. As a result, Hitler and his cronies took overt measures against Jews within the Reich, ignoring the possible reaction of other nations. During the night of November 9, fires flamed up all over the Reich: more than 200 synagogues were set on fire; 170 Jewish homes went up in flames; over 7,000 Jewish shops were looted; 36 Jews were killed and countless others physically abused and gravely injured. Twenty thousand Jews were arrested, 10,000 of whom were sent to Buchenwald alone. At that time the writer Valentin Senger was a fourteen-year-old boy living in Frankfurt. He lived through the Kristallnacht [the night of glass] and described it in his book *Kaiserhofstrasse 12:*

"Oi vay, will this bring heartache!" Mama said when the news came over the radio that a certain Grienspan [sic] had shot vom Rath, the Secretary of the German Embassy in Paris. The murdered man came from an old Frankfurt family. Mama raised her hands to her cheeks, and her eyes grew large with fear. "They've just been waiting for something like this to happen." After a while she went on, emphasizing every word. "Everything we have suffered in the past from the Hitler crowd will be nothing compared with what is going to happen now."

Mama was right as always. The next day, when I was on my

way to the place in Sachsenhausen where I worked, a young secretary met me on the Iron Bridge. "Have you heard, the synagogue in the Börneplatz is on fire, and on the Sandweg they are smashing the windows of Jewish stores and throwing everything out on the street?"

We arrived at the office. Everyone there was already very excited, they were all talking at once, and everyone had something different to report. Not only was the New Synagogue in the Börneplatz on fire, but all the synagogues were going up in flames, and all over the East End and the North End Jews were being driven out of their homes and all Jewish stores were being demolished.

I waited for the arrival of the member of the Hitler Youth who used to stand at the board in front of mine in the drafting room. He was in his final year of apprenticeship and was two years older than I. Often he came to work wearing his Hitler Youth uniform. As a sign of his rank as a platoon leader, a strip of braid extended in a curve from the shoulder tab on his tunic down to the middle button. He always knew before anyone else when some new action was going to be taken against the Jews.

Excited as I was, I could not afford to look suspicious or exhibit any more curiosity than the others. But I could not stand it any longer; I put on my jacket and ran to the Börneplatz. While I was still some distance away, I saw a huge cloud of smoke rising into the sky from the general direction of the synagogue.

And then I was standing in the square among the crowd, watching the flames shoot from the giant dome of the temple. SA men and auxiliary police were cordoning off the area around one hundred yards from the burning synagogue so that no one could get any closer to the site of the conflagration. In the forefront of the crowd, just inside the cordon, stood a group of Hitler Youth; they were grinning and laughing and making a celebration out of this horrible event.

But the people outside the cordon seemed disconcerted, and I did not hear any of them express a word of approval. A woman nearby was saying that she had seen Jews at the Zoological Gardens being transported out of town in trucks. A man said that he had just come from Friedberger Park and that the synagogue there was on fire, too, as was the Old Synagogue on All Saints Street.

Beside the circular building, which was blazing like a torch, stood two fire engines, one of them with a huge ladder that had not even been removed from the engine, and an equipment van. Several firemen were standing around holding firehoses, but they were not fighting the fire. Rather they merely extinguished the flaming rafters that fell onto the street. Obviously they had been ordered to let the synagogue burn down and to restrict their activities to preventing the fire from spreading to neighboring houses. . . .

Although I was surrounded by hundreds of curious people, I saw nothing but the flames and the smoke, and I could hear, as if he were standing right beside me, Papa's gentle, sad voice, "Howl, howl, evil winds." He was so close to me that I only needed to turn around in order to see him. And in my head ran the quavering refrain: "The winter will last a long time yet, the summer is still far away." I wept. The tears ran down my cheeks, and I did not care whether or not anyone saw me.

Slowly, I went back to the office. No one asked me where I had been. Half an hour later the Hitler Youth arrived. His hands and face were dirty.

"What's the news?" everyone asked him.

"What's the news? Let's hope that you already know all there is to know," he said.

But then he went ahead and told us about his part in the whole affair. The evening before his squad leader had warned him that something was going to happen that night and that he should be prepared to take part in a raid. At three o'clock in the morning someone got him out of bed, and half an hour later he was at the rendezvous point in the North End. Here the members of the Hitler Youth were divided into several groups, and then they set out toward the center of town. They systematically smashed the windows of Jewish shops in the streets assigned to them and destroyed everything inside. Then they forced their way into Jewish homes and drove the Jews out onto the streets. Here, too, they broke the windows and then threw all the furniture out the windows and onto the street.

The streets were covered with shards of glass, which gave the pogrom the name Kristallnacht.

The Jews who had been driven out of their homes were picked up by the SA and taken away.

The member of the Hitler Youth concluded his report with the observation: "We cut off one guy's beard and earlocks. Afterward he looked like a beet. Was that ever funny! And his eyes popped out like a frog's."

An older colleague asked him, "Were the Jews beaten too?"

"What do you mean by that?" asked the young platoon leader.

"Nothing. It's just that one hears all sorts of things."

"So you still feel sorry for *them?*"

His colleague said nothing. Insulted and, so to speak, misunderstood, the member of the Hitler Youth withdrew. Later he came over to where I was working at the drafting board in order to tell me more about his deeds of heroism. His troop of Hitler Youth had been assigned to the synagogue in Friedberger Park. Beside the park walls, across from the synagogue, a car loaded with several cans of gasoline was already waiting for them. So thorough preparations had been made for the arson raid. They poured the gasoline into the building through the main door and the shattered windows, and then set it on fire by lighting woolen cleaning rags soaked in gasoline. Twice they had to pour more gasoline into the building and light the fire again, before the synagogue finally went up in flames.

The Nazis described the events of that night as a spontaneous upwelling of anger against the Jews, triggered by the assassination in Paris. However, in reality the offensive had been planned down to the last detail, and the night known as Kristallnacht went down in history.

My father, who at that time was a prisoner in Buchenwald Concentration Camp, was there when the Jews were brought in, and after the war he told me how they were treated: They were beaten with rifle butts, the men's beards were cut off or burned off, SS men spit in their faces and forced them to kiss their boots or to lick them clean.

My father said, "You wouldn't believe what bestial things people are capable of, and you wouldn't believe all the things a human being can endure. Animals being led to the slaughter were better off than they were."

He spoke about this time only once. Afterward, despite my urging and my questions, he would never talk about it again.

After the Kristallnacht, those Jews who had not yet been arrested were placed directly under the control of the police. Overnight they had, so to speak, been placed outside the pale of the law and were now fair game. They could no longer appeal to a German court to protect their rights or afford them justice.

The following reports make it clear that the events of the Kristallnacht were not a spontaneous reaction by the German people:

Berlin No. 234-404, November 9, 2355

To all police stations and police headquarters
To all chiefs or deputies

This telegram is to be passed on [to all personnel] immediately, by the swiftest possible means.

1. In the immediate future action will be taken against Jews throughout Germany, and particularly against their synagogues. You are not to interfere with these actions. However, you are to cooperate with the security police to prevent looting and other excesses.

2. You are to take immediate measures to safeguard any important records that may be found in the synagogues.

3. You are to make preparations to arrest some 20,000 to 30,000 Jews throughout the Reich. The primary criterion of selection is that they be Jews of some wealth. More detailed orders will be issued later tonight.

4. If, during the coming actions, any Jews are found to be in possession of weapons, the most severe measures are to be taken against them. SS reserve troops, as well as the regular SS, may be called upon to participate in these joint actions. In any case, the necessary measures are to be taken to ensure that the actions are led by the State Police.

To Palatinate SA Group
Mannheim
(In your reply please include the date
and your letter-book number.)

At 3:00 A.M. on November 10, 1938, I received the following orders: "By the orders of the group leader, all Jewish synagogues within the territory of Brigade 50 are to be blown up or set on fire immediately.

"Neighboring houses inhabited by Aryans must not be damaged. This action is to be carried out in civilian clothes. Riots and looting are to be prevented. You are to report the completion of your assignment to headquarters or the brigade leader at any time before 8:30 A.M."

155

I immediately alerted the unit leaders and issued detailed instructions, and we began to carry out our orders at once. The following is a report of our achievements:

In the territory of
Unit 115
1. Synagogue in Darmstadt, Bleichstrasse — destroyed by fire
2. " in Darmstadt, Fuchsstrasse — " "
3. " in O./Ramstadt — interior and furnishings destroyed
4. " in Gräfenhausen — " "
5. " in Griesheim — " "
6. " in Pfungstadt — " "
7. " in Eberstadt — destroyed by fire

Unit 145
1. Synagogue in Bensheim — destroyed by fire
2. " in Lorsch, Hesse — " "
3. " in Heppenheim — destroyed by fire and explosives
4. " in Birkenau — destroyed by fire
5. Prayer house in Alsbach — " "
6. Meetinghouse in Alsbach — " "
7. Synagogue in Rimbach — interior and appointments completely destroyed

Unit 168
1. Synagogue in Seligenstadt — destroyed by fire
2. " in Offenbach — " "
3. " in Klein-Krotzenburg — " "
4. " in Steinheim am Main — " "
5. " in Mühlheim am Main — " "
6. " in Sprendlingen — " "
7. " in Langen — " "
8. " in Egelsbach — " "

Unit 186
1. Synagogue in Beerfelden — destroyed by explosives
2. " in Michelstadt — interior destroyed
3. " in König — " "

4. Synagogue	in Höchst im Odenwald	interior destroyed
5. "	in Gross-Umstadt	" "
6. "	in Dieburg	" "
7. "	in Babenhausen	" "
8. "	in Gross-Bieberau	destroyed by fire
9. "	in Fränk. Crumbach	interior destroyed
10. "	in Reichelsheim	" "

Unit 221

1. Synagogue	and chapel in Gr. Gerau	destroyed by fire
2. "	in Rüsselsheim	demolished and interior destroyed
3. "	in Dornheim	interior destroyed
4. "	in Wolfskehlen	" "

The Leader of Brigade 50 (Starkenburg)
Lucke, Brigade Leader

Report of Heydrich, Chief of the Security Police,
to Göring, the Premier of Prussia, dated November 11, 1938

. . . As of November 11, 1938, the reports received from the State Police stations up to this point may be summarized as follows:

Jewish stores and firms in countless cities have been looted. In every case stern measures were taken to prevent further looting. One hundred and seventy-four people were arrested for looting.

At the moment it is not yet possible to reduce to numerical terms the precise extent of the destruction to Jewish business and homes. Except where cases of arson are involved, the figures in the reports—815 stores destroyed, 29 department stores set on fire or destroyed by some other means, 171 homes destroyed or set on fire—represent only a fraction of the destruction that actually occurred. Because of the urgency of the need that reports be turned in as quickly as possible, those reports received until now have been restricted to supplying rather general data and say merely that 'many' or 'most of the shops were destroyed.' Thus the figures I have listed may well represent a mere fraction of the true figures.

The number of synagogues set on fire is 191, and an additional 76 were completely demolished. In addition 11 community centers, cemetery chapels, and the like were set on fire and 3 others completely destroyed.

Around 20,000 Jews were arrested, along with 7 Aryans and 3 foreigners. The latter were taken into custody for their own protection.

Deaths reported come to 36, and 36 people are reported to have suffered serious injury. The killed and injured are all Jews. The whereabouts of one Jew is still unknown. Among the Jews killed, one was a Polish citizen; there were two Polish citizens among the wounded.

Heydrich

The cynicism of the Nazis was so extrème that they forced the Jews themselves to pay for the damage inflicted on Jewish stores by the SA and the SS. This was an easy way for them to acquire Jewish property.

In addition, the Jews were forced to pay the sum of one billion marks in foreign bills of exchange to the German Reich.

Outside Germany there appeared a flyer signed by German emigrants, Communists, Social Democrats, writers, and artists. The rest of the world listened to their warning, but their voices did not reach into the German Reich.

Against War and Autarky, for Peace and Cooperation!

Hitler needs war to maintain his authority and to achieve the imperialistic goals of those whose interests he serves. The new Germany needs peace in order to fortify its newly won freedom and to achieve social and economic reconstruction. We will need the great and mighty power of peace in order to abandon the policy, so disruptive to peace, of interference in the internal affairs of other nations. Such a peace will bring to an end the unconscionable campaign of hate being waged against the Soviet Union. Law, not violence, ought to govern the national and private life of Germans, and law will also determine the nature of the relations developed among nations. International economic cooperation will replace the autarky so destructive of all aspects of economic life.

We have banded together to achieve these goals, feeling certain that those in our homeland who share our views will agree with what we have said. We appeal to all opponents of this bloody and infamous regime:

Try to work together and to work along with us!

Join your forces to ours in the common battle!

Let us form a united front to strike down the man who is the enemy of us all!

Our first goal is to overthrow Hitler and all the torturers of the German people!

For peace, freedom, and bread!

December 19, 1938.

Signed:

Rudolf Breitscheid
Albert Grzesinski
Max Braun
Professor Denicke
Toni Sender
Professor Siegfried Marck
Dr. E. Drucker
Professor Alfred Meusel
Alfred Braunthal
Professor Julius Lips

Emil Kirschmann
Dr. Hans Hirschfeld
Max Hofmann
Bruno Süss
Siegfried Aufhäuser
Karl Böchel
Alexander Schifrin
Richard Kirn
Bernhard Menne
Dr. Otto Friedländer

(Social Democrats)

Wilhelm Pieck
Wilhelm Florin
Walter Ulbricht
Franz Dahlem
Kurt Funk
Paul Merker
Willi Münzenberg

Ackermann
Weber
Bertz
Wilhelm Koenen
Philipp Daub
Hugo Gräf
Philipp Dengel

(Communists)

Willi Brandt
H. Diesel
K. Franz
R. Frey
Dr. Fried

J. Ewas
M. Koch
K. Sachs
J. Schwab
Th. Vogt

(For the Socialist Labor Party, SAP)

Lion Feuchtwanger
Arnold Zweig
Heinrich Mann

Professor Georg Bernhard
Ernst Toller
Professor E. J. Gumbel

Rudolf Olden
Balder Olden
Egon Erwin Kisch
Rudolf Leonhard
Professor Alfons Goldschmidt
Kurt Rosenfeld
Professor Anna Siemsen
Otto Lehmann-Russbüldt
Dr. Wolfgang Hallgarten
Bodo Uhse
Theodor Fanta
Wolf Frank

Dr. Felix Boenheim
Johannes R. Becher
Walter Schönstedt
Prof. Dr. J. Schaxel
Professor Fritz Lieb
Klaus Mann
Dr. Budzislawski
Kurt Kersten
Ernst Bloch
Wieland Herzfelde
Max Seydewitz

1939

On the street one day a school friend of mine was knocked down by a squad leader, the leader, that is, of a Hitler Youth unit. What had happened?

The Hitler Youth in our town used to march through the streets led by the band with their fanfares and drums; after the band came the standard-bearer and finally the three squads of troops. On that day my school friend, who was himself a member of the Hitler Youth, was not able to march with the others because his mother was sick and he had to do the shopping for her. Before crossing the street, he waited for the brown-uniformed column, whom he had only by chance failed to accompany that day, to pass by.

It was everyone's duty to raise his arm to salute the flag. My friend forgot to do so. Thereupon, the squad leader streaked out of the column and stretched the boy flat on the ground with two blows of his fist, so that my friend started bleeding from the mouth and nose. No wonder, for the squad leader was eighteen and very strong, whereas my school chum was only thirteen and slightly built.

There was no one to whom he could complain about what had happened, much less anyone to whom he could report the squad leader for having committed assault. No one would have thought that my friend was in the right—after all, as one of the Hitler Youth songs said, "For the flag is more than death."

In the Third Reich the failure to salute the flag was not a misdemeanor but the gravest crime.

A sequel to the whole affair occurred in school. We just happened to be reading Schiller's *William Tell*. In this play the tyrannical governor, Gessler, passes an edict declaring that the Swiss are to salute not only him but his hat when it is carried through the streets of the city.

The boy who had been knocked down by the squad leader

Paul Schneider, born on August 29, 1897, in Pferdsfeld near Kreuznach, was a Protestant minister whose ethical posture and liberal views soon brought him into conflict with the Nazi regime. After having been arrested several times, Pastor Schneider was sent to Buchenwald in 1937. Because he refused to salute the Nazi flag, the SS confined him in a bunker, subjected him to inhuman beatings, and finally murdered him on July 18, 1939.

asked our teacher why we learned in school that it was oppression when the Swiss had to salute Gessler's hat, and yet you got knocked down if you failed to salute the flag. After all, wasn't it really the same thing?

We all sat there, still as mice. We waited for the answer, but all our teacher said was, "Tell your father to report to the headmaster tomorrow at noon."

I never found out what happened during the conference. My

friend stubbornly refused to talk when we asked him about it, and after I noticed him crying when he thought no one could see him, we stopped asking him questions.

There were rumors that the headmaster had threatened to denounce the boy's father for the defamation of national symbols if he continued to demand that any amends be made to his son.

The case of the Lutheran minister Paul Schneider demonstrates that it could even cost one's life to fail to salute the Nazi flag.

Hitler was not satisfied with the terms of the Munich Pact, for it granted him only the German-speaking areas of Czechoslovakia, whereas he wanted the entire country.

He got it just six months later, and once again he had proved that his signature was worth something only as long as it continued to serve his goal of conquering all Europe.

The part of Czechoslovakia that remained after the cession of the Sudetenland contained only two other large racial groups, the Czechs and the Slovaks. German propaganda was aimed at causing dissension within the Czech nation. The Germans tried to convince the Slovaks that they were being oppressed by the Czechs.

On March 10, Slovakian Premier Tiso resigned from office, or more precisely, he was removed from office by the Prague government. Three days later he traveled to Berlin, where he was presented with a text written in the Slovakian language in which he, Tiso, declared that, effective immediately, Slovakia had become an independent state. After returning home, Tiso was supposed to telegraph this text back to Berlin, along with a postscript stating that Slovakia was requesting aid from the German Reich.

When Emil Hácha, the president of Czechoslovakia, learned what was going on, he hastened to Berlin and on March 14 pleaded with Hitler not to violate Czechoslovakian independence. Hácha was sixty-six years old and suffered from a heart condition. Hitler kept him waiting in the Adlon Hotel for four hours in order to put him in a compliant frame of mind. Then he was finally pressured so much that he signed a paper in which he trustingly placed the fate of the Czech people in the hands of the Führer of the Greater German Reich. Hitler had threatened that he would bomb Prague if Hácha did not sign. Actually

German troops had already crossed the Czech border as Hitler was dealing with him.

On March 15, German troops marched into what was left of Czechoslovakia, Bohemia and Moravia. Hitler followed in their wake, and at Hradčany Castle in Prague he proclaimed the "Protectorate of Bohemia and Moravia."

German emigrants who had taken refuge in Prague after 1933 were forced to flee again or, like Bertolt Brecht, had already fled earlier.

The Czech people were filled with impotent rage at these events. They felt that they had been abandoned by the entire world, for since the signing of the Munich Pact, the British and the French were no longer obligated to help them.

The German troops were followed by the SS and the Gestapo, just as they had been in Austria. An unprecedented wave of arrests rolled across the land. Anyone who did not join forces with the Nazis was considered suspect.

The Partition of Czechoslovakia

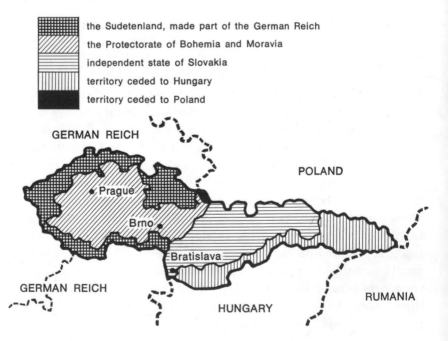

the Sudetenland, made part of the German Reich
the Protectorate of Bohemia and Moravia
independent state of Slovakia
territory ceded to Hungary
territory ceded to Poland

GERMAN REICH

POLAND

Prague

Brno

Bratislava

GERMAN REICH

HUNGARY

RUMANIA

Czechoslovakia had now been totally crushed, and Hitler graciously permitted Slovakia to become an "independent" nation, which remained his puppet until 1945.

On April 20, Hitler's birthday, a Slovakian delegation traveled to Berlin and paid homage to the German dictator.

The Czech nation had ceased to exist, the "thorn in the flesh of the German people" had been broken off. Bohemia and Moravia became a protectorate, governed by former German Foreign Minister von Neurath as Reich Protector.

From then on the Czech people were crushed by a government of unparalleled despotism, and Theresienstadt Concentration Camp, located north of Prague, became a place of terror to everyone in the land.

Now Hitler had his Skoda Works and all the rest of Czech industry besides. Czechs were forced to work in the munitions factories, and anyone who resisted was sent to serve as a forced laborer in the German Reich or even to a concentration camp.

A few days later, on March 23, German troops marched into the Memel region. This narrow strip of land had also once belonged to Germany and formed part of East Prussia, but the Treaty of Versailles had granted it to Lithuania. The sound of the fanfares heralding a special bulletin was issuing from our radio at shorter and shorter intervals.

My mother had changed completely since my father's arrest. She had become taciturn, her face had grown hard, and even to me she spoke harsh words that I would never have believed her capable of. Sometimes she even hit me when I came home and reported that Germany had acquired another piece of land. A polite distance existed between the neighbors and ourselves. Of course, they wanted to maintain the same relationship with my mother as they had done before my father's arrest, but my mother remained cool and did not allow any outsiders into the house.

Six months before, my father had disappeared without a trace, and we did not know where he was imprisoned. Every time we asked the police his whereabouts, they would tell us that they did not know where he was.

The chief of police in our town was an old school friend of my father's, but even he was unable to find out where my father was. He gave my mother a bit of friendly advice, suggesting that she stop trying to discover my father's whereabouts. He offered to tell her at once if he managed to find out anything through unofficial channels.

My grandfather was the solid center around which the rest of the family revolved. He detested the shouts of victory so much that he often used to say, "It makes me sick." During news broadcasts he left the kitchen and went out into the garden to smoke his pipe.

One day when my grandmother was talking with a neighbor woman at the window and could not find words enough to praise the genius of the Führer, my grandfather, pointing his pipe at my grandmother, said, "Boy, I don't know what kind of times we are living in. It used to be that when I got drunk, I woke up sober again the next day. Now people never get sober again at all. Boy, what times these are, what times. Maybe your father is better off than they are, after all; at least he is certain not to get drunk."

The majority of the people believed that Hitler was winning his victories for their benefit. Only a few saw through the fraud and recognized that Hitler was not promoting the interests of the people, but his, and his alone.

In fact, Hitler was indifferent to the fate of the German people, for to him the German people were only a means to an end: his mastery of all of Europe.

After his "peaceful" occupations of two sovereign nations, Austria and Czechoslovakia, Hitler felt safe. To be sure, the Western powers were furious at his rape of the truncated state of Czechoslovakia, but it did not look as if they were going to take serious steps against Germany.

On April 11, Hitler issued orders regarding the so-called White Situation. He was preparing to wage war against Poland.

When it became clear that Hitler had chosen Poland as his next victim, England and France issued certain guarantees. Both countries were prepared, if necessary through force of arms, to guarantee the independence of Poland, Rumania, and Greece.

At first Hitler did not take these guarantees seriously, for that year his prospects, both politically and militarily, looked rosy indeed. After conquering the empire of Abyssinia, Italy had also conquered Albania, and thanks to German military aid, the civil war in Spain was almost over. Austria had been incorporated into the Reich, Slovakia had become a vassal state, and Czechoslovakia had ceased to exist as an independent nation. Hitler had made such extensive preparations for war that the German Reich had become the strongest military power in Europe. The dictator Hitler was at the zenith of his power.

The English and the French were negotiating with the Russians for a defense against the Fascists, but the negotiations miscarried.

The Treaty of Versailles had guaranteed Poland access to the Baltic Sea. Thus a "corridor" now separated East Prussia from the rest of the German Reich. The Free City of Danzig was supervised by a high commissioner from the League of Nations and was an autonomous entity, i.e., it belonged neither to Germany nor to Poland.

Danzig became a source of contention. Hitler demanded the city, as well as a road and a railway track across the corridor that would link the rest of the Reich with East Prussia. Warsaw refused these demands, and Great Britain and France issued a guarantee that they would support Poland in case of war.

Hitler knew perfectly well that there was not a country in the world that would have complied with his demands; nevertheless, he refused to withdraw them, and relations between Germany and Poland became increasingly strained. Of course, this was just what Hitler wanted. He wanted the Germans to believe that he desired peace and that only the "wicked" Poles wanted a war.

The clash between German propaganda and Polish counter-propaganda led both countries to the brink of war, and confrontations occurred between Germans and Poles, particularly in areas that had formerly been German.

Naturally, according to the German propagandists, the Poles were always in the wrong because they had either caused these confrontations or had provoked the Germans until they were forced to strike back, or as this was officially termed by the Germans, "forced to defend themselves."

Of course, Hitler took advantage of these events. In the eyes of the world he wished to appear as a "mediator" who was intervening in these sometimes bloody confrontations in order to protect German lives from the Polish "barbarians."

It cannot be denied that many murders were committed around this time and that the murderers included both Germans and Poles. People had been goaded into a frenzy—the Germans by Nazi propaganda, the Poles by their overblown nationalism.

On April 28, Hitler once again delivered a major address to the Reichstag. In this speech he declared the nonaggression pact between Germany and Poland null and void and also suspended the naval agreement between Germany and Britain, which provided that the strength of the German Navy should be limited to 35 percent of the total tonnage possessed by the British.

In other words, Hitler had ceased to concern himself with these two treaties; he would attack Poland, and he intended to expand the German fleet.

The war, which for Hitler had been a certainty for years, edged closer. The negotiations between the British and French and Moscow disturbed him, for he did not want to run the risk of having to wage war on two fronts. Therefore, he let Stalin know that he was prepared to acknowledge Soviet interests "along the entire line extending from the Baltic Sea to the Black Sea." This was a chance for Stalin: Hitler was voluntarily offering him something that could not be wrested from the Western powers.

The German Foreign Minister to the Embassy in Moscow
Telegram
Urgent!
No. 189, August 20

Berlin, August 20, 1939, 4:35 P.M.
Arrival: August 21, 12:45 A.M.

Personal to the Ambassador:

The Führer orders you to contact Molotov immediately and give him the following telegram from the Führer to Herr Stalin:

Herr Stalin, Moscow.

1. I sincerely welcome the signing of the new German-Soviet trade agreement as the first step toward the reconstruction of German-Soviet relations.

2. The conclusion of a nonaggression pact with the Soviet Union has, in my view, established the outlines of German policy for a long time to come. In this pact Germany is once again adopting a political policy that proved advantageous to both na-

tions in past centuries. This being the case, the German Government is determined to carry this radical change of policy to its logical conclusions.

3. I find acceptable the draft of the nonaggression pact delivered to me by your Foreign Minister, Herr Molotov; however, I consider it a matter of the greatest urgency that we clear up as quickly as possible all remaining questions relating to the pact.

4. I believe that the question of the codicil desired by the Soviet Union can be cleared up most quickly, at least in its essentials, if a German statesman possessing full authority to negotiate were to come to Moscow to negotiate with you himself. The German Government knows of no other way in which the question of the codicil can be quickly clarified and defined.

5. The tension between Germany and Poland has become unendurable. The behavior of Poland toward a great power is such that the situation could reach a crisis any day now. In any case, Germany is resolved that from now on it will respond to these imputations by using all the means at its disposal to look after the interests of the Reich.

6. In my opinion it is expedient that we waste no time in implementing the intention of our two nations to establish new relations. Thus I repeat to you my suggestion that you receive my foreign minister on Tuesday, August 22, or, at the latest, on Wednesday, August 23. The German foreign minister has full authority to draw up and to sign the nonaggression pact as well as the codicil. In view of the international situation, it is impossible for the German foreign minister to remain in Moscow longer than one day or two at most. I would be pleased to receive your reply quickly. Adolf Hitler.

Ribbentrop

The Ambassador in Moscow to the Foreign Office
Telegram
No. 200, August 21
Urgent!
Top Secret

Moscow, August 21, 1939, 7:45 P.M.
Arrival: August 21, 9:35 P.M.
Concerning Telegram No. 199, dated August 21.

Text of Stalin's reply:

To the Chancellor of Germany, Herr A. Hitler.

Thank you for your letter.

I hope that the German-Soviet nonaggression pact will lead to a genuine improvement in the political relations between our countries.

The people of our two countries need to maintain peaceful relations; the consent of the German Government to conclude a nonaggression pact creates a basis for the elimination of political tensions and for the establishment of peace and cooperation between our nations. The Soviet Government has authorized me to inform you that it is prepared to receive Herr von Ribbentrop in Moscow on August 23.

> Signed:
> J. Stalin
> Schulenburg

On August 23, German Foreign Minister von Ribbentrop flew to Moscow, and after brief negotiations the German and Soviet foreign ministers signed a nonaggression pact containing a secret codicil, which consigned Estonia, Latvia, Lithuania, Finland, eastern Poland, and the Rumanian territory of Bessarabia to the Soviet sphere of interest.

Hitler thought that this move left him a clear field to seize Poland, for he did not believe that France and Great Britain would come to Poland's aid:

Secret Codicil

On the occasion of their signature of the nonaggression pact between the German Reich and the Union of Soviet Socialist Republics, the undersigned authorized agents of the two powers in question have, during the course of strictly confidential conversations, discussed the question of demarcating the spheres of interest of their respective countries in Eastern Europe. Their discussion has led to the following results:

1. In the event of a territorial and political alteration in the territories of the Baltic States (Finland, Estonia, Latvia, Lithuania), the northern border of Lithuania will represent the border between the German sphere of interest and that of the U.S.S.R. At the same time, both nations acknowledge the interests of Lithuania in the Vilna area.

2. In the event of a territorial and political alteration in the regions belonging to the state of Poland, the spheres of interest of Germany and the U.S.S.R. will be approximately defined by the courses of the Narew, Vistula, and San rivers.

The question of whether the interests of both nations make desirable the preservation of an independent Polish state, and the question of how the borders of this state would be defined, can ultimately be answered only in the course of the further development of the Polish situation. In any case, both governments will arrive at an amicable agreement regarding these questions.

3. With regard to southeastern Europe, the Soviet Government wishes to emphasize its interests in Bessarabia. The German Government declares its total lack of any political interest in these regions.

4. Both sides will observe the strictest secrecy regarding this codicil.

I can remember the day the pact was signed as if it were yesterday. Probably the reason this agreement caused such a sensation and stirred up so many people was that ever since 1933 it had been drummed into the heads of the Germans that they were waging a life-and-death struggle against the forces of Bolshevism. But now the Nazis had made a pact with the Russians. People did not understand this; they were rattled, and suddenly they began to have doubts about the Führer.

For the first time I saw my grandfather sitting next to the radio. He sat so close to it that he looked as if he were trying to climb right inside the loudspeaker, even though he was not at all hard-of-hearing. When the special bulletin was over, he turned around and looked at everyone else in the room who had listened with him, as if he were awakening from a deep sleep. Everyone waited for him to say something that would explain it all. This news was so shocking that we expected an old, experienced man who wanted nothing to do with Hitler's politics to tell us what this treaty with Moscow really meant. But my grandfather merely stood up and said, "I have to go back to the stable again; the gelding was very restless today."

That same evening I asked my grandfather why he had not commented on the news, and he replied, "Boy, am I supposed to tell them that there's going to be a war? They wouldn't believe me. So why tell them anything? Soon enough they'll know all about it themselves."

At the evening training sessions of the Hitler Youth, which, on my mother's advice, I attended now and then, we all asked someone to explain to us why Hitler had formed an alliance with his archenemy Stalin.

The squad leader—the same one who had knocked down my school chum—said that the explanation was really quite simple: To be sure, Hitler had always been against Bolshevism, but only against the Bolshevism in the German Reich, not that in the Soviet Union; therefore, the pact was logical, understandable, and even long overdue.

This was the simple way in which events of international political significance were explained. There was no doubt Hitler was given a free hand to proceed with his plans in the East. He no longer needed to fear that the Russians would prevent him from going to war with Poland.

And yet people continued to feel uneasy. On those rare occasions when one of us children dared to ask questions, our teachers did not know what to reply. They used to repeat the things that were said over the radio, which Goebbels controlled. The Führer, they said, must know what he was doing, and after all he was doing his best for the German people, and thus he had a right to make a pact with the devil himself if he wanted to. Our history teacher actually said this to us.

You could really feel sorry for some of the teachers. What they wanted to say was not permitted and what was permitted they ground out without conviction.

War was now inevitable because Hitler wanted it. On August 31, he issued Order Number One regarding the conduct of the war:

Berlin, August 31, 1939

Top Secret Command-Level Document

Now that all political means of bringing about a peaceable solution of the intolerable situation on Germany's eastern border have been exhausted, I have decided to solve the problem by violent means.

The attack on Poland is to be conducted in accordance with our preparations for the White Situation, allowing for certain modifications with regard to the Army, which has meanwhile almost completed its deployment.

Duty assignments and the goal of our operations remain the same.

Day of the attack: September 1, 1939

Time of the attack: 4:45 A.M

As far as the Western powers are concerned, we must leave to England and France all responsibility for the initiation of hostilities. For the time being minor border violations are to be dealt with on a strictly local level. The neutrality of Holland, Belgium, Luxembourg, and Switzerland, which we have promised to observe, is to be scrupulously respected. . . .

The Commander-in-Chief of the Wehrmacht
Adolf Hitler

However, Hitler still needed some immediate pretext for attacking Poland. No such pretext turned up on its own, and thus an incident had to be staged: Under orders from Chief of the Security Police Heydrich, SS Battalion Leader Naujocks, accompanied by some prisoners from German concentration camps who, like him, were dressed in Polish uniforms, attacked the radio broadcasting station in Gliwice, located near the Polish border. Now Hitler could stand up before the German people and claim, "Tonight, for the first time, regular Polish Army troops have started shooting on our territory. Since 5:45 we have been shooting back! From now on we will answer bombs with bombs. . . ."

At dawn on September 1, German troops crossed over the Polish border.

I can still remember just how Hitler sounded as we sat around the radio on September 1, for ever since daybreak we had been hearing the rumor that today the Führer planned to address the Reichstag.

No one cheered at the end of his speech, not even my aunt who had always cheered for Hitler; no one cried "Heil!" or turned somersaults with joy. Perturbation was written on everyone's face. No one spoke, and even the neighbors who had come to listen with us said nothing.

My grandfather wept. I could scarcely believe that I was seeing this old, worn-out man crying. No one asked him why he was crying. They were distressed because all of them knew what he had gone through during World War I. He had often told me about it.

No one displayed any enthusiasm. Not in school, not on the streets, not in the shops, not even among the Hitler Youth. No one dared to look anyone else in the face for fear that he might be asked what he thought about the war.

Of course, not everyone felt this way. A few of the boys in my class—we were thirteen years old—regretted that they were not older, for then they could have volunteered to join the Army; meanwhile, I consoled myself with the thought that the war would be over by the time I got out of school.

A few days later, when I went to the stable to help my grandfather feed the horses, he told me, "You know, for all I care they could go on fighting wars for as long as they wanted, if only it were not always the little people who had to foot the bill. But you don't understand these things yet."

Grandfather was wrong; I understood quite clearly, for my father, and after him my mother, had taught me well.

Three days after Hitler attacked Poland, Great Britain and France declared war on Germany.

The war with Poland was over in eighteen days. Only Warsaw, which had been surrounded and under siege for two weeks, continued to resist, and although this resistance could have no effect on the outcome of the war, Hitler ordered Warsaw to be bombed.

On October 6, Hitler submitted a peace proposal to the Western powers, but it was rejected by both France and England. The die had finally been cast in Paris and London: Hitler had to be eliminated. He not only represented a deadly peril to Europe, but to all mankind.

By October 9, Hitler had already ordered the attack on France, as well as on the neutral nations of Luxembourg, Belgium, and Holland. He regarded the war with Poland as only the first stage in his campaign to conquer Europe.

But he had miscalculated. Great Britain, which he always used to deride, was mobilizing its forces. Although the British Army was weak at the beginning of the war, for before 1939 there was no compulsory military service in Great Britain, it had the support of an international empire, which possessed inexhaustible supplies of raw materials, and a powerful navy, which controlled supply routes to the motherland and could supervise the activities of its German enemies.

In 1939, because of the many victories being won by the German Armed Forces, we children were often given time off from school, and naturally we were happy about that.

People who in the past had been opposed to Hitler were now reluctantly forced to acknowledge that he was a great general and statesman. After all, he had defeated Poland in only eighteen days.

Five days after the war began, British Prime Minister Chamberlain delivered an address to the German people in their own language over English radio:

> I regret being forced to say that no one in England any longer places the slightest trust in the word of your Führer. He promised to respect the Locarno Pact,[1] but he did not keep his promise. He also promised that he had neither the desire nor the intention of annexing Austria; here too he broke his word. He declared that he did not wish to annex Czechoslovakia and make the Czechs a part of the Reich, but he did it all the same. He also stated, after Munich, that he would make no further claims on European territory, and once again he broke his word. He promised that he did not intend to annex any provinces of Poland, and again he has not kept his word.

After the German victory over Poland, that country too was overwhelmed by the terrorist tactics of the SS: mass deportations, mass executions, forced labor for men, women, and children. The first concentration camps on Polish soil were erected and later were expanded and "perfected" for use as mass extermination camps. Henceforth, the German Reich intensified its campaign to exterminate all "life unworthy of living" coldly, brutally, mercilessly, bureaucratically.

[1] The Locarno Pact of 1925 was actually a series of treaties signed by European nations. The major treaty guaranteed most of the boundaries of Germany in the terms fixed by the Treaty of Versailles in 1919.—Tr.

Extract from the minutes of a conference
concerning the murder of the mentally ill,
held in Adolf Hitler's Chancellery on October 9, 1939
(Euthanasia Program)

Party Member Brack: "Today's discussion is devoted to final clarification: who and how? The two questions are closely related. Dr. Linden, a medical officer on the Board of Health, will report on the first question."

Party Member Dr. Linden: "Today registration forms are being sent to all nursing homes and mental hospitals along with a circular from the Minister of the Interior. . . . No suspicion can arise as to the true purpose for which the registration forms are being filled out, for the reason given in the circular is the need to consider everyone in the formation of our future economic plans."

Party Member Brack thanks Party Member Dr. Linden and expresses his views as to the number of cases that they can expect to handle. The number is derived from a computation based on the ratio 1000: 10: 5: 1. In other words, among every 1,000 people, 10 require psychiatric treatment; of these, 5 must be treated in a hospital ward. However, one of these five sick persons will be included in the procedure. In other words, out of every 1,000 people, one will be dealt with by the procedure. Expressed in terms of the total population of the Greater German Reich, this means that some 65,000 to 70,000 cases will fall into this category. This fact appears to have answered the question "Who?"

Party Member Professor Dr. Heyde expresses his views on the question "How?" The figure named by Party Member Brack coincides with his own computations. This figure eliminates the possibility of using injections, the method of treatment originally suggested by Party Member Professor Dr. Nitsche. For the same reason treatment involving the use of drugs must be ruled out. . . .

Party Member and Chief Administrative Adviser Werner states that the question has been discussed with Reich Criminal Investigation Department Head Nebe. Everyone agrees with Nebe that CO (carbon monoxide) represents the most suitable method.

Every kind of cruelty that people are capable of dreaming up was actually put into practice. One example of such cruelty is described in the account of a prisoner in Buchenwald, the concentration camp above whose entrance were written the words, "To every man his due":

Jakob Boulanger: Four Years in a Stand-Up Bunker (1939–1943) (For sixteen and a half hours a day, over a four-year span, the concentration camp guards made the socialist worker and resistance fighter J. Boulanger stand up in a bunker cell in Buchenwald—a torture that defies human imagination but which, nevertheless, was invented by human beings. Boulanger's account is one of the most shocking documents we possess in its revelation of the sadism of which the Fascists were capable; but it also testifies to the powers of resistance of a man whose life is rooted in his socialist beliefs.)

Our train arrived in Weimar late at night. We stayed in the railway cars until it got light. Then with shoves and blows we were made to form ranks. We marched double time to Buchenwald Concentration Camp on the Ettersberg.

My heart was pounding like mad. The six years of solitary confinement had taken a heavy toll. But I could not afford to break down.

My comrades hoped that at Buchenwald we would not be sent back to the bunkers. I was not so optimistic. They tried to convince me, saying, "You've already spent three years in a bunker, Jack! Now they'll put you in the regular camp for sure." Who can blame me for being only too ready to believe them.

We were climbing a fairly steep incline. To the left and right of our column were SS men with rifles and dogs. This road to the camp was known as Blood Street. Prisoners had constructed it. Thousands of them had died in the process.

"Come on, get going, you dogs! Left, two, three, four! Anyone who drops behind will be shot!"

The march was difficult, very difficult. If only we would get there!

At around nine o'clock we reached our destination. The SS had already assembled at the parade ground to welcome us. Now we were passing through the gates, above which, to mock the beaten, downtrodden, and abused, glittered the words: "To every man his due."

The senior prisoner of the camp, Ernst Frommhold (he was formerly the organizational leader of the Communist Party in Erfurt) had barely reviewed the group of new arrivals—he winked

177

at me as he went by—when the loudspeaker boomed: "Number 24073 to the gate!" This was my number. Now I knew that I was going to end up in the bunker again after all. Immediately thereafter, I heard them call the numbers of the sixteen comrades who had been with me in the bunker at Dachau.

At the gate stood Chief Platoon Leader Sommer. He was the most terrible of all the SS jailers I learned to know during my long imprisonment. Sommer led us into the bunker. We had to line up in the narrow corridor outside the cells. Cells, what am I saying! They were death chambers! Two meters long and one meter twenty wide, a space just large enough to house a corpse. And yet I was forced to live in this tomb for three and a half years.

Sommer asked each of us how many months he had already spent in a bunker. None of the others had spent more than twelve months there. Sommer bellowed, "Listen here! In ten months you won't be with me anymore, understand? You'll all have kicked the bucket by then!" Then the doors shut behind us.

I looked around at my cell. The walls were gray, the floor cement—a cement coffin. On the wall was a board that had been folded up and locked in position. In the evening this board became my bed. Ninety centimeters wide, one meter seventy long, hanging at an inclined angle, and without any raised area for my head! I had to sleep on this board without a blanket, a straw mattress, or a pillow. I used to use my shoes as a pillow. I wondered, Where am I supposed to sit when the board is folded up against the wall? After all, there's not even a stool here. Surely they'll give me one tomorrow.

But nothing of the kind happened. The board remained locked in position against the wall all day. I had to stand up—to stand up from morning until night. At first I was utterly beside myself. They expected a human being to remain on his feet all day long, a human being, moreover, who could walk only four steps back and forth! But there was nothing I could do about it. I had to stand up. From 4:30 A.M. until 9:00 P.M. All day long. And if Chief Platoon Leader Sommer decided not to lower my plank bed, then I had to stand up all night too. It was strictly forbidden to sit down on the floor. "Anyone who sits down on the floor," Sommer said, "will get twenty-five good ones on the ass!"

So, I thought, I have no choice but to keep standing from morning until night. But no, that's impossible too. If people stand up for too long, they get edema in their legs. Edema in the legs is tantamount to a death sentence, for naturally we will not receive any medical aid or be given any medication.

If bunker prisoners reported that they were sick, SS Medical Officer Dr. Hoven would turn up and say his little speech, "Well, we'll just prepare an injection for you, and then you'll feel better right away." And it was true, the prisoner soon felt better: He was released from his sufferings by death.

So one had to walk, to walk without stopping, up and down, four steps to the window, four steps to the door, four steps to the window, four steps to the door. Hour after hour, day after day, month after month, year after year. The spring came three times, summer, fall, and winter came three times, and I remained locked in this cement coffin. We were never allowed outside our cells like the convicts in a penitentiary, who could walk around in the fresh air for half an hour each day. We had no work, nothing to keep us busy, nothing to read. There was nothing to do but walk, walk up and down, four steps to the window, four steps to the door. . . .

At four or five o'clock in the morning, depending on his mood, the voice of Chief Platoon Leader Sommer would ring out, "Beds up!" Then you had to jump up at a single bound, lock the plank bed in position against the wall, take off your shirt, and, holding your chamber pot and mug, wait until the door of the cell was opened. Then everyone hurried into the washroom to empty his chamber pot and returned to his cell as quickly as he had come. We were not allowed to wash; this privilege was reserved to the SS.

And then began the eternity of the day. How long a minute is when one counts the seconds. And an hour! I used to count off 60 seconds 60 times, a total of 3,600 seconds. It seemed as if the hour would never end. Once again I counted 60 seconds 60 times. But the day is long, and time is timeless in the bunker.

It is depressing never to have anything to do. A human being must do, read, or work at something, regardless of what it is. This eternal inactivity, this total emptiness is a terrible torture. But the worst part is the brooding, the brooding about your situation. Every day you think about whether you are going to live through the next day; day after day you wonder how long you will remain buried alive in this stone vault and how long you will be able to endure the physical and emotional strain. Again and again, four steps to the window, four steps to the door, back and forth like the pendulum of a clock. For a time the routine can be soothing, but in the long run it almost drives a person insane.

So I assigned myself exercises to distract me from my tormenting thoughts—preferably exercises it took a long time to complete. For example, I thought about all the things that we, as members of the Party, had done right, and those that we had done wrong; in my mind I assumed the most diverse functions and thought up the subtlest rules for carrying out the conspiracies involved in our illegal work. I practiced reciting the alphabet backward as fast as I could; I solved mathematical problems, each one more complicated than the last.

But eventually every subject is exhausted. I lived in perpetual dread of running out of material. Hurry, try to find something else, I used to tell myself. And so I would make up some fantastic adventure tale. . . .

No one in Germany trusted anyone else anymore. Denunciation had become a patriotic duty and was a way of earning respect. A person had only to fail to raise his arm in salute, and immediately he was regarded with suspicion. Very few trials were held anymore, and in those cases that actually came to trial, the verdict had already been decided upon beforehand. The police, the Gestapo, and the SD (Sicherheitsdienst, or security police) had become the real judges. They decided questions of freedom and imprisonment, life and death. We children knew nothing whatever about all this or only heard rumors about it. I knew no more than the others, even though my father was in a concentration camp. The police had informed my mother of this fact in a few terse words. My father was in Flossenbürg Concentration Camp and was working in the granite quarries there.

One day after school my German teacher accompanied me home, for we lived on the same street. In front of my house he gave me a little package wrapped in newspaper. Imploringly he asked me not to show it to anyone or talk to anyone about it. The package contained a book, Stefan Zweig's *Sternstunden der Menschheit* [Hours of destiny in human history]. For me, this was the hour of destiny in my life; I began to read with aware-

180

ness. I began to develop an interest in history, and the history I read was very different from what we were taught at school. Connections became clearer to me; in short, I began to read the history of the vanquished rather than that of the victors. For the first time I had gained access to real literature.

I have often thought about why my teacher chose to give this book to me rather than to someone else. Perhaps it was because he knew that I liked to read but, in his opinion, was not reading the proper books. And perhaps another reason was that he knew my father was in a concentration camp and that I would not tell anyone that he had given me forbidden literature to read. After all, my mother had taught me that it was better to say one word too few than one word too many.

My German teacher succeeded in opening my eyes through literature. He had hidden his books, which it was worth his life to have in his possession, in the coal cellar, behind the stacks of wood stored up for the winter. He died in the mid-fifties in my Franconian homeland, a leached-out, old man. Although I had almost no money at the time, I boarded a train and traveled home to attend his funeral. When the minister who had confirmed me recognized who I was, he spoke to me. He asked why I had traveled such a long way to attend the funeral; had my old teacher really meant so much to me? "Yes," I replied, "I believe him to have been a great man." When I saw how surprised he looked, I added, "Back in those days when it could cost you your life not to cheer when you were ordered to, he did not cheer." The minister went away. A year later he died too. I did not attend his funeral. Once at church, at confirmation class, he boxed my ears because I had asked him whether it was God's will for my father to be in a concentration camp.

"All authority is derived from God," he said.

And I replied, "Then either there is something wrong with God or something wrong with the authorities."

Today I no longer remember how I got the courage to say that. In any case, my mother cried when she heard about the incident. She was afraid that I was going to end up in even more trouble than I was in already because my father, unlike other decent Germans, was not fighting in the war or working at home to support the war effort, but instead was "safe" behind barbed wire.

The "expansion" of the borders of the Reich and the beginning of World War II were not the only events that took place in 1939. For the Jewish population in Germany and in the areas it had "peaceably" conquered, this was a year of terror and persecution. After the Kristallnacht the number of emigrants increased until the emigration achieved the proportions of a mass exodus. Hundreds of thousands of Jews fled abroad in order to avoid arrest. On January 30, Hitler had already prophesied the extermination of the Jewish race if a war broke out. He set

---

Poster in German and Polish, listing German regulations regarding Polish Jews in Cracow:

<u>The District Leader of Cracow</u>

REGULATION

Identification of Jews in the District of Cracow

I hereby order that, as of December 1, 1939, all Jews in the district of Cracow above the age of twelve must wear a visible mark of identification while outside their homes. Jews who are only passing through the district are also subject to this ordinance for the duration of their stay.

This regulation defines as a Jew anyone

1. who is now or who in the past has been an adherent of the Mosaic faith,

2. or anyone whose father or mother now is or has in the past been an adherent of the Mosaic faith.

As a mark of identification, Jews are to wear on their upper arms, both on their clothing and their outer garments, a white armband that is inscribed on the outer, visible side with a blue star of David. The white background must be at least four inches wide, and the star of David must be large enough so that the opposite points of the star are at least 10 cm. apart. The angles must be at least 8 cm. wide.

Jews who fail to comply with this regulation will be severely punished.

The councils of elders are responsible for seeing that this regulation is carried out and particularly for supplying the Jews with marks of identification.

Cracow, November 18, 1939   Wächter
                                                                Governor

182

Der Distriktschef von Krakau

ANORDNUNG
Kennzeichnung der Juden im Distrikt Krakau

Ich ordne an, dass alle Juden im Alter von über 12 Jahren im Distrikt Krakau mit Wirkung vom 1. 12. 1939 ausserhalb ihrer eigenen Wohnung ein sichtbares Kennzeichen zu tragen haben. Dieser Anordnung unterliegen auch nur vorübergehend im Distriktsbereich anwesende Juden für die Dauer ihres Aufenthaltes.

Als Jude im Sinne dieser Anordnung gilt:

1. wer der mosaischen Glaubensgemeinschaft angehört oder angehört hat,

2. jeder, dessen Vater oder Mutter der mosaischen Glaubensgemeinschaft angehört oder angehört hat.

Als Kennzeichen ist am rechten Oberarm der Kleidung und der Überkleidung eine Armbinde zu tragen, die auf weissem Grunde an der Aussenseite einen blauen Zionstern zeigt. Der weisse Grund muss eine Breite von mindestens 10 cm. haben, der Zionstern muss so gross sein, dass dessen gegenüberliegende Spitzen mindestens 8 cm. entfernt sind. Der Balken muss 1 cm. breit sein.

Juden, die dieser Verpflichtung nicht nachkommen, haben strenge Bestrafung zu gewärtigen.

Für die Ausführung dieser Anordnung, insbesondere die Versorgung der Juden mit Kennzeichen, sind die Ältestenräte verantwortlich.

Krakau, den 18. 11. 1939.

gez. *Wächler*
Gouverneur

Szef dystryktu krakowskiego

ROZPORZĄDZENIE
Znamionowanie żydów w okręgu Krakowa

Zarządzam z ważnością od dnia 1. XII. 1939, iż wszyscy żydzi w wieku ponad 12 lat winni nosić widoczne znamiona. Rozporządzeniu temu podlegają także na czas ich pobytu przejściowo w obrębie okręgu przebywający żydzi.

Żydem w myśl tego rozporządzenia jest:

1) ten, który jest lub był wyznania mojżeszowego,

2) każdy, którego ojciec, lub matka są lub byli wyznania mojżeszowego.

Znamieniem jest biała przepaska noszona na prawym rękawie ubrania lub odzienia wierzchniego z niebieską gwiazdą sionistyczną. Przepaska winna mieć szerokość conajmniej 10 cm, a gwiazda średnicę 8 cm. Wstążka, z której sporządzono gwiazdę, winna mieć szerokość conajmniej 1 cm.

Niestosujący się do tego zarządzenia zostaną surowo ukarani.

Za wykonanie niniejszego zarządzenia, zwłaszcza za dostarczenie opasek czynię odpowiedzialna Radę starszych.

Kraków, dnia 18. XI. 1939.

(—) *Wächler*
Gubernator

183

up new work areas in concentration camps where the prisoners were forced to work to support the war effort. On May 15, a concentration camp was built at Ravensbrück, where 92,000 women had been murdered by the end of the war. After the invasion of Poland, more than two million Jews fell into the hands of the Germans. After the German military had committed acts of terrorism, looting, and murder, the German civil service continued to wage war against the Jewish people with laws, proclamations, and regulations. Now all Jews ten years of age or older had to wear the star of David.

The conquerors amused themselves by cutting off the beards of elderly Jews and by robbing and beating them up. Regulations followed thick and fast: Jews were forced to register all their property, pressed into forced labor, forbidden to live in certain districts of the city, barred from the use of any means of transportation. The Jews were to be robbed of everything they owned and deprived of all rights.

This picture of frightened Jewish children fleeing with their parents through a corridor of sneering SS men appeared in the English press. Step by step the way was being paved for the "Final Solution."

1940

I was confirmed on Palm Sunday, a week before Easter. We boys felt silly and even slightly ridiculous as we walked through town on our way to the church, dressed in long dark-blue or black trousers and black bow ties (in those days we used to call them "propellers").

In church the minister prayed. "Lord, protect the Führer, the German people, and our fatherland."

Many of the fathers of the boys to be confirmed had come to church dressed in their Army uniforms, but some were not there, for they had either fallen in the Polish campaign or had not been able to get leave in time.

A confirmation was the occasion for a major family celebration and definitely meant more in those days than it does today. All one's relatives came for the occasion if they possibly could.

I was given a wristwatch, and for the first time in my life I wore regular shoes and socks that had not been knitted at home but were made of a thin material and held up by garters. After I had been confirmed, my whole family sat around a long table covered with a white cloth. All of us were dressed in our best clothes, and I kept worrying that I might get a spot on the suit that my mother, by dint of many privations, had managed to save up the money to buy me.

Everyday commodities were already in short supply, and even with ration cards it was hard to get the things we needed.

The daily papers were already filled with lists of the dead, marked with the Iron Cross, beneath which were written the words: "Fallen for Führer, folk, and fatherland."

A few weeks later entire pages in the newspapers were covered with obituary notices, and my mother, who read her newspaper every day from back to front, often cried in a tone of disbelief, "What, him too?"

Some of my school friends had volunteered to join the Armed Forces. They were only fourteen years old, so naturally they were turned down. When I told my mother about them, she simply replied, "My God, these stupid boys, they can't wait to be shot dead."

After I finished school, I began a commercial apprenticeship at the Rosenthal Chinaware Works in Upper Franconia. Every day I used to ride my bicycle six kilometers to work; in winter I walked. I did not mind the trip even when the weather was bad, for I had grown up with this kind of hardship. We considered it a luxury to travel by train.

My best friends were attending secondary schools, and I did not see them as often as I had in the past.

At the Rosenthal Works I received an apprenticeship contract providing that during the first year of my apprenticeship I would be given a subsidy of 40 marks a month, during my second year, 80 marks a month, and during my third year, 120 marks a month.

Twice a week, in the evening, I attended business school in addition to the vocational school, where I learned typing, shorthand, bookkeeping, how to conduct a business correspondence, and English as the only foreign language.

Naturally, everyone at the office knew about my family background, but no one ever talked to me about it. Everyone was friendly and helpful, and the head clerk became a sort of fatherly friend.

After six months I was able to perform jobs that our training program had intended us to learn during our third year of instruction. I learned a great deal at Rosenthal's, and I read a great deal when I was at home.

I even continued to deliver newspapers so that I could use the money to buy books. As always, at harvest time I used to work in the evenings or on weekends for the farmers in our area. But now things had changed. In the past we had worked in order to get potatoes and other produce free, but now we were required to work for the farmers. In those days this was known as the Harvest Front.

At the age of fourteen I had become a "soldier in the harvest battle" and worked for twenty pfennigs an hour. The official

186

catch phrase was "fellow-citizens working on the land to ensure our food supply."

Labor was scarce because the men were forced to join the military. My four uncles were in the Armed Forces too, and sometimes they sent us letters. Without a return address, they were simply marked with a number, the number of the military post from which they were sent. This was a security measure designed to prevent the enemy from finding out where any particular military unit was stationed at a given time.

More and more women were forced to take over jobs that had formerly been performed by men.

A remedy was soon to be found for the shortage of labor, for just a few months later prisoners of war from Denmark, Poland, France, Holland, and Belgium began arriving in Germany, along with foreign workers, all of whom were put to forced labor.

On May 15, 1940, Heinrich Himmler, the Commander-in-Chief of the SS, had recorded his ideas about the future treatment of "foreign races," that is, those who were not German.

Some thoughts regarding the treatment of foreign races in Eastern Europe.

Our treatment of members of foreign races in the East must, as much as possible, be directed toward the recognition and cultivation of the individuality of these peoples—not only the Poles and Jews, but also the Ukrainians, the White Russians, the Góale people [of Poland], the Lemki [of the West Ukraine], and the Kashubians, and any more splinter groups we can discover.

What I mean to say is that it is very much in our interests to prevent the peoples of the East from joining forces and instead to divide them into as many fragments and splinter groups as possible.

But even within each racial group, it is not in our interests to encourage unity and greatness by, for example, gradually encouraging them to take pride in their nation and their native culture, but rather to break up each group into innumerable tiny fragments and particles.

Naturally we will employ members of all these races, particularly of small racial groups, as police officers and mayors.

Only the mayors and the local police should be permitted

187

to hold positions of leadership among these racial groups; among the Górale, the leaders will be the individual chiefs and tribal elders who, in any case, are already always feuding among themselves. We must not permit any consolidation of forces among the leaders, for only by dissolving the mishmash of races that makes up the fifteen million people of the General Government [i.e., Poland] and the eight million people in the Eastern provinces, will it be possible for us to sift through the various races; for our fundamental consideration must be to extract racially valuable stock out of this mishmash in order to take them to Germany to be assimilated.

For example, within a few years—I imagine in not more than four or five—the concept of the Kashubian race will have disappeared, for then a Kashubian people will no longer exist. (This is also, and most especially, true of the West Prussians.) I hope to see the idea of the Jew completely eradicated through some such technique as the mass migration of all the Jews to Africa or some other colony. Over a somewhat longer period it should also be possible to eliminate from our territory the concepts of such races as the Ukrainians, the Górale, and the Lemki. The same thing that can be said about these splinter races applies, on a correspondingly grander scale, to the Poles.

A fundamental question regarding the solution of all these problems is the question of education and thus of the sifting and classification of the young. The non-German population of Eastern Europe should not be allowed to receive any schooling beyond a fourth-grade elementary-school education. The exclusive purpose of such elementary schools would be to teach the following things:

Simple counting up to 500 at most, how to write one's name, and the doctrine that it is a divine commandment to obey Germans and to be honest, industrious, and well-behaved. I do not consider it necessary that these children learn how to read. . . .

Hitler also recorded his ideas:

No teacher should be allowed to come along and announce the need for the compulsory education of the subjugated peoples. The ability of Russians, Ukrainians, the Kirghiz people, and so on, to read and write, could only be damaging to us. For the ability to read and write makes it possible for intelligent people to acquire a certain knowledge of history, and thus would enable them to arrive at political conclusions that, in one way or another, would always be inimical to us.

On April 9, Germany had invaded Denmark and Norway, two small neutral nations.

On May 10, German armies were on the march in the West and once again attacked neutral countries—Luxembourg, Belgium, and Holland. The Western campaign had begun, and it continued until June 22. After the defeat of France, General de Gaulle formed a Provisional Committee of Free French in London.

The men who have commanded the French armies for so many years have formed a government.

Using the defeat of our armies as a pretext, this government has negotiated with the enemy to put an end to the fighting.

To be sure, we were and we still are being overwhelmed by the technological superiority of the enemy on land and in the air.

It was the tanks, the aircraft, and the strategy of the Germans, far more than their numbers, that caused us to retreat. The tanks, the aircraft, and the strategy of the Germans have overwhelmed our commanders-in-chief and driven them to the position they hold today.

But has the last word been spoken? Must we abandon hope? Have we suffered a final defeat? No!

Believe me, believe one who knows whereof he speaks and who tells you that France has not yet been defeated. The same means used to overwhelm us may one day bring about our victory.

For France is not alone! It is not alone! It is not alone! It has the support of a vast international empire. It can form a bloc with the British Empire, which rules the seas and which is still fighting on. It can, like England, make unlimited use of the vast industrial resources of the United States of North America.

This war is not being fought within the borders of our unhappy motherland alone. The outcome of this war has not been decided by the battle of France. This war is a world war. All our mistakes, all our hesitations, all our sufferings do not change the fact that there are means available in this world by which we can one day destroy our enemies. Although today we have been crushed by technological superiority, in the future we can be victorious by employing superior technological power. The fate of the world depends on our doing so.

I, General de Gaulle, who am at present in London, appeal to French officers and soldiers, those who are armed and those who are unarmed, those who are now on British soil or can make their way here, to contact me. I also appeal to the engineers and specially trained workers of the armaments industry who are now on British soil or can make their way here. Whatever happens, the flame of French resistance must not and will not be extinguished.

Tomorrow, like today, I will speak over Radio London.

On June 22, Germany signed an armistice agreement with France. The signing ceremony took place in the forest of Compiègne near Paris, in the same railroad car in which Germany and France had signed their armistice agreement at the end of World War I. Hitler had insisted on this location and this railroad car so as to blot out finally the humiliation of the Treaty of Versailles.

Just four weeks later, on July 21, Hitler had decided to attack the Soviet Union. The code name for the war plan outlining the Soviet campaign was Barbarossa.

We know about all this from the military log of General Halder, who at this time was the Army Chief of Staff and was privy to all secret plans.

However, if Russia is defeated, England's last hope will be gone. Germany will then be the master of Europe and the Balkans.

Resolved: In view of these facts, Russia must be finished off. Spring, 1941.

The faster we crush Russia the better. Operation makes sense only if we completely crush enemy straight off. Conquest of a certain amount of territory won't do the trick. Bogging down in winter risky. . . .

May, 1941. Five months to carry out [the operation]. Preferably some time this year.

But this won't be possible if we're to carry out a unified operation.

Goal: Destruction of Russia's vitality.

On September 27, Germany, Italy, and Japan signed the Berlin Pact. Italy had joined the war against France and Great Britain,

190

and as a result the war spread from Europe to Africa as well. Italy possessed African colonies such as Libya, Eritrea, the area now known as Somalia, and Ethiopia.

Smaller nations such as Hungary, Rumania, and Slovakia, which were dependent on Germany, also signed the Berlin Pact. The map shown here makes it clear that Germany more or less

---

Hitler's advance into the Balkans with the support of the Berlin Pact, which was signed by Slovakia, Hungary, and Rumania on November 23, 1940, Bulgaria on March 1, 1941, and Yugoslavia on March 25, 1941.

pressured them into doing so. Hitler needed a vast territory in which to deploy his forces for the war he planned to wage against the Soviet Union.

In the office at my firm hung a large map of Europe. One of the apprentices who had started his training at the same time as I did was a fanatical member of the Hitler Youth. At first he even used to come to the office wearing his Hitler Youth uniform, until the manager forbade it. This boy used to stick little colored flags into those places on the map that were occupied by German troops, so that he could trace the expansion of the German Reich.

Once I found myself alone with the head clerk, to whose political views I had not previously gained any clue. Suddenly he pointed at the map and said to me, "You know, it will all end when those armies are scattered across the whole of Europe; then the whole fantasy will simply collapse."

My colleague even stuck his little flags in the areas where German planes were dropping their bombs over England. After the conclusion of the Western campaign, Hitler wanted to risk invading England, and thus he had ordered it to be bombed almost around the clock. The propagandists called this the "air battle over England."

The terrible bombing attack on the English city of Coventry, which was virtually leveled to the ground in a single night, testified to the truth of Hitler's scornful slogan, "We'll wipe their cities off the map!"

However, the bombing attacks did not crush the British people's will to resist; instead they strengthened it.

Winston Churchill, who had formed a new government after Chamberlain's removal from office in 1940, coined a phrase that became famous: "I have nothing to offer but blood, toil, tears, and sweat." The more bombs dropped on England, the more determined the English people became to resist.

German losses of aircraft and pilots became so great that finally the battle of Britain had to be broken off, which put an end to Hitler's plan to invade England.

It has frequently been said that the battle of Stalingrad marked the turning point of the war and that from then on German troops were doomed to continual retreat, but I believe that the

192

loss of the battle of Britain represented the real turning point, for this loss made it impossible for Hitler to eliminate England as a nation and as an adversary. The British Empire remained intact.

Again and again the fanfares came on the radio to herald another special bulletin—for example, when enemy ships were sunk, enemy planes shot down, and enemy cities bombed.

As always, my grandfather, who was now gravely ill, went on driving his wagon into the woods or to the stone quarries. He had cancer. In the evenings when he rested wearily on the couch and no one else was in the room, he had me sit down beside him and tell him about my work at the office. Sometimes he would stroke my hand and say, "Let's hope that they'll have conquered themselves to death before you have to join that mob."

In Poland the annihilation of the Jews was being carried forward. On April 30, the first Jewish ghetto equipped with guards was set up in Lodz; on May 20, the concentration camp at Auschwitz was erected.

In the Ghettos

Ghettos are transit stations on the road to death, and for many people they are the final station.

At first the people continue to go to their usual places of employment in the Aryan part of town, and then in the evening they return to the ghetto. One day they find that the ghetto has been sealed off with barbed wire, and all the exits are guarded by armed sentries.

The sealing off from the outside world brings about economic disaster. The little businesses inside the enclosure can provide work for only a few people. Hundreds of thousands of people are imprisoned in a giant cage, abandoned to the certain death from starvation that Hitler has ordained for them. And more and more masses of people are continually crammed into the already overcrowded ghettos.

Confiscations, chicanery, looting, wild shooting sprees, and public executions here never end. But one plague is so terrible that all the others pale in comparison: hunger. Hunger is the song of lament of the beggars who sit on the street with their homeless families; hunger is the cry of the mothers whose new-born infants are dying. People fight each other until they draw blood for possession of a raw potato; children risk their lives to smuggle in a handful of turnips for which a whole family is waiting.

In the end, a little over two pounds of bread, seven and a half ounces of sugar, three ounces of jam, and one and a half ounces of lard represent a month's rations in the Warsaw Ghetto. Often spoiled food that has been rejected by the Wehrmacht is delivered to the ghettos. With industry and ingenuity people struggle to alleviate the misery. In primitive workshops, handcrafted products are laboriously turned out so that they can be exchanged for goods in the Aryan districts of the city. Useful kitchen implements are created from a piece of wood; brightly patterned kerchiefs are made from old bedsheets. With the connivance of the sentries, who extort enormous bribes from the starving people in return for their aid, whole wagonloads of food are smuggled into the ghetto. Nevertheless, the mortality rate continues to rise unabated. Typhus breaks out under these slum conditions. The carts that carry away the dead come more and more often. But it is impossible to observe the regulation of the German authorities that dead people not be allowed to lie in the street for longer than fifteen minutes. People dying of exhaustion lie down in the gutter, and those who are still alive pass right by them without turning around. Poverty, starvation, and despair gnaw their way deeper into the people until there is nothing left.

An even more terrible end awaits those who do not die here. In July, 1942, the transport of the Jews out of all the ghettos and into the extermination camps begins. Extermination through starvation is followed by extermination in the gas chamber. The members of the Jewish councils are forced to draw up the lists of those who are to be transported to the camps. Within a three-month period, 400,000 people are transported to Belzec and Treblinka from the Warsaw Ghetto alone. Mass shelters, hospitals, and children's homes are the first to be emptied. Then comes the turn of all those who are not working in war-related industries. In the beginning many homeless Jews volunteer to go to the camps just in order to get the half a loaf of bread and the tin of jam that have been promised to everyone during the journey. Their misery is so great that they have even ceased to fear the concentration camps, for they hope that there they may at least be given a plank bed to sleep on at night and a bowl of food.

Later, when the first rumors about the gas chambers filter into the ghettos, the Germans must employ the greatest brutality and violence in order to force the frightened people into the railroad cars. For days the city resembles a jungle in which people are being furiously hunted down. The streets echo with the curses of the police and the screams of the victims. People struggling with their hands and feet to resist are struck bloody blows and dragged to the transfer points. Hundreds of them are forced into each of the cattle cars, and many die in the course of the journey. When Treblinka becomes too overcrowded, the lead-sealed trains are left standing on the track for days until all the people inside have suffocated.

In the summer of 1943, all the ghettos except Lodz (the Germans call it Litzmannstadt) are finally torn down. Only a few companies of Jewish prisoners in forced labor camps are left, but sooner or later they too will follow the path that leads to the gas chambers or the ditches where they will be shot in mass executions.

Later 350,000 Jews died in the Warsaw Ghetto, which was erected on October 16 of this year. A deeply moving document about the life of Jews in rural areas is the diary of little David Rubinowitsch, who later died in the gas chamber at Treblinka at the age of fourteen:

The Diary of a Child

March 21, 1940. Early this morning I walked through the village where we live. From some distance away I saw a notice on the wall of the store; I hurried over to read it. The new announcement said that Jews are no longer permitted to ride in cars or other wheeled vehicles (we were forbidden to travel by train a long time ago).

April 4, 1940. Today I got up earlier than usual because I wanted to go to Kielce. After breakfast I left the house. I felt sad walking the paths through the fields all alone. After four hours on the road, I arrived at Kielce. When I entered my uncle's house, I saw everyone sitting there looking very depressed, and I was told that all the Jews were being moved out of certain streets, and I was overcome by sadness too.

April 5, 1940. I could not sleep all night; strange thoughts kept going through my head. After breakfast I went home.

June 9, 1940. Today the German Army were practicing. All the troops spread out over the fields, set up machine guns, and shot at each other.

June 18, 1940. The police searched our house for anything of a military nature. The policemen asked me where these things were, and I kept saying that there weren't any and that was all I knew. So they found nothing and went away again.

August 5, 1940. Yesterday the guard from the community around Dorfschulzen drove up and told us that all Jews and their families were supposed to go to Dorfschulzen and be registered. At seven in the morning we were already there. We stayed for several hours, for the oldest members of the community were selecting a council of Jewish elders. Then we went home.

August 12, 1940. Ever since the war started I have been studying alone at home. When I think about how I used to go to school, I feel like crying. But today I am supposed to stay put and not go anywhere. And when I think about all the wars taking place in the world, and how many people are being killed every day by bullets, gas, bombs, epidemics, and other enemies of mankind, I do not feel like doing anything anymore.

September 1, 1940. Today is the first anniversary of the day the war began. I am thinking about everything we have already had to go through in this short time, how much suffering we have already endured. . . .

July 10, 1941. Times are very hard. It is difficult to live through every hour. In the past we always had a small supply of food, at least enough to last a month. But now it is hard to buy food enough to last a single day. Not one day goes by during which someone does not come to beg at our door, someone who wants only something to eat, which now is the hardest thing of all to obtain.

January 8, 1942. This afternoon I learned that in Bodzentyn there are two more victims among the Jews. One of them died at once; the other was wounded. They arrested the wounded man and took him to the guardhouse in Bieliny, where they will beat him to death.

January 11, 1942. Since early morning it has been snowing heavily and very cold; today it reached minus 20 Celsius. As I watched the wind sweeping across the fields, I noticed that the village guard was putting up an announcement. I immediately

196

went over to read the news. There was no news in the announcement; the guard simply said that he was bringing some announcements to the village mayor that stated that all the Jews were going to be taken out of all the villages and shipped somewhere else. When I told my family about it, we were all very depressed. Now, in the middle of a hard winter like this, they were going to transport us somewhere else? Where can we be going? Now it is our turn to endure terrible suffering. The Lord God alone knows for how long.

1941

I was fifteen years old the first time I saw a human being die.

My grandfather had collapsed in the stable where he was feeding the horses. We carried him into the house, where he lived on for another four weeks in unspeakable agony.

One evening when I came home from the office, my mother told me, "Grandfather is dying. We're going in to say good-bye." Everyone was assembled in the living room—my grandmother, my mother, two aunts, an uncle who happened to be home on leave, and I. Grandmother led us into the bedroom. I could hardly recognize my grandfather anymore. Each member of the family took his hand, which he was no longer able to lift himself. Later the minister arrived and prayed at the foot of the bed. Two hours later my grandfather was dead.

I had not only lost my beloved grandfather, I now had one less friend and teacher in the world. Everything I know about nature and life I learned from him.

In the funeral procession I walked in the first row between Grandmother and my youngest uncle, who had come to the funeral dressed in his uniform. His name was Max too, and before 1933 he had been a member of the SPD (Social Democrats). Three weeks after Grandfather's burial he was dead too; he had fallen for Führer, folk, and fatherland in Russia. My uncle was the first man in our little town to die in Russia.

My uncle was not married, so the military authorities sent a little package containing his belongings to my grandmother. There was not much in the package: a pocket watch, a couple of yellowed photographs, a little notebook with nothing written in it, a larger photograph of his former fiancée, twenty marks and a note addressed to me that said: "Dear Max, look after Grandmother. Be brave." I kept this note, and even today I sometimes puzzle over the meaning of that "Be brave." Was he perhaps already convinced of the senselessness of this war?

In 1941, the war grew into a worldwide conflagration.

On February 8, the Afrika Korps was set up under the command of General Rommel. This corps was needed to support the Italians in the fighting along the Mediterranean coast of North Africa.

On April 6, German troops overran Yugoslavia and Greece. This campaign continued until April 21 and for Germany was the "least bloody" campaign of the war.

Hitler and Mussolini intended to create their own sort of new order in southeastern Europe.

Hitler occupied all the Balkan states, thus securing his right flank and clearing the way for the attack on the Soviet Union he had been planning for so long.

On June 22, German troops, ranged all the way from Rumania in the south to the Baltic Sea in the north, crossed the border into the U.S.S.R. without any previous declaration of war. Although the U.S.S.R. had observed its treaty obligations, Hitler once again violated his. The bloodiest, cruelest, most hopeless war in European history had begun. Hitler was now attempting to realize his plans to conquer "living space" in the East. The German troops made rapid progress. By December, 1941, they had won several battles, surrounded Leningrad and placed it under siege, and occupied the "new living space" of the Ukraine.

Now once again the propagandists in the Reich concentrated on the Russian people. They proclaimed that Russians were inferior human beings, were in fact subhuman, and that Russian prisoners of war were not entitled to any legal rights. It was permissible to allow them to starve to death, shoot them, or force them into slave labor. Their right to live a life worthy of a human being was no longer acknowledged:

Just as the night revolts against the day, just as light and shadow are eternal enemies—so the greatest enemy of man, the master of the earth, is man himself.

The subhuman man [*Untermensch*]—that creation of nature appearing wholly identical in all biological respects, with hands, feet, and a species of brain, with eyes and a mouth, is in reality something quite different, a dreadful creation, a mere first draft of a human being with facial features resembling those of human beings—but mentally and spiritually inferior to any animal. The inner life of one of these people is a hideous chaos of wild and uninhibited passions: a nameless will to destroy, desire in its most primitive form, the most manifest vileness.

A subhuman—and nothing more than that!

For not every person who wears a human face is like every other. Woe to him who forgets this!

All the great works, thoughts, and arts on earth were invented, created, and perfected by man. He thought and designed, for him there was only one goal: to work his way up into a higher existence, to create something new when what was old was not enough, to replace what was inadequate with something better.

Thus culture developed.

Thus the plow, the tool, the house were invented.

Thus man became social and so developed the family, the people, the state. In this way man became good and great. In this way he rose far above all other living creatures.

In this way he became akin to God!

But the subhuman man existed too. He hated the work of the other man. He raged against him, secretly as a thief, openly as a blasphemer—and a murderer. He joined forces with his own kind.

The beast called unto the beast.

The subhuman creature never kept the peace; he never gave the others any rest. For he needed twilight and chaos.

He shunned the light of cultural progress.

In order to survive he needed the swamp, he needed Hell, but not the sun.

And this underworld of subhuman creatures found its leader: the eternal Jew! . . .

Issued by the Central Office of the SS

Thus we will once again emphasize that we were compelled to occupy, secure, and establish order in a given region; we will say that in the interests of the native population we were forced to provide for law and order, food, methods of transportation, and so on, and that it is for these reasons that we stepped in and took charge. It should not be apparent that we are thereby paving the way to take charge permanently! Nevertheless, we can and will take any measures necessary—shootings, deportations, etc. . . .

Basically it comes down to cutting up this gigantic cake into manageable slices, so that first we can control it, second we can administer it, and third we can exploit it. : . .

We must cling to one iron principle: Anyone who is not a German must never be permitted to carry a weapon! . . . The area around Leningrad is being claimed by the Finns; the Führer wants to reduce Leningrad to rubble, and then turn it over to the Finns.

July 16, 1941
Minutes of a conference with Adolf Hitler

Once again the SS followed in the wake of the German troops. They shot the political commissars attached to all major units of Soviet troops. How Hitler planned to deal with the conquered Russians is revealed in a memorandum written on May 2, 1941, describing the decision to plunder the economic resources of the occupied territories, and the resulting starvation of millions of Russians is cynically taken into consideration.

1. The war can be continued only if, by the third year, all Armed Forces are fed from Russia.

2. No doubt millions of people will starve if we strip the country of everything we need.

3. The most important factors are the recovery and transport of rape seed and oil cake, and only secondarily of grain. Presumably the troops in Russia will consume all the available lard and meat.

4. Industrial activity may be permitted to resume only in areas deficient in needed supplies.

Notes of a secret conference held on May 2, 1941

And Hitler himself explained how the subjugated people were to be treated:

Vaccinations and other prophylactic medical measures are not under any circumstances to be administered to the non-German population. Thus they must be persuaded that vaccinations and so forth are very dangerous things. . . . Of course, schools must be provided for them, but they must pay if they wish to attend them. They must not be allowed to learn anything more in these schools than, at most, how to read traffic signs. Generally speaking their instruction in geography should be restricted to the fact that

202

the capital of the Reich is called Berlin and that everyone must go to Berlin once during his life. In addition to these things, it will be quite sufficient if the non-German population learns to read and write a little German. Instruction in counting, arithmetic, and that sort of thing is unnecessary.

The first great massacre of the Russian campaign took place in Kiev, where, on September 28, no fewer than 34,000 people were shot, beaten to death, and mowed down with machine guns.

In 1970, in response to an invitation from the Soviet Writers' League and my Moscow publishers, I went to the Soviet Union, where I visited Kiev and saw the ghastly place known as Babi Yar (meaning "the ravine of the virgins"), where the massacre took place. The city of Kiev has now expanded to include the ravine, which in 1941 was still many kilometers from the city.

There was not much to see. A stone stood there bearing a Russian inscription stating that one day a memorial was to be built at this place.

In Kiev I met an old woman who in September, 1941, had managed to climb out from under a mountain of dead bodies during the night, and who, despite the area's being strictly guarded and her own severe wounds, succeeded in dragging herself back to Kiev. There she told everyone what had really happened at Babi Yar, for the Germans had announced that they were merely using the ravine for shooting practice.

Attack Group A Concerning Mass Murder in the U.S.S.R.

It was to be expected from the beginning that the Jewish problem in the East would not be solved by pogroms alone. On the other hand, the purge carried out by the security police, in conformity with our basic orders, had the most extensive possible elimination of the Jews as its goal. . . .

Appendix 8. Summary of the number of executions carried out so far:

	Jews	Communists	Total
Lithuania	80,311	860	81,171
Latvia	30,025	1,843	31,868
Estonia	474	684	1,158
White Ruthenia	7,620	—	7,620
	118,430	3,387	121,817

In addition:

Jews eliminated during pogroms in Lithuania and Latvia	5,500
Jews, Communists, and partisans executed in Muscovy	2,000
Mentally ill persons executed	748
	130,065
Communists and Jews liquidated along the frontier by the state police and the Tilsit Division of the SD	5,502
	135,567

Through this woman who had survived the massacre at Babi Yar, the world found out what had actually taken place at Kiev. But Goebbels, the untiring liar for Hitler, spoke on the radio and dismissed her tale as a horror story dreamed up by enemy propaganda.

I am convinced that the majority of the German people accepted what Goebbels said, for no one could believe that German men were capable of such atrocities.

On July 31, Hermann Göring assigned to Reinhard Heydrich, Chief of the Ministry of Security and an unscrupulous master of the technology of power, the task of transporting all the Jews in occupied Europe to concentration camps and arranging for them to be murdered there.

On September 23, the first experimental gassings actually began at Auschwitz. At first automobile exhaust fumes were used, and later the poisonous gas Zyklon B. The exhaust fumes produced by diesel engines were pumped through pipes into barracks constructed especially for this purpose. The people locked inside the barracks died an agonizing death:

In the fall of 1941, in obedience to special secret orders, the Gestapo singled out the Russian politruks [political instructors assigned to units of the Soviet Armed Forces], commissars, and special political officials from among the other prisoners in the prisoner-of-war camps and took them to the nearest concentration camp for liquidation. Small groups of this kind were always arriving at Auschwitz and shot to death either in the gravel pit

204

next to the main administration buildings or in the courtyard of Blockhouse II. While I was on a business trip my second-in-command, SS Company Commander Fritzsch, on his own initiative, had employed gas to execute some of these Russian prisoners of war. He did so by cramming the Russians into the individual cells located in the cellar and ordering his men, wearing gas masks, to throw Zyklon B into the cells; this caused immediate death. The firm of Tesch & Stabenow had frequently employed the gas Zyklon B at Auschwitz to exterminate vermin, and thus there was always a supply of the gas canisters stored in the administration buildings. . . . The next time Eichmann came to visit the camp, I reported to him how the Zyklon B had been used, and we decided that we would use this gas for future mass exterminations. . . .

I remained in command at Auschwitz until December 1, 1943, and I would estimate that at least 2,500,000 victims were executed and exterminated there in the gas chambers and the crematoria; at least another half million died of starvation and disease, so that the total number of dead was approximately 3,000,000. This figure represents approximately 70 or 80 percent of all prisoners sent to Auschwitz; the others were especially chosen to serve as slave labor in the industries run by the concentration camp.

Rudolf Höss
Commandant of Auschwitz Concentration Camp

On September 1, a police ordinance went into effect decreeing that every Jew living in Germany had to wear a yellow star of David on his clothing.

A Jewish family was living in our town, and until the Kristallnacht in 1938, they had run a small ready-to-wear clothing store. In 1938, their business was closed and they were forbidden to engage in any form of employment. I do not know what they lived on, perhaps on savings or on donations from Jewish friends.

The first time I saw the yellow star of David, it was being worn by the husband and father of this Jewish family. Even from a long distance away one could see it shining on his threadbare coat. People turned away to avoid him. I stood still because I thought the star was some special type of military decoration. I wanted to approach the man to get a better look at the star, but just at that moment my mother came out of the butcher shop and held me back. She hissed in my ear, "Stay here, that can be dangerous." But perhaps she also believed that I might humiliate the old man even more if I walked up and gaped at his star.

1. Jews of the age of six and above are forbidden to appear in public without a star of David.

2. The star of David must be a six-pointed star, the size of the palm of a man's hand, made of yellow material outlined in black, on which is written in black the inscription "Jew." It is to be sewn onto clothing on the left side of the chest in such a way that it is clearly visible.

None of the people working at my office was happy when the war against the U.S.S.R. began, even though I am certain that all our employees were anti-Communist. All day long the head clerk went around looking depressed and got angry at the apprentice who every morning zealously moved the little flags on the map farther toward the East. Our head bookkeeper now read the newspaper from back to front, just like my mother. The last pages were filled with the lists of the dead decorated with the Iron Cross.

One day while he was busy working, the head bookkeeper received a phone call. I can still remember how he turned pale, dropped the receiver, and stiffly walked out of the office. He did not return for three days. His eldest son had been killed in Russia.

My mother took an intense interest in the course of the war. She devoured the newspapers, and when she was listening to the news on the radio she looked as if she were trying to climb inside. She was not interested in military matters but in something quite different: I was getting bigger and older, and it was now clear to my mother that the war had ceased to be a little excursion at the end of which we would gain a glorious victory. Obviously, it was going to be a long war, and she was afraid that I would be drawn into it at last. She sometimes asked me whether I felt quite well and whether I was suffering from any ailments that might have excused me from military duty.

Naturally, I was feeling quite well; I engaged in sports and gymnastics, played handball, was a long-distance runner, and in the winter I used to ski.

I went on long bicycle trips with my school friends into the Fichtelgebirge, the Bavarian woods, or even across the border into the woods of Bohemia. We used to sleep on straw in the barns and then work for a day for the farmer in order to earn our food. The war was very far away from this peaceful and quiet landscape, and you could almost forget that bloody battles were being fought in the East.

While time seemed to stand still for us, the SS were executing people in the gas chambers, people were being tortured in prison basements, all the Jews in the Reich were being shipped off to Poland to be gassed there, and in this year alone 11,405 "left-wing intellectuals" were arrested, many of whom did not survive their captivity.

Sometimes I even forgot that my own father was leading a wretched existence in one of these camps.

But reality soon caught up with us. When we spent the night at some farm, we saw only women and children as a rule, for the men were off fighting in the war. The men we did see were prisoners of war or forced laborers—French, Belgian, Dutch, and sometimes even Czech.

When I arrived home on December 7, my mother ran out to meet me, waving her arms about and looking very excited. She told me that she had heard over the radio that Japanese planes had bombed the American naval base at Pearl Harbor and destroyed a portion of the American fleet.

I immediately got out my atlas and looked for Pearl Harbor. The naval base was located on the Hawaiian island of Oahu.

Extract from Roosevelt's Speech of December 9, 1941

The course that Japan has followed for the past ten years in Asia has paralleled the course of Hitler and Mussolini in Europe and in Africa. Today it has become far more than a parallel. It is collaboration—actual collaboration—so well calculated that all the continents of the world, and all the oceans, are now considered by the Axis strategists as one gigantic battlefield.

In 1931, ten years ago, Japan invaded Manchukuo—without warning.

In 1935, Italy invaded Ethiopia—without warning.

In 1938, Hitler occupied Austria—without warning.

In 1939, Hitler invaded Czechoslovakia—without warning.

Later in 1939, Hitler invaded Poland—without warning.

In 1940, Hitler invaded Norway, Denmark, the Netherlands, Belgium, and Luxembourg—without warning.

In 1940, Italy attacked France and later Greece—without warning.

And this year, in 1941, the Axis powers attacked Yugoslavia and Greece, and they dominated the Balkans—without warning.

In 1941 also, Hitler invaded Russia—without warning.

And now Japan has attacked Malaya and Thailand—and the United States—without warning. . . .

And what we all have learned is this:

There is no such thing as security for any nation—or any individual—in a world ruled by the principles of gangsterism. . . .

Your government knows that for weeks Germany has been telling Japan that if Japan did not attack the United States, Japan would not share in the division of spoils with Germany when peace came. She was promised by Germany that if she came in she would receive the complete and perpetual control of the whole of the Pacific area—and that means not only the Far East, not only all of the islands in the Pacific, but also a stranglehold on the west coast of North, Central, and South America. . . .

We are now in the midst of a war, not for conquest, not for vengeance, but for a world in which this nation, and all that this nation represents, will be safe for our children. We expect to eliminate the danger from Japan, but it would serve us ill if we accomplished that and found that the rest of the world was dominated by Hitler and Mussolini.

We are going to win the war and we are going to win the peace that follows.

Three days later, on December 11, Hitler declared war on the United States. Italy followed suit. I was listening to the radio and heard Hitler say in his address to the Reichstag: "If it is the will of Providence that the German people not be spared this struggle, then I will be grateful to Providence for having appointed me leader in a historic contest, which for the next five hundred or one thousand years, will decisively affect not only

German history but also the history of Europe, and indeed of all mankind."

My mother listened attentively, but strangely enough she did not seem as depressed as she usually was when we heard about new declarations of war and new campaigns. Instead, she seemed to be relieved. In fact, she became almost cheerful and said, "So, boy, now you won't have to get into the war. Now the war will be over soon. In a couple of weeks the Americans will have chased Hitler to the devil."

She was mistaken. The war was destined to go on for years yet and to claim many more millions of human lives.

In December, the first camp designed for the regular gassing of prisoners was built in Chelmno near Poznán in Poland.

Naturally, we knew nothing about this. I am certain that the majority of Germans knew nothing about what was going on in the East behind the front lines. And if some bit of information did leak out, Goebbels would speak on the radio and claim that the "rumors" were nothing but wicked enemy propaganda. Indeed, the bits of information we did receive seemed so incredible that people preferred to believe Goebbels' refutations.

As always, our daily concern was what we would eat on the following day. Living in the country as we did, we were better off than the people in the cities. We had a large garden where we could grow vegetables, and the farmwork we did also brought in some supplies. But, by 1941, the general food situation had already become very difficult. For a long time there had been no luxury goods such as coffee, which was used as a medium of exchange on the so-called black market.

We had been using ration cards ever since the war began. In return for each coupon, one received a certain quantity of bread, meat, or vegetables. The food was weighed and measured to determine its nutritive value in terms of calories. I still remember how I looked in my little dictionary to find out what a calorie really was, but all it said was that a calorie was a "thermal unit," and I could not make much sense out of that.

The food situation for people living in the German-occupied countries of Europe was much worse. Every day each person of the following nationalities was given a limited ration of calories:

Poles	800 calories
Belgians	950 calories
Norwegians	1,500 calories
French	1,600 calories
Dutch	1,900 calories
Germans	2,500 calories

The number of calories allotted to each group is an indication of how the Nazis rated their relative importance. Farmers in the German Reich who held back food supplies for the lean years were hauled before a summary court of justice. They were charged with being antisocial parasites and sentenced. Then they were either sent to a concentration camp or shot immediately. On the other hand, foreigners were treated in accordance with one of Hitler's favorite phrases: The Nazis made short work of them by shooting them without a trial.

A terrible famine broke out in Greece and claimed thousands of victims. Conditions in Yugoslavia were equally dreadful. Hitler and Mussolini had divided the country up into little states: Croatia, Serbia, and Montenegro were "independent," and the rest of Yugoslavia had been divided between Germany and Italy. Resistance groups, some Conservative and some Communist, fought the occupation troops and often each other as well.

> Digging the ditches consumes the greatest amount of the time, whereas the actual shooting can be conducted quite rapidly (100 men, 40 minutes). . . . Initially my soldiers were not affected. However, by the second day it was already apparent that some of them do not have the nerve to carry out executions over a prolonged period. My personal impression is that one does not experience any emotional inhibitions during the actual shooting. However, such inhibitions do develop when, after days of witnessing the executions, one reflects about them in the peace of the evening.
>
> Report by First Lieutenant Walther
> concerning executions carried out near Belgrade
> on November 1, 1941

The man who was later to become known as Marshal Tito began a partisan war that German troops were never able to get under control.

1942

Swaggering, lofty, out of touch with reality, Hitler had spoken in his declaration of war on the United States of the Providence that had willed this conflict.

He was accustomed to counting in spans of a thousand years and referred to his empire as "The Thousand-Year Reich." Fortunately, it lasted for only twelve years. His policies had always been designed with a view to avoiding the need to fight on two fronts at once; but now he was waging war on many fronts, all at the same time.

In the East he had to face the U.S.S.R., in the West, Great Britain and the United States, which even at that time was the greatest food producer in the world.

However, at first it looked as if the war would turn out just as Hitler had hoped. His Japanese allies were winning victories throughout Eastern Asia. In a single sweep they conquered Hong Kong, the Celebes, Borneo, Singapore, New Guinea, the Solomon Islands, and the Philippines, and they were now advancing toward the borders of India and Australia.

England was having serious problems, for the Japanese Navy and Air Force had acquired virtually complete control of the entire Indian and Pacific oceans.

The German armies in Russia launched major offensives. They advanced to Stalingrad on the Volga River and penetrated the Caucasus region. Although Italy had lost all its colonies except Libya to the English, Japan and Germany were now at the zenith of their military power.

But the United States was preparing to strike back. Thanks to the superiority of their air force, it was not long before the Americans, overcoming Japanese resistance, began to win back island after island, and gradually the superior material resources of the United States made their presence felt in Europe too.

Within the Reich efforts were stepped up to follow through

with Hitler's plan to annihilate the Jews under the cover of a war. On January 20, a conference was held in Berlin, in the course of which the decision was made to murder all the Jews. The Wannsee Conference held to determine "the final solution of the Jewish problem" established with bureaucratic precision exactly how an entire people were to be wiped out of existence.

The possibility of a mass migration of the Jews has now yielded to another possible solution, which we duly obtained the Führer's permission to carry out: the evacuation of the Jews into the East.

This action actually represents a mere evasion of the problem, but it is enabling us to gain some practical experience of great importance in relation to the final solution of the Jewish problem.

When we speak of the final solution of the problem of European Jewry, we are speaking in terms of around eleven million Jews. . . .

The final solution will involve the transportation of the Jews to the East, in a suitable manner and under the appropriate leadership, to enter the labor force. After the men have been separated from the women, able-bodied Jews will be formed into large labor units and taken to regions in the East where they will work at road construction; in the process a large number of them will doubtless be eliminated by natural means.

Those who may manage to survive since they will undoubtedly represent the hardiest portion, will have to be dealt with accordingly, for, having undergone a process of natural selection, these Jews would, if they were to be set free, serve as a germ cell for the building of a new Jewish race. (Consider the lessons of history.)

The practical implementation of the final solution will make it necessary for us to comb through Europe from the West to the East. The housing problem and other socio-political exigencies will require that we proceed first within the Reich, including the Protectorate of Bohemia and Moravia.

From then on the ovens in the extermination camps burned day and night. Soon there were not enough camps to house all the Jews, and new ones had to be built. The death camp of Belzec was built on March 16.

212

On May 27, Reinhard Heydrich, Himmler's second-in-command and the Reich Protector of Bohemia and Moravia, who had instituted a reign of terror in the truncated remnants of Czechoslovakia, died as a result of wounds inflicted by Czech patriots who had thrown a bomb at him in the street.

The Germans responded to the assassination with an inhuman act of retaliation. The assassins, who without the knowledge of the villagers had hidden for a couple of days in the village of Lidice, were captured. The Germans shot all the men in the Czech village, sent the women to Ravensbrück Concentration Camp, and gassed eighty-one of the eighty-three children.

The more brutal the terrorism practiced by the German occupation forces in the conquered lands, the stronger the people's resistance became. In the past there had been only isolated resistance groups, but now all the groups were being organized into an army.

German supply routes, military outposts, and munitions and supply depots were attacked. The Germans responded with mass arrests and the shooting of hostages, men, women, and children alike. The inhabitants of entire villages were executed, as in the French village of Oradour-sur-Glane, in 1944, or the Yugoslavian village of Borysowka.

Report from the State Police Headquarters in Prague
regarding retaliatory measures
taken against the village of Lidice, 1942
Copy
Secret State Police

Prague, June 24, 1942

State Police Headquarters Prague—L—
Retaliatory measures against the village of Lidice

In obedience to the Führer's orders, retaliatory measures were carried out against the village of Lidice in Bohemia because fugitive Czech agents, who had parachuted into the area from English planes, fled to this village and received aid from villagers with relatives in the Czech Legion in England and from a large number of the other villagers.

The village, consisting of 95 houses, was burned to the ground; 199 male citizens over the age of fifteen were shot on the spot; 184 women were sent to Ravensbrück Concentration

Camp, 7 women to the police prison at Theresienstadt, 4 pregnant women to the hospital in Prague; 88 children were sent to Lodz, whereas 7 children under the age of one year were taken to a children's home in Prague. Three children are being taken back to the old Reich to be raised as Germans. One gravely ill woman is still in the hospital in Kladno.

Signed:
Dr. Geschke

Report of the French Government (Vichy)
to Commander-in-Chief in West

June, 1944

On Saturday, June 10, a unit of SS, who probably belonged to the division Das Reich, which was present in the area, burst into the village, which they had already completely surrounded, and ordered the populace to assemble at the marketplace. The people were informed that they had been denounced for concealing explosives in their village and that a house search and identity check was to be carried out.

The men were ordered to split up into four or five groups, and each of these groups was then locked inside a barn. The women and children were taken to the church and locked in. It was around two o'clock in the afternoon. Soon the sound of machine-gun salvos was heard, and the entire village, as well as the surrounding farms, was set on fire. The homes were kindled one after another. Given the size of the village, it must surely have taken several hours to carry out this operation.

Throughout this time the women and children, who could hear the noise of the inferno and the bursts of machine-gun fire, were very frightened. At five o'clock German soldiers entered the church and placed on the Communion rail a mechanism for asphyxiating people, consisting of a sort of box from which there projected burning fuses. In a short time the air was no longer breathable, but someone nevertheless succeeded in opening the door to the sacristy and thus revived the suffocating women and children. Then the German soldiers began shooting through the church windows. Thereupon, they burst into the church to finish off the last survivors with their submachine guns and scattered a combustible substance all over the floor.

Only one of the women managed to get away. She had climbed up to one of the windows, intent on escape, when the cries of a mother who wanted to give this woman her child at-

tracted the attention of one of the guards. He fired at her, wound-
ing her gravely. She managed to save her life only by pretending
to be dead, and later her wounds were tended in a hospital in
Limoges.

At around six o'clock that evening German soldiers stopped
the local train, which was traveling nearby, and ordered the
passengers who were going to Oradour to get off the train. They
mowed them down with their submachine guns and threw their
corpses into the inferno. . . .

Of course, the people of many Russian towns—those who were
opposed to Bolshevism or even openly fought it—welcomed the
German troops as liberators and believed that the coming of the
Germans, who, especially in the Ukraine, enjoyed a good reputation, would result in a better life for them all. But soon the
inhumane conduct of the occupation forces drove the Russians
into the ranks of the partisans.

On June 10, all the Jewish schools still left in the Reich were
closed down; on June 12, Himmler approved the so-called General Plan for the East, which provided that all the natives of
Eastern Europe were to be relocated to Siberia. Poland and the
European part of Russia were to be opened up for German settlement.

This plan, conceived as the Germanization of Eastern Europe,
also provided for the decimation of thirty million Slavs:

> The plan makes it clear that this program cannot be carried
> out overnight and that the German settlement of this territory
> will not be achieved until some thirty years after the war. It fol-
> lows from the plan that 14,000,000 non-German natives will re-
> main in the area. It appears extremely unlikely that within the
> anticipated thirty-year span these people will actually have
> changed their nationality and become Germanized, for in terms
> of the present plan the number of German settlers will still be
> relatively small. . . .
>
> If we start with the assumption that 14,000,000 non-Germans
> will remain in the areas in question, as the plan provides, this
> means that some 46,000,000 to 51,000,000 people would have to
> be relocated. The estimate in the plan, that only 31,000,000 peo-
> ple would have to be resettled, cannot be correct. . . .
>
> Thus the plan provides for the resettlement of 80 to 85 per-

cent of the Polish people. In other words, depending on whether one estimates the population of Poland as 20,000,000 or 24,000,000 people, between 16,000,000 and 20,400,000 Poles will have to be resettled, whereas between 3,000,000 and 4,800,000 Poles will remain in the area of German settlement. . . .

Once the industrial regions of the Kuznetsk Basin, Novosibirsk, and Karaganda start working at their full capacity, a large, technically skilled labor force will be needed. Why should Walloon engineers, Czech technicians, Hungarian industrial tradesmen, etc. not carry on their activities in Siberia? We could then justly speak of Siberia as a territory for European settlement and as a reserve source of raw materials. . . .

According to the plan of the Reich Ministry of Security, the West Ukrainians are also to be transferred to Siberian territory. The figure of 65 percent has been suggested. . . .

The plan provides that 75 percent of the White Ruthenians will be resettled. . . .

Our aim is not simply the destruction of the Moscow regime, a goal that, because it has been conceived in purely historical terms, will, once it has been achieved, never bring about a permanent solution of the problem. Instead, we must destroy the vitality of the Russian people and thus destroy Russian national characteristics themselves, in order to achieve the fragmentation of the Russians. Only if the problems involved here are consistently interpreted from a biological standpoint, and particularly in terms of racial biology, and only if German policies in the East conform to this interpretation, will it be possible for us to avert the danger posed by the Russian people. . . .

In the current view, a large portion of the Czechs—that is, those who appear to be racially unimpeachable—will be integrated into German culture. It is estimated that approximately 50 percent of the Czechs will fall into this category. . . .

Future German policy regarding Eastern Europe will reveal whether we are willing to ensure the Third Reich a permanent and secure foundation. In any case, if the Third Reich is indeed to endure for a thousand years, we must plan its future for generations ahead.

Erich Wetzel

On June 30, Hermann Göring had declared: ". . . it is a matter of indifference to me if you say that your people are dropping dead from hunger. Let them do so, as long as no German has to drop dead from hunger . . . if people starve, then it will not be Germans who starve but others . . . as far as the people in the occupied territories are concerned, I am interested only in those who work in munitions factories or help to supply food; they must be given just enough to eat so that they can do their work. . . ." The Nazis could hardly have made a clearer statement of their contempt for human beings; nothing mattered to them but the representatives of the "German master race."

On July 22, the death camp of Treblinka in Poland was completed. In the course of the next few years millions of people died in the gas chambers there. The dead were not all Jews, but represented virtually every group that did not conform to the racial delusions of the German rulers, such as Gypsies, religious minorities, Jehovah's Witnesses, resistance fighters, Communists, and Socialists.

Hitler, Himmler, and Göring had only one plan in mind for the Soviet Union: "Exploit them, starve them, resettle them, hang them, shoot them, gas them," and the special units of the SS acted accordingly.

Not only were there resistance groups in the occupied countries, but also groups who founded Nazi parties there; for example, this happened in Norway, Belgium, and Holland.

Between August, 1942, and the beginning of 1943, the Gestapo arrested one hundred and thirty members of a resistance group to whom the Nazis had given the name The Red Choir. The German writer Günther Weisenborn was a member of this group, which was led by Chief Administrative Adviser Arvid von Harnack and by Harro Schulze-Boysen, an officer in the Reich Ministry of Aviation. Thirty-one men and eighteen women were executed, and most of the others were sentenced to long terms in prison.

On November 23, the tide of the war began to turn.

The Russians surrounded Stalingrad, which at that time contained a German army of 220,000 men.

The first American troops landed in North Africa and opened a second front against Italy and Germany. But Hitler and Goebbels never flagged in their efforts to convince the German people that the Americans were milksops who would sneak away and hide in the sand the moment the first shot was fired.

The German soldiers soon knew better. Under the pressure of American superiority in tanks and aircraft, they were gradually forced to yield their position in North Africa.

Within the Greater German Reich many people still believed that Germany would ultimately be victorious. They remained devoted to Hitler. He was still their god, their statesman, and their general, all wrapped up in one. Every meter of ground the Germans won reawakened their hopes; every sunken enemy ship, every enemy plane shot down was greeted with cheers.

I was now sixteen years old, too young for military service but already old enough not to be unconcerned about it. I did not eagerly volunteer as many of my school friends did, for the hope of my grandfather and my mother that the war would be over before I had to carry a gun had taken root in me and grown stronger.

My fellow apprentice at the office continued to move his little flags back and forth across the map of Europe. A year before, when the Japanese had entered the war, a map of the world had appeared beside the map of Europe. At least there was one good thing about this: it taught me geography. In those days anyone who looked at a map of the world could easily come to the conclusion that Japan and Germany controlled half of it.

One day I arrived at the office half an hour earlier than my colleague. At home I had fashioned some little flags out of cardboard and matches, and I planted them on the map of the world in all the countries that were at war with Japan, Germany, and Italy. These countries included all of North, Central, and South America, the entire continent of Africa (for after all, most of the African countries were either French or British colonies), the Near East, India, and Australia. Now the map looked very different from the way it had before.

When my zealous colleague arrived at the office, he saw the change at once and was so angry he almost burst. But he could not prove that I was the one who had played this trick on him. He shouted at me, "I'm going to report you." But the head clerk, who was standing at his high desk and who had grinned approvingly when he saw the change in the map, called to him, "Quiet down there. I'm the only one who's allowed to yell here."

The marks of hunger were becoming more evident even in our

region, which was a sort of peaceful island in the middle of Germany. We had enough to eat, but fruit and vegetables were not available. Of course, you could fill up on potatoes alone, but just having a full stomach does not mean that you are getting the proper nourishment. You could buy very little with your money because the value of currency had dropped. Foodstuffs had become the current medium of exchange.

For example, if you wanted a new inner tube or a new tire for your bicycle, you had to pay for it with produce. Two years previously I had built a large rabbit hutch and sometimes kept as many as thirty rabbits at a time. They supplied us with meat. I procured food for the rabbits from farmers, and in addition I rented a roadside ditch that I was allowed to mow in order to gather additional food for them. And there were always enough scraps.

In the garden I built a goat pen in which I kept two goats, which supplied us with milk, and my mother had six hens and a couple of geese, so that we were almost "self-supporters," as it used to be termed in those days.

At night school I continued to learn about tax laws, property rights, bookkeeping, accounting, shorthand, and typing. In my vocational school we were only taught things relating to the war, and what represented the proper conduct for a member of the German master race. Once I met the Hitler Youth leader on the street. We started talking, and he asked why I had stopped attending the evening training sessions and never turned up at roll call; after all, he said, it couldn't be because I did not have a uniform. The German people, he told me, were now engaged in a struggle for their very existence, and so everyone would generously overlook it if I turned up at roll call dressed in lederhosen or some other form of civilian dress. I asked him why we had already been waging war against the U.S.S.R. for over a year, despite the fact that we had concluded a nonaggression pact with the Soviets. His answer was simple, a parroted piece of the party line: Essentially the German people were waging war against international Jewry, and there were more Jews in the Soviet Union than anywhere else.

He was one year older than I, and he believed everything he heard over the radio and all the lies his brown-uniformed leaders told him. He was one of the millions of young Germans who had been stupefied and incited to a frenzy. I carefully refrained from telling him so.

That year my mother began to listen regularly to Radio London. This offense was punishable by death. If one were really lucky, one would "merely" be sent to a concentration camp.

At nine o'clock at night she would drape a thick blanket around the radio and stick her head underneath it. Afterward she would tell me the news the "enemy broadcasters" had announced in German.

I was never permitted to listen with her. Obstinate to the core, she would send me out of the room, saying that if she were caught, she could still prove that I had nothing to do with it. Her logic made a lot of sense to me.

Thus my mother learned about the atrocities committed inside the Reich and beyond the German borders. Now she knew what was really going on in the concentration camps, and she learned that the Germans were not the only ones who were winning victories but that the Allies were also making headway. And yet she was disappointed by the Americans because, in her opinion, they were taking too long to defeat the Germans. We also heard about the first major bombing attacks on German cities, and the

Prisoners working in the stone quarries at Flossenbürg Concentration Camp

news sounded very different from the ranting of Joseph Goebbels, who described the bombing attacks as acts of terrorism directed against German civilians because they killed women, children, and old people. Suddenly Goebbels was insisting on humanitarian principles that he himself had forgotten long ago.

One Sunday, in 1942, my mother and I rode our bicycles to Flossenbürg, where my father was imprisoned in the concentration camp. It was a thirty-kilometer journey. We finally decided to find out what a concentration camp looked like. But we did not even get within shouting distance of it, for long before we arrived we met up with some SS guards who were patrolling the road and who drove us away with their rifles in their hands. We saw no prisoners, only the stone quarries. However, later I learned that the prisoners used to work in these quarries until they dropped. They were not only Germans, they were people of many other nationalities.

After the war my father told me how the prisoners had named the paths along which they were forced to drag the heavy stones, and on which, if they collapsed from hunger and exhaustion, they would simply be shot. They called the paths Heaven Street, Stairway to Heaven, or Blood Street.

My father used to walk along one of these paths day after day. But on that Sunday we saw nothing of the cruelty the guards enjoyed inflicting on the prisoners behind the barbed wire and thick walls. Dense forest, a peaceful landscape, the old ruins above Flossenbürg—that was all. It was one of those days when the world seems to be profoundly at peace. But then we glimpsed two watchtowers through the fir trees behind which the camp lay concealed in its valley: the Valley of Death.

1943

On January 8, the Soviets demanded the surrender of General Paulus, the Commander-in-Chief of the German Sixth Army, which was under siege in Stalingrad. Paulus, in obedience to Hitler's orders, refused. Then, on January 10, the Soviets launched their attack on Stalingrad. By January 31, this senseless battle was over, and this was the beginning of the end of the war.

The battle of Stalingrad cost the lives of 146,000 German soldiers, and 90,000 more were taken prisoner, many of whom never returned home again.

The Führer has promised faithfully that he will get us out of here; the announcement was read aloud to us, and we all firmly believed it to be true. I still believe it, for after all, I have to believe in something. If it isn't true, what would be left for me to believe in? . . . All my life, or at least for eight years of it, I have always believed in the Führer and had faith in his word. It is terrible to see how the men here are beginning to doubt him, and it shames me to hear words to which I can say nothing in reply because all the facts suggest that they are true.

If what we have been promised is not true, then Germany will be lost, for in this case no one will keep his word anymore. Oh, these doubts, these horrible doubts; if only they go away soon.

I was horrified when I saw the map. We are completely alone, cut off from any outside aid. Hitler has just left us sitting here. This letter still has a chance of getting mailed if we are still in control of the airfield.

I don't know how we can get out of here. Really it isn't my job to know. We marched on orders, we shot on orders, we starved on orders, we die on orders, and we'll also march out again on orders. Actually we could have marched out a long time ago, but the strategists have not yet agreed on what to do. Soon it will be too late, if it isn't too late already. But we will certainly march on orders once again. Probably even in the same direction we were headed, but this time without weapons and under different leaders.

. . . that is why you should know the truth. The truth is in this letter. The truth is knowing about this terrible battle being waged under hopeless conditions. Misery, hunger, cold, resignation, doubt, despair, and a horrible death. More about it I will not say.

My personal guilt for the state things are in cannot be denied. But it stands in the ratio of one to seventy million, a low ratio, but one that nevertheless exists. I am not trying to evade my responsibility, and I believe that by giving up my life I will have atoned for my guilt. . . . I am not a coward but am merely sad that I cannot furnish any greater proof of my courage than to die for this useless, not to say criminal, cause.

(These letters from unknown soldiers were confiscated and opened in late January, 1943, in obedience to orders from the Führer's headquarters because the Nazis wanted "to determine the mood in the fortress of Stalingrad." The addresses and the names of the men who had written the letters were removed.)

In the past the Western powers had toyed with the idea of offering Germany a so-called peace with honor if it agreed to surrender, but the idea was rejected at the conference that Roosevelt and Churchill held in Casablanca from January 14–26. They now demanded the unconditional surrender of Germany.

Not only were the resistance groups in the occupied countries continually gaining strength in their fight against this senseless war that was daily claiming more and more lives, but the resistance within the German Reich was also growing stronger day by day.

A resistance group had been formed in Munich. This group, which was known as the White Rose, was led by the brother and sister Hans and Sophie Scholl and by the university professor Kurt Huber. With the aid of fellow students who shared their views, they composed handbills in which they appealed to people to resist the National Socialist regime. Thousands of copies of the publications of the White Rose were distributed in the university towns of Munich, Stuttgart, Frankfurt am Main, Freiburg, Vienna, and Hamburg. The group was betrayed and its members were executed.

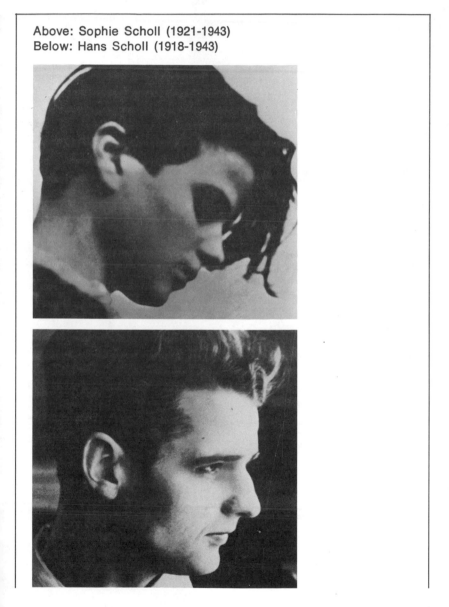

Above: Sophie Scholl (1921-1943)
Below: Hans Scholl (1918-1943)

Kurt Huber (1893-1943)

Appeal to All Germans!

The war is nearing its foregone conclusion. As it did in 1918, the German government is attempting to divert everyone's attention by pointing out the growing threat posed by submarines, while meanwhile the armies in the East are steadily retreating and we are awaiting an invasion in the West. American armament has not yet reached its peak, but already her forces surpass any that has ever existed in the past. With mathematical certainty Hitler is leading the German people into the abyss. *Hitler cannot win the war; he can only prolong it!* His guilt and the guilt of his henchmen has infinitely exceeded any degree that human beings can measure. Their just punishment advances nearer and nearer.

But what are the German people doing? They do not see and they do not hear. Blindly they follow their seducers to perdition. "Victory at any price!" these seducers have written on their flags. "I'll fight to the last man," Hitler says, and all the while the war has already been lost.

Germans! Do you and your children want to suffer the same fate meted out to the Jews? Do you want to be measured by the same standard as those who have led you astray? Are we to remain forever a people who are hated and rejected by everyone in the world? No! Therefore you must sever yourselves from the National Socialist subhumanity! Prove by your actions that you disagree with their policies! A new war of liberation is beginning. The best Germans are fighting on our side. Break the shell of indifference in which you have encased your hearts! Make a choice *before it is too late*!

Do not believe the National Socialist propaganda that has instilled the dread of Bolshevism in your very bones! Do not believe that the welfare of Germany is linked, for better or for worse, with the victory of National Socialism! A band of criminals cannot win any German victories. Sever yourselves, *while there is still time*, from everything National Socialism stands for. Later a terrible but just judgment will be pronounced on all those who, instead of making a choice, behaved like cowards and went off and hid.

What can we learn from the results of this war, which has never been an expression of the true Germany?

The imperialistic conception of power, whichever side it comes from, must be prevented from doing any harm ever again. Unilateral Prussian militarism must never again be allowed to come to power. Only wide-scale cooperation among the peoples of Europe can lay the groundwork on which we can begin to rebuild. All centralized authority of the type that the Prussian state has attempted to exercise in Germany and Europe must be nipped in the bud. The Germany of the future must be based on a federal structure. Only a healthy federalistic system of government is capable of infusing new life into the debilitated continent of Europe. The working classes must be liberated, by means of a rational socialism, from the state of abject slavery in which they now live. The phantom of an autarkistic economy must disappear from Europe. Every people, every individual has a right to the goods of this world!

Freedom of speech, freedom of religion, the protection of the individual citizen against the despotism of criminal and violent governments—these are the foundation stones of the new Europe.

Support the resistance movement, circulate the handbills!

This handbill mentions the submarine warfare that Hitler had initiated in order to bring England to its knees. Any vessel found within an area demarcated by the Germans—even if it belonged to a neutral nation—could be sunk by German U-boats without any previous warning. On February 18, Goebbels, speaking from the Sports Palace in Berlin, declared total war. We heard his speech on the radio:

> I ask you: Do you want total war? Do you want a war that, if necessary, will be more total and more radical than we can possibly imagine at this moment? . . .
>
> If we have ever loyally and steadfastly believed in victory, then we do so in this hour of national reflection and inner resolution. We see victory lying before us, within our grasp; we must only reach out and seize it. We must only resolve to subordinate all other concerns to the service of victory. This is the commandment of the hour.

At that time I did not know what total war really meant: the curtailment of civilian life and the concentration of everyone's energies on the war effort. I thought, "What is he talking about? This war is already total."

On March 13, an attempt to assassinate Hitler, planned by a group of Army officers when they were in the middle of Russia, misfired because the bomb failed to detonate. On April 5, the members of another resistance group were arrested. The minister Dietrich Bonhoeffer and his brother-in-law, Hans von Dohnany, had helped with the preparations for the unsuccessful attempt to assassinate Hitler in March, 1943. Later both men were executed in Flossenbürg Concentration Camp.

The war in Africa was lost. In March, General Rommel had been relieved of his command. Afterward it was only a matter of time before the Western Allies would leap across the Mediterranean from Africa to Sicily and Italy. It had now become militarily feasible for them to launch an invasion. The British and American air forces, combined with their naval forces, now had absolute control of the Mediterranean, even though the Germans still held the island of Crete and some of the other Greek islands. Supply routes through Yugoslavia were no longer secure. Fuel shortages grounded more and more German aircraft.

On June 11, Heinrich Himmler ordered the destruction of the Warsaw Ghetto, which at this time was still inhabited by 70,000 Jews who were working in munitions plants. The Jews had pro-

Jewish children in the Warsaw Ghetto in 1943.

cured weapons through underground channels and used them to defend themselves against the systematic evacuation of the ghetto. Around 12,000 Jews died fighting the SS, another 7,000 were gassed with smoke candles [fumigating candles], and the rest were sent to the extermination camp of Treblinka to die in the gas chambers.

After it had been conquered, the ghetto was torn down and reduced to rubble.

SS Leader Jürgen Stroop wrote a report of the systematic smashing of the Warsaw Ghetto uprising and turned the report over to Himmler after the action was completed. This document, which still exists, reveals once again the brutal contempt for human life of Hitler's "master race."

On June 19, Goebbels proudly declared the city of Berlin "Jew free." He had hereby carried out his duty as the Nazi District Leader of Berlin.

At a meeting of SS group leaders in Poznán (Poland), Heinrich Himmler declared:

> An SS man must observe one absolute principle: We must behave with honesty, decency, loyalty, and true comradeship toward members of our own blood, but not toward anyone else. What happens to the Russians, what happens to the Czechs is all the same to me. Those members of other nations who possess

A b s c h r i f t !
F e r n s c h r e i b e n

Absender: Der ₴- und Polizeiführer im Distrikt Warschau

Warschau, den 8. Mai 1943

Az.: I ab St/Gr - 16 07 - Tgb.Nr. 624/43 geh.
Betr.: Ghetto-Großaktion

An den

Höheren ₴- und Polizeiführer Ost
₴-Obergruppenführer und General der Polizei Krüger
o.V.i.A.

K r a k a u

Verlauf der Aktion am 8.5.43, 10.00 Uhr:

Das gesamte Gebiet des ehem. jüdischen Ghettos wurde heute von Durchkämmungsstoßtrupps nach vorhandenen Bunkern und Juden durchsucht. Wie schon vor einigen Tagen gemeldet, halten sich z.Zt. noch das Untermenschentum, die Banditen und Terroristen in Bunkern auf, in denen durch die Brände die Hitze unerträglich geworden ist. Diese Kreaturen wissen nun genau, daß es nur eines gibt, entweder sich verborgen zu halten, solange es geht oder an die Erdoberfläche zu kommen, dabei aber den Versuch zu machen, möglichst die sie bedrängenden Männer der Waffen-₴, der Polizei und der Wehrmacht zu verwunden bzw. umzulegen.

Die im gestrigen FS gemeldete Auffindung der Lager des Bunkers der sog. engeren "Parteileitung" wurde am heutigen Tage wieter verfolgt. Es ist gelungen, den Bunker der Parteileitung zu öffnen und etwa 60 Banditen, die schwer bewaffnet waren, zu packen. Es gelang, den stellv. Leiter der jüdischen militärischen Organisation "ZWZ" und seinen sog. Stabschef zu fangen und zu liquidieren. In diesem Bunker waren etwa 200 Juden untergebracht, 60 davon wurden erfaßt, 140 durch große Einwirkung von Nebelkerzen und durch Anlegung großer Sprengladungen an verschiedenen Stellen vernichtet. Durch die Nebelkerzen waren bereits ungezählte Tote von den hervorgebrachten Juden gemeldet. Wenn der Kampf gegen die Juden und Banditen in den ersten 6 Tagen schwer war, so muß festgestellt werden, daß nunmehr die Juden und Jüdinnen erfaßt werden, die die Träger des Kampfes dieser Tage waren. Es wird kein Bunker mehr geöffnet, ohne daß von den darin sich befindenden Juden mit den ihnen zur Verfügung stehenden Waffen, lMG., Pistolen und Handgranaten Widerstand geleistet wird. Heute wurden wiederum eine ganze Anzahl Jüdinnen erfaßt, die in ihren Schlüpfern entsicherte und geladene Pistolen trugen.

Nach gemachten Aussagen sollen sich noch etwa 3 - 4000 Juden in den unterirdischen Löchern, Kanälen und Bunkern aufhalten. Der Unterzeichnete ist entschlossen, die Großaktion nicht eher zu be-

Copy of the Official Report of the destruction of the Cracow ghetto:

Copy
Telegram

From: SS Leader and Chief of Police in the District of Warsaw

Warsaw, May 8, 1943

Departure time: I from St/Gr—4:07 P.M.—Log No. 624/43 gen.
Regarding: The major action in the ghetto

To the
Supreme SS Leader and Chief of Police in the East
SS Senior Group Leader and Supreme Commander of Police Krüger
To be delivered immediately

Cracow
Course of the action on May 8, 1943, 10:00 A.M.:

Today the entire area of the former Jewish ghetto was thoroughly searched by a raiding party for any existing bunkers and Jews. As I reported several days ago, some of these subhumans, bandits, and terrorists are still holed up in bunkers in which the fires have produced unendurable heat. These creatures are fully aware that they have only one choice: either to remain hidden as long as possible or to come to the surface and attempt, if they can, to wound or kill those members of the Waffen-SS, the police, and the Army who are pressing them.

Today we followed through on our search, already mentioned in yesterday's telegram, for the bunker supply depots of the so-called inner party leadership. We succeeded in opening the bunker of the party leaders and seized some sixty heavily armed bandits. We also succeeded in capturing and liquidating the Deputy Leader of the Jewish military organization, the "ZWZ," and his so-called chief of staff. Around 200 Jews had taken shelter in this bunker; 60 of them were captured; 140 were killed by the use of a large number of smoke candles and by explosive charges detonated at various points. The Jews we brought out reported that the smoke candles had already killed countless numbers of people. Although the first six days of our struggle against the Jews and bandits were difficult, the Jews and Jewesses who were the mainstays of the revolt are now being captured. We can no longer open any bunker without meeting with resistance from Jews armed with any available weapons—machine guns, pistols, and hand grenades. Today we once again captured a large number of Jewish women who, in their sweaters, were carrying loaded revolvers with the safety catch already released.

According to the statements we heard, some 3,000 to 4,000 Jews enden, bis auch der letzte Jude vernichtet ist.

Insgesamt wurden heute aus Bunkern 1 091 Juden erfaßt, im Feuer-
kampf wurden etwa 280 Juden erschossen, ungezählte Juden in den
43 gesprengten Bunkern vernichtet. Die Gesamtzahl der erfaßten
Juden erhöht sich auf 49 712. Die noch nicht durch Feuer ver-
nichteten Gebäude wurden heute angezündet und dabei festgestellt,
daß sich immer noch vereinzelte Juden irgendwie im Mauerwerk oder
in den Treppenhäusern versteckt halten.

Eigene Kräfte:

Einsatzkräfte:	Deutsche Polizei	4/101
	TN	1/6
	Sipo	2/14
	Pioniere (WH)	3/69
	Waffen-SS	13/527

Absperrkräfte:	bei Tag	bei Nacht
Deutsche Polizei	1/87	1
Waffen-SS	–	1/
Trawniki	160	–
poln. Polizei	1/160	1/160

Eigene Verluste: 2 Waffen-SS tot
2 Waffen-SS verwundet
1 Pionier verwundet

Ein am 7.5.43 verwundeter Angehöriger der Orpo ist heute seinen
Verletzungen erlegen.

Erbeutet wurden etwa 15 - 20 Pistolen versch. Kalibers, größere
Bestände an Pistolen und Gewehrmunition, außerdem eine Anzahl
von in den ehem. Rüstungsbetrieben selbstgefertigten Handgranaten.

Ende der Aktion: 21.30 Uhr, Fortsetzung am 9.5.43, um 10.oo Uhr.

F.d.R.:

SS-Sturmbannführer.

Der SS- und Polizeiführer
im Distrikt Warschau

gez. Stroop

SS-Brigadeführer
u. Generalmajor der Polizei.

are still hiding in underground holes, canals, and bunkers. The undersigned is resolved not to conclude this large-scale action until the last Jew has been destroyed.

Today a total of 1,091 Jews were removed from the bunkers and captured; approximately 280 Jews were shot during the exchange of gunfire; countless Jews were killed in the 43 bunkers we blew up. The total number of Jews captured has risen to 49,712. The buildings not yet destroyed by fire were set on fire today, and as a result we discovered that a few Jews were still hiding somewhere inside the masonry or in stairwells.

Our forces:

Attack forces:

German police		4/101
Trawniki [Polish auxiliaries]		1/6
Security Police		2/14
Military Engineers (Winter Aid)		3/69
Waffen-SS		13/527

Sentry Cordon	During day	At night
German police	1/87	[illegible]
Waffen-SS	—	
Trawniki	160	—
Polish police	1/160	1/160

Our losses: 2 Waffen-SS dead
2 Waffen-SS wounded
1 Military Engineer wounded

Today a member of the local police, wounded on May 7, 1943, died of his wounds.

We seized fifteen or twenty pistols of various calibers, large stores of pistol and rifle ammunition, and a quantity of home-made grenades manufactured in former munitions plants.

Action concluded at 9:30 P.M., to be resumed on May 9, 1943, at 10:00 A.M.

I personally testify
to the accuracy of this report:

Jürgen Stroop

SS Battalion Leader

SS Leader and Chief of Police
in the Warsaw District
Signed: Stroop
SS Brigade Leader
and Major General of Police

good blood of our type, we will assimilate, if necessary by stealing their children and raising them among Germans. Whether other peoples live in a state of prosperity or die of starvation interests me only to the degree that we may need them as slaves for our culture; otherwise I have no interest in them at all. Whether or not ten thousand Russian women collapse from exhaustion while constructing an antitank trench interests me only as to whether or not the trench is completed for Germany. We will never be brutal and heartless when it is not necessary to be so: this is clear. We Germans, who are the only people in the world who have a decent attitude toward animals, will also adopt a decent attitude toward these human beasts, for it is a crime against our own blood to worry about them and to instill ideals in them so that our sons and grandsons will have even more trouble keeping them under control. If someone comes to me and says, "I can't build the antitank trench with children or women. That would be in-human, for it would kill them," then I must reply, "You are a murderer of your own blood, for if the antitank trench is not constructed, then German soldiers will die, and they are the sons of German mothers. They are of our blood." This is the attitude which I would like to instill and—I believe—have instilled in the members of the SS, as one of the holiest laws of the future. Our concern, our duty, lies with our people and our blood. For them we must be concerned, for them we must think, work, and fight, and for nothing else. We may be indifferent to everything else. I wish the SS to adopt this attitude toward the problem of all for-eign, non-Germanic peoples, above all, the Russians. Everything else is hogwash.

I would like to emphasize particularly one sentence from this speech: "We Germans, who are the only people in the world who have a decent attitude toward animals, will also adopt a decent attitude toward these human beasts."

Thousands of people—"human beasts," as Himmler called them —were dying in the gas chambers every day. It may be that other peoples had not such a decent attitude toward animals, but they may have had a decent attitude toward people instead.

The movie theaters were showing more and more films that encouraged the Germans to stick it out, i.e., films about German history designed to show that the Germans had always been vic-torious in the end, even if at first the situation looked hopeless. Naturally Frederick II, known as Frederick the Great, was highly suitable for this purpose. Goebbels commissioned many films of this type. Veit Harlan, the official film director of the Third Reich, was just the right man for the job; he had also directed the film *Jud Süss* [an anti-Semitic propaganda film].

> I hereby commission you to produce a major film to be called *Kolberg*.[1] Using the city in the title as an example, this film is to show that a people united at home and at the Front can defeat any adversary. I authorize you to request all the aid and support you need from the Armed Forces, the Government, and the Party; you have only to point out to them that the film I am hereby ordering you to make will serve to build up morale and thus will serve the war effort.

On July 25, the Italian dictator, Mussolini, was overthrown, which brought an end to the Fascist regime in Italy. Mussolini was taken to the mountain fortress of Gran Sasso d'Italia, whence he was rescued on September 12 by German paratroopers under the command of Otto Skorzeny. That same day he was flown to Hitler's headquarters in Rastenburg, East Prussia.

I can still remember quite clearly the newsreel photos—the beaming faces of the paratroopers, whose sortie to liberate Mussolini was being celebrated as an act of supreme heroism. Skorzeny was held up as a model to German youth.

The movie public were deeply touched and thought, "See, the Führer doesn't leave his friends in the lurch!"

My mother, who was with me at the movies, said on the way back home, "Hitler will be overthrown just like Mussolini. But let's hope that no one sets him free again!"

No bombs were falling on my home country, the Fichtelgebirge, and there were no soldiers around; here the world still looked as if everything were normal. We boys had good times with our friends as usual and sometimes also with girls. But for the girls we were only foolish boys because we were not in uniform.

Many of my school friends who were lucky enough to have stayed in school long enough to have a chance to pass their war-

---

[1] Kolberg is a Pomeranian city on the Baltic, now part of Poland. After the Prussians had suffered decisive defeats by the French during the Napoleonic Wars, Kolberg endured a six-month's siege and held out until peace had been concluded in 1807. A few years later Prussian troops helped to defeat Napoleon.—Tr.

time *Abitur* examinations at the end of secondary school were unhappy because they were not yet running around in a uniform. Some girls even openly called us cowards because we were still living at home.

My mother used to comfort me by saying, "Don't pay any attention; being made fun of by some silly geese is still a lot better than being shot and killed. Remember that. And don't forget: Howl like the wolves, but not too loudly, because that would attract attention. Now the only important thing is to survive."

The Allies landed in Sicily. The leap to the European continent had succeeded.

In the German news reports such a far-reaching event as the invasion was described as if it were no more than a minor mischance that would be all cleaned up in a short time. But my mother knew better, for she still listened to Radio London every night.

On August 24, Heinrich Himmler, the man who had said that only we Germans knew how to treat animals decently, became Reich Minister of the Interior and thus, after Hitler, the most powerful man in the German Reich.

Now there were no more limitations imposed on his racial mania. The extermination machinery was running in high gear, gassings were carried on around the clock, and there were not enough ovens to burn up all the corpses, so they were simply thrown into mass graves, as at Treblinka.

Eyewitness Accounts of the Massacres of Jews
a) In Rovno
I, Hermann Friedrich Gräbe, testify under oath: From September, 1941, until January, 1944, I was executive manager and chief engineer of a branch of the Josef Jung Construction Firm of Solingen whose headquarters were located in Sdolbunov in the Ukraine. As such it was my duty to visit the firm's construction sites. In addition to other sites, my firm was working on a construction site in Rovno in the Ukraine.

During the night of July 13–14, 1942, all the inmates of the Rovno Ghetto, which still housed some five thousand Jews, were liquidated.

The following is a description of how I came to witness the

destruction of the ghetto and the action carried out during the night and in the morning:

. . . Shortly after 10:00 P.M. the ghetto was surrounded by a large complement of SS and about three times that number of Ukrainian militiamen, and the electric arc lamps that had been set up in and around the ghetto were turned on. Then the SS and militia broke up into groups of four or six, and each group would break into, or try to break into, the houses. If the doors and windows were locked and the people in the house did not open the door in response to shouts and loud knocking, the SS or militiamen smashed the windows, forced the doors open with beams and crowbars, and entered the houses. No matter where they were or what they were doing, regardless of whether they were dressed or lying in bed, the people in the houses were all driven out onto the street. Most of the Jews refused to leave their homes and tried to resist, in which case the SS and militiamen used force. By dint of many kicks and blows with whips and rifle butts, they finally succeeded in emptying out the houses. The people were driven out of their homes in such haste that in some cases small children who had been asleep in bed were simply left behind. Out on the street the women wailed and cried out for their children, and children were crying for their parents. This did not prevent the SS from hitting the people and driving them along the street on the double until they arrived at the waiting freight train. One railroad car after another was filled with people; the screams of the women and children, the lashing of the whips, and the sound of rifle shots never ceased for a moment. Individual families or groups had barricaded themselves in particularly well-built houses whose doors could not be staved in with beams and crowbars, so these were blown open with hand grenades. The ghetto was directly adjacent to the railroad in Rovno, so young people tried to escape the ghetto area by crossing the railroad tracks and the little stream beyond. Since this area was not illuminated by the electric lights, flares were sent up to light the landscape. All night long the beaten, harried, and wounded people made their way along the brightly lit streets. Women were carrying dead children in their arms; children were dragging and tugging the bodies of their dead parents along the streets by their arms or legs, all on their way to the train. Again and again the cry "Open up! Open up!" echoed through the ghetto.

I left briefly at around 6:00 A.M., leaving behind Einsporn and several other German workmen, who had meanwhile returned. I believed that the greatest danger was now past, which is why I risked doing so. Shortly after I left, Ukrainian militiamen forced their way into the house at Bahnhofstrasse 5, dragged out seven Jews and took them to a rendezvous point inside the ghetto. When I returned, I managed to prevent any more Jews from being removed from this house. Then I went to the rendezvous point to save the seven. On the streets I was forced to travel, I saw dozens of corpses of every age and both sexes. The doors of the houses stood open; the windows had been smashed. In the streets lay stray bits of clothing—shoes, stockings, jackets, caps, hats, coats, and so on. At the corner of one house lay a baby less than a year old whose skull had been crushed. Blood and brains had spattered onto the wall of the house and covered the area surrounding the child. All it had on was a little shirt. . . .

b) Near Dubno

. . . (October 5, 1942) The men, women, and children of all ages who had climbed down out of the trucks were ordered to undress by an SS man who was holding a riding whip or a dog whip and were then forced to set down each article of clothing—shoes, outer garments, and underwear—in a separate place. I saw a pile of what I estimate must have been eight hundred to a thousand pairs of shoes and great stacks of underwear and other clothing. These people undressed without weeping or crying out, stood together in family groups, kissed and said good-bye to each other, and waited for the signal from another SS man who was standing by the pit and was also holding a whip in his hand. During the fifteen minutes that I was standing beside the pits, I did not hear anyone complain or plead for his life. I observed a family of around eight people, consisting of a man and a woman who were both around fifty, several of their children, who were approximately one, eight, and ten years old, and two grown-up daughters between twenty and twenty-four. An old woman with snow-white hair was holding the one-year-old in her arms, singing to him and tickling him. The baby was gurgling with pleasure. The married couple watched them with tears in their eyes. The father was holding the hand of a boy about ten years old and talking to him softly. The boy was trying hard not to cry. The father pointed his finger at the sky, stroked the boy's head, and seemed to be explaining something to him. Then the SS man beside the pit called something to his comrade. The latter picked out around twenty

238

people and ordered them to stand behind the pile of earth. The family I have mentioned was among them. I can still remember very clearly a black-haired and slender girl who, as she passed close by me, pointed at herself and said, "Twenty-three years old!" I walked around the pile of earth and stood in front of the huge grave. The people were stacked so densely on top of each other that only their heads could be seen clearly. From almost all of the heads blood was streaming down onto the shoulders. A few of those who had just been shot were still moving. Some of them lifted their arms and turned their heads to show that they were still alive. The pit was already three quarters full. I would judge that it contained around 1,000 people. I looked back at the man who had shot them. An SS man, he was sitting on the ground at the edge of the narrow end of the pit, his legs dangling down inside it with a submachine gun across his knees, and he was smoking a cigarette. The people, totally naked, were walking down a staircase that had been dug into the mud wall of the pit and made their way, sliding, across the heads of the people lying below until they reached the place to which the SS man had pointed. They lay down in front of the dead or wounded people, and some of them stroked those who were still alive and spoke to them softly. Then I heard a series of shots. I looked into the pit and saw the bodies twitching or the heads already resting quietly on the bodies that lay before them. Blood was running down the napes of their necks. I was surprised that I was not ordered to move away, but I noticed that two or three post-office workers in uniform were also standing nearby. The members of the next group had already been chosen, climbed down into the pit, lined up beside the other victims, and were shot. When I walked back around the pile of earth, I saw that another shipment of people had just arrived. This time there were sick and infirm people among them. An old, very lean woman with fearfully thin legs was being undressed by several other people who were already naked, while two people held her up. Apparently the woman was paralyzed. The naked people carried her around the pile of dirt. I left with Moennikes and drove back to Dubno.

Next morning, when I visited the construction site again, I saw around thirty naked people lying between thirty and fifty meters from the pit. Some of them were still alive and were staring vacantly into space; they did not seem to notice either the cold of the morning or the employees of my firm, who were standing around them. A girl around twenty years old spoke to me and asked me to give her some clothes and help her to escape. Then we heard the sound of a car approaching rapidly, and I saw that it was a squad of SS. I left and went over to my construction site. Ten minutes later we heard the sound of several shots fired in the area of the pit. The Jews who were still alive had been forced to throw the corpses of the others into the pit, and then they themselves had to lie down inside it so that they could be shot in the back of the neck.

I am making the foregoing statements in Wiesbaden, Germany, on November 10, 1945. I swear by God that I have told the absolute truth.

Fried Gräbe

Eyewitness Accounts of Mass Executions in the Gas Chambers

a) Extract from the Gerstein Report

. . . On the following day we traveled to Belzec. A little railroad station had been built especially for the camp on a hill just north of the Lublin-Lvov highway, directly west of the line of demarcation. South of the highway were a few houses bearing the inscription "Special Waffen-SS Squad at Belzec." The real commandant of this institution for murder, Police Captain Wirth, had not yet arrived, and therefore Globocnek introduced me to SS Company Commander Obermeyer (from Pirmasens). That afternoon Obermeyer let me see only the things that it was absolutely necessary for him to show me. I saw no dead people that day; but in the August heat the stench permeating the entire area was truly pestilential, and there were millions of flies all over. Right next to the little railway station with its two tracks, was a large barracks, the so-called checkroom, containing a large counter on which valuables were to be placed. Next came a room filled with some one hundred chairs, the barbershop. Then one went outside and walked along a little avenue surrounded by birch trees and fenced in on both sides by a double wall of barbed wire. Along the avenue were signs saying: "To the inhalation rooms and the bathrooms!" We came to a kind of bathhouse decorated with geraniums. Then we climbed a small staircase and saw three rooms each on the right and the left. The rooms were about five meters square, one meter ninety high, with wooden doors like the doors of a garage. In the rear wall, which one could not see clearly because of the darkness, were large wooden doors leading to a loading platform. On the roof, as an "ingenious little joke," was a star of David! In front of the building was a sign which said, "Heckenholt Foundation"! That was all I got to see that afternoon.

Next morning, shortly before 7:00 A.M., I was told, "The first shipment will be arriving in ten minutes!" And, in fact, a few minutes later the first train arrived from Lvov. It consisted of forty-five freight cars and contained 6,700 people, 1,450 of whom were already dead upon arrival. Children, hideously pale and anxious, their eyes full of mortal fear, looked out from behind the barred windows; I saw men and women too. The train enters the station. Two hundred Ukrainians fling open the doors and lash the people out of the cars with their leather whips. A giant loudspeaker issues further orders: Take off all clothes, even glasses and artificial limbs, etc. Deposit valuables at the check-room counter, without any check-out slip or receipt. The loudspeaker tells them to tie their shoes together carefully (because of the textile goods collection), for otherwise no one could have found the two shoes which belong together in the pile of shoes, which is over twenty-five meters high. Then the women and girls are sent to the barber, who with two or three slashes of his shears cuts off all their hair and hides it inside potato sacks. "The hair is going to be used for some special purpose by the U-boats, for caulking or something like that," I am told by the SS sub-platoon leader on duty.

Then the procession begins. Led by a very pretty young girl, they walk along the avenue, all naked, men, women, and children, without their artificial limbs. I myself am standing with Captain Wirth up above on the ramp between the gas chambers. Mothers holding their infants against their breasts climb up the stairs, hesitate, and enter the death chambers! At the corner stands a strong SS man who tells the unfortunates in a clergyman's voice, "Nothing at all is going to happen to you! When you get into the rooms, you must simply breathe deeply; this expands your lungs, and this inhalation is necessary because of the diseases and epidemics." When they ask him what is going to happen to them, he replies, "Well, naturally, the men have to work building houses and highways, but the women will not have to work. But if they want to, they can help out with the cleaning and in the kitchen." A few of the wretched people experience a slight glimmer of hope that is just enough to prevent them from resisting as they walk the few steps into the chambers. Most of them know what is going to happen, for the smell has clearly informed them of their fate! So they climb the little staircase, and then they see everything. Mothers with their children at their breasts, small naked children, adults, men and women, all of them naked. They hesitate, but then they enter the death chambers, driven forward by the others behind them or by the leather whips of the SS. Most of them do not say a word. A Jewish woman about forty years of age, with flaming eyes, calls down on the murderers the blood guilt for the blood that is being shed here. She receives five or six blows in the face with a riding whip from Captain Wirth personally, and then she too disappears into the chamber. Many people are praying. I pray along with them; I press myself into a corner and cry aloud to my God and theirs. How glad I would have been to have entered the chamber with them, how glad I would have been to have died their death along with them! Then the others would have found a uniformed SS officer in their gas chambers. They would have treated the whole thing as an accident, and no one would ever have mentioned the incident again. Thus, I am not yet permitted to die; first, I must tell everyone what I have seen here. The chambers are filling up. "Stuff them in good and proper"—those are Captain Wirth's orders. The people are standing on each other's feet. Between 700 and 800 people crammed into an area of twenty-five square meters in a room whose volume is around forty-five cubic meters. The SS push them in until they cannot possibly cram in one more person. The doors are closed. Meanwhile, the others are waiting outside in the open air, with no clothes on. Someone tells me, "That's the way we do it even in the winter!" "Yes, but they could catch their death of cold!" I say. "Yes, that's exactly what's supposed to happen!" an SS man tells me. Now I finally understand why the whole establishment is called the Heckenholt Foundation. Heckenholt is the diesel-engine driver, a minor technician who also built the installation. The people are going to be killed with diesel exhaust fumes. But the diesel is not working! Captain Wirth arrives. Obviously he is embarrassed by the fact that this had to happen today, while I was here. Oh; yes, I see everything! And I wait. My well-behaved stopwatch kept a perfect record. Fifty minutes, seventy minutes— the diesel engine won't start! The people are waiting in their gas chambers. In vain. We can hear them crying, sobbing. . . . Captain Wirth strikes the Ukrainian who is supposed to help Sub-

242

Platoon Leader Heckenholt run the diesel, twelve or thirteen times in the face with his riding whip. After two hours and forty-nine minutes—the stopwatch recorded the time exactly—the engine starts. All this time the people have been alive inside the four chambers—four times 750 people occupying a volume of four times forty-five cubic meters! Another twenty-five minutes go by. That's right, many of them are dead now. One can see that by looking through the little window when the electric light illuminates the chambers for a moment. After twenty-eight minutes only a few are still alive. Finally, after thirty-two minutes, they are all dead!

The men on fatigue duty open the wooden door from the other side. Even the Jews among them have been promised their freedom and a certain rate per thousand of all the prisoners' valuables in return for carrying out their ghastly jobs. The dead are standing upright, pressed tightly together, inside the chambers, like so many basalt columns. There was no room for them to fall down or even bend forward. Even in death one can still recognize the families. Their hands, rigid in death, are still clutching each other, so that it is difficult to separate them and clear out the rooms for the next batch. The corpses—damp with sweat and urine, soiled with feces or with menstrual blood on their legs—are thrown out the door. The corpses of children fly through the air. Time is short, and the riding whips of the Ukrainians whistle as they lash the members of the work detail. Two dozen dentists open the mouths of the dead with hooks and search for gold. Bodies whose teeth contain gold go to the left, those without gold to the right. Other dentists use hammers and pliers to dig the gold teeth and crowns out of the jaws.

Captain Wirth is everywhere at once. He is in his element. Some members of the work detail check the genitals and the anuses for gold, diamonds, and other valuables. Wirth calls me over, "Just lift this tin full of gold teeth and see how much it weighs, and these were all collected just yesterday and the day before!" In an incredibly vulgar and base manner he told me, "You wouldn't believe all the gold and brilliants"—he pronounced the word with two l's—"and dollars we find every day. But see for yourself!" Then he led me to a jeweler who was in charge of all these treasures and showed them to me. Then I was shown the former head of the Warehouse of the West in Berlin and a violinist: He was a captain in the old Imperial Austrian Army, a

243

Knight of the Iron Cross First Class, and now he's the senior prisoner in the Jewish work detachment! The naked corpses were placed on wooden handbarrows and dragged only a few yards away to pits some 100 meters long, 20 meters wide, and 12 meters deep. After some days the corpses began to decay and a short time later crumbled away so that a new layer could be thrown on top of them. Then ten centimeters of sand were strewn on top so that only a few heads and arms could still be seen sticking out. At one of these places I saw Jews climbing over the corpses and working inside the graves. I was told that by mistake someone had failed to undress those people in one trainload who had arrived dead. Naturally, not to lose the valuables and textile goods they might have taken into the grave with them, this mistake had to be rectified. Neither at Belzec nor at Treblinka was any effort made to count the numbers of the dead or to record their names. The only numbers recorded were estimates based on knowledge of the average capacity of one of the railroad cars. . . . Captain Wirth asked me not to suggest in Berlin that any changes be made in his facilities and simply to leave everything as it was, in its present well-coordinated state, which had proved its worth over the course of time. . . .

Everything I have said is literally true. I am completely conscious, before God and all mankind, of the extraordinary implications of my statements and hereby swear a solemn oath that nothing I have recorded is fictitious or invented, but that everything occurred exactly as I have stated. . . .

b) The Gas Vehicles

The people who died in the gas chambers at Auschwitz died more quickly than those killed in the gas vehicles at Minsk, for the corpses of the dead at Auschwitz bore no marks of disfiguration. At his trial in Nuremberg, Rudolph Höss, who murdered millions of people in the death camp at Auschwitz, stated that it took his victims eight minutes to die.

And what was the situation at Minsk?

As soon as a new transport train arrived at its destination, the people inside were allowed to disembark calmly and peacefully. To their great amazement no one bullied them or shouted at them. Then they were driven in trucks to a meadow about eight miles away, where relatively attractive-looking "mobile homes" were waiting for their new lodgers.

As soon as everyone who had arrived in this shipment had

assembled at the meadow, an SS officer would address them all, saying something like this:

"You have been brought here because we trust you more than we do the Russians. You will be driven to our SS properties and put to work there. You will remain there until the end of the war, at which time we will make further plans. You need not be concerned: nothing is going to happen to you. You have nothing to fear. Are there any people among you with specialized skills, especially radio technicians? We need you here."

Then young, strong-looking men were picked out and set apart from the others—a total of forty men from among a thousand men, women, and children: forty out of a thousand! The others were forced to climb into the trucks disguised as mobile homes. From a distance these vehicles actually looked like real mobile homes. Windows, curtains, shutters, and even a chimney had been painted on the outside. When I saw one of these chimneys for the first time, I was struck by the fact that it had been painted very recently and that, unlike the vehicle, it showed no signs of wear. And then I learned the hideous reality.

When the vehicle was filled with so many people that no one else could fit inside, the iron doors clanged shut, and then, yes, then the engine was started and the exhaust pipe conducted the deadly gas inside the vehicle.

In order to complete their ghastly work as quickly as possible, the drivers ran the engines as hard as they could—perhaps too they were trying to drown out the screams of the unfortunate beings inside—and thus a smaller amount of gas entered the vehicle than had been predicted, so that the people inside were not gassed to death but suffocated instead. Their death agony must have been horrible indeed, for all the corpses, without exception, were stained with blood which had exuded from their eyes, ears, noses, and mouths.

For a long time I did not understand why the SS officer used to address such a soothing speech to the candidates for death before they were executed. The mystery was finally cleared up when I read in a report by SS Medical Officer and SS Deputy Company Commander Becker that "as far as is practicable," the attempt should be made to prevent the victims from getting upset, for in this way death would result more quickly. Thus, it was not compassion that motivated the reassuring speech, but rather the desire to bring about death more swiftly—to make a quicker job of it. . . .

Even in the regular concentration camps, like Buchenwald or Dachau, which were not labeled extermination camps but only labor camps, the ovens burned day and night.

The concentration camps were not used exclusively for the destruction of human lives. The prisoners were also exploited in the most inhumane way by being forced to work in SS-owned industries. Almost all the plants in the SS German Industrial Enterprises combine adjoined concentration camps whose inmates were forced to serve as slave labor. The following "profitability estimate" drawn up by cynical bureaucrats on the basis of their studies of the living and dead prisoners of Sachsenhausen Concentration Camp reveals the inconceivable brutality of the SS.

Average daily profit per prisoner: 6 reichsmarks
  minus the cost of food   —.6 reichsmark
  minus the cost of deprecation
    of clothing   —.1 reichsmark
Average length of life: 9 months
270 days × 5.3 reichsmarks = 1,431 reichsmarks

The income received from a prisoner's corpse was shamelessly computed in the following terms:
1. Gold from teeth
2. Clothing
3. Valuables
4. Money
  minus cremation costs   (2 reichsmarks)
  Average net profit   +200 reichsmarks
  Total profit after nine months   1,631 reichsmarks
  plus additional proceeds to be obtained
  from the bones and the sale of the ashes

People living in my area were perfectly aware of the existence of concentration camps, but certainly they did not know what really went on there, and they did not know about the extermination camps. After all, the death camps were located far away in Poland, in regions to which only the "elect" had access.

That year a former teacher of mine returned home. Although he was walking on crutches because he had lost his right leg, he nevertheless looked very proud as he hobbled through town dressed in his uniform.

Once we met on the main road as I was returning home from the office. He looked at me with amazement and incredulity, raised his arm in the customary Nazi salute, and said loudly, "Heil Hitler!"

I replied, "Grüss Gott, Teacher."

"So von der Grün, you're still at home shirking your duty?"

"I'm still at home," I said, "but not because I'm shirking my duty; it's because I'm only seventeen."

And then he said something that made my mother burst into a resounding peal of laughter when I told her about the encounter: "Remember, von der Grün, every day when you are not fighting for the Führer is a day wasted!"

My God, and people like him had taught us! Yes, there were people who had had *both* their legs shot off and who nevertheless had not yet understood anything. Today there are still people in the Federal Republic of Germany who do not want to understand and who deny everything that happened, even the concentration camps and the mass extermination of millions of people. For them these are still, as Goebbels said, "horror stories." How these people dare to dismiss countless documents out of hand remains a mystery.

The king of Italy, who, after Mussolini's fall from power, had assumed command of the Italian troops and formed a new government, declared war on Germany. This happened on October 13, the same day I was called up to serve in the Reich Labor Service; by this time I was seventeen and a half. A few days before, although I had not yet served my full three years of apprenticeship, I had taken my commercial assistant's examination.

In those days, who expected the observance of the legally prescribed training period? Soldiers were more important.

I was sent to Lower Bavaria, and my mother went with me to the railroad station. She did not cry but was completely calm. She did not talk to me either, which was another bad sign. As I climbed into the train to Straubing carrying a small suitcase, which contained my few belongings, she put her arms around me. I was startled, for we had never been demonstrative, and especially not when we were out in public. In our family people did not show their feelings; that was something that only actors did in the movies.

She whispered in my ear, "Put up a good front, the way I have always taught you. Be careful not to attract attention. Don't be pushy about anything."

No one in the Labor Service was over eighteen. We learned to march and salute with our spades. The spade was the worker's weapon. We used to march, singing cheerfully, through the landscape of Lower Bavaria, and we helped the farmers in their fields or at least gave them as much help as they needed at this time of year. We dug trenches for air-raid shelters and were allowed to play war games and stand up very stiff and straight in the presence of our superiors, who every day referred to us at "wretched idiots." We learned discipline, which in military jargon simply meant drill.

But despite my mother's warning, I attracted attention by my skill in sports and by the knowledge of history and literature that I displayed when we all got together in the evening. These attainments did not sit well with our Labor Service leaders.

One day after evening roll call a Labor Service leader took me aside and told me that he had been ordered to report the names of people who wished to volunteer to become paratroopers. He said that he wanted to suggest my name.

The last thing I wanted was to volunteer to join a military unit. I asked him for time to think, for the coming weekend my mother said she was going to visit me for the first time in seven weeks.

She brought me a suitcase full of food. Eggs, ham, cake, and delicacies, which at that time could no longer be obtained by honest means. She was not allowed to enter the camp, and so I was granted one day's leave, and we met at an inn.

At once I told her about the Labor Service leader's proposal, meanwhile gobbling down all the food like a starving man. But she was neither angry nor suspicious. She simply smiled, and then she said something that surprised me so much that I stopped eating.

"You've had a stroke of luck. Go ahead and volunteer. Then you'll get into a special unit, and in special units it takes longer to train you. Then, once you've joined up, you should volunteer for every special course that's offered. After all, you're not stupid; you have a good head on your shoulders. But don't be too pushy about it because that attracts attention and often ends up producing just the opposite result from what you wanted. As long as you are still being trained for something, you won't have to shoot a gun, and other people won't be shooting at you. The war isn't going to last much longer; the Americans are advancing faster now."

This made a lot of sense to me. I followed her advice until the war was over.

1944

The more rapidly the "Thousand-Year Reich" deteriorated, the more brutal became the reign of terror in the Reich and in the occupied countries.

Between April and June a new wave of arrests swept across Europe, with 176,670 people imprisoned or deported, including more than 20,000 Germans. The Balkan countries were the hardest hit, for there all the Jews were seized and transported to the extermination camps in Poland.

A bloodlust had seized the Nazis, as if they believed that the slaughter of defenseless people could somehow halt the disintegration of the Reich.

On June 6, the Allies landed in northern France. The greatest military invasion in the history of warfare had begun. The Atlantic Wall, whose praises Goebbels had sung in such grandiloquent terms, collapsed just a few hours after the Americans and British had landed. German losses, including the wounded, the injured, and those who had been taken prisoner, amounted to 400,000 men.

It was only logical that partisan activity should now increase. In Yugoslavia under Marshal Tito, and in Russia too, the partisans had organized themselves into regular military units. In these countries, as well as in France, German troops behind the front lines no longer felt safe.

Increasingly harsh measures were employed against partisans by the German Army as well as by the SS Field Marshal Hugo Sperrle, the Commander-in-Chief on the Western front, issued the following orders:

2.) To achieve this I order:
   A. Any unarmed soldier who strays outside the guarded area around his barracks is to be punished without regard to any extenuating circumstances. Any man who does not have a pistol

must carry a rifle or a carbine. Any man who does not have either of these weapons must carry a submachine-gun.

B. If a unit is attacked in any way, either while the men are on the march, in their barracks, or anywhere else, it is the obligation of their leader to institute countermeasures immediately, on his own authority. Among these countermeasures are the following:

a) Shoot first, ask questions later!

If innocent people are also killed in the process, it is regrettable, but the terrorists alone are to blame.

b) The area surrounding the place of the attack is to be immediately cordoned off, and all civilians in the area, regardless of their rank or identity, are to be arrested.

c) Any houses from which shots have been fired are to be burned down at once.

Only after these or similar on-the-spot measures have been taken should a report be turned in to military command headquarters and the SD (Security Police), whose responsibility it is to pursue the matter further, employing equally rigorous measures. . . .

In evaluating the conduct of energetic commanding officers, the highest priority must under all circumstances be placed on the decisiveness and rapidity with which they have taken action. Severe punishment is to be meted out only to the spineless and indecisive commanding officer, for by his conduct he endangers the security of his troops and diminishes respect for the German Armed Forces. In view of our present situation, no measures adopted can be so harsh as to merit punishment. . . .

I had taken my mother's advice and volunteered for the paratroopers. For this reason, I was discharged early from my term in the Labor Service, then spent three days at home, and finally, when I received my mobilization orders, reported to my barracks at Gardelegen near Magdeburg.

My training proceeded according to plan: infantry training, then paratroop training, and at this point, like my comrades, I could have been sent to serve in a front-line unit. But then one evening a captain came to our room and, while everyone else in the room was frozen with awe, asked me whether I would like to become a radio operator.

Even today I do not know how he happened to choose me.

Perhaps because I was the only one who, like him, used to listen to classical music. I passed the initial test and began my training one week later.

I was transferred from Gardelegen to Cologne-Ostheim. While I was being trained as a radio operator, it was discovered that I had a talent for encoding and decoding radio messages.

Radio messages were not transmitted, as they say in the technical jargon, "in the clear" or "in plain text," for if they had been, an enemy listening in on the transmission would know what was happening on the other side. Thus every day we were given a code into which we had to translate the plain text. Quite logically, the radio messages we received had to be decoded again, and naturally this had to be done quickly, for not only minutes but seconds could mean the difference between life and death.

This special training once again won me a reprieve. Every night, while I was in Cologne, I heard the enemy planes flying into the Reich. During bombing attacks we soldiers had to take care of the women and children and get them into air-raid shelters or into makeshift slit trenches that had been constructed especially for this purpose. The women were often dead tired, for most of them worked all day in the munitions plants. The children in our arms just went on sleeping. Often they were not even aware of what was going on around them.

Before the enemy planes dropped their bombs, the "Christmas trees" fell. These were bunches of flares, which turned the night into day, for all German cities had been observing such a strict blackout for years now that it was almost impossible for any pilot to find a target at night.

One night after the All Clear signal, when we left the bunker and went outside again, we found that our camp and our barracks were no longer standing. A short time later all of us, some 120 young men, were loaded onto a train and shipped off to southern France. Our training continued on the border of the town of Angoulême. There I caught a glimpse of another reality of life under the Nazis.

As a warning, the entire company was taken to witness a court-martial. The accused was a young man about my age. He had written home that the rations were poor, his superior officers brutal, and that the war was senseless. His letter had been intercepted and opened. Any one of us could have written a letter like this, for after all everything he said was true.

He was sentenced to death for undermining Army morale. At the time I thought that the whole thing had simply been staged in order to intimidate us and refused to take the trial seriously. But the next day my platoon leader, who worked with me at the radio set, told me that the sentence had been carried out that same day.

My God! I thought, when I heard this ghastly news; why didn't he have a mother like mine who had drummed into my head: "Never write anything but good news. If you're all right, then say, 'I'm fine,' but if you're having a hard time, then write, 'I'm feeling very well.' "

Letters written home by German soldiers were often opened and read in order to detect "enemies of the State" or simply to gather information about troop morale.

When my training had been completed, I, along with my comrades, was stuck in a cattle car and shipped off to Brittany, which was already being invaded by the Allies. I was assigned to a station in a mobile radio van that was parked in a small woods near the town of Quimper.

It must have been the beginning of August, for the fruit was not yet ripe. I was seated inside my radio van listening to the peeping sounds coming over my earphones, when I heard shouting outside the van. It was strictly forbidden to leave the radio set during a transmission, so I could not go and see what was happening outside. Suddenly someone flung open the door behind me and yelled in English, "Hands up!"

Now I knew what had happened. I stood up, raised my arms, and turned around.

For the first time in my life I came face to face with a black man. He signaled to me to get out of the van, grinned at me and said, "Okay, boy, the war is over for you."

He signed to me to sit down, then drew a box of chocolate from inside his uniform, and handed me a piece.

It was the first time in months that I had eaten chocolate. If only nothing goes wrong now, I thought, then I'll have survived.

Along with my three comrades from the radio van, I was sent

to a large prisoner-of-war camp near Brest. We stayed there for barely a week, and then during the night we were loaded onto a ship. There were around one thousand prisoners of war on board. In England—I no longer remember in which port—we all disembarked and were crammed into freight trains.

After a long trip that to me seemed endless, the train finally stopped in Scotland, near Glasgow. But I stayed in this camp for only four weeks. Once again we boarded a ship, and soon Europe lay behind me.

Four days later our ship arrived in New York harbor. As I stood on deck that night I saw, for the first time in five years, a city whose lights were all lit. My God, I thought, and Hitler believed that he could defeat this America. He must be insane.

I was destined to remain in the United States for three years.

All I knew about the subsequent course of events in Europe was what I read in the American newspapers or heard on the radio.

I was still in France on July 20, when the attempt was made to assassinate Hitler. Colonel Claus von Stauffenberg had placed a bomb in the Führer's headquarters in Rastenburg. But Hitler survived the explosion and was only slightly injured.

That same evening Claus Schenk, the Count von Stauffenberg, and his fellow-conspirators were shot to death with submachine guns.

After the assassination attempt, Hitler, maddened with fury, had sworn that he would wipe out "these traitors" and their entire families. The manhunt that then began and was conducted under the direction of a special commission of 400 officials went on for several months. Ten members of von Stauffenberg's family and eight members of Goerdeler's [1] family ended up in Buchenwald at the same time. The official SS report states that there had been 7,000 arrests. Later the resistance fighter Fabian von Schla-

[1] Carl Friedrich Goerdeler (1884-1945), jurist and politician. Worked in Nazi administration and supported strong, authoritarian government until 1937, when he began to protest Nazi policies. Became leader of the non-Communist resistance movement against Hitler in 1939 and planned to become Chancellor himself if Hitler was overthrown. Wanted a strong central government but also a parliamentary, constitutional one. Executed after the assassination attempt on Hitler in July, 1944.—Tr.

Claus Schenk, Count von Stauffenberg (1907-1944)

brendorff testified concerning the torture to which he was subjected during his captivity:

One night I was taken out of my cell for interrogation. Several people were present in the interrogation room. I was told that this was my last chance to confess. When I continued to deny my guilt as I had in the past, they resorted to torture. The torture was carried out in four stages. During this inhuman procedure everyone present expressed approval with scornful cheers. The first torture session came to an end when I fainted. No act of violence they inflicted on me induced me to confess a single word or to give them the name of a single one of my political comrades. After regaining consciousness, I was taken back to my cell. The guards welcomed me with unmistakable expressions of sympathy and horror. On the following day I suffered a heart attack. The prison doctor was summoned. Filled with suspicion, but incapable of putting up any resistance, I endured his ministrations. Then I lay there for several days until I was once again able to leave my bed and move around. The result of my recovery was a repetition of the torture.

People of all nationalities continued to be murdered and gassed in the concentration camps. In 1944, the camps—not counting the extermination camps—contained a total of 524,277 prisoners. On July 24, the extermination camp of Maidanek was freed by Soviet troops—the first of the camps to be liberated by the Allies.

Theresienstadt Concentration Camp in Czechoslovakia was partially "liquidated"; in other words, 18,404 Jews were transported from there to Auschwitz to be gassed. This happened on September 28.

For years physicians conducted medical experiments on people in the camps. Prisoners who survived these experiments became cripples or invalids for life. I myself know several people who were subjected to such experiments and who now live on a scanty pension.

S. Rascher, M.D.
SS Company Commander

Munich, February 17, 1945

To the Reichsführer of the SS
and Chief of German Police,
Herr Heinrich Himmler
Berlin SW 11
Prinz-Albrecht-Strasse 8
Honored Reichsführer:

The enclosed appendix represents a brief summary of the results obtained in my experiments with restoring warmth, through the application of animal heat, to human beings whose body temperature has been markedly reduced.

At the moment I am attempting, through experiments on human beings, to prove that people whose body temperature has been lowered by dry cold can be restored to normal just as quickly as those whose temperature was reduced by placement in cold water. SS Medical Officer and SS Group Leader Dr. Grawitz strongly doubted that this was possible, and it was his opinion that I would have to prove my thesis by performing one hundred successful experiments. Up to this point, by compelling them to remain outdoors unclothed for a period of between nine and fourteen hours, I have cooled the body temperature of around thirty people to between 27° and 29° [80° and 84° F.]. After a period of one hour (the time it took to transport them to the facilities), I placed the subjects in a hot plunge bath. Up to now, despite the fact that their hands and feet were partially frostbitten, the patients have in every case been restored to their normal body temperature within a period of an hour at most. The day after the experiment some of the subjects exhibited a slight debility accompanied by a low fever. I have not yet observed any case in which death has resulted from this extraordinarily rapid method of restoring body heat. I have not yet been able, honored Herr Reichsführer, to carry out your recommendation that the patients be warmed up again by means of a sauna; for in December and January the weather was too warm to conduct experiments outdoors, and now the camp is quarantined because of typhoid fever, and thus I have not been able to take the subjects to the SS sauna. I have been vaccinated against typhoid fever several times and am now conducting the experiments in the camp myself, despite the presence here of typhoid fever. The simplest solution would be to transfer me to the Waffen-SS, in which case I would travel to Auschwitz with Neff, and there, in a country where people often freeze to death, I could quickly clarify the question of restoring body heat by conducting a large-scale series of experiments. Auschwitz is in every respect more suitable than Dachau for the conduct of such a series of experiments, for it is colder there, and the great size of the camp area means that the experiments would attract less attention in the camp than they do here (the subjects yell a lot when they are very cold).

If, honored Herr Reichsführer, it meets with your approval that these experiments, which have important ramifications with regard to our land forces, should be carried out quickly at Auschwitz (or Lublin or some other camp in the East), I ask you most humbly to issue me the necessary orders soon so that we can take advantage of the remaining days of winter cold.

> With sincere gratitude,
> and bidding you 'Heil Hitler!'
> I am your most obedient and devoted servant,
> S. Rascher

In the final months before the collapse of Germany, a number of prominent prisoners were quickly murdered. Often they had been in captivity since 1933, like, for example, the Communist politician Ernst Thälmann.

On the afternoon of August 17, 1944, a telephone call came from the central telephone exchange, with the order to get the ovens ready. . . . At around eight o'clock that evening the prisoners were locked inside their barracks adjoining the crematorium. The overseer, Jupp Müller, issued orders that no one was to leave quarters. Müller and the stoker, Heinz Rohde, had in turn been given these orders by the commanding officers.

Nevertheless, I left my quarters through the air shaft and got out into the crematorium courtyard. I hid behind a slag heap. . . . At ten minutes after midnight the two officers in charge of the crematorium emerged and opened the courtyard gate to admit a large passenger car. Three men in civilian clothes got out; two of them were obviously guarding the third, who was walking between them. I saw the prisoner only from the rear. He was tall, broad-shouldered, and bald. I could see that because he was not wearing a hat.

Meanwhile, the other SS men had come into the courtyard and were standing beside the entrance to the crematorium. The men in civilian clothes made their prisoner precede them as they walked toward the door. The moment he had passed through the lane of SS men and was entering the crematorium, three shots were fired at him from the courtyard.

Then all the SS men and the two men in civilian clothes entered the crematorium and closed the door behind them. About three minutes later a fourth shot was fired inside the crematorium. Apparently this was the customary *coup de grace*.

Around twenty or twenty-five minutes later the noncommissioned officers left the crematorium. I heard Hofschulte say to Otto, "Do you know who that was?" Otto replied, "That was the Communist leader, Thälmann." . . .

On the following morning, August 18, 1944, when I cleaned the ovens and removed the ashes, all I found was a pocket watch that had been tempered in the fire. From the color of the ashes I could tell that the dead man had been burned with all his clothes on.

On December 16, when the Allies were already in Belgium and

Holland, the Germans launched their final offensive in the Ardennes. Within a few days the German forces had been smashed. Hitler's last hope of driving the Allies out of France failed miserably. Those German armies that were still in fighting trim had been defeated, and they had lost 100,000 men, 600 tanks and cannons, and 1,600 planes.

The American newspapers reported the launching of the German offensive in the Ardennes. Many of my fellow-prisoners in the camp at Monroe, Louisiana, actually believed that in a few days German troops would be marching into Paris. So strong was the spell of Nazi propaganda, even separated by an ocean. After all, they had been fed this propaganda for twelve years.

We had very good accommodations at the camp. We slept in beds on clean white sheets, and we were given plenty to eat. The American guards treated us well and were even friendly toward us. The Nazi propaganda machine had told us daily that soon America, too, would begin to suffer from the effects of the war. None of this was true, for every day we were given meat, fruit, vegetables, salad, and white bread—things we had only dreamed about in Germany. We prisoners of war were fed better than the German soldiers at the front.

America could even afford to waste food, while in Germany and in the German-occupied countries people were starving—and starving to death. There were several playing fields in the camp where, during our free time, we used to play soccer and handball. We needed sawdust to mark the fields. One day when I asked the American commandant for a few bags of sawdust so that we could mark out the fields for our games, he was at a loss to know what to do at first. Where could he get sawdust when there were no sawmills in the area? However, he himself was a sports enthusiast, so he gave us two bags of pure wheat flour, and on another occasion he gave us a bag of powdered sugar.

Mad as this may sound, it is true. In Germany the prisoners were stretching their arms through the barbed wire and begging the people outside for a piece of bread or a potato, but the people outside had nothing to eat themselves.

Yet in the southern United States we were strewing wheat flour and powdered sugar over a soccer field.

260

1945

From February 4 to February 11, Roosevelt, Churchill, and Stalin held a conference at Yalta in the Crimean peninsula, in the course of which they decided to divide Germany and Berlin into zones of occupation after the war. The ultimate result of this conference is the fact that today there are two separate German states, the DDR [the Deutsche Demokratische Republik], the German Democratic Republic, and the BRD [Bundes Republik Deutschland], the Federal Republic of Germany.

In Germany once again everyone was mobilized to enter the war effort; women were drafted into the Volkssturm [people in arms], and fifteen-year-old boys in the Hitler Youth were sent off to fight in the war.

On April 4, Buchenwald Concentration Camp was liberated by its own inmates, two days before the arrival of the American soldiers. By the end of the war Buchenwald had housed some 239,000 prisoners, of whom around 56,000 did not survive their captivity. Suffering unspeakable torments, they worked in the branch offices of the camp, in the munitions plants of firms like Krupp, Wintershall, IG Farben, Junkers, the Lignite-Petroleum Company [Braunkohle-Benzin, AG], and others. During the years 1941 and 1942, thousands of Soviet prisoners of war were murdered at Buchenwald.

President Roosevelt died on April 12. On the following day all the inmates of our POW camp were ordered to assemble, and the American commandant told us about the president's death.

A man around forty years old, who was standing next to me in line, whispered to me, "Now we'll win the war."

I could hardly believe my ears; he had not learned anything yet. As if the outcome of the war depended on a single man. But he was not the only one who had such notions; many believed the same thing because they were not aware of how a Western

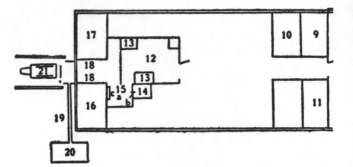

**Execution Facilities in the Horse Stable
at Buchenwald Concentration Camp**
1 = Vehicle arriving with prisoners
2 = Storage room for straw
3 = Storage room for horse feed
4 = Room where prisoners about to be executed took off their clothes
5 = Table for the prisoners' valuables and identification tags
6 = Loudspeakers
7 = Radio room
8 = SS dressing room
9 = SS dining hall
10 = SS lounge
11 = Toilet

---

democracy functioned. They always judged things in terms of Germany, where everything revolved around a single person, the Führer. In the United States Harry S. Truman assumed President Roosevelt's duties and continued to carry out the policy of his predecessor: to end the war and to abolish Fascism.

On April 25, Soviet and American troops met at the Elbe River near Torgau. All German territory that was not already occupied by Soviet and Allied troops was now divided into two parts. But the insane war continued, and as my mother later assured me,

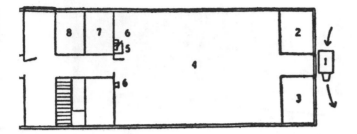

12 = So-called doctor's office
13 = Tables for medical instruments
14 = SS "shooting gallery" containing an opening
    through which the SS could fire at a target in Room 15
15 = Execution chamber containing a drain for flushing blood (a),
    a wooden partition for the SS man holding the water hose (b),
    and a target that could be draped with a curtain (c).
16 = Storeroom for sawdust
17 = Storeroom for straw
18 = Piles of dead bodies
19 = Gutter through which blood was drained out
20 = Refuse pit
21 = Vehicle for carrying away corpses

---

there were actually still people in our town who believed in the ultimate victory of Germany.

As they marched toward Berlin, both the Allied and the Soviet troops made ghastly discoveries.

In many concentration camps the prisoners had been mowed down with machine guns shortly before the arrival of the Allied troops. The sight of these victims intensified the resolve of the victorious powers to show the defeated Germany no mercy.

On April 30, Hitler committed suicide in the bunker of the

Above: Gotha Concentration Camp
during Eisenhower's visit on May 3, 1945.
Below: Two rows of mass graves containing dead prisoners
at Nordhausen Concentration Camp, May 3, 1945.

Chancellery in Berlin, along with Eva Braun, whom he had married just a short time before. Gasoline was poured over the two corpses and they were set alight. The "greatest general of all time," as the Nazi propagandists used to call him, had chosen this way to avoid being called to account.

That same day Goebbels, too, committed suicide along with his wife and children.

Hitler left a will in which he stated: "Above all I call on the leaders of the nation to ensure the strict observance of the racial laws and to engage in a merciless struggle against international Jewry, the poisoner of all the peoples of the world."

On May 9, Germany finally signed an unconditional surrender. Hundreds of thousands of German soldiers became prisoners of war.

That day, when we came back from working in the fields, we were not allowed to return to our barracks but had to wait in the main courtyard of the camp until all the work details had reported in. Then the American captain stood before all the prisoners and spoke a single sentence, "The war is over in Europe."

Did we cheer? I don't remember. All I remember is that I was thinking about my mother and my father. Were they still alive? The captain had consciously spoken only of the war in Europe, for the war had not yet ended for the United States. Not until atomic bombs were dropped on Hiroshima on August 6 and on

German prisoners of war marching along the highway on March 29, 1945.

Nagasaki on August 9 did the East Asian war against Japan finally come to an end.

While we were in the United States, we gradually learned about the hideous crimes the Germans had committed against the Jews and other peoples. Scarcely a week went by in which we were not ordered to watch a film in which we saw pictures taken in the concentration camps by American or Soviet camera teams.

Many of my fellow-prisoners used to start crying and leave. But others, after they had seen the film, left the theater and laughed in the faces of the American soldiers, for they thought that all these pictures were horror stories invented by the enemy, just as Goebbels, with his cunning propaganda, had for years been teaching them to believe. In discussions that went on all day long, they attempted to grasp the inconceivable fact that even German soldiers were capable of performing acts of inhuman atrocity.

The Germans had murdered millions of people. One of the

A German soldier shooting a Polish Jew and her child.

worst of these Germans, Rudolf Höss, who had been commandan at Auschwitz, maintained, right up to the time of his execution the pose that he had been an ordinary, well-disciplined bureau crat who had merely been following orders.

Deposition of the Commandant of Auschwitz

I, Rudolf Ferdinand Höss, having duly and legally sworn to tell the truth, hereby declare and testify to the following facts:

1. I am forty-six years old and have been a member of the NSDAP [the Nazi Party] since 1922; a member of the SS since 1934; a member of the Waffen-SS since 1939. On December 1, 1934, I became a member of the SS Guard Unit, the so-called Death's-Head Squad.

2. From 1934 on, without interruption, I participated in the management of concentration camps and served at Dachau until 1938; then I served as adjutant at Sachsenhausen from 1938 to May 1, 1940, at which time I was appointed Commandant of Auschwitz. I remained in command at Auschwitz until December 1, 1943, and I would estimate that at least 2,500,000 victims were executed and exterminated there by means of gassing and cremation; at least 500,000 more died of starvation and disease, which makes a total of approximately 3,000,000 dead. This figure represents approximately 70 to 80 percent of all the prisoners sent to Auschwitz; the remainder were especially chosen to serve as slave labor in the camp industries. Among the executed and cremated persons were approximately 20,000 Russian prisoners of war. . . . The rest of the victims included approximately 100,000 German Jews and a vast number of inhabitants—also mostly Jews—of Holland, France, Belgium, Poland, Hungary, Czechoslovakia, Greece, and other countries. Approximately 400,000 Hungarian Jews were executed by us at Auschwitz alone during the summer of 1944.

6. The Final Solution of the Jewish problem meant the total extermination of all the Jews in Europe. In June, 1942, I was ordered to introduce improvements to facilitate the extermination of prisoners at Auschwitz. At that time three other extermination camps already existed in Poland: Belzec, Treblinka, and Wolzek. These camps were under the operational command of the security police and the SD. I visited Treblinka to determine how the exterminations were carried out. The commandant at Treblinka told me that he had liquidated 80,000 people over a six-month

267

period. His principal responsibility was the liquidation of all the Jews from the Warsaw Ghetto. He used carbon-monoxide gas, and in his opinion his methods were not very effective. Thus when I built the extermination facilities at Auschwitz, I used Zyklon B, a crystallized form of prussic acid, which we used to throw inside the gas chamber through a small opening. Depending on climatic conditions, it took the people inside the gas chamber between three and fifteen minutes to die. We knew when the people were dead because they stopped screaming. Usually we waited for half an hour before opening the doors and removing the corpses. After the corpses had been removed from the gas chamber, our special units took the rings off their fingers and extracted the gold from their teeth.

7. Another way in which I improved on the facilities at Treblinka was by building gas chambers that could hold 2,000 people at a time, whereas each of the ten gas chambers at Treblinka could hold only 200. We selected our victims in the following way: Two SS medical officers were responsible for examining the prisoners as the transports arrived at Auschwitz. The prisoners had to walk past one of the doctors, and as each one went by, the doctor would give a signal indicating his decision. Those who appeared suitable for work were sent into the camp. The others were immediately sent to the extermination facilities. All young children, without exception, were exterminated, for because of their youth they were incapable of working. Yet another way in which we improved on the system at Treblinka was this: At Treblinka the victims almost always knew that they were about to be killed, but at Auschwitz we attempted to fool them by telling them they were simply going to be deloused. Naturally, they were often aware of our true intentions, and thus we frequently had to cope with mutinies and other difficulties. Very often the women tried to hide their children underneath their clothing, but when we discovered the children, they were naturally sent to the gas chamber. We were supposed to carry out the extermination in secret, but the stench of decay produced by the round-the-clock cremation of the bodies—a stench that actually made people feel nauseous—permeated the entire area, and all the people living in the communities surrounding the camp knew that people were being exterminated at Auschwitz.

> Sworn testimony
> of Concentration Camp Commandant Höss
> in Nuremberg on April 5, 1946

These were not horror stories but the plain, unvarnished truth, and while we were in the United States we learned only a fraction of that truth. But even when, little by little, people all over the world found out about the German atrocities, our American guards continued to treat us very decently. We ran our own affairs in the camp, we were always given good food, and we had radios, a movie theater, newspapers, and a large number of books.

We were paid for our work in the farmers' fields and received coupons with which we could purchase cigarettes, toilet articles, stationery, chocolate and nonalcoholic beverages at the camp canteen.

In the United States I began to read the German literature that had been banned in Germany from 1933 to 1945. I learned to know the writers whose books the Nazis had cast into the flames: Döblin and Kesten, Brecht and Werfel, Zweig and Thomas Mann, Heine and Tucholsky, Anna Seghers and B. Traven; I could fill pages and pages with their names.

We began to hope again and planned what we would do when we got back to Germany. The war had been lost, but in the United States, far away from home, we could not imagine what was really going on in Germany. Even the infrequent letters we now began to receive from there gave us no clear idea of what conditions were like back home. Many of us had no idea where our families were or even whether they were still alive.

The first letter from my mother, in which she wrote me that she and my father were fine, reached me shortly before Christmas, 1945. It had taken four weeks to arrive.

She expressed herself with great caution regarding the situation after the collapse of the Third Reich. Since she had written that she was very well indeed, I knew that she was having a hard time, but my father was alive.

When the war ended, I was not yet nineteen. I dreamed of a career at the Rosenthal Chinaware factory, where I had served a good apprenticeship. Perhaps I would become a head clerk or even a manager. I wondered whether the old head clerk who sometimes used to wink at me was still alive.

During the day we prisoners worked in the fields on endless numbers of farms. We picked cotton, tomatoes, and peanuts, chopped sugar cane, and chopped down tall trees. Actually I was quite content except for the fact that I suffered from the heat, which was like that of a hothouse. But I got used to that too.

On November 20, the war-criminal trials began in Nuremberg. Those on trial were the Nazi leaders who had not escaped the responsibility for their crimes by suicide.

The balance sheet of the war, which today, once again, many people who are apparently incapable of learning anything believe to have been some sort of accident and not a deliberate war of aggression, was drawn up:

Total number of casualties	54,800,000
Number of this total who died fighting on the various fronts	27,000,000
(i.e., 24% of all the soldiers involved were killed)	
Number of people killed of various nationalities	
Soviet Union	20,300,000
Asian nations (especially Japan)	13,600,000
Poland and the Balkans	9,010,000
Germany	6,600,000
Western Europe	1,300,000
Italy and Austria	750,000
U.S.A.	229,000
Missing persons	3,000,000
Total losses	54,789,000

The cost of waging the war and of damages inflicted: around 1,350 billion dollars
21,000,000 people deprived of homes and property as a result of bombing attacks
45,000,000 people evacuated, imprisoned, or deported from their native lands
2,672,422.5 tons of bombs dropped on Europe

Shortly before February, 1948, when I once again set foot on German soil, I met men my own age who believed that the Germans would have won the war if Hitler had been informed of everything that was taking place in the Reich. Just as, after World War I, the Germans developed the legend that they had been "stabbed in the back," so among prisoners of war in the United States a new legend was springing up: "If only the Führer had known about all these things, then. . . ." Unfortunately, many of these people who simply refuse to learn are still alive, and another generation of them is growing up to take their place. I fear that they never informed themselves about the truth or they did not wish to be informed. Today we are once again reading in the newspapers almost daily about extreme right-wing or neo-Fascist movements, some of them old and some new. Many people do not take them very seriously because, so they believe, these groups represent only a tiny minority.

But Hitler began with only seven disciples.

BIBLIOGRAPHY OF SOURCES

Anrich, Gerold, *Das Flaggenbuch, mit Bildern von Gudrun und Adrian Cornford,* Otto Maier Verlag, Ravensburg, 1978
(Abbreviated: Anrich)
Antifaschistischer Widerstand, der Deutsche, 1933–1945 in Bildern und Dokumenten, ed. by P. Altmann, H. Brüdigam, B. Mausbach-Bromberger, M. Oppenheimer, Röderberg-Verlag, Frankfurt am Main, 1975
(Abbr.: *Antifaschist. Widerstand*)
Das sind unsere Lieder: Ein Liederbuch, ed. by Hein and Oss Kröher, illustrations by Gertrude Degenhardt, Büchergilde Gutenberg, Frankfurt am Main, 1977
(Abbr.: *Das sind unsere Lieder*)
"Die Ballade von den Säckeschmeissern," all rights reserved to VEB (Volkseigner Betrieb) Deutscher Verlag für Musik, Leipzig. See also *Das sind unsere Lieder*
Dokumente zur deutschen Geschichte 1924–1929, ed. by W. Ruge and W. Schumann, Röderberg-Verlag, Frankfurt am Main, 1977
(Abbr.: *Dok. z. dt. Gesch. 1924–1929*)
Dokumente zur deutschen Geschichte 1929–1933, ed. by W. Ruge and W. Schumann, Röderberg-Verlag, Frankfurt am Main, 1977
(Abbr.: *Dok. z. dt. Gesch. 1929–1933*)
Dokumente zur deutschen Geschichte 1933–1935, ed. by W. Ruge and W. Schumann, Röderberg-Verlag, Frankfurt am Main, 1977
(Abbr.: *Dok. z. dt. Gesch. 1933–1935*)
Dokumente zur deutschen Geschichte 1939–1942, ed. by W. Ruge and W. Schumann, Röderberg-Verlag, Frankfurt am Main, 1977
(Abbr.: *Dok. z. dt. Gesch. 1939–1942*)
Dokumente zur deutschen Geschichte 1942–1945, ed. by W. Ruge and W. Schumann, Röderberg-Verlag, Frankfurt am Main, 1977
(Abbr.: *Dok. z. dt. Gesch. 1942–1945*)
Das Dritte Reich: Seine Geschichte in Texten, Bildern und Dokumenten, two vol., ed. by Heinz Huber and Artur Müller, Verlag Kurt Desch, Munich, 1964
(Abbr.: *Drittes Reich*)

Eine Ziffer über dem Herzen: Erlebnisbericht aus 12 Jahren Haft, by Michael Tschesno-Hell, Berlin, 1957. All rights retained by author. See also: *Proletarische Lebensläufe: Autobiographische Dokumente zur Entstehung der Zweiten Kultur in Deutschland*
(Abbr.: *Eine Ziffer über dem Herzen*)

"Es gibt keinen jüdischen Wohnbezirk in Warschau mehr": *Stroop Bericht,* Hermann Luchterhand Verlag, Darmstadt and Neuwied, 1960 and 1976
(Abbr.: "Es gibt . . .")

Frohes Lesen: Fibel für Stadt und Land, Hanover, 1935
(Abbr.: *Frohes Lesen*)

Der gelbe Stern: Die Judenverfolgung in Europa 1933 bis 1945, ed. by Gerhard Schoenberner, Bertelsmann Verlag, Gütersloh, 1960, 1978
(Abbr.: *Gelber Stern*)

Geschichtliche Weltkunde, vol. 3, ed. by W. Hug, Verlag Moritz Diesterweg, Frankfurt am Main, 1976
(Abbr.: *Geschichtl. Weltkunde*)

Graf, Oskar Maria, *An manchen Tagen: Reden, Gedanken und Zeitbetrachtungen,* Frankfurt am Main, 1961, and Süddeutscher Verlag, Munich. Excerpts quoted from Wildermuth, Rosemarie (ed.), *Als das Gestern heute war: Erzählungen, Gedichte und Dokumente zu unserer Geschichte (1789–1949),* Ellermann Verlag, Munich, 1977
(Abbr.: Graf/Wildermuth)

Hillgruber, A., *Die Auflösung der Weimarer Republik,* Hanover, 1960, p. 29; excerpt quoted from *Geschichtliche Weltkunde,* vol. 3, Verlag Moritz Diesterweg, Frankfurt am Main, 1976
(Abbr.: Hillgruber)

Hofer, Walther (ed.), *Der Nationalsozialismus: Dokumente 1933–1945,* Fischer Taschenbuch Verlag, Frankfurt am Main, 1957
(Abbr.: Hofer)

Kästner, Erich, *Kästner für Erwachsene,* ed. by Rudolf Walter Leonhardt, S. Fischer Verlag, Frankfurt am Main, 1966
(Abbr.: Kästner)

Kesten, Hermann, *Die Kinder von Gernica,* Limes Verlag, Wiesbaden, 1948
(Abbr.: Kesten)

Kogon, Eugen, *Der SS-Staat: Das System der deutschen Konzentrationslager,* Europäische Verlagsanstalt, Frankfurt am Main, 1965
(Abbr.: Kogon)

Krautkrämer, E./ Radbruch, E., *Wandel der Welt,* Bad Homburg, 1976, p. 161; excerpt quoted from *Geschichtliche Weltkunde,* vol. 3, Verlag Moritz Diesterweg, Frankfurt am Main, 1976

(Abbr.: Krautkrämer/Radbruch)

Kühnl, Reinhard (ed.), *Der deutsche Faschismus in Quellen und Dokumenten,* Pahl-Rugenstein Verlag, Cologne, 1975, 1977 (second, expanded edition)
(Abbr.: Kühnl)

Langhoff, Wolfgang, *Die Moorsoldaten,* Verlag Neuer Weg, Tübingen, 1973
(Abbr.: Langhoff)

Lieder gegen den Tritt, ed. by Annemarie Stern, Asso Verlag, Oberhausen, 1974
(Abbr.: *Lieder*)

Picker/Ritter, *Hitlers Tischgespräche in Führerhauptquartier,* Bonn, 1951, p. 116, from the conversation on the evening of July 22, 1942; excerpt quoted from *Geschichtliche Weltkunde,* vol. 3, Verlag Moritz Diesterweg, Frankfurt am Main, 1976
(Abbr.: Picker/Ritter)

Proletarische Lebensläufe: Autobiographische Dokumente zur Entstehung der Zweiten Kultur in Deutschland, vol. 2, 1914–1945, ed. by Wolfgang Emmerich, Rowohlt Taschenbuch Verlag, Reinbek, 1975
(Abbr.: *Prolet. Lebensläufe*)

Reichsführer! . . . *Briefe an und von Himmler,* ed. by Helmut Heiber, Deutsche Verlagsanstalt, Stuttgart, and Deutscher Taschenbuch Verlag, Munich, 1970
(Abbr.: *Reichsführer*)

Sachsenhausen: Dokumente, Aussagen, Forschungsergebnisse und Erlebnisberichte über das ehemalige Konzentrationslager Sachsenhausen, ed. by the Komitee der Antifaschistischen Widerstandskämpfer der DDR, VEB Deutscher Verlag der Wissenchaften, Berlin, 1974
(Abbr.: *Sachsenhausen*)

Schönstedt, Walter, *Kämpfende Jugend,* Berlin, 1932; new edition, Oberbaum Verlag, Berlin, 1971

Schütze, Alfred, *Marschtritt Deutschland,* Stuttgart, 1939
(Abbr.: Schütze)

Senger, Valentin, *Kaiserhofstrasse 12,* Hermann Luchterhand Verlag, Darmstadt and Neuwied, 1978
(Abbr.: Senger)

Serke, Jürgen, *Die verbrannten Dichter,* Beltz Verlag, Weinheim and Basel, 1977
(Abbr.: Serke)

Seydewitz, Max, *Es hat sich gelohnt zu leben,* Dietz Verlag, Berlin (East Germany), 1976

Der Tag, September 4, 1928, excerpt quoted from *Geschichtliche Welt-*

kunde, vol. 3, ed. by W. Hug, Verlag Moritz Diesterweg, Frankfurt am Main, 1976

Tausk, Walter, *Breslauer Tagebuch 1933–1940,* Röderberg-Verlag, Frankfurt am Main, 1977
(Abbr.: Tausk)

Tucholsky, Kurt, *Gesammelte Werke,* vol. 3, 1929–1932, ed. by Mary Gerold-Tucholsky and Fritz J. Raddatz, Rowohlt Verlag, Reinbek, 1969
(Abbr.: Tucholsky, vol. 3)

Weimarer Republik, ed. by Kunstamt Kreuzberg, Berlin, and the Institut für Theaterwissenschaft of the University of Cologne, Elefanten Press, Berlin and Hamburg, 1977
(Abbr.: *Weimarer Republik*)

Weinert, Erich, "Das Wunder vom 1. Mai 1929," from E.W., *Das Zwischenspiel,* Berlin (East Germany), 1956, in: Rudolf Walbinger (ed.), *Mit Spott gegen Kaiser und Reich,* Aufbau Verlag, Berlin (East Germany), 1971

Wildermuth, Rosemarie, ed., *Als das Gestern heute war: Erzählungen, Gedichte und Dokumente zu unserer Geschichte (1789–1949),* Ellermann Verlag, Munich, 1977
(Abbr.: Wildermuth)

SOURCES OF QUOTATIONS

SOURCES OF PHOTOGRAPHS

Bildarchiv Preussischer Kulturbesitz, Berlin: pages 16, 26, 28, 67, 72, 73, 74, 75, 77, 86, 87, 114, 116, 117, 183, 226, 229, 256, 264, 265, and back cover

Das Dritte Reich: Seine Geschichte in Texten, Bildern und Dokumenten (2 vol.), ed. by Heinz Huber and Artur Müller, Verlag Kurt Desch, Munich, 1964: page 220

Der Gelbe Stern: Die Judenverfolgung in Europa 1933 bis 1945, ed. by Gerhard Schoenberger, Bertelsmann Verlag, Gütersloh, 1960, 1978: pages 64, 182,

Faschismus (Renzo Vespignani), ed. by the Neue Gesellschaft für Bildende Kunst and the Kunstamt Kreuzberg, Elefanten Press, Berlin, 1976: page 113

Kunst im Dritten Reich: Dokumente der Unterwerfung, (Exhibition Catalogue), Frankfurter Kunstverein, Frankfurt am Main, 1974: page 115

Mytze, Andreas W.: page 93

Ullstein-Bilderdienst: pages 30, 100, 118, 225, 266, and front cover

concentration camps (*cont.*)
 Theresienstadt, 165, 257
 Treblinka, 195, 217, 229, 236,
  244, 267, 268
 Wolzek, 267
culture, Nazi, 18, 19, 67-76, 83,
 101, 112-114, 141-145, 234-235
Czechoslovakia, 136-139, 145-148,
 163-165, 166, 167, 207; map, 164

d'Arguto, Rosebery, 97
Daladier, Edouard, 148
Danzig, 167
de Gaulle, Charles, 189-190
Denmark, 187, 189
Dohnany, Hans von, 228

East Germany. *See* German Democratic Republic
economy, 16, 23, 27, 28-31, 35-37,
 41, 48, 122-123, 126-127, 131,
 219. *See also* labor, unemployment
education, 33, 83, 88, 116-119,
 150-151, 180-181, 202-203; of
 non-Germans, 188-189. *See also*
 propaganda
elections, 23, 37, 55, 59, 65, 80
Enabling Act, 66, 122
England. *See* Britain
Estonia, 170, 203
euthanasia program, 105, 176, 204
experiments, human, 257-258
extermination, camps, 63, 175,
 194-195, 204-205, 209, 212, 217,
 229, 240-245, 257, 267-268; of
 mentally ill, 105, 176, 204; of villages, 213-215

Federal Republic of Germany
 (BRD), 106, 114, 261
Feuchtwanger, Lion, 68, 74

Finland, 170
France, 101, 108, 128, 166, 167,
 168, 170, 173, 174, 187, 189-190,
 207, 251, 260
Franco, Francisco, 110
Franck, James, 75
Frank, Leonhard, 68, 73
Freud, Sigmund, 69

German Association of Veterans,
 44
German Democratic Republic
 (DDR), 261
German Girl's League, 85
German National People's Party,
 24, 37, 38, 44
German Popular Front, 125
German-Soviet non aggression
 pact. *See* USSR
German Women's Association, 85,
 87
Germanization, 188, 215-216, 229,
 234
Gestapo, 33, 104, 132, 139, 164,
 180, 204
Globke, Hans, 105-106
Goebbels, Joseph, 15, 16, 62, 67,
 76, 77, 89, 114, 115, 172, 204,
 209, 217, 221, 228, 229, 251, 265
Goerdeler, Carl Friedrich, 255
Göring, Hermann, 33, 63, 65-66,
 67, 77, 94, 133, 204, 216
Gräbe, Fried, 236-240
Graf, Oskar Maria, 68, 70-71
Greece, 166, 200, 210, 228
Groener, Wilhelm, 53
Grosz, George, 114
Grynspan, Herschel, 151
Guernica, 110-111

Hácha, Emil, 163
Harlan, Veit, 235

282

285

ABOUT THE AUTHOR

Born in Bayreuth in 1926, Max von der Grün grew up in the Fichtel-gebirge region of Germany, which lies along the Czech border. After finishing school, he completed a commercial apprenticeship and was then inducted into the labor service and thence into the Army. In August, 1944, von der Grün was taken prisoner by the Americans and spent the next three years in POW camps in the United States. Von der Grün describes those three years as his university, for besides working on farms and in quarries he read widely and deeply. After his release, he returned home and worked as a clerk in a building firm, doing construction work on the side to earn extra money.

In 1951, von der Grün went to the Ruhr district and became a coal miner. A serious accident in 1955 hospitalized him for three months and became the theme of his novel *Irrlicht und Feuer* (Will-'o-the-Wisp and Fire). The novel, published in 1963, enraged the mining industry and resulted in von der Grün's being blacklisted. He has been a free-lance writer ever since.

Mr. von der Grün has published a number of novels, some of which have been made into films, and has written screenplays, short stories, and a book for children. He has traveled widely in both Eastern and Western Europe, and in 1977 he again came to the United States, this time at the invitation of Oberlin College to teach there for a semester.

ABOUT THE AUTHOR

Nick Drake is the author of two critically acclaimed novels featuring Rahotep: *Nefertiti: The Book of the Dead*, which was shortlisted for the Crime Writers' Association Best Historical Crime Novel Award, and *Tutankhamun: The Book of Signs*. He is also a screenwriter and an award-winning poet. He wrote the screenplay for *Romulus, My Father*, which starred Eric Bana and won best film at the Australian Film Awards 2007.

TRIALS OF THE WORD

The imaged Word, it is, that holds
Hushed willows anchored in its glow.
HART CRANE, "VOYAGES VI"

TRIALS OF THE WORD
Essays in American Literature and the Humanistic Tradition
R. W. B. LEWIS

New Haven and London   *Yale University Press*   *1965*

FOR GLADYS BALDWIN BARR AND STRINGFELLOW BARR

My dear Oak and Winkie:

Not all these poets and novelists are among your favorites, but I want to dedicate the book to you because of my enduring affection for you both, and because for many years you have led me along fascinating paths of literature and history. I am especially grateful to you, Winkie, for introducing me to the great traditions of Western humanism. And I am especially grateful to you, Oak, because when I was an undergraduate you gave me the best advice a fledgling critic could receive—advice I try to pass on to my own students. What you said was: "Be a little tentative."

Your devoted nephew.

PREFACE

Most of these essays were written in the last five or six years, and most of them—the long concluding essay is the exception—were written at the suggestion of an editor or the chairman of some literary symposium. I hope I may be forgiven for taking as my title a phrase I have used before, though in a less conspicuous place (as the title of a subsection in another book). Like the benighted fellow in Frost's poem, I like having thought of it so well, I cannot resist saying it again. But it is, I think, apt for my intentions here. For these are in fact trials—that is, attempts or essays, efforts to come to terms with certain phenomena made up of words, to explore certain phases of the language of literature. They are also tests of certain hypotheses about the nature of poetry and fiction (the essays on Whitman and Conrad, for example) and about the relation between the available forms of literature and the observable forms of life (as in the discussions of Hawthorne and James and of Edith Wharton). But they do not derive, so far as I can retrospectively make out, from any very stringent theory about literature itself; and, in any case, I prefer to move toward theory by exemplifying it rather than by elaborating it as it were in cold blood.

But just as one has temperamental preferences, so one has congenital and recurring interests; one is drawn all helplessly, time and again, to the same center of imaginative attraction. What attracts me, more often than not, is the tug of the transcendent: or, rather, the fertile tug-of-war between the transcendent and the concrete. I am drawn to testing the energy of the Word within the word—to watching any imaginative attempt to body forth "the imaged Word," in Hart Crane's phrase—in order to see how or to what extent the reality of the natural and phenomenal and human world may, through the resources of the literary arts, appear (in Crane's fine figure) to be anchored in and receive its illumination from the Word-made-image.

To put it differently, I tend to focus upon those phases of a work of literature in which what have to be called religious considerations are overtly or secretively paramount. But this volume is by no means a contribution to that field of study known as "religion and literature"; nor is the religious element explored, any more than the religious viewpoint at work, by any means unequivocally Christian. My present notions about all this are set forth as plainly as possible in the essay called "Hold on Hard to the Huckleberry Bushes," which is as close as the volume comes (and not very close at that) to a theoretical statement. The problem is one of cultural history and its relation to the perennial human consciousness; and two quotations come to mind in aid of explanation, as providing a dialectic—thesis and antithesis— which I am happy to embrace. The first is from Edmund Wilson at his terse and hard-spoken best: "The word *God* is now archaic, and it ought to be dropped by those who do not need it for moral support" (from "Religion," in *A Piece of My Mind,* 1956). The second is from Melville, offering Mr. Wilson a cautionary answer a century in advance: "Take God out of the dictionary, and you would have Him in the street." And there indeed, or so these essays will sometimes suggest, is where the banished Word has to be looked for in the modern epoch: in the streets, and in the exacerbated experiences of the men and women who walk them. It is to be looked for, that is, in the poetic and fictional representations of those places and persons and experiences; and it is to be found above all in the artistic evocation, the summoning into being by drama and metaphor, of a lurking elusive force that had otherwise been known to us only by negation, in the void and in the blasphemy. These are perhaps hard sayings, even dark sayings; but the discussion of *The Wings of the Dove,* among several others, may bring them closer to the light. But to be concerned with modern literature is, I believe, to be deeply concerned with the devious ways in which the irrepressible religious consciousness finds expression in the midst of its resolutely secular and frequently very ordinary materials.

These essays proceed, as well, from the assumption that American literature is a sizable and intermittently handsome body of writing, and that the case for its importance—much less for its existence—need no longer be argued. No doubt it has its own distinctive features and vocabulary, its own obsessions and quirky angles of vision; it manifests its own kind of masterpiece and minorpiece and contains writings that triumph or fail in a specifically American manner and idiom. I await, without impatience, the day when our universities will have departments of American, as they now have departments of English and of French. Nonetheless, the greatest writings by American authors continue to be definable in relation to the whole body of Western literature —to the whole long humanistic tradition. In part, this is simply a matter of common sense. But in part it is due to the unrivaled hospitality of the American imagination to the literatures of other nations. For all its occasional parochialism and its periodic bursts of cultural nativism, American literature at its most original and adventurous is also the most international, the most cosmopolitan, the most *Western* of the literatures of the Western world. This may be merely the inevitable obverse of parochialism; it is, anyhow, a quality rather to be taken into account than to be bragged about. If, for example, T. S. Eliot's *The Waste Land* in the previous generation and Saul Bellow's *Herzog* in our own are unmistakably American products, it is exactly because both the poem and the novel reveal such an extravagant appetite for the whole range of Western literature, philosophy, and theology, and for seizing again upon the archetypal human dilemmas embodied therein. The analogy with the external historical process is obvious. Much has been said, in echo of Henry James, about the complex fate of being an American, though I should suppose it was a fate complex enough merely to be a human being under the modern circumstances; but it may be the peculiar and the rather terrible fate of the modern American that he feels himself required by history to assume the burden of representative Western man. This has been the disconcerting tendency our literature has reflected, resisted, and abetted—as, in the final essay, I mean to imply.

By way of footnote, I might add that the traditional aspect of this volume would have been a bit more visible if I had included one or two other essays which had been in my original table of contents: essays, in particular, on Virgil's *Aeneid* and Shakespeare's *Pericles*. I was persuaded by my editors—I think rightly—to omit those essays in the interest of symmetry and of chronological focus. They await the accumulation of further trials and other words.

R.W.B.L.

New Haven, Conn.
March 8, 1965

"Walt Whitman: Always Going Out and Coming In" was the introduction to the Whitman section in *Major Writers of America,* edited by Perry Miller (New York, Harcourt, Brace & World, Inc., 1962). The essay on Melville's tales and poems was the introduction to *Herman Melville: a Reader* (New York, Dell Publishing Co., 1963); and that on *The Confidence-Man* was the Afterword to the New American Library Signet edition of the novel (New York, 1964). "Hawthorne and James: The Matter of the Heart" first appeared in *Centenary Essays* (Columbus, Ohio, Ohio State University Press, 1964). "Hold on Hard to the Huckleberry Bushes" was published in *The Sewanee Review,* Vol. LXVII, No. 3 (Summer, 1959). The essay on *The Wings of the Dove,* delivered at the Modern Language Association meeting in December, 1956, was published by *Modern Fiction Studies* (Spring, 1957). "Edith Wharton and *The House of Mirth*" served as introduction to the Houghton Mifflin Riverside edition of Mrs. Wharton's novel (Boston, 1963). "Malraux and His Critics" appeared in *Malraux: a Collection of Critical Essays,* edited by the author (Englewood Cliffs, N.J., Prentice-Hall, 1964). "The Sense of Fair Play" and "Days of Wrath and Laughter" are published here for the first time. I am most grateful to the publishers and editors concerned for permission to reprint.
    The lines from "Skunk Hour" on page 187 are from *Life Studies,* © 1956, 1959 by Robert Lowell; reprinted by permission of Farrar, Straus, and Giroux and Faber and Faber. The other lines on pages 187–88 are from *Lord Weary's Castle,* Copyright © 1944, 1946 by Robert Lowell; reprinted by permission of Harcourt, Brace & World, Inc., and Faber and Faber.

CONTENTS

TRIALS OF THE WORD

WALT WHITMAN:
ALWAYS GOING OUT
AND COMING IN

Walt Whitman is the most blurred, even contradictory figure in the classical or mid-nineteenth-century period of American Literature. Recent scholarship and criticism have been clearing things up a good deal; but both the poet and his work remain something of a jumble. For a number of decades, Whitman was the most misrepresented of our major poets; and the misrepresentation began with Whitman himself, in the last twenty-five years of his life. It was during those years, from 1867 onward, that Whitman —initially a very self-exposed and self-absorbed poet—became willfully self-concealing, while at the same time he asserted in various ways an entity, a being, a persona radically other than the being that lay at the heart of his best poetry.

The chief mode of such concealment and assertion was not creative; it was editorial. Whitman wrote little poetry of lasting value after "Passage to India" (1871); what he did do in those later years was constantly to reshuffle the contents of his expanding book: to disperse the poems out of their original and effective order, to arrange them in new and fundamentally misleading groups, to suppress some of the more telling and suggestive of the items, and to revise or delete a series of key passages. The result of this process was a serious shift of emphasis whereby the authentic Whitman was gradually dismembered and replaced by a synthetic entity that was more posture than poet, more mere representative than sovereign person. It, or he, was the representative—in nearly the conventional political sense— of a rather shallowly and narrowly conceived democratic culture:

a hearty voice at the center of a bustling and progressive republic, a voice that saluted the pioneers, echoed the sound of America singing, itself sang songs of joy that foretold the future union of the nation and the world and the cosmos, chanted the square deific, and wept over the country's captain lying cold and dead on the deck of the ship of state. Other and truer aspects of Whitman continued to exert an appeal, especially in certain lively corners of Europe. But in the English-speaking world, it was primarily the bombastic, or, as his disciples sometimes said, the "cosmic" Whitman that was better known; and it was this Whitman that was either revered or—in most literary circles after the advent of T. S. Eliot—dismissed or simply disregarded.

So much needs to be said: for our first task is to disentangle Whitman, to separate the real from the unpersuasive, to separate the poet from the posture. To do that, we have, first of all, to put Whitman's poems back into their original and chronological order. It might be argued that we have no right to tamper with the poet's own editorial judgment; that *Leaves of Grass* is, after all, Whitman's book and that we are bound to take it in the order and the form he eventually decided on. The answer to this proposition is that there is no satisfactory way around the critical necessity of discriminating among Whitman's successive revisions of his own work, of appealing from the Whitman of 1867 and 1871 and later to the earlier Whitman of 1855 and 1856 and 1860. The dates just named are all dates of various editions of *Leaves of Grass;* and the latter three, the ones we appeal to, are those of the editions in which most (not all) of the real Whitman is to be found. This Whitman is a great and unique figure who is also the recognizable ancestor of many significant poetic developments since his creative prime—from *symboliste* poetry to imagism to more recent neoromantic and, less interestingly, "beat" writing; a chief, though by no means the only, American begetter of Wallace Stevens and Hart Crane, to some extent of Ezra Pound (as he once reluctantly confessed), and to an obscure but genuine degree of T. S. Eliot.

The importance of chronology, in Whitman's case, cannot be exaggerated. Without it, we can have no clear sense of Whitman's development as a consciousness and as a craftsman: an affair of far graver concern with Whitman than with many other poets of his stature. For, as I shall propose, the development of his consciousness and his craft, from moment to moment and year to year, is the very root of his poetic subject matter. It is what his best poems are mainly about, or what they re-enact: the thrust and withdrawal, the heightening and declining, the flowing and ebbing of his psychic and creative energy. Whitman's poetry has to do with the drama of the psyche or "self" in its mobile and complex relation *to* itself, to the world of nature and human objects, and to the creative act. What is attempted here, consequently, is a sort of chart of Whitman's development—in the belief that such a chart is not simply a required preliminary for getting at Whitman, but, rather, that it is the proper way to identify the poetic achievement, and to evaluate it. And in a case like Whitman's, the chart of the development is not finally separable from the graph of the life, or biography; the biographical material, therefore, has likewise been distributed among the successive commentaries on the editions of Whitman's single lifelong book.

I: 1855

When *Leaves of Grass* was published on July 4, 1855, Walt Whitman, now thirty-six years old, was living in Brooklyn, with his parents and brothers, earning an occasional dollar by carpentering. Both his family and his carpentry served as sources of allusion and metaphor in the poetry; but neither—that is, neither his heredity nor his temporary employment—help much to explain how a relatively indolent odd-jobber and sometime journalist named Walter Whitman developed into Walt Whitman the poet. His mother, whom he salutes in "There Was a Child Went Forth" for having "conceiv'd him in her womb and birth'd him" (the birthday being the last day in May 1819; the place, rural Long Island), was of Dutch and Quaker descent, not especially cultivated, and remembered by her son, in the same poem of 1855, as quiet and mild and clean. His father was a farmer of deteriorating fortunes, temper, and health: "manly, mean, anger'd, unjust" in his son's account; and it is a psychological curiosity that the father died within a week of the son's first public appearance, or birth, as a poet. Other members of the family were sources of that compassionate intimacy with the wretched and the depraved reflected, for example, in "Song of Myself":

> *The lunatic is carried at last to the asylum a confirm'd case . . .*
> *The prostitute draggles her shawl, her bonnet bobs on her tipsy*
> *and pimpled neck . . .*
> *Voices of the diseas'd and despairing and of thieves and dwarfs.*

Two of Whitman's brothers were diseased, one of them dying eventually in an insane asylum and the other (who was also a drunkard) married to a woman who became a prostitute. Yet another brother was a congenital idiot; and one of Whitman's sisters suffered from severe nervous melancholy. From these surroundings emerged the figure who, in the carpentering imagery of "Song of Myself," felt "sure as the most certain sure, plumb in the uprights, well entretied, braced in the beams"; a figure who not only felt like that but could write like that.

So remarkable and indeed so sudden has the appearance of Whitman the poet seemed, and out of so unlikely and artistically inhospitable a background, that literary historians have been driven to making spectacular guesses about the miraculous cause of it: an intense love affair, for instance, with a Creole lady of high degree; an intense love affair with an unidentified young man; a mystical seizure; the explosive impact of Emerson or of Carlyle or of George Sand. The literary influences can be documented, though they can scarcely be measured; with the other guesses, evidence is inadequate either to support or altogether to discount them. But perhaps the problem itself has not been quite properly shaped. Whitman's poetic emergence was remarkable enough; but it was not in fact particularly sudden. Nor was the career, seen retrospectively, as haphazard and aimless as one might suppose. Looked at from a sufficient distance, Whitman's life shows the same pattern of thrust and withdrawal, advance and retreat, that pulsates so regularly in the very metrics as well as the emotional attitudes of his verses; and to much the same effect. Up to about 1850, when he was thirty-one, Whitman—like the child in the autobiographical poem already quoted—was always going forth, always brushing up against the numberless persons and things of his world, and always *becoming* the elements he touched, as they became part of him. After 1850, he withdrew for a while into the privacies not only of his family but, more importantly, of his own imagination, in touch now with what he called the "Me myself"—his genius, or muse. It was this latter union between man and muse that, by 1855, produced the most extraordinary first volume of poems this country has so far seen.

One of the things Whitman did not become was a scholar, or even a college graduate. His school days, all spent in the Brooklyn to which his family moved in 1823, ended when he was eleven.

Thereafter he was apprenticed as a typesetter for a Long Island newspaper; and characteristically, the boy not only worked at the job, he *became* a typesetter, and typesetting became a part of his imagination. The look of a printed page and the rhetoric of punctuation were integral elements in his poetry—the printing of which he actually set with his own hands or carefully supervised. Between 1831 and 1836, Whitman occasionally wrote articles as well as set type for the paper; and he continued to compose fugitive little pieces from time to time during the five years following, from 1836 to 1841, while he was teaching in a variety of schools in a variety of Long Island villages. Writing, too, became part of him; and Whitman became a writer—at least by intention, announcing very firmly in a newspaper article of 1840, that he "would compose a wonderful and ponderous book . . . [treating] the nature and peculiarities of men, the diversities of their characters. . . . Yes: I *would* write a book! And who shall say that it might not be a very pretty book?"

In 1841, Whitman moved into New York City, where he was absorbed especially by what he called "the fascinating chaos" of lower Broadway, and by the life of saloons and theaters, of operas and art museums.[1] Operatic techniques and museum lore went into his later verses; but what Whitman became at this stage was that elegant stroller, or *boulevardier,* known as a dandy. This role persisted during the five years passed as reporter for a number of New York newspapers; and even after he returned to Brooklyn in 1846 and became editor of the *Eagle,* he came back by ferry to stroll Manhattan on most afternoons. But he was a dandy much caught up in public and political affairs. Among the personae he took on was that of the political activist, an ardent Freesoiler in fact, arguing the exclusion of Negro slavery from the territories with such editorial vehemence that the newspaper's owner fired him in February 1848. Within a matter of

1. Of special importance to Whitman were the Brooklyn Art Union, established by a group of Brooklyn painters about 1850, and the Egyptian Museum at 629 Broadway, in Manhattan. Whitman wrote an article about the former for the *New York Evening Post* in February, 1851; he was personally acquainted with several of the younger painters involved, and he was particularly observant of their techniques for handling light and color. Through visits to the Egyptian Museum, meanwhile, and through considerable study under the supervision of his friend, the Museum's proprietor, Dr. Abbot, Whitman became remarkably well versed in Egyptology—allusions drawn from which are frequent and suggestive in *Leaves of Grass.*

days, however, Whitman left for what turned out to be a three-month stay in New Orleans, where he served as assistant editor to that city's *Crescent*. It was there that rumor once assigned him the affair with the Creole lady, that soul-turning initiation into love that is said to have made a poet of him. The legend is almost certainly baseless; but something did happen to Whitman nonetheless. During the long weeks of travel, passing over the vast stretches of land and along the great rivers and the lakes (all that "geography and natural life" he catalogues so lavishly in the 1855 Preface), Whitman had his first encounter with the national landscape, and became (it may be hazarded) another of the personalities announced in *Leaves of Grass:* an American.

Back in Brooklyn, Whitman accepted the post of editor-in-chief on the liberal *Freeman* and stayed with it till he resigned in political outrage the following year. He had clearly "become" a journalist, an uncommonly able and effective one; his best poetry sprang in good part from a journalistic imagination—"I witness the corpse with its dabbled hair, I note where the pistol has fallen." At the same time, the forthgoing impulse was nearly—for the moment—exhausted. After expressing his sense of both national and personal betrayal by the Fugitive Slave Law in 1850, Whitman withdrew from the political arena; withdrew from active or regular journalism, and from the life of the city. He moved back to his family and commenced a leisurely existence in which, according to his brother George, "he would lie abed late, and after getting up would write a few hours if he took the notion"— or work at "house-building" for a bit, with his father and brothers, if he took that notion. Now he became a workman; and it was in the role of working-class artisan that he presented himself both in the verses of the 1855 *Leaves of Grass* and in the portrait which appeared as substitute for the author's name in the front of the volume.

For Whitman, I am suggesting, the act of becoming a poet was not a sudden or an unpredictable one. He had always been in process of becoming a poet, and the figures he successively became, from his school days onward, were not false starts or diversions, but moments in the major process. Typesetter, reporter, dandy, stroller in the city, political activist, surveyor of the national scenery, skilled editor, representative American workman: none of these was ever fully replaced by any other, nor were all at last replaced by the poet. They were absorbed into the poet; and if they do not explain the appearance of genius (nothing can explain that), they explain to some real degree the kind of writing—observant, ambulatory, varied, politically aware, job-conscious—in which *this* particular genius expressed itself.

Signs and symptoms of the poet proper, however, can also be isolated over a good many years. The determination to write a "wonderful" book, in 1840, has already been mentioned; but that was presumably to be a philosophical disquisition in prose. In the early 1840s, the writer-in-general became a writer of fiction, and Whitman contributed a number of moralistic short stories to different New York periodicals, all signed by "Walter Whitman" and none worth remembering. Not much later than that, certainly not later than 1847, Whitman's aspiration turned toward poetry. He began to carry a pocket-size notebook about with him; in this he would jot down topics for poems as they occurred, experimental lines, and trial workings of new metrical techniques. The process was stepped up from 1850 onward. In June 1850, the New York *Tribune* published two free-verse poems by Whitman, the second—later called "Europe: The 72d and 73d Year of These States," on the uprisings of 1848—to be included as the eighth item in the 1855 *Leaves of Grass*. It was probably in 1852 that he composed, though he did not publish, a fairly long poem called "Pictures," which had everything characteristic of his genuine poetry except its maritime movement. And in 1854, the repeal of the Missouri Compromise, and the arrest in Boston of a runaway slave named Anthony Burns, drew from Whitman a forty-line satiric exclamation that would comprise the ninth poem in the first edition—later called "A Boston Ballad."

These creative forays were increasingly stimulated by Whitman's reading, which was not only wide but, as evidence shows, surprisingly careful. He had reviewed works by Carlyle, George Sand, Emerson, Goethe, and others for the Brooklyn *Eagle*. He had known Greek and Roman literature, in translation, for years. "I have wonder'd since," he remarked in *A Backward Glance* (1888), "why I was not overwhelm'd by these mighty masters. Likely because I read them . . . in the full presence of Nature, under the sun . . . [with] the sea rolling in." (The comment suggests much of the quality of Whitman's poetry, wherein a natural atmosphere and sea rhythms help provide fresh versions of ancient and traditional archetypes.) It should be stressed that Whitman's literary education at this time, though it was by no means skimpy, was fairly conventional. It included the major English poets, Shakespeare and Milton especially, but it did not include Oriental writing or the literature of the mystical tradition or that of German idealism—except as those sources reached him faintly through his occasional readings in the essays of Emerson. This is probably to be reckoned fortunate: Whitman's mystical instinct, during his best creative years, was held effectively in check by a passion for the concrete, a commitment to the actual; and discussion of his "mysticism" is well advised to follow his example. Whitman became acquainted, too, with such American writers as Longfellow and Bryant, both of whom he came later to know personally. In addition, he took to making extensive notes and summaries of a long list of periodical essays, mostly dealing with art and artists.

"Art and Artists," in fact, was the title of an essay which Whitman himself read to the Brooklyn Art Union in 1851. And it was here that he first developed his large notion of the artist as hero—of the artist, indeed, as savior or redeemer of the community to which he offers his whole being as champion (sacrificial, if necessary) of freedom and humanity and spiritual health. "Read well the death of Socrates," he said portentously, "and of greater than Socrates." The image of the modern poet as godlike—even Christlike ("greater than Socrates")—was to run through and beneath Whitman's poetry from "Song of Myself" to "Passage to India"; and often, as here, it drew added intensity from Whitman's disillusion with other possible sources for that miraculous national transformation scene he seems to have waited for during most of his life. It was an extravagant notion; but it was one that anticipated several not much less extravagant images, in the twentieth century, of the artist as hero. It was this image, anyhow, that Whitman sought to bring into play in the whole body of the 1855 *Leaves of Grass* and particularly in "Song of Myself."

The first edition contained a long Preface introducing the poet-hero, who is then imaginatively created in the poems that follow. There were twelve of the latter, unnumbered and untitled and of varying length, with unconventional but effective typography—for example:

> *The atmosphere is not a perfume . . . . it has no taste of the*
> *distillation . . . . it is odorless,*
> *It is for my mouth forever. . . . I am in love with it.*

The first and by far the longest entry was, of course, the poem that in 1881 was labeled "Song of Myself." It is in part genuine though highly original autobiography; in part, it is a form of wish projection. We may think of it, among many other things, as a free-flowing recapitulation of the two processes I have been describing —the process by which a man of many roles becomes a poet, and the process by which the poet becomes a sort of god. There are as many significant aspects to "Song of Myself" as there are critical discussions and analyses of it; if the comment here is mainly limited to the enlargement of its central figure—that is, to the question of its structure—it is because the structure tends to confirm one's sense of Whitman's characteristic movement both in life and in poetry. For if, again, this strange, sometimes baffling, stream-of-consciousness poem does have a discernible structure, an "action" with a beginning, middle, and end, it is almost certainly one that involves the two events or processes just named.

More than one astute reader, while acknowledging a typical pulse or rhythm in the poem, a tidal ebb and flow, has nonetheless denied to it any sustained and completed design. But it may be ventured, perhaps, that "Song of Myself" has not so much a single structure as a number of provisional structures—partly because Whitman, like Melville, believed in a deliberate absence of finish in a work of art; more importantly because of what we may call Whitman's democratic aesthetic. Just as the political activist was absorbed into the poet at some time after 1850, so, and at the same moment, a practical concern with the workings of a democratic society was carried over into the aesthetic realm and applied to the workings of poetry, to the writing and the reading of it. The shape of "Song of Myself" depended, in Whitman's view, on the creative participation of each reader—"I round and finish little," he remarked in *A Backward Glance,* "the reader will always have his or her part to do, just as much as I have had mine." In a real sense, the poem was intended to have as many structures as there were readers; and the reason was that Whitman aimed not simply to create a poet and then a god, but to assist at the creation of the poetic and godlike in every reader.

Like Emerson, Whitman was here giving a democratic twist to the European Romantic notion of the poet as mankind's loftiest figure. For both Emerson and Whitman the poet's superiority lay exactly in his representativeness. "The poet is representative," Emerson had said, in his essay "The Poet." "He stands among partial men for the complete man, and apprises us not of his wealth, but of the common wealth." This is what Whitman meant when he spoke of "the great poet" as "the equable man"; and it is what he asserted in the opening lines of "Song of Myself":

> *I celebrate myself and sing myself*
> *And what I assume you shall assume.*

As one or two commentators—notably Roy Harvey Pearce[2]—have rightly suggested, "Song of Myself" is the first recognizable American epic; but, if so, it is an epic of this peculiar and modern sort. It does not celebrate a hero and an action of ancient days; it creates (and its action *is* creative) a hero of future days—trusting thereby to summon the heroism implicit in each individual.

Considered in these terms, as the epic consequence of a democratic aesthetic, "Song of Myself" shows a variable number of structural parts. This reader discovers but does not insist upon the following. The invocation leads, in Sections 1 and 2, into a transition from the artificial to the natural—from perfume in houses to the atmosphere of the woods; uncontaminated nature is the first scene of the drama. Next comes the recollection of the union—mystical in kind, sexual in idiom—between the two dimensions of the poet's being: the limited, conditioned Whitman and the "Me, myself," his creative genius, what Emerson might have called the Over-Soul. This was the union that was consummated somehow and sometime in the early 1850s, and out of which there issued the poem in which the union was itself reenacted.

There follows a long portion, continuing at least through Section 17, where—as a result of union—the *man* becomes a *poet,* and by the very act of creation. What is created is a world, an abundant world of persons and places and things—all sprung into existence by the action of seeing and naming:

> *The little one sleeps in its cradle,*
> *I lift the gauze and look a long time . . .*
> *The suicide sprawls on the bloody floor of the bedroom,*
> *I witness the corpse with its dabbled hair . . .*
> *Where are you off to, lady? for I see you.*

2. *The Continuity of American Poetry* (Princeton, N.J., 1961), especially pp. 59–82.

The democratic aesthetic is most palpably at work here. What we take at first to be sheer disorder, what some early reviewers regarded as simple slovenliness and lack of form, is in fact something rather different. It is the representation of moral and spiritual and aesthetic equality; of a world carefully devoid of rank or hierarchy. In "Song of Myself," this principle of moral equivalence is not so much stated as "suggested" (one of Whitman's favorite words), and suggested by "indirection" (another favorite word)—by the artfully casual juxtaposition of normally unrelated and unrelatable elements, a controlled flow of associations.[3] Thus:

> *The prostitute draggles her shawl, her bonnet bobs on her tipsy*
> *   and pimpled neck . . .*
> *The President holding a cabinet council is surrounded by the*
> *   great Secretaries,*
> *On the piazza walk three matrons stately and friendly with*
> *   twined arms,*
> *The crew of the fish-smack pack repeated layers of halibut in*
> *   the hold,*
> *The Missourian crosses the plains toting his wares and his*
> *   cattle*

and so on. In the 1855 Preface, Whitman was willing to make the case explicit: "Each precise object or condition or combination or process exhibits a beauty." And he there illustrated the idea in a succession of still more surprising incongruities: "the multiplication table . . . . old age . . . . the carpenter's trade . . . . the grand-opera."

When, therefore, toward the end of this phase of the poem, the speaker begins to claim for himself the gradually achieved role of poet, it is as the poet of every mode of equality that he particularly wishes to be acknowledged. The announcement runs through Section 25:

> *I play not marches for accepted victors only, I play marches*
> *   for conquer'd and slain persons . . .*
> *I am the poet of the Body, and I am the poet of the Soul. . . .*
> *I am the poet of the woman the same as the man . . .*
> *I am not the poet of goodness only, I do not decline to be the*
> *   poet of wickedness also.*

3. Cf. the essay on Whitman by David Daiches in *The Young Rebel in American Literature*, ed. Carl Bode (New York, 1960).

The *poet* now makes ready for the second great adventure, the long journey, as we may say, toward *godhood*. By way of preparation, he undergoes a second ecstatic experience in Sections 26 and following: an experience of an almost overpoweringly sensuous kind, with the sense of touch so keen as to endanger his health or his sanity: "You villain touch! . . . . you are too much for me." The poet survives, and in Section 33 he is "afoot with [his] vision." In the visionary flight across the universe that is then recounted, the poet enlarges into a divine being by *becoming* each and every element within the totality that he experiences; while the universe in turn is drawn together into a single and harmonious whole since each element in it is invested in common with a portion of the poet's emergent divinity. It is no longer the prostitute who draggles her shawl, the President who holds a cabinet council, the Missourian who crosses the plain: it is "I" who does all that:

> *I anchor my ship for a little while only . . .*
> *I go hunting polar furs and the seal . . .*
> *I am the man, I suffer'd, I was there . . .*
> *I am the hounded slave, I wince at the bite of dogs.*

And the "I" is itself no longer the individual man-poet; it is the very force or *élan vital* of all humanity.

The journey lasts through Section 33; and in its later moments, as will be noticed, the traveler associates especially with the defeated, the wretched, the wicked, the slaughtered. Whitman's poetic pores were oddly open, as were Melville's, to the grand or archetypal patterns common to the human imagination—so psychologists such as Carl Jung tell us—in all times and places; and the journey of "Song of Myself" requires, at this point, the familiar descent into darkness and hell—until (Section 33) "corpses rise, gashes heal, fastenings roll from me," and an enormous resurrection is accomplished. But what gets reborn, what "troop[s] forth" from the grave is not the poet simply; it is the poet "replenish'd with supreme power," the poet become a divine figure. Just as, by the poetic act of creating a world, the man had previously grown into a poet; so now, by experiencing and, so to speak, melting into the world's totality to its furthest width and darkest depth, the poet expands into a divinity. He has approximated at last that "greater than Socrates" invoked by Whitman in 1851; he has become that saving force which

Whitman had proposed was to be the true role of the American poet. It is the divinity who speaks through Sections 39 to 51, proclaiming his divine inheritance ("Taking to myself the exact dimensions of Jehovah," etc.), performing as healer and comforter ("Let the physician and the priest go home"), exhorting every man to his supreme and unique effort. For it is a divinity who insists at every turn that he speaks but for the divine potential of all men. And, having done so, in Section 52 he departs.

Wallace Stevens, the most sophisticated among Whitman's direct poetic descendants, once specified his ancestor's recurrent and dual subject matter in the course of a resonant salute to him in "Like Decorations in a Nigger Cemetery":

> *Walt Whitman walking along a ruddy shore*
> *. . . singing and chanting the things that are part of him*
> *The worlds that were and will be, death and day.*

"Death and day," with its corollary "life and night," is as apt a phrase as one can think of for the extremes between which Whitman's poetry habitually alternates. "Song of Myself" is Whitman's masterpiece, and perhaps America's, in the poetry of "day"—"the song of me rising from bed and meeting the sun"—while "To Think of Time" or "Burial Poem," as Whitman once called it, belongs initially to the poetry of "death," and "the Sleepers" to the poetry of "night." But although both the latter, in their very different ways, explore in depth the dark undergrounds of experience, both return—as "Song of Myself" does—with the conviction of a sort of absolute life. "I swear I think there is nothing but immortality": so ends the meditation in "To Think of Time." And such is the determining sense everywhere in the 1855 edition; we shall shortly have occasion to contrast it with the sense of things in the edition of 1860. It may be helpful, meanwhile, to glance at the 1855 poem "There Was a Child Went Forth," to see how Whitman's characteristic psychological movement was reflected in his poetic technique— how the shifting play of his consciousness was reflected in the shifting play of his craft.

"There Was a Child Went Forth" is Whitman's most unequiv-ocal account of the thrust toward being. It is a poem about growth, about burgeoning and sprouting; and it grows itself, quite literally, in size and thickness. The difference in the sheer physical or typographical look of the first and last stanzas is an immediate clue to the poem's thematic development. Yet what the poet enacts, on the technical side, is not an altogether uninterrupted increase in substance and vitality. The process is rather one of alternation, of enlarging and retracting, of stretching and shrinking—in which, however, the impulse toward growth is *always* dominant. The quantitatively shrunken fourth stanza, for example, is flanked by the longer eight-line stanza that precedes it and the longest or eighteen-line stanza that follows it and completes the poem's swelling motion: giving us a process in fact of stretching-shrinking-stretching. The same process is present more artfully still within the first stanza, with its rhythmic shift from short line to longer line to still longer and back to shorter once again; but where the line that contains the quantitative shrink is nonetheless a line accentuated by the word "stretching"—"Or for many years or stretching cycles of years." The psychic stretching is thus quietly affirmed at the instant of technical shrinking; and it is the stretching impulse that triumphs and defines the poem.

The same effect is accomplished metrically. "There Was a Child Went Forth" is what is now called free verse; and no doubt the word "free" in this context would have had, had Whitman known the whole term, a political aura, and become a part of his democratic aesthetic. Whitman was the first American poet to break free from the convention of iambic pentameter as the principal and most decorous meter for poetry in English; in so doing he added to the declaration of literary independence—from England, chiefly—that had been triumphantly proclaimed for his generation in Emerson's "The American Scholar" and was the predictable artistic consequence of the political fact. Whitman's was a major gesture of technical liberation, for which every American poet after him has reason to be grateful; every such poet, as William Carlos Williams (a manifest heir of Whitman) has said, must show cause why iambic pentameter is proper for him. But it was not an act of purely negative liberation; it was emancipation with a purpose. It freed Whitman to attempt a closer approximation of metrics and the kind of experience he naturally aimed to express; and it made possible an eventual and occasional return to older and more orderly metrics—to possess them, to use them freshly, to turn them to the poet's established poetic intentions. The long uneven alternations I have been describing could hardly have been conveyed by recurring five- and four-stress lines. Whitman instinctively depended, not on the regular alternating current of the iambic, but on an irregular alternation of *rising* and of *falling* rhythms—which corresponded happily to the rise and fall of the felt life, to the flowing and ebbing—and the rising rhythm, once again, is always in command:

There was a child went forth.

And in the poem's conclusion—when a world and a child have been brought fully to interdependent life—the rhythm settles back in a line that neither rises nor falls; a line that rests in a sort of permanent stillness; a subdued iambic of almost perfectly even stress—a convention repossessed in the last long slow series of monosyllables broken only and rightly by the key words "became," "always," and "every":

These became part of that child who went forth every day, and who now goes, and will always go forth every day.

It is not possible to invoke the imagery of stretching and shrinking without being reminded of sexual analogies, and thereby of the sexual element so prevalent in Whitman's poetry. That element was notably, even blatantly more central to the 1856 edition—it was about several poems in this edition that Thoreau, otherwise much taken with Whitman, said that "It is as if the beasts spoke"—and it operated most tellingly in 1860. Still, it was evident enough in 1855 to startle sensibilities. "Song of Myself" exhibits a degree of sexual bravado mixed with a trace of sexual nostalgia. But the sexual aspect is more apparent in the poem that inhabits the world where Freud and Jung would look for signs of the sexual impulse—the world of dreams. "The Sleepers"—or "Sleep-Chasings," according to its 1860 title—is not only a poem of night and death—"I wander all night in my visions . . . the white features of corpses"—it is a poem of profound psychic disturbance, as the speaker makes clear at once in a superb line that gained force from the 1855 typography: "Wandering and confused . . . . lost to myself . . . . ill-assorted . . . . contradictory." A portion of sexual shame contributes to the uncertainty and deepens the sense of terror—the terror, as Richard Chase has usefully hazarded, of the ego, or conscious self, confronting the id, or the unconscious, and being threatened by extinction.[4] But, in the manner typical of the first *Leaves of Grass,* the poem moves to the discovery of solace amid fear, of pattern amid the random. Descending through the planes of night, "The Sleepers" encounters in its own heart of darkness sources of maternal comfort and spiritual revelation. Guilt is transcended and harmony restored. The adjectives of the opening stanza—"wandering and confused, lost to myself, ill-assorted, contradictory"—are matched and overcome by the adjectives of the poem's close: "sane," "relieved," "resumed," "free," "supple," "awake." There has occurred what Jung would call the "reintegration of the personality"; the ill-assorted psyche has become whole again after passing through what Jung would also call the "night journey." In "The Sleepers," Whitman displayed once more his remarkable talent for arriving by intuition at the great archetypes. And the night journey concludes in that confident recovery of day, that perfect reconciliation with night, that is the distinctive mark of the edition of 1855.

II: 1856

The second edition of *Leaves of Grass* appeared in June 1856, less than a year after the first. There had been several more printings of the latter; and, indeed, during the intervening months Whitman was mainly occupied with the new printings and with reading—and writing—reviews of his work. He still lived with his family in Brooklyn, but he had virtually given up any practical employment. He had "no business," as his mother told Bronson Alcott, "but going out and coming in to eat, drink, write and sleep."[5] The same visitor from Concord quoted Whitman himself as saying that he only "lived to make pomes." Over the months he had made twenty new ones, and included them all in the considerably expanded second edition.

Conventional norms of printing crept back a little into this edition. All the poems, old and new, were now numbered and given titles, the new poems always including the word "poem" —a word that obviously had a magical power for Whitman at the time. Among the poems added were: "Poem of Wonder at

4. *Walt Whitman Reconsidered* (New York, 1955), pp. 54–57.
5. Roger Asselineau, *The Evolution of Walt Whitman* (New York, 1960), pp. 92–93.

the Resurrection of Wheat"—to be known more tamely as "This Compost"; "Bunch poem"—later "Spontaneous Me"; and "Sundown Poem"—later "Crossing Brooklyn Ferry." The physical appearance of the poems had also become a trifle more conventional, as the eccentric but effective use of multiple dots was abandoned in favor of semicolons and commas. The poetry lost thereby its vivid impression of sistole and diastole, of speech and silence, of utterance and pause, always so close to Whitman's psychic and artistic intention: for example, "I am the man . . . . I suffered . . . . I was there" gets crowded together by punctuation and contraction into "I am the man, I suffer'd, I was there." But the earlier mode of punctuation might well have become exceedingly tiresome; and Whitman, in any event, had arrived at that necessary combination of originality and convention by which the most vigorous of talents always perpetuates itself.

For the rest, the new poems dilate upon the determining theme and emotion of the first edition. There is still the awareness of evil, both general and personal: "I am he who knew what it was to be evil/ . . . Had guile, anger, lust, hot wishes I dared not speak/ . . . the wolf, the snake, the hog, not wanting in me" (an unmistakable and highly suggestive borrowing from *King Lear,* III.iv.87 ff.—Whitman drew more on literary sources than he or his critics have normally admitted). There is even a fleeting doubt of his own abilities—"The best I had done seem'd to me blank and suspicious"—a note that would become primary in the 1860 edition. But by and large the compelling emotion is one of unimpeded creative fertility, of irresistible forward-thrusting energy. It registers the enormous excitement of the discovered vocation and of its miracle-making nature: Whitman's response to the experience of having published his first volume and to the headiest of the reviews of the book. Contrary to some reports, including Whitman's forgetful old-age account, the first edition had a reasonably good sale; and among the many reviews in America and England, some were admiring, some were acutely perceptive, and one or two were downright reverential and spoke of Whitman as almost that "greater than Socrates" he had been hoping to become. Much the most stirring for Whitman, of course, was the famous letter from Emerson, which found *Leaves of Grass* "the most extraordinary piece of wit and wisdom that America has yet contributed," with "incomparable things said incomparably well in it." One sentence from this letter—and without Emerson's permission—adorned the back cover of the 1856 edition: "I greet you at the beginning of a great career."

The tone of the new poems, consequently, was one of achieved and boundless fertility. This is the poetry of day and the poetry of unending flow. The feeling, indeed, is so large and intense as to produce a sense of profound awe: a sense, almost, of terror. That sense arises from Whitman's convinced and total association of his own fecundity ("Spontaneous Me") with that of nature at large ("This Compost"), an association itself enough to intoxicate one. It arises, too, from Whitman's startling view that the creative accomplishment—of the man-poet and of nature—issues from something superficially ugly or shameful or diseased or dead. "Spontaneous Me" mingles two kinds of poems: those that result from the artistic act and those that are involved with the physical act. The act of love, the expression of sexual energy, whether metaphorical or physical, whether heterosexual or homosexual, carries with it a sweeping sensation of shame ("the young man all color'd, red, ashamed, angry"). But the experience fulfills itself in triumph and pride, just as Whitman had deliberately expanded the erotic dimension of the new volume in triumph and pride; it leads to a great "oath of procreation," procreation in every sort; it ends in a full consciousness of wholesome abundance. In much the same way, nature, in "This Compost," reproduces life each spring out of the rotting earth: "Every spear of grass rises out of what was once a catching disease." The conduct of nature—creating life out of death, health out of sickness, beauty out of foulness, "sweet things out of such corruption"—provided Whitman with an example, an analogy to his own creative experience, so immense as to terrify him.

The terror, needless to say, did not disempower but electrified him. The most far-ranging and beautiful of the new poems, "Crossing Brooklyn Ferry," shows Whitman writing under the full force of his assurance—of his assured identification with the *élan vital* of all things. The interplay of the self and the large world it thrusts forward into is on a scale not unlike that of "Song of Myself"; the flow of the consciousness merges with the flow of reality. Every item encountered is a "dumb beautiful minister" to Whitman's responsive spirit; all the items in the universe are "glories strung like beads on my smallest sights and hearings." The complex of natural and human and created objects now forms a sort of glowing totality that is always in movement, always frolicking on. "Crossing Brooklyn Ferry" presents a vision of an entirety moving forward: a vision that is mystical in its sense of oneness but that is rendered in the most palpable and concrete language—the actual picture of the harbor is astonishingly alive and visible. And the poem goes beyond its jubilant cry of the soul —"Flow on river!"—to reach a peace that really does surpass any normal understanding. Whitman was to write poetry no less consummate; but he was never again to attain so final a peak of creative and visionary intoxication.

III: 1860

Whitman, as we have heard his mother saying, was always "going out and coming in." She meant quite literally that her son would go out of the house in the morning, often to travel on the ferry to Manhattan and to absorb the spectacle of life, and would come back into the household to eat and sleep, perhaps to write. But she unwittingly gave a nice maternal formula to the larger, recurring pattern in Whitman's career—the foray into the world and the retreat back into himself and into a creative communion with his genius. The poetry he came in to write—through the 1856 edition just examined—reflected that pattern in content and rhythm, and in a way to celebrate the commanding power of the outward and forward movement. The early poetry bore witness as well, to be sure, of the darker mode of withdrawal, the descent into the abysses of doubt, self-distrust, and the death-consciousness; but it was invariably overcome in a burst of visionary renewal. The poetry of 1855 and 1856 is the poetry of day, of flood tide.

The 1860 *Leaves of Grass,* however, gives voice to genuine desolation. In it, betimes, the self appears as shrunken, indeed as fragmented; the psyche as dying; the creative vigor as dissipated. The most striking of the new poems belong to the poetry not of day but of death. A suggestive and immediate verbal sign of the new atmosphere may be found in the difference of title between so characteristic a poem of 1855 as "There Was a Child Went Forth" and perhaps the key 1860 poem, "As I Ebb'd with the Ocean of Life." Yet the case must be put delicately and by appeal to paradox. For, in a sense, the new death poetry represents in fact Whitman's most remarkable triumph over his strongest feelings of personal and artistic defeat. There has been a scholarly debate over the precise degree of melancholy in the 1860 edition, one scholar emphasizing the note of dejection and another the occasional note of cheerfulness; but that debate is really beside the point. What we have is poetry that expresses the sense of loss so sharply and vividly that substantive loss is converted into artistic gain.

During the almost four years since June 1856, Whitman had once again gone out and come back in; but this time the withdrawal was compelled by suffering and self-distrust. Whitman's foray into the open world, beginning in the fall of 1856, took the form, first, of a brief new interest in the political scene and, second, of a return to journalism, as editor-in-chief of the Brooklyn *Daily Times* from May 1857 until June 1859. In the morning, he busied himself writing editorials and articles for the newspaper; in the afternoon, he traveled into New York, to saunter along lower Broadway and to sit watchful and silent near or amid the literati who gathered in Pfaff's popular Swiss restaurant in the same neighborhood. In the evening, he continued to write—prolifically: seventy poems, more or less, in the first year after the 1856 edition and probably a few more in the months immediately following. Then there occurred a hiatus: a blank in our knowledge of Whitman's life, and apparently a blank in his creative activity. We cannot say just when the hiatus began—sometime in 1858, one judges. It ended, anyhow, at some time before the publication in the December 1859 issue of the New York *Saturday Press* of a poem called "A Child's Reminiscence," its familiar title being "Out of the Cradle Endlessly Rocking."

On the political side, Whitman's disenchantment was even swifter than usual. The choices offered the American public in the election of 1856—Buchanan, Frémont, and Fillmore—seemed to him false, debased, and meaningless; and he called—in an unpublished pamphlet—for a president who might play the part of "Redeemer." His disappointment with the actual, in short, led as before to an appeal for some "greater than Socrates" to arise in America; and, also as before, Whitman soon turned from the political figure to the *poet,* in fact to himself, to perform the sacred function, asserting in his journal that *Leaves of Grass* was to be "the New Bible." (Not until 1866 would the two aspirations fuse in a poem—"When Lilacs Last in the Dooryard Bloom'd"—that found a new idiom of almost biblical sonority to celebrate death in the person of a Redeemer President, Abraham Lincoln.) Meanwhile, however, Whitman's private and inner life was causing him far more grief and dismay than the public life he had been observing.

A chief cause for Whitman's season of despair, according to most Whitman biographers, was a homosexual love affair during the silent months: an affair that undoubtedly took place, that was the source at once of profound joy and profound guilt, and that, when it ended, left Whitman with a desolating sense of loss. Such poems as "A Hand-Mirror" and "Hours Continuing Long, Sore and Heavy-Hearted" testify with painful clarity both to the guilt and to the subsequent misery of loneliness. At the same time, poems such as "As I Ebb'd with the Ocean of Life" and "So Long!" strike a different and perhaps deeper note of loss: a note, that is, of poetic decline, of the loss not so much of a human loved one but of creative energy—accompanied by a loss of confidence in everything that energy had previously brought into being. There had been a hint of this in "Crossing Brooklyn Ferry" in 1856— "The best I had done seem'd to me blank and suspicious"—but there self-doubt had been washed away in a flood of assurance. Now it had become central and almost resistant to hope. It may be that the fear of artistic sterility was caused by the moral guilt; but it seems no less likely that the artistic apprehension was itself at the root of the despair variously echoed in 1860. If so, the apprehension was probably due to a certain climacteric in Whitman's psychic career—what is called *la crise de quarantaine,* the psychological crisis some men pass through when they reach the age of forty. Whitman was forty in May 1859; and it was in the month after his birthday that he wrote two aggressive and, one cannot but feel, disturbed articles for the Brooklyn *Daily Times*—on prostitution and the right to unmarried sexual love—that resulted in his dismissal from the paper. Characteristically dismissed, Whitman characteristically withdrew. But no doubt the safest guess is that a conjunction of these factors—*la quarantaine,* the temporary but fearful exhaustion of talent after so long a period of fertility, the unhappy love affair—begot the new poems that gave "death and night" their prominence in the 1860 edition.

The edition of 1860 contained 154 poems: which is to say that 122 had been composed since 1856, and of these, as has been said, seventy by the summer of 1857. Most of the other fifty, it can be hazarded, were written late in 1859 and in the first six months of 1860. It can also be hazarded that among those latter fifty poems were nearly all the best of the new ones—those grouped under the title "Calamus," the name Whitman gave to his poetry of masculine love. These include "Scented Herbage," "Hours Continuing," "Whoever You Are," "City of Orgies," "A Glimpse," "I Saw in Louisiana," "Out of the Cradle," "As I Ebb'd" (published in the April 1860 issue of the *Atlantic Monthly* as "Bardic Symbols"), and "So Long!"

"A Hand-Mirror" records a feeling of self-loathing almost unequaled in English or American poetry. And it is representative of the entire volume in its emphatic reversal of an earlier work and an earlier course of feeling. In "This Compost," in 1856, Whitman was seized with a wonder verging on terror at the capacity of nature and of man to produce the beautiful out of the foul or shameful; here, in 1860, he is smitten with the dreadful conviction of having, in his own being, produced the foul and the shameful out of the potentially beautiful. "Hours Continuing Long, Sore and Heavy-Hearted" is a statement of pain so severe, so unmitigated, that Whitman deleted the poem from all subsequent editions of *Leaves of Grass*. These poems of pain are uncommonly painful to read; and yet, in the other major new poems of 1860, we find Whitman executing what might be called the grand Romantic strategy—the strategy of converting private devastation into artistic achievement; of composing poetry of high distinction out of a feeling of personal, spiritual, and almost metaphysical *ex*tinction. Keats's "Ode on a Grecian Urn" offers an example of the same, at one chronological extreme; as, at another, does Hart Crane's "The Broken Tower."

That strategy is, indeed, what the 1860 edition may be said to be about; for more than the other versions of *Leaves of Grass,* that of 1860 has a sort of plot buried in it.[6] The plot—in a very reduced summary—consists in the discovery that "death" is the source and beginning of "poetry"; with "death" here understood to involve several kinds and sensations of loss, of suffering, of disempowering guilt, of psychic fragmentation; and "poetry" as the awakening of the power to catch and to order reality in language. What had so fundamentally changed since 1855 and 1856 was Whitman's concept of reality. In 1855, as we have seen, the thought of death led to a flat denial of it: "I swear I think there is

6. See the Facsimile Edition of the 1860 text, edited with an introduction by Roy Harvey Pearce (Ithaca, N.Y., 1961).

nothing but immortality." But in "Scented Herbage" of 1860 he arrives at an opposite conclusion: "For now," as he says, "it is convey'd to me that you [death] are . . . the real reality." If Whitman's poetic faculty had formerly been quickened by his sense of the absolute life, it now finds its inspiration in the adventure of death. In "So Long!" Whitman confesses to the death of his talent: "It appears to me that I am dying. . . . My songs cease, I abandon them." Yet in "Scented Herbage" poetry is identified as the very herbage and flower of death, as Baudelaire had a few years earlier identified poetry as the flower of evil; his new poems, for Whitman, are "growing up above me above death." By 1860 Whitman had reached the perception of Wallace Stevens—in "Sunday Morning" (1923)—that "death is the mother of beauty."

Stevens' phrase might serve as motto for the 1860 edition; as it might also serve for another of the several titles for the poem that was first called "A Child's Reminiscence," then "A Word Out of the Sea," and finally (in 1871) "Out of the Cradle Endlessly Rocking." Whatever else occurs in this in every sense brilliant poem, there unmistakably occurs the discovery of poetic power, the magical power of the word, through the experience —here presented as vicarious—of the departure and loss, perhaps the death, of the loved one. It is one of the most handsomely *made* of Whitman's poems; the craft is relaxed, firm, and sure. Only an artist in virtuoso control of his technical resources would attempt a poem with such effortless alternation of narrative (or recitatif) and impassioned aria, such dazzling metrical shifts, such hypnotic exactitude of language, not to mention a narrative "point of view" of almost Jamesian complexity: the man of forty recalling the child of, say, twelve observing the calamitous love affair of two other beings, and the same man of forty projecting, one assumes, his own recent and adult bereavement into the experience of an empathic child. Whitman, by 1860, was very impressively the poet in that word's original meaning of "maker," in addition to being still the poet as inspired singer; and "Out of the Cradle Endlessly Rocking"—for all its supple play of shadows and glancing light—will bear the utmost weight of analysis. But it has perhaps been sufficiently probed elsewhere,[7] and I will instead take a longer look at "As I Ebb'd with the Ocean of Life."

7. For example, in the four essays by Stephen E. Whicher, Paul Fussell, Jr., Richard Chase, and Roy Harvey Pearce contained in *The Presence of Walt Whitman*, ed. R. W. B. Lewis (New York, 1962).

We will not be far wrong, and in any case it will illuminate the pattern of Whitman's career, if we take this poem as an almost systematic inversion of the 1855 poem "There Was a Child Went Forth," as well as an inversion of a key moment—Sections 4 and 5—in the 1855 "Song of Myself." As against that younger Whitman of morning and of spring, of the early lilacs and the red morning-glories, here is the Whitman of the decline of the day and of the year—a poet now found "musing late in the autumn day" (the phrase should be read slowly, as though the chief words were, in the older fashion, divided by dots). All the sprouts and blossoms and fruit of "There Was a Child Went Forth" are here replaced, in the poetically stunning second stanza by:

> *Chaff, straw, splinters of wood, weeds, and the sea-gluten,*
> *Scum, scales from shining rocks, leaves of salt-lettuce, left*
>   *by the tide;*

to which are added, later, "A few sands and dead leaves," "a trail of drift and debris," and finally:

>   *loose windrows, little corpses,*
> *Froth, snowy white, and bubbles,*
> *(See, from my dead lips the ooze exuding at last . . . .)*

The poem's rhythm, instead of pulsating outward in constantly larger spirals (though it seems to try to do that occasionally), tends to fall back on itself, to fall away, almost to disintegrate; no poem of Whitman's shows a more cunning fusion of technique and content. It is here, quite properly, the falling rather than the rising rhythm that catches the ear. As against:

> *There was a child went forth,*

we now hear:

> *Where the fierce old mother endlessly cries for her castaways*

—a dying fall that conveys the shrinking away, the psychological slide toward death, the slope into oblivion that the poem is otherwise concerned with.

The major turn in the action appears in the grammatical shift from the past tense of Section 1 ("As I ebb'd," etc.) to the present tense of Section 2 ("As I wend," etc.). It is a shift from the known to the unknown, a shift indeed not so much from one moment of time to another as from the temporal to the timeless, and a shift not so much accomplished as desired. For what produces in the poet his feeling of near-death is just his conviction that neither he nor his poetry has ever known or ever touched upon the true and timeless realm of reality. The essential reality from which he now feels he has forever been cut off is rendered as "the real Me." To get the full force of the despondent confession of failure, one should place the lines about "the real Me" next to those in Sections 4 and 5 in "Song of Myself" where Whitman had exultantly recalled the exact opposite. There he had celebrated a perfect union between the actual Me and the real Me: between the here-and-now Whitman and that timeless being, that Over-Soul or genius that he addressed as the Me myself. *That,* I suggest, was Whitman's real love affair; that was the union that was consummated in 1855 and that ended—so Whitman temporarily felt—in disunion three or four years later; "the real Me" was the loved one that departed. And now, divorced and disjoined from the real Me, the actual Me threatens to come apart, to collapse into a trail of drift and debris, with ooze exuding from dead lips. (So, by analogy, a Puritan might have felt when cut off, through sin, from the God that created him.)

Still, as Richard Chase has insisted, this poem is saved from any suggestion of whimpering self-pity by the astonishing and courageous tone of self-mockery—in the image of the real Me ridiculing the collapsing Me:

> *before all my arrogant poems the real Me stands yet untouch'd, untold, altogether unreach'd,*
> *Withdrawn far, mocking me with mock-congratulatory signs and bows,*
> *With peals of distant ironical laughter at every word I have written,*
> *Pointing in silence to these songs, and then to the sand beneath.*

It is an image of immeasurable effect. And it is, so to speak, a triumph over its own content. Anyone who could construct an image of the higher power—the one he aspires toward—standing far off and mocking him with little satiric bows and gestures, comparing and consigning his verses to the sandy debris under his feet: such a person has already conquered his sense of sterility, mastered his fear of spiritual and artistic death, rediscovered his genius, and returned to the fullest poetic authority. Within the poem, Whitman identifies the land as his father and the fierce old sea as his mother; he sees himself as alienated no less from them than from the real Me, and he prays to both symbolic parents for a rejuvenation of his poetic force, a resumption of "the secret of the murmuring I envy." But the prayer is already answered in the very language in which it is uttered; Whitman never murmured more beautifully; and this is why, at the depth of his ebbing, Whitman can say, parenthetically, that the flow will return.

IV: 1867

If Whitman, by the spring of 1860, had not been "rescued" by his own internal capacity for resurgence, he would, more than likely, have been rescued anyhow by the enormous public event that began the following April with the outbreak of a national civil war. During the war years, Whitman "went forth" more strenuously than in any other period of his life, and he immersed himself more thoroughly in the activities and sufferings of his fellows. The immediate poetic fruit of the experience was a small, separately published volume of fifty-three new poems, in 1865, called *Drum-Taps,* with a *Sequel to Drum-Taps*—containing "When Lilacs Last in the Dooryard Bloom'd"—tacked on to the original in 1866. Both titles were added as an Appendix to the fourth edition of *Leaves of Grass* in 1867, which otherwise contained only a handful of new poems. Several of Whitman's war poems have a certain lyric strength, either of compassion or of sheer imagistic precision; and the meditation occasioned by the death of Lincoln is among his finest artistic achievements. Nonetheless—and however remarkable and admirable his human performance was during the war—it was in this same period that Whitman the poet began to yield to Whitman the prophet, and what had been most compelling in his poetry to give way to the misrepresentation and concealment that disfigured *Leaves of Grass* over the decades to follow.

Until the last days of 1862, Whitman remained in Brooklyn, formally unemployed, making what he could out of earnings from *Leaves of Grass,* and—once the fighting had started—following the course of the war with the liveliest concern. He was initially very much on the side of the North, which he regarded as the side of freedom, justice, and human dignity. But as time went on, he came to be increasingly on the side of the nation as a whole, more anxious to heal wounds than to inflict them—and this, of course, is what he literally turned to doing in 1863. In December of the previous year, he learned that his younger brother Jeff had been wounded. Whitman journeyed south at once, found his brother recuperating satisfactorily near Falmouth, Virginia, and stayed for eight memorable days among the forward troops in the battle area. It was only eight days, but the spectacle of horror and gallantry of which he was the closest eyewitness had an enduring, almost a conversionary effect upon him. He came back north only as far as Washington; and from that moment until 1867, he spent every free moment in the military hospitals, ministering to the needs of the wounded. He became, in fact, a "wound-dresser," though a dresser primarily of spiritual wounds, bearing gifts, writing letters, comforting, sustaining, exhorting; he became, indeed, the physician-priest with whom, in "Song of Myself," he had associated the figure of the poet.

He made a living in Washington through a series of governmental jobs: as assistant to the deputy paymaster for a while; as clerk in the Indian Bureau—a position from which he was summarily dismissed when the bureau chief read *Leaves of Grass* and pronounced it unpardonably obscene; finally in the office of the Department of Interior. Here he stayed, relatively prosperous and content, until he suffered a partly paralyzing stroke in 1873. It was in the same year that, traveling north, ill and exhausted, he settled almost by accident in Camden, New Jersey, where he lived until his death in 1892.

In short, when Whitman went forth this time, or was drawn forth, into the American world of war, he was drawn not merely into New York City but into the center of the country's national life; to the actual battlefields, to the seat of the nation's political power, to the offices of government, to the hospitals, and into the presence of the men who carried on their bodies the burden of the nation's tragedy. It is not surprising that the outer and public life of the country absorbed most of his energy; it is only regrettable that, as a result, and in the course of time, the solitary singer disappeared into the public bard, into the singer of democracy, of companionship, the singer not of "this compost" but of "these States." This was the figure celebrated by William Douglas O'Connor in a book written as an angry and rhapsodic

defense of Whitman at the time of his dismissal from the Indian Bureau; a book which, in its title, provided the phrase which all but smothered the genuine Whitman for almost a century: *The Good Gray Poet* (1866).

There had been a faint but ominous foreshadowing of the good gray poet in the 1860 edition: in the frontispiece, where Whitman appeared for the first time as the brooding, far-gazing prophetic figure; in the first tinkerings with and slight revisions of the earlier poems; and in the group of poems called "Chants Democratic," the volume's major blemish. The 1867 edition had no frontispiece at all; but now the process of revising, deleting, and rearranging was fully at work. A number of the "Calamus" poems on manly love, for example, were removed from *Leaves of Grass* once and for all: those which acknowledged or deplored his erotic attraction to another man—including "Hours Continuing." The sexuality of "Song of Myself" and "The Sleepers" was toned down by deleting in particular the orgasmic imagery in both of them. Much of the bizarre and the frantic was taken out of the 1856 and 1860 poetry, in the interest, as Roger Asselineau has put it, of placing "the accent on the poet-prophet rather than on the lover."[8] In a general way, it was the intense and personal *self* of Whitman that got shaded over by the new editing—that self, in its always rhythmic and sometimes wild oscillations, that was the true source and subject of the true poetry. The private self was reshaped into the public person, and the public stage on which this person chanted and intoned became the major subject of the would-be national bard. Whitman became less and less the original artist singing by indirection of his own psychic advances and retreats; he was becoming and wanted to become the Poet of Democracy. No longer the watchful solitary, he was changing into the Poet of Comradeship.

It should not be assumed that, because these were postures, they were necessarily false or worthless; they were simply uncongenial to Whitman's kind of poetry. In the same year, 1867, that *Leaves of Grass* unveiled the prophet of the democratic culture, Whitman also published in the New York *Galaxy* a prose essay called "Democracy," where he set forth much of the evidence that, a few years later, went into the longer essay

8. *The Evolution of Walt Whitman,* p. 196.

"Democratic Vistas"—as cogent and searching an account of the conditions of democracy in America, and of their relation to the life of letters, as any American has ever written. But what Whitman could do with this material in prose, he could not do effectively in verse. The democratic element in the early poems was, as has been suggested, an aesthetic element. It was part of the very stress and rhythm of the verse, implicit in the poet's way of looking at persons and things, in the principle of equality in his catalogues and the freedom of his meters, in the dynamic of his relation to his readers. Tackling democracy head on in poetry, Whitman became unpersuasive, even boring.

In the same way, Whitman's poems about the actual war were least striking when they were least personal. There is critical disagreement on this point, but in one reader's opinion, Melville wrote far more authentic war poetry because he had what Whitman did not—a powerful sense of history as allegory. In "The Conflict of Convictions," for example, Melville could suggest the thrust and scale of the struggle in a frame of grand tragedy and in a somberly prophetic mode that the aspiring prophet, Whitman, could never approach. Whitman, the man, had entered the public arena, but his muse did not follow him there; and the enduring poems culled from the war are rather of the intimate and lyrical variety—tender reminiscences or crisp little vignettes like "Cavalry Crossing a Ford," where the image is everything.

There appears among these poems, however, like an unexpected giant out of an earlier age, the work that is widely regarded as Whitman's supreme accomplishment: "When Lilacs Last in the Dooryard Bloom'd." This poem does not, in fact, have quite the artistic finality of "As I Ebb'd" or "Out of the Cradle"; or, rather, its finality is more on the surface, where it is asserted, than in the interior and self-completing pulse of the verses. But, like the other two poems just named, "When Lilacs Last in the Dooryard Bloom'd"—a string of words, D. H. Lawrence once said, that mysteriously makes the ear tingle—has to do with the relation between death and poetry. The death of Lincoln provided the occasion, and the emergent grief of an entire nation served as large but distant background. What is enacted in the foreground, however, is what so often summoned up Whitman's most genuine power: the effort to come to terms with profound sorrow by converting that sorrow into poetry. By finding the language of mourning, Whitman found the answer to the challenge of death. By focusing not on the public event but rather on the vibrations *of* that event—vibrations converted into symbols —within his private self, Whitman produced one of his masterpieces, and perhaps his last unmistakable one.

V: 1871 and Later

The transformation that both Whitman's figure and his work had slowly undergone was acknowledged by Whitman himself in his Preface to the fifth edition of *Leaves of Grass,* which had two identical printings in 1871 and 1872, while Whitman was still in Washington. The earlier editions, he said, had dealt with the *"Democratic Individual"* (the italics are his); in the new edition, he is concerned instead with the "Vast, composite, electric *Democratic Nationality."* It was never clear just what the latter entity amounted to; and in any case, Whitman was not able to make it susceptible to satisfactory poetic expression. It became the subject not of poetry but of oratory and rant—elements that had always been present in Whitman's work but that, for the most part, had hitherto been sweetened by music and, as it were, liquified by verbal sea-drift.

Oratory and rant were unhappily notable even in the most interesting of the new poems added to the 1871 edition, "Passage to India." But the case of "Passage to India" is peculiar. It was stimulated by several public events (including, for one, the opening of the Suez Canal), stimuli usually dangerous for Whitman unless he could instantly personalize them, as here he could not. The poem not only bespeaks the ultimate union of all times and places and peoples but finds in that condition a universal reality; and as Richard Chase has remarked, "Whenever [Whitman] headed for the universal he was headed for trouble." The poem moves swiftly away from the tough entanglements of the concrete that were the vital strength of works as different as "Song of Myself" or "Crossing Brooklyn Ferry" or "As I Ebb'd"; and, arriving at a realm of bodiless vapor, Whitman can only utter such bodiless lines as: "the past—the infinite greatness of the past!"—which is an exclamation without content. Yet "Passage to India" is interesting, because, while providing an example of Whitman's bombast, it is also technically most accomplished. It completes a kind of parabola of Whitman's craftsmanship: from 1855, where consciousness and craft were discovering each other; through 1856 and 1860, where power and technique were very closely fused; to the later sixties, where technique almost superseded content. The technique in question is primarily a manipulation of sound patterns, something too involved to be analyzed here in detail: an extremely skillful distribution of sheer sounds, without any regard for substance. "Passage to India" is interesting too, by way of historical footnote, for the obsessive effect it was to have more than fifty years later on Hart Crane. It virtually supplied the initiating force for *The Bridge,* especially for the "Atlantis" section, the first portion of his symbolist epic that Crane composed.

Whitman spent the last nineteen years of his life in Camden, New Jersey. He made a partial recovery from the stroke of 1873, but then suffered further seizures from time to time until the one that carried him off. In between these bouts, he continued to "go out" as much as he could: to nearby Philadelphia frequently, to Baltimore and Washington, to New York, and once —in 1879—to Kansas, Colorado, and Canada. Otherwise he remained in Camden, writing short and generally trivial poems, a great amount of prose, and countless letters to friends and admirers all over the world. His old age was punctuated by a series of controversies about him in the public press: in 1876, for example, when a clamor from England to raise a subscription for Whitman was countered by a verbal assault upon him in the New York *Tribune* by Bayard Taylor. The charge was almost always obscenity; in the instance mentioned, the charge only aroused the English to greater efforts, and Whitman was so encouraged as to feel, in his own word, "saved" by the contributions —then and later—of Rossetti, Tennyson, Ruskin, Gosse, Saintsbury, and others. Longfellow and Oscar Wilde, old Dr. Holmes and Henry James, Sr., were among the visitors to his Camden home. He became the genius of the city; and his birthday became an annual celebration. It was amid such flurries of support and defamation, idolatry and contempt, that the old man—cheerful and garrulous to the end—succumbed at last to a horde of diseases that would have killed most men many years sooner.

Whitman *was,* as M. Asselineau says of him, a "heroic invalid." But it may be that his physical and psychological heroism as a man was what produced, by overcompensating for the terrible discomforts he felt, the relentless optimism of so much of his writing in the last two decades—optimism not only about himself and his condition, but about America and about history: for which and in which every disaster, every betrayal was seen by Whitman as a moment in the irresistible progress of things toward the better. The "word signs" of his poetry after 1867 became, as Whitman himself remarked in *A Backward Glance O'er Travel'd Roads* (1888), "Good Cheer, Content and Hope," along with "Comradeship for all lands." Those were also the words that fixed and froze the popular understanding of the poet.

Mention of *A Backward Glance,* however, reminds one that Whitman's most valuable work after 1867 tended to be in prose rather than in verse. The sixth edition of *Leaves of Grass,* printed in 1876 and called the "Centennial Edition" (America's centennial—America now being Whitman's subject), added almost no significant new poetry; but it did include the remarkable essay "Democratic Vistas." The latter poises a noble emphasis upon individual integrity against the moral squalor of a society that was already an impossible mixture of chaos and conformity; and in its plea for "national original archetypes in literature" that will truly "put the nation in form," it presents one of the great statements about the relation between art and culture. The next or seventh edition, that of 1881–82, contained the fine little image of the copulative collision of two eagles—an image based on a written description of such an event by Whitman's friend John Burroughs—and a poem that, with two others, gave cause for the suppression of the entire volume, following a complaint by the Society for the Prevention of Vice. But this edition was also characterized by endless revisions and expurgations and, now especially, regroupings of earlier poems: the process whereby the old man steadily buried his youth. In the same year, though, Whitman also published a separate volume of prose: *Specimen Days and Collect.* In it, along with *Specimen Days* and the several indispensable prefaces to *Leaves of Grass,* were "Democratic Vistas," Civil War reminiscences, and Whitman's annual lecture on Lincoln. *A Backward Glance* first appeared in 1888; the following year it served as the Preface to, and was the one memorable new piece of writing in, the *Leaves of Grass* of 1889.

Though it is indeed memorable and even beguiling, *A Backward Glance* is also somewhat misleading. The real motivations and the actual achievement of *Leaves of Grass* lie half-forgotten behind the comradeship, good cheer, and democratic enthusiasm of the ailing elderly bard. Like F. Scott Fitzgerald, Whitman could have said, though one cannot imagine him doing so, that he had found his proper form at a certain moment in his career, but that he had then been diverted into other forms, other endeavors less appropriate to his talent. The fact that it was in these other forms that Whitman's reputation got established make the development more lamentable. At his best, Whitman was not really the bard of the democratic society at all; nor was he the prophet of the country's and the world's glorious future. He was, perhaps, the poet of an aesthetic and moral democracy. But he was above all the poet of the self and of the self's swaying motion —outward into a teeming world where objects were "strung like beads of glory" on his sight; backward into private communion with the "real Me." He was the poet of the self's motion downward into the abysses of darkness and guilt and pain and isolation, and upward to the creative act in which darkness was transmuted into beauty. When the self became lost to the world, Whitman was lost for poetry. But before that happened, Whitman had, in his own example, made poetry possible in America.

1961

MELVILLE AFTER *MOBY-DICK*

"Failure is the true test of greatness," Herman Melville remarked in his essay on Hawthorne (1850). He was speaking of the artist's need to risk defeat by constantly attempting more demanding and original creative enterprises; and, like Faulkner in our day, Melville always honored the daring failure over the safe success. "If it be said," he contended (half anticipating Faulkner's remark about Hemingway), "that continual success is a proof that a man wisely knows his powers, it is only to be added that, in that case, he knows them to be small." Melville must have known his own powers to be great ones: he was, at the very moment, in the midst of his most powerful work and spectacular critical failure, *Moby-Dick*. But just as he had a zest for the overreaching artistic effort, so Melville grew to have a special psychological affinity with defeat, almost a bias toward it. "Praise be to God for the failure!" is the motto of one of his slighter stories;[1] and in *The Encantadas* he located his symbol of worshipable humanity "not in the laureled victor, but in this vanquished one," Hunilla, the Chola widow. It is in a context of such affinities and beliefs that the writing here examined is to be measured.

I: Tales and Poems

For the most part, the stories and poems written after *Moby-Dick* represented new directions for Melville's imagination, new challenges to his shaping power; and they were written during what are generally regarded as Melville's long years of failure, neglect,

1. "The Happy Failure: A Story of the River Hudson" (1854).

and silence—following the large misunderstanding of *Moby-Dick* and the critical catastrophe of *Pierre* (1852). Some of the items were no doubt, as Melville said about his book-length poem *Clarel* to an English admirer, "Eminently adapted for unpopularity," given the habits and expectations of the American reading public in Melville's lifetime. But, while the imagery of defeat and of physical wreckage and spiritual ruin abounds, Melville's work after *Pierre* and in media other than the novel comprises an extraordinarily successful achievement. It is a body of work, moreover, that expresses a steadily deepening tone of authority —even, perhaps, of metaphysical and religious authority. In those buried years, Melville came to speak in all eloquence with what Scott Fitzgerald would call "the authority of failure."

Still, it is useful to approach that achievement and that authority from the moment of Melville's encounter with Nathaniel Hawthorne. They met in 1850, not long after Melville, in the immensity of his enthusiasm for *Mosses from an Old Manse,* contributed the essay on Hawthorne to the *Literary World.* Most of what Melville had to say in that essay—his metaphysical expostulations, his insight into Shakespearean tragedy, his passion for paradox as the great vehicle of truth, his search for the robustly native American writer, his sense of the fellowship of creative genius the world round—this tells us, of course, a good deal more about Melville's view of life and of art than about Hawthorne's. But as a result of "Hawthorne and his Mosses," there developed between the two men the most illuminating relationship in the history of American literature; not the less illuminating because it was strained and flawed and doomed to brevity; and not less because, although each had much to teach the other (Melville felt that "this Hawthorne has dropped germinous seeds into my soul"), the writers were in fact moving in almost exactly opposite directions.

Melville's letters chart the course of this curious friendship. "When the big hearts strike together," he wrote Hawthorne, "the concussion is a little stunning." But Melville had a more avid taste than did Hawthorne for intellectual and emotional concussion; as, one feels sure, he did for the "ontological heroics" he speaks of looking forward to enjoying with the older man. On Melville's side, the relationship reached its peak of intensity in the almost uncontrollable and mystical excitement with which he acknowledged Hawthorne's reception (evidently both discerning and sympathetic) of *Moby-Dick*. At that instant, Melville felt Hawthorne to be a "divine magnet" to whom "my magnet responds"; he felt that "the Godhead is broken up like the bread at the Supper," and that he and Hawthorne were the pieces. Hawthorne did not have the temperament to reply in kind; and in the following year, when Melville was being so savagely belabored in the press for *Pierre,* the friendship seems to have gone stale—perhaps, as one or two critics have suggested, because neither Hawthorne nor anyone else could have supplied Melville with the kind of protection and comfort he thought he needed. The last extant letter is dated November 1852; and shortly thereafter Hawthorne went abroad for a long stay. The two men met at least once again in 1856, when Melville stopped off for a few days with the Hawthornes in Liverpool; but Melville was to believe that they had been "estranged in life/ And neither in the wrong." Such was the burden of Melville's "Monody," a poem that is almost certainly Melville's obituary both to Hawthorne and to their friendship.

But, as I have said, these two enormously gifted spirits were moving in opposite directions from the moment they met; and it was only Melville's constant fascination with the mating of opposites that made any friendship at all possible between them. To begin with, Melville, in 1850, had five novels behind him (*Typee, Omoo, Mardi, Redburn,* and *Whitejacket*); he was occupied with *Moby-Dick* and after that with *Pierre;* but his novelistic aspirations were becoming ever more thwarted, and within a couple of years his energies and interests would turn decisively toward the shorter form, toward the story or tale or novella. In 1850, Hawthorne, on the other hand, was done with the shorter form; he had behind him a number of masterful stories and tales, and his endeavors in this vein had reached their climax and end in that very great novella *The Scarlet Letter;* he had, indeed, already advanced into the field of long fiction and had almost completed the first of his "novels," *The House of the Seven Gables.* By the time (in August 1852) that Melville urged Hawthorne to make a tale similar to Hawthorne's own "Wakefield," out of the "Agatha anecdote," the proposal was in every sense anachronistic. Hawthorne was right, in his evasive but kindly way, to suggest instead that Melville should undertake the thing. And Melville did, though without success; it was his first invasion of the short story, and it led swiftly enough to *Bartleby* and *The Encantadas.*

More importantly, Melville and Hawthorne congenitally moved in opposite directions of mental and imaginative inquiry: as one sentence in Melville's letter about "Agatha" reminds us. Concluding his ruminations, Melville tells Hawthorne: "You have a skeleton of actual reality to build about with fulness & veins & beauty." The remark bespeaks Melville's customary method: that of beginning with the actual, the bare bones of the case, often with the personally experienced, and then enlarging by the resources of art toward fullness and beauty. His writing at its best seems to be palpably thickening and stretching, as the actual gives birth to some breath-taking glimpse into the generalized condition of man. Melville's characteristic accomplishment (for example, in *The Encantadas*) was to move from a sort of journalistic immediacy to an exposure of some grave and permanent principle or element that must be at work (even if perniciously at work) in human experience; his creative torment was the awareness, which he often dramatized, that the effort so to expand, to enlarge, was incalculably difficult. Such, however, was neither Hawthorne's accomplishment nor his torment. Although he did of course draw upon the actual and his own experience, nonetheless, and especially in his shorter fiction, Hawthorne habitually began with some perennial human impulse and then sought for the concrete terms by which he might embody it. Hawthorne, in a word, really did approach the allegorical mode, though little that he wrote can be classed as pure allegory; but Melville, for all his allegorical hints and leanings, approached rather the form of the fable. All the difference between them can be suggested by comparing Hawthorne's "Wakefield" (which Melville so admired) and Melville's *Bartleby*. Both are accounts of self-impelled isolates; Wakefield is "the Outcast of the Universe," and Bartleby seems "alone, absolutely alone in the universe." But Hawthorne's capital letters point to a fixed type of human situation that he is, primarily, trying to illustrate; while much of the odd charm of *Bartleby* is its tantalizing escape from fixity. Bartleby remains a mystery just because he is irredeemably an individual, not finally and fully explicable by any general theory of human conduct, toward which the creative effort nonetheless inclines.

Hawthorne must have taught Melville a good deal about the formal possibilities of fiction; and his talent for the dark insinuation must have encouraged Melville in his desire (as he says about Shakespeare in the Hawthorne essay) to express the "deep far-way things in him," to probe "the very axis of reality." Hawthorne's fiction also provided Melville with the major example in America of the poetic resource by which such probing could be attempted—the resource of the complex symbol. On his part, Hawthorne was perhaps reminded by Melville of the inestimable value of the particular, the potent vitality of the immediate: certainly, *The Blithedale Romance,* the only work of fiction that Hawthorne began and completed during the years in question, is by all odds his most "realistic" work, the one most rooted in the actual. But then they moved on, in literally and physically opposite directions—Hawthorne away from the obscurity of a customs house into the bright light of quite considerable popularity; Melville away from his own considerable popularity toward the obscurity of his own eventual job as a customs inspector—and between them there fell a silence.

When Melville said in *The Encantadas* that he worshiped humanity not in the figure of the victor but in the figure of the vanquished, he was giving precise statement to the tragic sense that possessed him in the 1850s. It is a sense that communicates more directly to our own age of wholesale wreckage and defeat —when the laurels go so often and so resoundingly to the worst of men and of causes—than it did to the confident America of Melville's time. Melville, like Albert Camus (who said, via Dr. Rieux in *The Plague,* that "I feel more solidarity with the vanquished than with the saints"), found human dignity in the little dark corners of life; not among the powerful and successful, but among the oppressed, the afflicted, the defeated; among the victims of God or of nature or, simply of "things." In the character of Captain Ahab, Melville had offered a titanic image of magnificent defeat; but in the tales of the fifties, the focus was rather on the touching and forlorn.

Bannadonna, the arrogant Renaissance architect in *The Bell-Tower,* pursues his tragic course in the classical manner; he is the person of exceptional abilities and overweening pride who brings upon himself his own violent destruction. Ironically, this was the only short story of Melville's reprinted during his lifetime —reprinted twice, in fact, and once under the general title of *Little Classics: Tragedy.* Melville's genuinely classic conception of tragedy would find expression in his Civil War poetry; but ın the years immediately following *Pierre,* he evinced an un-classical involvement with pathos. More representative than Bannadonna, at this time, are persons like Bartleby, "a bit of wreck in mid-Atlantic"; or Hunilla, with her tearless bleak en-durance; or Jimmy Rose, transformed at a stroke from a wealthy man-about-town to a sandwich-filching parasite—"poor, poor Jimmy—God guard us all—poor Jimmy Rose!"; or the blank-looking girls in the infernal papermill, with their pallid cheeks and pale virginity; or Benito Cereno, almost literally shocked to death by his encounter with evil. Vanquished ones like these characterize Melville's collection of short stories, *The Piazza Tales* in 1856, and make incarnate in their variously pathetic ways Melville's then current estimate of life.

Instances of physical collapse or decay are often associated with these cases of human misfortune. The fall of the tower of Bannadonna in an earthquake is sheer melodrama; but elsewhere we observe the "sad disrepair" of Don Benito's ship, the *San Dominick,* which looks as though put together and launched from Ezekiel's valley of dry bones, and the awe-inspiring barrenness of the cindery Encantadas which seem to be Ezekiel's valley itself. We can watch Melville, in his letter to Hawthorne about the proposed "Agatha anecdote," lingering with mournful af-fection over a projected account of the slow decay of Agatha's mailbox and the post on which it stands:

> To this *post* they must come for their letters. And, of course, daily young Agatha goes—for seventeen years she goes thither daily. As her hopes gradually decay in her, so does the post itself and the little box decay. The post rots in the ground at last. Owing to its being little used—hardly used at all—grass grows rankly about it. At last a little bird nests in it. At last the post falls.

The passage does, indeed, reflect Melville's continuing taste for Gothic moldering, along with his alertness to what he called "the linked analogies"—between the concrete (the post and the box) and the soul of man (Agatha's hopes). But, at the same time, the lines quoted suggest another significant aspect—namely, the source and the nature of Melville's idea of defeat.

It is easy enough to say that Melville's sensitivity to failure in the mid-fifties was the direct consequence of his own "failure" as a novelist, after several years of considerable "success." What is important is Melville's view of just what had happened, of where the failure lay. In his view, the point was not only that his last two novels had failed to sell widely—though this was a fact of great· seriousness to him (dollars, as he said, always damned him). It was not only that American critics did not like his work, or neglected it—though Melville shared with many another American writer a much higher regard for British than for American critics and reviewers. What had really happened, Melville evidently believed, was something rather different. What had failed was an effort at communication. A recurring motif during these years, accordingly, is the motif of the undelivered letter or the misapprehended sign.

In *Benito Cereno,* both the wretched Spanish nobleman and members of his crew attempt to convey by sign language the reality of their desperate situation; and good Captain Delano fails consistently to receive their messages. Closer to the "Agatha" passage above and probably carried over from its rhetoric is the picture of the island "post-office" in *The Encantadas:*

> It may seem very strange to talk of post-offices in this barren region, yet post-offices are occasionally to be found there. They consist of a stake and a bottle. The letters being not only sealed, but corked. They are generally deposited by captains of Nantucketers for the benefit of passing fishermen, and contain statements as to what luck they had in whaling or tortoise-hunting. Frequently, however, long months and months, whole years glide by and no applicant appears. The stake rots and falls, presenting no very exhilarating subject.

A still less exhilarating subject and the most memorable example of this theme occur at the end of *Bartleby,* when the narrator reports the rumor that Bartleby had at one time worked as a subordinate clerk in the Dead Letter Office in Washington. What could be more terrible for a man prone to hopelessness like Bartleby, the narrator asks, than the business of "continually handling these dead letters, and assorting them for the flame. . . . On errands of life," he adds, appalled, "these letters speed to death."

So Melville's letters of life—his novels—had in his view of the matter sped to death, undelivered, unread by the addressee, the public; destined only to be destroyed. Melville felt that he had somehow failed to deliver the messages that shaped themselves so urgently in his imagination; and for a writer as profoundly personal and expressive as Melville, a failure of this kind was apt to be devastating. He could not—like Henry James and to some extent like Hawthorne—rest in satisfied contemplation of his own created objects; nor, once those objects were, metaphorically, destroyed, could he assuage his spirit in contemplation of the ideal that the object had made concrete—as he admires Hawthorne for seeming to say in "The Artist of the Beautiful." But what he could do, and what in these stories he did do, was to convert his sense of the failure of communication into a central fictional theme; and to make expert shorter fiction out of the failure of his longer fiction. It was a courageous undertaking indeed; and it has been properly celebrated by Hart Crane, in his poem "At Melville's Tomb," as the artistic effort by which Melville is to be identified:

> *Often beneath the waves, wide from this ledge*
> *The dice of dead men's bones he saw bequeath*
> *An embassy. Their numbers as he watched,*
> *Beat on the dusky shore and were obscured.*

Crane had to explain to his editor that his intention had been to relate the bones of dead mariners, men who failed to reach the shore alive, with "certain messages undelivered," certain experiences not finally communicated; both the bones and the messages beat on the dusky shore and get obscured. The passage is complex; but it testifies in its oblique way to an essential aspect of Melville, as well as to the sureness of Crane's understanding of it.

To formulate success and failure in terms of communication is, needless to say, to find the focus of human experience in the question of community—that is, of the relation between the individual and community. The tales of the fifties contain some of the most extreme and disturbing images of isolation that modern literature has recorded; and they are the more disturbing because, Bannadonna apart, these luckless men and women are not cut off from humanity through pride, like Ahab ("and Ahab stands alone among the millions of the peopled earth"), or through some sinful act, like Coleridge's mariner. They are rather the victims of a calamity: of a flaw in the psychological mechanism, like Bartleby; of an altogether "absurd" accident, like Hunilla; of the brutality of other men, like Benito Cereno. And, conversely, the one story in the group that breathes an air of perfect contentment is itself an image of perfect community—the account of an evening spent in a London men's club, *The Paradise of Bachelors*. This semifictional fusing of several dinners at the Elm and the Erechtheum Clubs in December 1854 is Melville's worldly, even lip-smacking counterpart to James's "The Great Good Place"; and it offers a Melvillean ideal of genial masculine companionship: "It was the very perfection of quiet absorption of good living, good drinking, good feeling, and good talk. We were a band of brothers. Comfort —fraternal, household comfort, was the grand trait of the affair." One should probably not make too much of the celibate aspect of the English Paradise; for what Melville rejoices in is less the absence of women—of the heterosexual element—than the absence of families ("You could plainly see that these easy-hearted men had no wives or children to give an anxious thought"). And, beyond that, the situation so handsomely set forth is a mode of sexless companionship, in the basic meaning of "companionship" as a deep sharing of nourishment, of both physical and spiritual bread. It is the antithesis of the situation of Bartleby and the others.

In the course of his sketches of isolation and defeat, Melville observes and dramatizes a variety of responses among those for whom there is no Erechtheum Club available. At one extreme is Don Benito, who summons up the courage to plunge out of his confinement and rejoin humanity in the friendly boat of Amasa Delano (a moment reminiscent of the scene Melville selected for special praise in *The House of the Seven Gables,* "where Clifford . . . would fain throw himself forth from the window to join the procession"); but thereafter the Spaniard yields to the horror of his experience and slides helplessly toward death. At quite another extreme is the Chola widow, that "lone shipwrecked soul," whose isolation is absolute, whose plight is the most hideous— and whose fortitude is the most enduring. Somewhere in between is the canny, unashamed adjustment of Jimmy Rose, who emerges from his spell of self-concealment after the disaster, "to crawl through life, and peep among the marbles and mahoganies for contumelious tea and toast"; and Bartleby, who, bit of unsalvageable wreckage that he is, yet continues to utter his brief refusal, who says, "No," to the end—not, "No! in thunder," as Melville imagined Hawthorne saying, but, "No," in a soft intractable undertone.

It has been sufficiently suggested, I trust, that these portraits of the vanquished and victimized are not themselves instances of *artistic* failure or of *literary* defeat. On the contrary, the tales of the fifties represent a very far reach in shorter American fiction: though we have to remove them some distance from the enormous shadow of *Moby-Dick* before their qualities become visible. *Jimmy Rose* may be not much more than an anecdote, though it is carried beyond its slender limits by a surprisingly appropriate verbal vigor. Even *The Bell-Tower,* while "literary" in a bad sense of the word, keeps stirring the edges of our imagination by the hint of a meaning (about cultural history, about race and sex) much more interesting than the moral so heavily insisted on. *The Tartarus of Maids* is a story of perhaps exaggerated reputation that threatens to bore us with the strained comedy of its sexual and anatomical allegory; but, again, the narrative tends to slip out of its frame of contrived fantasy to touch some ultimate in human, and especially in feminine, degradation, some final reduction of the female in a mechanized world to a sexless and, as it were, devaginated thing. These are stories that reward our best attention; once read, they refuse to be dislodged from their little niches in our memory. But three other stories do more than that: they add to our store of imaginative understanding and of beauty; once read, they become part of the way we look into life and appraise it. These, of course, are *Bartleby, The Encantadas,* and *Benito Cereno.*

About *Bartleby,* the least ought to be said; for it is a fable, almost a parable, something that depends, for our satisfaction, on remaining intact. It provides an image in steady slow motion of the gradual extinction of spirit, of the dissolution of all but the fact of will in a single human psyche—not the will *toward* anything, not active desire, but the faculty itself. Bartleby is a voluntary phantom, the dim underside of Captain Ahab. His thinning actuality is perceived in its contrast with the Dickensian fullness of urban life, the Wall Street office, the two volatile clerks and the impish call-boy, the busy activities of the legal profession, and the prudent and well-intentioned narrator. Seen from that vantage point of cozy normality and unquestioning conformity, Bartleby flickers with ever-decreasing light and ever-increasing mystery. The narrator's final exclamation ("Ah, Bartleby! Ah, humanity!") suggests that in the declining person of Bartleby he —and Melville—had identified some type of human character and experience; but all that has been identified is the mystery of life.

The story's mild paradox is that it is the narrator's failure to make contact with Bartleby ("It was his soul that suffered, and his soul I could not reach") that leads him to a sense of common humanity; he feels "a fraternal melancholy." A glimpse of fraternity is thus stimulated by the discovered absence thereof; what is shared is an awareness of darkness; and at the end all we know is that we know nothing.

The Encantadas offers the inquiring reader a more strenuous problem of judgment. If *Bartleby* is all compact, *The Encantadas* is all meandering sketchiness; and nothing is less clear, at first sound, than its exact tone. A contemporary reviewer referred to the work as "a series of charming descriptions," as though it were a contribution to pastoral literature; but we shall not be far wrong if we take it, instead, as a sustained and conscious exercise in the antipastoral mode. The pastoral is an account of the world in its unfallen state, as nostalgically imagined after the fact of the fall (the definition can arguably hold even for the Virgilian pastoral); but Melville's key contention here is that "In no world but a fallen one could such lands exist." *The Encantadas* is not—as was so much American writing contemporary with Melville—an artistic transformation of the actual and fallen world; it is an extension of it. It surveys a certain terrain and certain objects and experiences to conclude, as Cardinal Newman once concluded after surveying human history, that the data collected showed the human race must be "implicated in some terrible and aboriginal calamity."

Melville searches the islands for signs of the absolute consequences of just such an aboriginal calamity; as Charles Darwin, by a suggestive coincidence, had earlier explored the same islands for material to use in his study of the biological rise of man. Indeed, Melville's sketches of the Galapagos archipelago (a thick cluster of islands some six hundred miles west of Ecuador) are at once a scientific description, in the Darwinian manner, and an adumbration of the moral and social world that is the so-called civilized home of modern man. That home is kept present to our minds by the story's allegorical tendency (we should not use a stronger word), which is indicated throughout by the quotations from Melville's favorite allegorical poem, *The Faerie Queene,* and finds its most vivid expression in the hallucination at the end of Sketch First, when a "scene of social merriment" seems to fade into a scene of lonely, haunted woods, and the representative of the Encantadas, a gigantic tortoise, crawls across the ballroom floor. Not only the tortoise with his reminder of mortality, but equally the heroic Hunilla, the Calibanesque Oberlus, the pirates and ghosts and lizards, the "runaways, castaways, solitaries, gravestones etc.": all these beings (Melville suggests) inhabit not only the faraway Galapagos, as a matter of scientific fact; they also inhabit—metaphorically—our modern civilization, they inhabit our drawing rooms, they inhabit our personalities.

The power of *The Encantadas,* in short, derives—as so often with Melville—from its linked analogies, from the creative relation between the abundant concrete and the range of moral and psychological and metaphysical implication. No work of Melville's is so close in its narrative strategy to *Moby-Dick,* a book that was once also praised for being, so to speak, a charming description of whaling voyages. In *Moby-Dick,* we have the leisurely and thorough account of whaling, its history and geography and folklore, the exact dimensions of the various species of whales and their heads and members, the techniques of harpooning; so, in *The Encantadas,* we attend to the skimpily known history of the islands, the reports of visiting frigates, the names and dates of the chief authorities, a survey of the landscape and of plant and animal life, the blurry reports of settlements, uprisings, and freebooting. Like *Moby-Dick,* too, the shorter work—while, similarly, throwing off a steady shower of allegorical sparks— gathers dramatic momentum and bursts into a sudden new vitality toward the end. The dramatic focus of *The Encantadas* is the successive appearances and stories of the Chola Widow Hunilla and the Hermit Oberlus in Sketches Eighth and Ninth, a pairing of images in a sort of dyptich.[2] The opposite possibilities they represent have already been stated fairly flatly at the opening of Sketch Second, where, speaking of the tortoise, Melville remarks that "dark and melancholy as it is up the back, [it] still possesses a bright side. . . . Enjoy the bright . . . but be honest, and don't deny the black. Neither should he, who cannot turn the tortoise from its natural position . . . for that cause declare the creature to be one total inky blot" (compare this with the "Try-Works"

2. The word "dyptich" (which means, of course, a two-paneled painting) has been used by commentators to describe the fictional work in which Melville sets opposite anecdotes or symbols side by side under a dual title. There are several such among the stories of the fifties, *The Paradise of Bachelors* and *The Tartarus of Maids* being perhaps the most memorable.

meditation in *Moby-Dick).* Hunilla and Oberlus were in fact actual human beings, one a Peruvian and the other an Irishman; they come to us as living individuals; but within the prepared atmosphere of allegory they also enlarge into symbols of the human potential—that of grandeur amid defeat and that of bestial degradation. Hunilla, utterly alone except for her dogs and the transient brigands by whom she has been periodically assaulted, embodies what there is of spiritual brightness in the grim hell of the actual; Oberlus has become an animal and an isolate by choice.

Opposition, to speak colloquially, was Melville's middle name; and contrariety is no less central in *Benito Cereno.* Here we have one of modern literature's great enactments of the greatest of all oppositions, to the perennial eye of the poet: that between appearance and reality—concretely, between the apparent situation on board the *San Dominick,* the apparent relation between black man and white man, between slave and master, obedience and command; and the reality of all that. Melville's handling of his story—wherein the slow-witted, kindhearted American, Amasa Delano, boards the Spanish ship, explores it, talks with the Captain and his Negro "servant" Babo, and departs without ever gaining more than the most fleeting impression of the truth—has been much praised. The protective innocence of Delano has been analyzed, and the depths of Babo (the slave who has in fact seized command by means of horrifying violence) have been sounded with various psychological instruments. Melville's exploitation of the element of color in this story has likewise been admired; and his creative techniques studied by comparing the novella to its easily available source in Delano's *Narrative of Voyages and Travels.* But another aspect is still worth considering—that is, whether and how the central opposition is "resolved."

Superficially, the resolution occurs when the narrative of the apparent situation—presented through the undiscerning eyes of Amasa Delano—is followed by the narrative of what had really happened, in the deposition made by the ailing Don Benito at the court in Lima, during the trial of the Negroes. That legal document has caused critical trouble and has resulted, for example, in a hostile verdict on *Benito Cereno* by Newton Arvin, in the best critical study of Melville yet written. The charge is that the deposition is a dry letdown after the murky excitements of the longer section that precedes it, and that in any case Melville had shirked his artistic responsibility by bringing in the (actual) court testimony and laying it down flat in his pages. As to the letdown, the deposition will probably prove engrossing enough, if read without prejudice. But as to the artistic problem, the documentary pages may well comprise one of Melville's happiest strokes. For Melville's point in thus juxtaposing these two so different narrative modes and voices is this: *that neither version of the events contains the truth.* No reader doubts that Delano's version is false, that he got everything wrong way round; but we should recognize, I think, that Benito Cereno's version is equally flawed by an inadequacy of perception, equally remote from the whole reality of the adventure. The remoteness, in the second case, is conveyed precisely by the language of the deposition—by those abstractions of the legal vocabulary that evade all contact with the blood and stuff of experience. We are presumably intended to accept the Spaniard's statements of the external facts, the process of revolt and of massacre, the names and numbers of those that killed or were killed. But for Melville facts were not truth and, wrongly handled, could be an obstacle to truth. The Spaniard was quite unequipped by his aristocratic temperament to grasp the motives at work, the raging desire of the Negroes for freedom, the murderous animosity that slavery begot in them; as Captain Delano was unequipped by his temperament to grasp the force and presence of evil. Neither narrative, accordingly, rises to the truth of the affair; and yet this is a curious instance of two wrongs making a right—or, rather, of two falsehoods making a truth between them. As our minds play back and forth between the two versions, we find each making us more and more aware of what is false in the other. And so the truth comes finally into view, as contained in the continuing tension between alternate versions, in a subtly and knowingly unresolved duplicity.[3]

Another complaint against *Benito Cereno* is an alleged lack of political morality on Melville's part: as though he had failed to indicate sympathy with the Negroes' lust for freedom; as though he were blind to the evil of slavery. But it is Don Benito who is blind to that evil, not Melville. Melville was profoundly aware not only of the slavery issue but of its ambiguities and complexities,

3. Much the same view of *Benito Cereno* has been made persuasively by Allen Guttmann in "The Enduring Innocence of Captain Amasa Delano," *Boston University Studies in English,* 5 (Spring, 1961).

and his awareness is conveyed in a doubleness of narrative mode whereby moral guilt and moral myopia are subtly distributed to all participants in the drama. It can be noted, meanwhile, how frequent is the theme of insurrection in the tales of the fifties; the notion of revolt pressed hard upon Melville's imagination. In addition to the bloody uprising of the slaves in *Benito Cereno,* we recall the mutiny of the lawless mariners against the Dog-King, in Sketch Seventh of *The Encantadas.* Bartleby himself is a sort of passive, unconquerable *homme révolté.* And though, in the uncannily prophetic climax of *The Bell-Tower,* it is the machine that mysteriously turns on the man and destroys him, Melville supplied a motto for the story that points to the analogy intended and relates *The Bell-Tower* unexpectedly and very closely to *Benito Cereno:* "Like negroes, these powers own man sullenly; mindful of their higher master; while serving, plot revenge." More generally still, Melville—as I have been stressing on almost every page—was singularly attuned to conflict as the very definition of experience; to opposition and ambiguity intensifying betimes into frightful collision, and with neither side (to adopt his remark about Hawthorne and himself) altogether in the wrong. No American writer was better prepared to measure the full significance of the quarrel over slavery that led to rebellion and, in 1861, grew into armed conflict with the outbreak of the national Civil War.

But if he was prepared to take its measure, he was only partially prepared to express his understanding of the conflict in the literary genre to which he was now turning—the genre of lyric and narrative poetry. After the failure of *Pierre,* Melville had applied himself to the shorter fictional form; now, after another effort in the longer mode (*The Confidence-Man,* 1857) and another critical and financial failure, he abandoned prose fiction completely and wrote nothing but poetry until, more than thirty years later, he came back to prose for the last time to write that rusty masterpiece, *Billy Budd.*

To be sure, the poetry Melville began to compose in the late fifties was not the very first he had ever attempted. There is evidence that he had tried his hand at verse at least two decades earlier, while the first of his extant poems date from 1849 in the semisatirical poetastings of *Mardi.* But it was in 1859 that his wife wrote guardedly to her mother: "Herman has taken to writing poetry. You need not tell any one, for you know how such things get around."[4] Jocularly assuming the same attitude, Melville wrote his sea-captain brother Tom in 1862 that "some villian [sic] & secret enemy of yours" had set afloat the "cursed report" that Tom "had begun to take to—drink?—Oh, no, but worse—to sonnet-writing." Melville promised to quash the rumor, since he himself had been innocently responsible for it. On the particular voyage after which the rumor got started, it was Herman Melville, his brother's guest aboard Tom's ship, the *Meteor,* who had been heard discussing poetry and reciting it—on one "romantic moonlight night," as he said in the same letter, "repeat[ing] to you about three cables' length of [my] verse." The verses in question were presumably among those later included as separate lyrics in the long narrative poem *Clarel* in 1876, and those gathered under the heading "Fruit of Travel of Long Ago" in a volume called *Timoleon* in 1891. But another comment in the letter to Tom Melville indicates the source of a rather different kind of poetry. "Do you want to hear about the war?—The war goes bravely on. McClellan is now within fifteen miles of the rebel capital, Richmond. . . . But when the *end*—the wind-up—the grand pacification is coming, who knows." It was the eventual fall of Richmond to General Grant three years later that provided the impulse, Melville was to say, to an entire volume of war poetry, published in 1866 as *Battle-Pieces and Aspects of the War.*

The author of *Battle-Pieces* had, then, a certain experience in the writing of poetry. But it was a painful and private business; no more than any other gifted contemporary could Melville count on an established native poetic craft, upon a set of living conventions and resources he could possess himself of, and exploit for his own purpose. By the early 1860s, American poetry was getting worse, not better. After the limited yet crucial breakthrough of Emerson and Thoreau, the superb but unpublished poems of Emily Dickinson, and the magnificent achievements of the early Whitman (a poet Melville seems not yet to have known, though the evidence is unclear), American poetry was following the other arts into the dreary decades of dehydrated idealism and truthless, Europeanized sentimentality from which it would only be rescued, near the turn of the century, by Edwin Arlington Robinson. And

4. Cf. Mrs. Melville again to her mother in 1875: "Pray do not mention to *any one* that he is writing poetry [i.e., *Clarel*]—you know how such things spread, and he would be very angry if he knew I had spoken of it—and of course I have not except in confidence to you and the family."

so, as Robert Penn Warren has remarked (*Selected Essays*) in the best discussion we have of Melville as a poet, while "it must be admitted that he did not learn his craft, the point is that the craft he did not learn was not the same craft which some of his more highly advertised contemporaries did learn with such glibness of tongue and complacency of spirit." Glibness and complacency had no part in the disturbed, often awkward but sometimes dazzling poetry that Melville wrote out of so much of his craft as he did manage to acquire.

Indeed, the characteristic effect of his best poetry, like that of his best prose, is that of a struggle with incompatible materials and intractable language suddenly releasing an insight and an idiom of remarkable poise and beauty. But it was too compound a beauty, too dependent on contrariety, to appeal to Melville's contemporaries; *Battle-Pieces,* though not entirely overlooked, had a most indifferent success. Melville's poetic achievement is of the sort that the present generation, because of historic experience and critical fashions, has learned to appreciate; for it derived from an imagination alert to paradox and contradiction and to the large mythic action detectable amid the jostling immediacies of life. That was the imagination summoned to a supreme creative effort by the supreme contradiction of a Civil War. It was not only war as such, it was fratricidal war, the condition of a whole people doing desperate battle with itself, that galvanized the poetic genius of the man for whom communal fraternity was so potent an ideal. It was fratricidal war, moreover, seen as a tragic drama of deeply traditional quality and of mythic importance. It was because he so envisioned the war and because, in *Battle-Pieces,* he gave shape and substance to his vision that Melville deserves to be called *the* Civil War poet.

The contrast with Whitman and his *Drum-Taps* is worth pausing over, since between them Melville and Whitman examined in poetry the two great aspects of the war. The poetry that came out of Whitman's front-line experiences and his service in the military hospitals in Washington is not, strictly speaking, war poetry; it is, rather, wound poetry, the poetry of hurt, of pain and courage, of love and healing and death. *Drum-Taps* records the war in its immediate and fragmentary effects upon the bodies and spirits of individual soldiers, and in its moments of comradeship in the camp or on the march. Melville, in *Battle-Pieces,* looked at the terrible course of events from a much greater distance; and as the final sentence of his prose supplement to the volume declares, he saw the war as a "great historic tragedy" which he prays "may not have been enacted without instructing our whole beloved country through terror and pity." That last phrase tells us that by "tragedy" Melville had in mind something thoroughly specific and traditional: a catastrophe of immense significance, with a traditional rhythm and (so he prays) a traditional outcome. But by referring to the war as a "great *historic* tragedy," Melville was no less precisely locating the area of its tragic action: which was not only, not primarily in what happened to the bodies and spirits of individual soldiers, but in what happened to the body and spirit of "our whole beloved country." The tragic hero of *Battle-Pieces* is America itself.

Battle-Pieces as a whole, therefore, may be thought of as a tragic drama expanding in the direction of a tragic epic, where the fate not of an individual but of an entire nation is fearfully at stake—though an epic composed of more or less separate lyric and narrative poems of varying length and uneven merit. Most of those poems deal with particular moments in the war, but before getting down to particulars Melville establishes a vast setting that reaches almost to a totality of space and time (as epic poets habitually frame their human action in a huge perspective of history and of the gods). He begins with the ominous image (in "The Portent") of the future veiling its face, even as the hangman's cap veils the face of John Brown; goes on to musings about "The tempest bursting from the waste of Time/ On the world's fairest hope linked with man's foulest crime" ("Misgivings"); and from those clashing superlatives proceeds to a sort of absolute spatial and temporal reference in the apocalyptic vision ("The Conflict of Convictions") of "strong Necessity . . . heap[ing] Time's strand with wrecks," of an event so large and convulsive that the very gulfs will bare their "slimed foundations"—whereafter, *perhaps,* "the throes of ages" may "rear/ The final empire and the happier world." But perhaps the dire opposite will come to pass, perhaps "power unanointed may come"—sheer power without grace— and an America that has become mighty by abandoning the dream of its founders. Meanwhile, behind the historic American struggle, Satan and Raphael are glimpsed in the background carrying on their timeless war between evil and good.

Within so universal a context and with such grand alternatives in the offing, the actualities of the war and its aftermath are then dramatized in roughly chronological order, from 1860 through April 1866. After the cosmic tonalities of the opening poems, Melville narrows his focus to the first march into Virginia; to land battles, such as Shiloh, Malvern Hill, the Wilderness; naval battles, such as those involving the *Temeraire;* the draft riots in New York in July 1863 ("The House-top," a powerfully impressive poem); the experience of the prison camp; the fall of the southern capital; the emancipated slave; the returning soldiers and those who failed to return ("The Slain Collegians" from north and south alike); retrospective memorial verses; the confrontation of the postwar American world and an urgent plea for understanding and reconciliation.

We make out—amid these vivid, shocking, and somber particulars—a steadily unfolding "action" of a very familiar kind. It is a movement from youth to age, from innocence to experience, from hope to horror, from life to death; with rebirth, new knowledge and a renewal of hope rather prayed for than affirmed at the end. It is the entire country, as I have said, that is passing through this multiple movement—the country sometimes seen in its manyness, as a northerner or a southerner, a college-boy officer or a dead soldier, a prisoner or a slave, sometimes seen in its oneness, as in the poem called "America" which concluded *Battle-Pieces* proper (before the so-called memorial verses) and which rehearses a good part of this action. But we find a synecdoche of the whole process, an enactment in small, in the last stanza of "The March into Virginia":

> *But some who this blithe mood present,*
> *   As on in lightsome files they fare,*
> *Shall die experienced ere three days be spent—*
> *   Perish, enlightened by the vollied glare.*

Among other things, the lines testify to a movement from romantic illusion to violent disenchantment, as the young men who marched away "with fifes, and flags in mottoed pageantry" ("Ball's Bluff"), while "The banners play, the bugles call/ The air is blue and prodigal" come up against the reality of the guns on the battlefield. But even more than disenchanted, the young men, in Melville's phrasing, are *experienced* and *enlightened*. The former word reminds us that Melville saw the progress of those chivalric soldiers in the familiar terms he had already dramatized in his fiction; as a development from innocence to experience. The

second italicized word, which Melville uses with all the cunning
of a metaphysical poet, indicates that in the present instance (as in
the case of *Pierre* but not that of *Redburn*), Melville looked upon
the development as tragic. For the word "enlightened" not only
contrasts ironically with the "lightsome" manner of departure,
and not only images the literal and physical lighting up of the
scene by the cannon-fire, at the moment of death. It combines
both effects with the notion of spiritual illumination, the awareness kindled by experience; and it is, thus, a Shakespearean pun
that confirms a Shakespearean sense of tragic action—a catastrophe which, even as it occurs, begets a new perception.

The same traditionally tragic idea—the idea of enlightenment
bred out of horror and death either witnessed or experienced—
appears at many turns in *Battle-Pieces*. In "The College Colonel,"
after the splendid simile of the regimental remnant filing home
like castaway sailors crawling ashore,[5] Melville goes on to contrast
the searing new consciousness of the young officer with the shouts
of the welcoming crowds and the wreaths thrown at him from the
gay balconies. It is not, Melville says, a mode of self-pity; though
he has lost a leg and his arm is in splints, nonetheless "self he
has long disclaimed." It is rather an insight into a more general
and more terrible truth, the truth that came to him in the Wilderness and the field hospitals; the kind of truth Ishmael arrives at in
Moby-Dick when he discovers that, although the visible spheres
were formed in love, the invisible spheres were formed in fright.
A similar point is made abruptly by another brilliantly exploited
word in "Shiloh," where, in parentheses, Melville exclaims, "What
like a bullet can undeceive!"—not merely kill, but educate; in-
struct the soul by the removal of illusion. The education achieved
in death by the soldiers at Shiloh is what Melville prays will be
achieved by "our whole beloved country," when, in the supplement he expresses his wish that "the great historic tragedy may
not have been enacted without *instructing*" America "through
terror and pity."

Instructed, one notices, not only through terror, but through
terror and pity; not only made aware of the horror that lies close
to the heart of experience, but simultaneously ennobled by compassion for suffering humanity. By the end of the Civil War, Mel-

5. "Their mates dragged back and seen no more" in the second stanza
of "The College Colonel" is probably the immediate Melvillean source of
Hart Crane's poem "At Melville's Tomb," quoted above, p. 43.

ville had in fact somewhat revised the formula he had attributed to Ishmael in *Moby-Dick*. He felt now that, if one could indeed penetrate through love to fright, one might also move beyond the discovered fright to a new form of love. The soldiers at Shiloh who were enemies in the morning become friends at eve, as they lie dead together: this is the final accomplishment of the undeceiving bullet. And the collegians who "went from the North and came from the South" as mortal foes end up by lying down "midway on a bloody bed," like lovers after the battle. "Woe for the homes of the North," Melville sighs; and then, after a typographically indicated pause, "And woe for the seats of the South:/ *All* who felt life's spring in prime . . . All lavish hearts *on whichever side"* (italics added).

One of the great qualities of *Battle-Pieces* is its powerful rise toward a comprehensive pity; toward the conviction that, however foul a crime slavery may have been, nonetheless of the two parties to the struggle, of the two halves of America that had been "estranged in life" (again to quote the poem on Hawthorne), neither had been completely in the wrong. "Calvin's creed"— that is, the doctrine of natural depravity—is as much "corroborated" by the northern draft riots (in "The House-top") as by southern slavery; and Melville's sympathy and admiration for the southerners increases through his description of Stonewall Jackson and Sherman's march through Georgia. It is in the intensity of his hope that all America may be so moved, so educated through terror to a new and durable sense of fraternal love, that Melville—after the expressed grief over "all lavish hearts" quoted above—concludes *Battle-Pieces* proper with "America." Here, in a dream of hope, he sees a dead America, a composite of all the dead at Shiloh and Malvern Hill and the other battlefields, returning to "promoted life." The reborn country—so runs the dream— will have been purified through suffering; will have acquired through pain a sobering knowledge; will have reached a certain wisdom that henceforth will ballast its hope. America will represent "youth matured for age's seat"—for, like so many individual heroes in the fiction of Melville and his contemporaries, America itself will have at last grown up.

An America so matured—"its lashings charmed and malice reconciled," to quote once more from Hart Crane's poem— would, for Melville, be like the greatest of poems. In Melville's view, every great poem, like every other genuine work of art, resulted from the artist's struggle to harmonize opposites; every poem involved a sort of creative Civil War. Such is the burden of the remarkable little poem called "Art": where Melville declares that the creation of "pulsed life" and the achievement of form require that "unlike things must meet and mate"; and where, after giving some examples of the meeting of unlike things (love and hate, audacity and reverence, and so on), he concludes:

> *These must mate,*
> *And fuse with Jacob's mystic heart,*
> *To wrestle with the angel—Art.*

Every conflict man endures, accordingly, is analogous to the conflict involved in the creative process; and vice versa. Almost everything that Melville ever wrote—since it was a confrontation of contraries—can thus be taken as a paradigm of the struggle of the artist.

We should keep those burgeoning analogies in mind as we consider the poetry of Melville published after *Battle-Pieces*. *Clarel* apart, Melville saw to the publication of two privately financed and printed volumes (twenty-five copies each) in the last three years of his life: *John Marr and Other Sailors* in 1888, and *Timoleon* in 1891. The former consisted of twenty-five "sea-pieces," to use Melville's phrase, written during the years when Melville earned his small living as a customs inspector on the New York docks—an appointment he was forced to accept in the year *Battle-Pieces* appeared, 1866. "The Maldive Shark" and "The Berg" were included in *John Marr*. Of the forty-two items in *Timoleon*, a little more than half seem to have been written in the relatively few months remaining to Melville after he was able to retire from the customs job in 1887; among these were "After the Pleasure Party," "In a Garret," "Art," "Shelley's Vision," and "Fragments of a Lost Gnostic Poem." The rest of the book consisted of verses collected under the subtitle "Fruit of Travel of Long Ago" and were presumably written as an immediate result of Melville's travels in Europe and the Near East in the late '50s; "In a Bye-Canal," "Milan Cathedral," and "Greek Architecture" form a part of this group. But a good many of Melville's poems—such as "The Rusty Man," the two Camoens pieces, and "Pontoosuce"—were not published until the Constable Edition of 1924. All in all, Melville's shorter poems comprise a volume of considerable bulk. And when we add to it *Clarel* and finally the novella *Billy Budd* (the latter also not published till 1924), we find in the literary production of Melville's last decades a body of work of great richness, power, and variety—and something that belies the usual impression of long lingering years of creative silence on Melville's part. Melville was a practicing writer quite literally till the day he died.

But he was a writer steadily given to meditation about the drama of creativity, about the nature of the art-work, about the dilemmas of the artist. The first of these provides the subject both of "Art" and "In a Garret"—the key words of each of which are, respectively, "grapple" and "wrestle": robust verbs to suggest the strenuous difficulty of the enterprise, the agony of creation. "Milan Cathedral" and "Greek Architecture" are among several poems in which Melville associates the grand work of art with religious worship, or reverence for the transcendental "idea." Elsewhere, Melville addresses himself to the figure of the artist by taking on the guise of other poets: in "Shelley's Vision," for example, and in the double salute to the sixteenth-century Portuguese writer, Luis de Camoens, whose epic, the *Lusiads,* had so invigorating an effect on Melville's two epic endeavors, *Moby-Dick* and *Battle-Pieces.*

A more characteristic Melvillean statement about the artist, however, may be found slightly hidden beneath the apparent subjects of "The Maldive Shark," "In a Bye-Canal," and "The Berg." For here we encounter again Melville's conviction that the artist must risk disaster by facing up constantly to new challenges. Like the pilot fish, he must be willing, metaphorically, to "lurk in the port of [the maldive shark's] serrated teeth," and find "asylum in the jaws of the Fates." Melville felt, with all justice, that he had done so; and in "In a Bye-Canal," he could claim:

> *Fronted I have, part taken the span*
> *Of portents in nature and peril in man.*
> *I have swum—I have been*
> *'Twixt the whale's black flukes*
>   *and the white shark's fin.*

It is one of the most effective passages in Melville's poetry, or any other nineteenth-century poet; the entire stanza should be read as a superbly compressed chapter of autobiography. But Melville knew that anyone, artist or man, who tried to swim " 'twixt the whale's black flukes/ and the white shark's fin" risked total destruction; and "The Berg" is a tough-worded dream image of such an event. Yet behind it one feels the force of Melville's persistent belief that, as he said in his essay on Hawthorne, failure —however disastrous—is the true test of greatness.

All these poems bring other highly animated themes into play with the theme of art—for instance, in "The Berg," the idea of nature itself as lumpish, lumbering and, especially, deadly indifferent in its massive destructiveness. But probably the richest concatenation of themes appears in what is in other respects as well Melville's finest lyric poem, "After the Pleasure Party." In this easily misunderstood work, preoccupations with art, science, religion, sexual love, and celibacy—each element in various modes—mingle together; and thematic language from other poems turns up here in vitalizing new contexts. The phrase "enlightened, undeceived" takes us back to "The March into Virginia" and "Shiloh," and to the notion of education through the shocking experience. The line "Few matching halves here meet and mate" echoes the poem "Art" so strikingly as to suggest an intimacy approaching equivalence between the sexual dilemma (the immediate reference here) and the creative dilemma. Despite these guideposts, however, "After the Pleasure Party" is worth a slightly extended look.

The title is itself a mild play on words. "Pleasure party" is a now archaic colloquialism roughly equal to "picnic"; but juxtaposed with the meditation on sexual passion that follows, the word "pleasure" takes on a strongly erotic overtone. The poem's construction, much reduced, is this: after a day's outing on the slopes overlooking the northern Mediterranean, a mature woman who had devoted herself to the intellectual life reflects on the relative value of her celibate devotion to knowledge as against the enjoyment of heterosexual love; for she has been greatly aroused by another member of the party, and has experienced a storm of jealousy over a pretty peasant girl on whom her loved one had looked with obviously physical desire. The woman's tormented interior monologue continues for twelve stanzas. It is followed by two stanzas in which the poet comments directly. Then the monologue is resumed, as at another time and place, in stanza fifteen. The poem concludes with ten last lines of rumination by the poet, and his plea to all virgins to pray for "Urania" and to beware lest, in their virginity, they too offend the love god.

By referring to his troubled heroine as Urania, the goddess of astronomy, Melville evidently intends to indicate the woman's particular scientific profession—she had for long peered through the "reaching ranging tube," the telescope, at such constellations as Cassiopeia. The allusion to "Vesta struck with Sappho's smart" does not mean that this virginal intellectual has been stirred by Lesbian passion; the object of her love is quite plainly (in stanzas eight and nine) a "He," whose presence has the effect upon her of the young person in Sappho's famous ode ("Like to a god" etc.). She compares herself as a "plain lone bramble"—who can yet thrill to the spring—with the allegedly sly girl whose "buds were strung" on briars; and this "floral" imagery reaches its climax in the wonderfully shameless eroticism of the Marvellian couplet: "I'd buy the veriest wanton's rose/ Would but my bee therein repose." As the poem proceeds, the meditation enlarges from the particular incident and the particular erotic surge into a general puzzlement about the fact of sex—or, better, the mystery of sex and its division. And finding that "fair studies charm no more," the woman sets off in search of some other source of physical and spiritual peace, contemplating the convent life and then praying instead to an "armed Virgin," "mightier one," to protect her against the bodily urges the vengeful Amor continues to visit upon her. "Fond appeal," Melville concludes with cleareyed compassion; for there is no escape from the "sexual feud" that "clogs the aspirant life."

The above remarks are merely introductory to this very remarkable poem, and scarcely touch its subtle density of language and symbol—for example, the way the woman's dream of being "throned" alongside Cassiopeia (mythologically, a queen) leads to the realization that in fact she is more like an idiot in a cell "crowned" with straw rather than gold; that she has, so to speak, been uncrowned by sex, so that Melville can later say in parentheses that Rome is a suitable place for her since Rome is "for queens discrowned a congruous home." Nor is there space to inspect the elaborating contrast between pagan and Christian religion and religious art. One can only observe that in "The Pleasure Party," as elsewhere, Melville does not attempt to resolve the fierce contradictions his poem introduces. He holds them in balance, matching and mating them in a form, a pulsed created life that, for Melville, was the perennial ambition of art. Such a form was art's way of representing the ultimate nature of reality, which, as he says in "Pontoosuce" (sometimes called "The Lake"), is itself a mating of opposites, a "warmth and chill of wedded life and death." "Pontoosuce," like "The Pleasure Party," is one of the poems wherein Melville presents his vision of the final truth about things, the very core of his tragically achieved understanding. When we have read works like these and reached that core, we are prepared to alternate Melville's own name with the name of Shakespeare in the final stanza of " 'The Coming Storm' ":

> *No utter surprise can come to him*
> *Who reaches Shakespeare's core;*
> *That which we seek and shun is there—*
> *Man's final lore.*

1962

II: *The Confidence-Man*

The action of this most deceptive and carefully composed of Melville's novels takes place on the first of April, between dawn and midnight on the Feast of All Fools; and by a startling coincidence the book was published on the first of April, in the year 1857. Melville had finished *The Confidence-Man* the summer before, and he was by this date staying at the Hotel Luna in Venice, nearing the end of a long trip through England, the Middle East, and Italy. Very possibly, he was at work on one of the two poems about Venice (the second being the superb lyric "In a Bye-Canal") that he would eventually include in the volume of verses called *Timoleon*. He had, anyhow, already turned from fiction to poetry, and with a kind of finality; until the novella *Billy Budd* more than thirty years later, Melville's statement of the rendingly opposed forces that beset his imagination would find expression only in lyric and narrative poetry. His portrait of a "flock of fools, under this captain of fools, in this ship of fools" —to borrow the wooden-legged passenger's acerbic and echoing words (chapter iii)—thus marked the end of the great fictional period. It had begun in 1846 with *Typee* and reached its apogee with *Moby-Dick* in 1851; had continued through *Pierre* in 1852, *Israel Potter* in 1855, and the remarkable tales of the mid-fifties. Now, by way of rehearsing what he had learned and of displaying the skills he had acquired during that period, Melville, in a mood oddly blended of comedy and controlled ferocity, explored for one final time the human world he had lived through.

The Confidence-Man was also the last of Melville's writings to gain critical attention. But commentary, if it started late, has in recent years become torrential; it is by now excessive in range and discord of opinion even for Melville criticism. Extraordinary claims have been made for it, extraordinary hostility voiced against it; and extraordinary theories propounded to account for it.[6] Certainly it is not an easy book to read. At first glance, it seems rather to bulge and thicken than to progress; one has the impression of a number of dimly identifiable persons who simply "talk and keep talking," as the character known as the cosmopolitan once puts it; and who "still stand where [they] did." But it is an almost irresistibly easy book to reread. The second or third time round the deck, one enjoyably makes out a good deal of the intricate pattern of the Confidence Man's tricks, disguises, and sophistics. One also makes out something at least of the deeply meaningful artistic trickery of Melville, as he moves his picaresque protagonist through the series of encounters aboard the river steamer named with such apt inaptness the *Fidèle* on that long April day.

The Confidence-Man is in some sort a satire, but of a peculiar variety. Its titular hero, for example, is the agent and source of satire, rather than—as in Voltaire's *Candide,* with which it has been misleadingly compared—the incarnate object or victim of it. The object of the satire, indeed, is hard to determine. In one of the few extant letters that refer to *The Confidence-Man,* Melville reported (September 15, 1857) that he was looking about for "a good, earnest subject" for a lecture, and offered the following underscored possibility: *"Daily Progress of man towards a state of intellectual & moral perfection."* No doubt that recurring

6. Critical opinions up to 1954 have been collected and examined by Elizabeth S. Foster in the invaluable introduction to her own definitive edition of the novel. A second round-up through 1961 has been made by Daniel G. Hoffman in *Form and Fable in American Fiction;* Mr. Hoffman adds some stimulating suggestions drawn from his knowledge of such archetypal figures in American writing as the devil and the confidence man. Among still more recent studies, one should mention H. Bruce Franklin's *The Wake of the Gods,* which argues the case for Hindu mythology as the key to the novel's structure and meaning.

American illusion is being detonated by the book; but only as it existed in the minds of readers in the nation at large, or as it was being noisily asserted in the hustings. Virtually no one of the *Fidèle's* passengers believes in man's moral progress, least of all the Confidence Man. He proclaims it only as a part of his strategy, which resembles the strategy suggested later by Huey Long (a striking modern and real-life descendant of Melville's complex hero); Long, it will be recalled, once said that when fascism came to America, it would come in the guise of antifascism. Misanthropy likewise enters the world of Melville's novel in the guise of its opposite, philanthropy. (In the same way, the Confidence Man, a master of irony and a brilliant satirist, denounces both those modes of discourse—"never could abide irony," he says to Pitch; "something Satanic about irony. God defend me from Irony, and Satire, his bosom friend." And in the midst of his dizzying changes of costume and personality, he pauses to inveigh against inconsistency of character.) Within the novel, a belief in human perfectibility is not an active illusion; it is one of many masks or hypocrisies. And the book's emergent theme, as I shall hope to show, is the theme of charity.

If *The Confidence-Man* should thus be initially distinguished from *Candide,* it is the recognizable and awe-inspiring ancestor of several subsequent works of fiction in America: Mark Twain's "The Man Who Corrupted Hadleyburg" and *The Mysterious Stranger,* for example; and, more recently, Nathanael West's *The Day of the Locust,* Faulkner's *The Hamlet,* Ralph Ellison's *Invisible Man,* John Barth's *The Sot-Weed Factor,* Thomas Pynchon's *V.* Melville bequeathed to those works—in very differing proportions—the vision of an apocalypse that is no less terrible for being enormously comic, the self-extinction of a world characterized by deceit and thronging with impostors and masqueraders, and the image of the supreme tempter (the "super-promiser," as West called him) on the prowl through that world, assisting it toward its promised end. These books and others comprise the continuing "anti-face" of the American dream, the continuing imagination of national and even universal disaster that has accompanied the bright expectancy of the millennium. It is a vast prospect, either way; and *The Confidence-Man* announces at the start the vastness, indeed the totality, of its scope. It will deal, we are told, with nothing less than the entire human race.

After the brief, puzzling view of a flaxen-haired deaf-mute, whose arrival (to which I shall return) coincides with the rumor that "a mysterious impostor from the East" may also be coming aboard the steamer, the narrative turns to inspect the horde of passengers and sees them as including "all kinds of that multiform species, man." They are compared to "Chaucer's Canterbury pilgrims" and to "those Oriental ones crossing the Red Sea towards Mecca;" for a while we are allowed to suppose that these mid-western and mid-century Americans may be intended to resemble the members of St. Augustine's Pilgrim City, the great community of the faithful moving through this earthly world en route to the heavenly and eternal City of God. But we are soon enough disturbed by the awful suspicion that the pilgrim species of this novel is heading in quite an opposite direction.

To chart the course of the pilgrimage, we can begin by noticing the characteristic direction of the book's *prose:* observing what dark periods and unsettling climaxes the prose habitually moves toward. *The Confidence-Man,* I have been trying to insist, is a novel, and should be read as such, rather than as a philosophical dialogue or a contribution to intellectual history (though, like most of Melville's writings, it contains important ingredients of both). It is a novel, moreover, that wears the mask of comedy: primarily, as Melville suggests at the end of the first of several fascinating reflections on the art of fiction (chapter xiv), a "comedy of thought." But the comic technique serves to draw us on through intellectual laughter to something like intellectual panic. Consider, for instance, the description of the woman Goneril, in the story about her in chapter xii:

> Goneril was young, in person lithe and straight, too straight, indeed, for a woman, a complexion naturally rosy, and which would have been charmingly so, but for a certain hardness and bakedness, like that of the glazed colors on stone-ware. Her hair was of a deep, rich chestnut, but worn in close, short curls all round her head. Her Indian figure was not without its impairing effect upon her bust, while her mouth would have been pretty but for a trace of moustache. Upon the whole, aided by the resources of the toilet, her appearance at distance was such, that some might have thought her, if anything, rather beautiful, though of a style of beauty rather peculiar and cactus-like.

The whole tone, purpose, and strategy of *The Confidence-Man* are in those sentences, with their parade of notations and counter-notations, and the final flurry of phrases that modify, hesitantly contradict, and then utterly cancel one another out, leaving not a rack of positive statement behind. Goneril is in fact repellent: flat-chested, with a baked face and matted hair, heavily made-up, moustached and prickly-looking: *or is she?* As her physical actuality is blurred and dissolved by Melville's prose, we belatedly remember that Goneril probably does not even exist, but is simply an invention of the Confidence Man himself in his guise as "the man with the weed."

Or take Melville's analysis of the gentleman with the gold sleeve buttons in chapter vii. He had, Melville tells us with a straightforward air, the "very good luck to be a very good man"; although, Melville adds, he could not perhaps be called righteous, and righteousness was indeed—St. Paul is cited as the authority —a quality superior to goodness. Still, Melville goes on, the gentleman's goodness, if falling short of righteousness, should even so not be regarded as a *crime;* or anyhow (pressing the argument onward) not a crime for which the poor fellow should be sent to jail, since after all he might have been innocent of it. This is mental and moral sabotage. Amid all those pre-Jamesian qualifiers and circlings, Melville is of course insinuating that the gentleman with the gold buttons is not good at all: that his alleged goodness is no more than willful, self-protective innocence, thus reinforcing an earlier hint that the gentleman was the kind who refused to dirty his hands in the dilemmas of ethical choice, and was moral brother to history's most notorious hand-washer, "the Hebrew governor"—Pontius Pilate. Before Melville's prose is through with him, this very good man is lumped with those responsible for the crucifixion of Christ; and Melville has delivered himself of a very searching moral insight.

In short, the first and most accomplished of the confidence men in the novel is the author; and his first potential victim is the inattentive reader. The drastic aim of Melville's comedy of thought is to bring into question the sheer possibility of clear thinking itself—of *knowing* anything. The aim is a sort of intellectual derangement, by arousing and deploying what Whitman called the terrible doubt of appearances; doubt every which way; doubt of the gold-buttoned gentleman's goodness and of Goneril's beauty, and then doubt of that doubt. Out of these particular and playful doubts, there gradually arise the more fateful ones, those which shake our foundations: doubt about goodness and beauty as existent realities anywhere in the world of man; doubt about the benevolence of God and of nature, or, for that matter, about the cruelty and hostility of either; doubt, in the outcome the most desperate of all, about the remaining capacity for genuine friendship or charitable love between man and man.

The prose is perfectly designed to bring into view a world of dubious and mutually doubting humanity; one that is dominated, though by no means exclusively populated, by cheats and impostors. As we move about the *Fidèle,* we catch a glimpse of riverboat gamblers. We meet an old soldier whose physique was ruined by a long stretch in the tombs, but who passes for a heroic and charity-imploring veteran of the Mexican war. We encounter a mean-spirited miser, and a callow, conceited college student (needless to say, a sophomore, or wise fool). We are introduced to swindlers, hypocrites, and falsifiers, like Charles Noble and Mark Winsome and Egbert; and, in Egbert's perverse moral fable, we hear of the unspeakable Orchis and his relentless ruination of his no less oddly named "friend," China Aster. We witness the efforts of a young boy who is skilled in corruption beyond his years. So suspicious are the passengers of each other and so expert is Melville at infecting us with a nearly universal skepticism, that we cannot be sure but what some of the apparently decent and goodhearted persons, like the two clergymen in chapter iii, may not also be practitioners of pious fraud.[7]

Most of these are types one could find on a Mississippi steamer something over a century ago, products and representatives of the bustling, greedy, inventive American Middle West; the book's solid sociological basis should never be neglected, nor its running implicit contrast with other times and manners in the American East. But the passengers surveyed are also representative of the pilgrim species, man, in Melville's immeasurably disenchanted —yet not altogether hopeless—view of him. They are the constituents of an appalling human world: a radically "fallen" world, and a splintered one; a wolfish world, wherein the crafty and utterly self-regarding denizens are intent chiefly on fleecing one another. In this world, as in the apocalyptic vision of Albany in *King Lear,* humanity has at last begun to "prey upon itself/ Like

7. H. Bruce Franklin has explored the evidence for this possibility and for comparable ones.

monsters of the deep." It is our world in the process of becoming our hell. And, what is the same thing, the pilgrimage on which the species, man, has here embarked is a pilgrimage not to the Christian shrine or the Moslem Mecca but to a midnight hell on earth of man's own devising. Moving through that cosmos, eventually towering over it, is another figure, the book's ambiguous hero: *the* Confidence Man, for whose visitation the race of small-time confidence men has made itself ripe and ready.

The Confidence Man makes eight appearances in all: seven in fairly rapid succession over the first half of the book, and continuing in the single majestic role of the cosmopolitan throughout the latter half. As Black Guinea, a crippled Negro with a tambourine (in chapter iii), he names the roles he will go on to assume, in a pretence of naming people who know him and will vouch for him: "a werry nice, good ge'mman with a weed, and a ge'mman in a gray coat and white tie, what knows all about me; and a ge'mman wid a big book, too; and a yarb doctor . . . and a ge'mman wid a brass plate" and so on. In the course of time, we meet most of the gentlemen named and in the order listed. It is a part of Black Guinea's guile (or, more simply perhaps, of Melville's forgetfulness) that he also includes several references —to a soldier, a man with a yellow vest, other unspecified "ge'mmen"—who do not show up or, if they do, are not masks of the title figure.[8] But the others appear, ply their trade, and disappear with a sort of rhythmic dishonesty.

In each of his early guises, the Confidence Man exerts one distinctive kind of appeal, represents a parody or debasement of one phase of humanity and performs one sort of symbolic function. The developing pattern would be worth examining in detail, but here we need only remind ourselves of the general progression. The man with a weed in his hat—a spurious emblem of mourning—wears the mask of private misfortune; he spins his melancholy tale of domestic misery (including the bizarre depravities of his "wife," Goneril) and touches the kindly merchant

8. Melville helps us detect the so-to-speak genuine masks of the Confidence Man by a number of devices: for example, by showing the man with the weed in possession of a business card we have seen Black Guinea surreptitiously acquiring; by having the various *personae* loudly vouch for each other; by a similarity of names—John Ringman (a man who is a ringer of changes), John Truman, Frank Goodman.

for money. The man in the gray coat and white tie is the enthusiastic spokesman for the highly organized and public "business" of charity, and for the profit that can accrue from exploiting the multiple pains of mankind; he works effectively on the gold-buttoned passenger and on a "charitable lady." The representative of the Black Rapids Coal Company bespeaks another phase of the business world; he sells stocks to a miser, a sophomore, and the merchant and writes their names in his big book (which we suspect of being the ledger of the damned). The Herb Doctor is the healer as fraud; he plays gainfully on the terrors and the sentiment of the miser, a sick person, and an old soldier; but he is rebuffed by a suffering backwoods "Titan" and by a staunchly morose Missouri bachelor named Pitch. Returning as a sycophantic Philosophical Agent wearing a brass plate, the Confidence Man has another go at Pitch, this time by a more devious and appropriate (because more intellectual) brand of salesmanship, and manages to sell him a nonexistent lad who will be the perfect boy-of-all-work on Pitch's plantation.

The Philosophical Agent concludes the first half of the adventure by announcing his departure from the *Fidèle* at a "grotesquely-shaped bluff" known as "the Devil's Joke"; and it is shortly after this that the Confidence Man re-enters in the role he will retain, that of Frank Goodman, a fantastically garbed "cosmopolitan." Nudged by these proper names, the essential question about the Confidence Man comes into full and alarming prominence. *Are* all his tricks and bluffs and bilkings the grotesque April Fool's jokes of the Devil? The question "grows in seriousness" as the masquerade goes forward; partly because the cosmopolitan himself (Melville twice uses the phrase about him in the later portions of the book) grows in seriousness—and in stature and mystery. For it is this book's ominously joking version of the question that energized Melville's writings, drove and destroyed his Ahab, and unremittingly obsessed his mind. Is the supreme force in the universe a force of good or one of evil? Does one find love at the heart of things, or does one find horror? Is the Confidence Man a devil, or is he a savior? Pitch uses the precise adjective about him when he calls him (chapter xxiv) not a moral but a *"metaphysical* scamp"; for he seems, as the chapters pass, to loom above us, demanding nothing but the largest and most ultimate interpretations. We confront him in his role as cosmopolitan the way Axel Heyst confronted the mysterious trio approaching his remote island in Conrad's *Victory;* their appearance, Heyst felt, was:

> like those myths current in Polynesia, of amazing strangers, who arrive at an island, gods or demons, bringing good or evil to the innocence of the inhabitants—gifts of unknown things, words never heard before.

The Confidence Man—who was "in the extremest sense of the word, a stranger," as Melville says about him—is also an amazing and ambiguous creature of myth; though it is a main feature of the world he invades that it has little innocence left in it and only scattered examples of moral conscience. *As* a creature of myth, the Confidence Man is to some extent Melville's American embodiment of one of the most engaging of the great archetypal figures: namely, the trickster god, especially as that figure took the name of Hermes in Greek mythology. Hermes was a god of travelers, and in this capacity he also escorted the souls of the dead into the underworld. He was, to use modern terms, the god of gambling, and the deity of financial profit, the one involved in commercial dealings—particularly in shady ones. Hermes was the muse responsible for inspiring the rhetoric of salesmanship; he had a modest musical talent; and he was an adept of the daring and elaborate prank.[9] The resemblance to the Confidence Man is impressive; and Melville's hero (like the fictional descendants mentioned earlier) can be related in similar terms to other avatars of the trickster god in European folklore. But the Confidence Man is somehow a more dangerous, at once a twistier and a more portentous figure than Hermes; and his multiform character contains archetypal aspects of quite different orders.

In a book dense with diabolic hints and allusions, the Confidence Man seems to be at least a species of devil: say, a Protestant and even Miltonic devil. His voice is seraphic; and he quotes, sometimes slyly misquotes, Scripture to his purpose. Time and again he is associated with the figure of the snake: so frequently, indeed, that one inevitably begins to doubt the implication. As the cosmopolitan, he appears—like Satan in Melville's favorite biblical text, the book of Job—from coming and going on the earth, and from walking up and down in it; he is "king of

9. See, for example, the *Larousse Encyclopedia of Mythology,* introduction by Robert Graves (New York, 1959), pp. 133 ff.

travelled good-fellows." But the fact is that Melville is of this devil's party: more knowingly than Milton was thought to be by William Blake; and we recall that Milton's Satan is honored by Melville (in chapter xliv) as one of the few radically "original characters" in literature, along with Hamlet and Don Quixote.

The Confidence Man was evidently conceived by Melville as just such an original character: as, when we meditate the matter, the results he achieves can indicate. If the Confidence Man's intention is to deceive for profit, he is only indifferently successful. The man with the wooden leg spots him at once as a sham: "some white operator betwisted and painted up for decoy." The Herb Doctor is assaulted by the Titan. Pitch resists the Confidence Man in two of his disguises, and recognizes him at the third encounter for what he is: "Jeremy Diddler No. 3." Charles Noble is horrified when the cosmopolitan beats him to the draw in asking for a loan (they have been trying to get each other softened up by drink); and Mark Winsome and his disciple combine in a long and chilling refusal of financial assistance. There is a kind of cynicism, a kind of hard-won moral harshness, a kind of moody intelligence, and a kind of rock-like egotism against which the Confidence Man's deviltry seems powerless. But of course the Confidence Man is not really interested in money, though he is extremely interested in the interest evinced in money by others. The wooden-legged man touches a part of the truth when he rebukes the passengers for thinking, as he puts it, that "money . . . is the sole motive to pains and hazard, deception and deviltry, in this world. How much money did the devil make by gulling Eve?" The Missouri Bachelor adds his own similar and bemused reflection: "Was the man a trickster, it must be more for the love than the lucre. Two or three dirty dollars the motive to so many nice wiles?"

The human species in the novel, and in this respect it is emphatically the American species, is intensely money-minded; and it is in fact money-mindedness (rather than, say, optimism or innocence) that is the important first half of the book's theme and the first object of its satire—an evidently ineradicable money-mindedness that plays steadily though obliquely into the Confidence Man's hands. For the motive of *his* nice wiles is something different. His motive is to trick, beguile, maneuver, or force each and every person he accosts to declare himself: to announce, whether consciously or not, his own fundamental moral and

intellectual nature. In this, Melville's hero is unreservedly successful every time: and no less successful with the Titan and Pitch,
with the wooden-legged man and with Mark Winsome, than he
is with his more obvious victims. He has, in short, exactly the
same prodigious effect as that attributed by Melville to the great
original in literature.

The latter, Melville claims, "is like a revolving Drummond-
light, raying away from itself all round it—everything is lit by it,
everything starts up to it (mark how it is with Hamlet)."[10] Mark
how it is, too, with the Confidence Man. His own consciousness
may or may not be a darkened one; but his effect upon others
is incandescent. Everyone he meets "starts up to him," the moral
reality of each is lit by contact with him. This man of many masks
is after all the great unmasker; this unrivaled obfuscator is the
great illuminator; this customarily bland mock optimist is a great
satirist in action. And if the spectacle uncovered by his wiles is
for the most part a dreadful one, several more goodly qualities are
also forced into the open. The merchant's essential if flawed
kindliness is made apparent. The stricken Titan, as we have seen,
is driven to exhibit his outraged integrity. And Pitch, an attractive
figure throughout, is stung by the Herb Doctor's mealymouthed
statement of his position on slavery (chapter xxi: a splendid instance of self-erasing prose) into a passionate and prophetic
expression of political morality:

> "Picked and prudent sentiments. You are the moderate man,
> the invaluable understrapper of the wicked man. You, the
> moderate man, may be used for wrong, but are useless for
> right."

The passengers on board the *Fidèle,* we may say, get the Confidence Man they deserve. And this, I venture, is the explanation
of the novel's opening chapter, and the simultaneous appearance
of the deaf-mute and of the placard describing the impostor from
the East. The Confidence Man is prepared to offer himself either
way. When he appears in the first sentence "suddenly as Manco
Capac at the Lake Titicaca," in the guise of a lamb-like defective,

10. From the OED: *"Drummond light.* 1854. The lime-light or oxyhy-
drogen light (invented by Capt. T. Drummond, R.E., *c* 1825), wherein a
blow-pipe flame, *e.g.* of combined oxygen and hydrogen, impinges on a
piece of pure lime, and renders it incandescent."

intimations of divinity hover in his features and conduct and in the metaphoric language used about him.[11] The deaf-mute, pleading for charity, is manhandled, rejected, and forgotten. He retires to his spot on the forecastle with an aspect "at once gentle and jaded," a sort of weary and disillusioned but still gentle-spirited Christ. After a brief interval (long enough, one presumes, to "betwist" and paint himself), the Confidence Man returns in his alternative or trickster role; and from Black Guinea to the Philosophical Agent, he performs as impostor, outconning the con-men and deviously eliciting those occasional declarations of intellectual and moral firmness.

As the cosmopolitan, however, the Confidence Man is more and other than an impostor. He becomes a figure of almost palpably greater dimension; as though now composed of larger and more resplendent versions of the two alternative roles he had previously practiced. He is, we may suppose, an outsize embodiment of the major contradictions in the universe and in man: or so he is willing to insinuate (in chapter xlii) when the barber, startled by what for an instant he had taken for "a sort of spiritual manifestation," exclaims in relief that the cosmopolitan "is only a man."

> "*Only* a man? As if to be but a man were nothing. But don't be too sure what I am. You call me *man,* just as the townsfolk called the angels who, in man's form, came to Lot's house; just as the Jew rustics called the devils who, in man's form, haunted the tombs. You can conclude nothing absolute from the human form, barber."

All the enigmas are there—human versus inhuman; angel versus devil—and we can conclude nothing absolute. But that is not the same as saying that we can conclude absolutely nothing. Melville has offered a long-range advance hint in the multiple analogy suggested at the end of the second chapter: between the crowd of passengers—"these varieties of mortals [who] blended their varieties of visage and garb;" mid-America—"the dashing and all-fusing spirit of the West;" and the great river—"the

11. Elizabeth S. Foster informs us that Manco Capac was a Peruvian god, a child of the sun—the deaf-mute, we remember, appears at sunup—and the legendary founder of the Inca Empire. His earthly career began with his sudden manifestation at Lake Titicaca.

Mississippi itself, which, uniting the streams of the most distant and opposite zones, pours them along, helter-skelter, in one cosmopolitan tide." We have to learn, as the novel unfolds, never to place complete trust in any individual statement by author or character; but it is impossible not to add a fourth term to the analogy. It is, needless to say, that of the dashing and confident cosmopolitan himself, with his garb of many colors, his shifting visage, his all-fusing character, his multizoned citizenship. He really is Everyman—that is, Everyman as All-men; manifesting to a splintered world the grand human potential for demonism or divinity, summoning mankind to choose.

It is, finally, exactly in his all-fusing personality that the cosmopolitan bespeaks and tests the human capacity *for* fusion: for friendship, for the intimate and organic relation between man and man, for free participation in a human community. No one of his tests is failed more absolutely; and it is that failure that darkens and renders more deeply "serious" the closing sections of the book. One way, indeed, to trace the growth in seriousness from the first half of the novel to the second is to follow the development in focus from what the man in the gray coat calls the *business* of charity to what we ourselves might call the *virtue* of charity. Of all the interrelated words and terms and themes that are central to *The Confidence-Man*—confidence, faith, trust, nature, goodness, and so on—it is probably charity that is the chief victim of Melville's dialectical battering. This is hardly surprising: for charity in its traditional Christian or Pauline sense—the self-giving love between man and man—had always been for Melville the supreme human resource, the supreme human counter-measure, in a wolfish and maddeningly ambiguous world; and Melville's commitment to it was passionately manifested in his fiction, his letters and his marginalia, as well as in his life. He was all the more alert to the way charity had been reduced to its narrower and materialistic if no less traditional meaning, not of self-giving but of money-giving (as the man in the gray coat indicates, institutionalized money-giving). Charity in this lowly sense is the source of much of the hoaxing in the earlier episodes, when money is handed over and withheld with all the air of a debased ritual. But meanwhile, in addition to those sordid exposures, the many debates about the degree of goodness in man, in nature, and in God have been pointing up the urgency of the issue of charity in its higher sense. This is what is finally at stake in the cosmopolitan's encounters, in the relationships enacted, and in the long anecdotes exchanged.

The most fully dramatized form of charity is the displayed capacity for genuine friendship; and it is of this that the stories both of Charlemont (chapter xxxiv) and Orchis and China Aster (chapter xl) provide such bleakly negative demonstrations. The lengthy report on Colonel John Moredock (whose historic career is adjusted to Melville's fictional needs) is a more generalized example: that, namely, of obstinate if courageous and honorable hatred toward an entire segment of the human race, the whole breed of Indians; the latter appear as so many devils to be exterminated, and in dealing with them Colonel Moredock exhibits extreme versions of all the qualities opposite to the virtue of charity. The fascinations of Colonel Moredock's adventurous career and the complexities of his character are such that his story, for a while, runs away from the novel, and becomes uncommonly absorbing and memorable for its own sake. But the other two tales are more sharply related to the book's major theme. Charlemont—and the cosmopolitan tells his story immediately after his "boon companion" Charles *Noble* has agitatedly rejected a request for money—was a man too much possessed of a fragile dream of friendship. In the crisis, he does not dare put his ideal to the test, and so vanishes till he has recovered those material fortunes upon which, as he secretly and desperately believes, all friendship is actually grounded. The story of Orchis is, in itself, an extended study in the hypocrisies of friendship; but it gets its vibrations from the comically bewildering dramatic context within which it is being recited.

Egbert offers his account of the systematic destruction of one friend by another as a moral lesson against borrowing or lending among friends. Part of the dramatic irony at work here is that Egbert is as it were the human application of the idealism of his master Mark Winsome:[12] an idealism that, though opposite in force, has curiously similar consequences in practice to the reported idealism of Charlemont. At the same time, and at the

12. At some remove, the figure of Mark Winsome seems to be a satire on Emerson, or on the Emersonian kind of idealist. But Winsome no more represents Melville's rounded view of Emerson than the Colonel Moredock story represents his view of Indians—or, for that matter, Black Guinea his view of the Negro.

cosmopolitan's request, Egbert has assumed the role of Charles Noble: that is, of the false friend whose recent conduct had given rise to the story of Charlemont. The various scenes and stories thus mirror and parody each other; and in the dialectical squeeze that results, the sheer possibility of the most minimal of friendships seems altogether to evaporate. It is the fulfillment, the final confirmation, of what had been implicit in the novel's opening scene: when the deaf-mute's plea for charity—a plea carried by scribbled phrases from St. Paul—was greeted with derision and violence.

We come thus to the novel's ending: to the solitary pious old man discovered reading the Bible by the light of a single and strangely decorated lamp. A mysterious boy, a sort of apprentice devil apparently, sells the old man protective devices against the world's deceitfulness and thievishness, in which, the old man has only just declared, he does not believe; while a voice from one of the bunks cries out about the Confidence Man and about the apocalypse. The last lamp is extinguished; and the Confidence Man "kindly [leads] the old man away" into the darkness. There is without doubt a sense of terrible and total finality about the scene. The closing questions of *King Lear,* those uttered by Edgar and Albany, come insistently to mind: "Is this the promis'd end?/ Or image of that horror?" An already darkened world had shown itself radically devoid of the one human impulse that might relight it and redeem it: the impulse of charity. The last scene, with its heavily and somberly ceremonial atmosphere, seems to be enacting a ritual of cosmic obliteration. Perhaps it is; perhaps the Confidence Man, having induced the human species into freely choosing its own damnation, is now ready to escort it with all courtesy down to the underworld.

But Melville does have one more thing to say: that "Something further may follow of this Masquerade." There is no implication here that Melville contemplated writing additional episodes; it is hard to name a novel that so completely comes to its end as does *The Confidence-Man.* It is not the novel but the Masquerade it has been describing that may continue. The ambiguous power represented by the Confidence Man may make another visitation: may at some future time enact again what Hart Crane called God's "parable of man." *This* visitation could scarcely end anywhere except in absolute darkness; for though the human species did not know it, it had been edging into darkness all along. The next time may be different: but Melville does not encourage us to think so. He only makes it clear that the Confidence Man is not the bringer of darkness; he is the one who reveals the darkness in ourselves. Whether this is the act of a devil or an angel may not, when all is said and done, really matter.

1964

HAWTHORNE AND JAMES:
THE MATTER OF THE HEART

The Bostonians is Henry James's single major effort at a novel not only set entirely on the American scene but populated exclusively by American characters; and it is hardly surprising that, when he came to write it, James's imagination should be more than usually hospitable to the good influence of his major American predecessor in the art of fiction. The Hawthorne aspect of *The Bostonians* is pervasive: so much so that James's novel seems at times to be composed largely of cunning rearrangements and inversions—on a lower mimetic level (to borrow Northrop Frye's category) and at a later moment in history—of ingredients taken over from Hawthorne. The several similarities between *The Blithedale Romance* and *The Bostonians,* as between novels dealing respectively with the New England reformist temper before and after the Civil War, have been sufficiently pointed out, and we may accept them as among the valid commonplaces of American literary history. But what is striking is that *The Bostonians* carries forward and downward more interestingly yet from *The Scarlet Letter,* and that it significantly perverts elements derived from *The House of the Seven Gables.* I even suspect that James, for the fullness of his artistic effect, may have depended upon our having the novels of Hawthorne in mind: as, for example, Thomas Mann in *The Magic Mountain* depended upon the reader's recollection of the *Odyssey* and the *Divine Comedy,* on each of which he was ringing a number of ironic and terrible changes. If my suspicion of James is correct, it was splendidly continental and un-American of him: the more so because, when the American writings are juxtaposed, they bring into prominence compulsions and strategies that have become generic to American fiction, in good part because Hawthorne made it possible for James to see those phenomena as generic to any imaginative view of that American world which, in *The Bostonians,* James for the first and last time explored in depth.

They bring into view, among other equally absorbing things, what I find no way to avoid calling the American theme; in James's case, we might call it his own local treatment of the intranational theme. One likes to assume that American fiction has displayed a sufficient variety of themes; none of the novels in question is inclined to reduce reality to a single phase or anything as abstract as a theme, still less a theme transfixed and further reduced by a patriotic adjective. But it remains true that one idea more than another has agitated American novelists from Hawthorne's generation to our own, and that this idea is what Hawthorne defined as "the sanctity of a human heart." We should cling to Hawthorne's remarkable and precise wording of the formula, and not shrink the matter to a mere question of "identity" or some polemic for the rights of personality. Understood as Hawthorne and James understood it, wrapped in unmistakable if ambiguous religious connotations, the formula has had an almost explosive power of suggestion for the novel in America (and, from Whitman onward, for poetry too).

It has appeared there, persistently, as a kind of touchstone for human behavior and social organization. True and false human relationships have been identified by appeal to it. It is what is at stake when everything is at stake: what has most aroused novelists when they seek to dramatize the periodic clash between new ideas and old; the real issue in fictionalized moments of historic social crisis and ideological change. It is or has been made to seem the measure of progress and reaction, what threatens the old and is threatened by it. It is or has been made to seem the first of all sacraments in any vital religion, what blasphemes the established order and is blasphemed by it. It is even implicated in the distinction of genres to which American fiction has been prone: allegory, legend, romance, satire, the realistic novel. To these large contentions, a whole range of American writers could testify, though I shall not summon them to do so. I want only to reflect, by means of a few notes and notations, on the extent to which Hawthorne and—following him—James felt the radical force of the heart's sanctity; and on how, by making that force palpable in narrative, they showed what the American novel can grapple with and how much it can accomplish. I shall be addressing myself to what Hawthorne's generation called a writer's talent as much as to his genius, his craft as much as his vision; nor do I expect to say anything very new. But the occasion is ceremonial: a time for reaffirmations.[1]

I

In *The Scarlet Letter*, as in *The Bostonians*, the theme of the heart's sanctity is closely associated with a question about the condition of women, and that question in turn arises out of a supple play of historical perspectives. The patterning becomes evident in the course of the opening scene: though fully so, I shall suggest, rather to the attentive reader than to the actors in the drama. Among the latter, it is Dimmesdale who, for his own mixed private purposes, comes closest to sounding the theme: when, according to John Wilson's report, he argues that "it were wronging the very nature of woman to force her"—as Hester Prynne is being forced—"to lay open her heart's secret in such broad daylight, and in presence of so great a multitude." Hawthorne has already let us know that he shares Dimmesdale's attitude and goes beyond it, and that in his opinion enforced public exposure wrongs not only the nature of woman but human nature generally, that it violates some urgent, perhaps some sacred, principle of life: "There can be no outrage, methinks, against our common nature . . . more flagrant than to forbid the culprit to hide his face for shame." Unlike Dimmesdale, who is wholly encased within what he believes to be a changeless theocratic structure, Hawthorne is there speaking out of a historical perspective. His voice is that of the humane nineteenth-century New England spirit as it broods over the New England of two centuries earlier; and it is the same spirit that had been quick to observe, and from the same historical vantage point, the awesome dignity as well as the cruelty of Hester's punishment: "On the other hand, a penalty, which, in our day, would infer a degree of

1. The occasion was the centenary of Hawthorne's death—May 16, 1964—and a gathering in Columbus, Ohio, sponsored by the Ohio State University Press, which also honored the date by publishing a volume of *Centenary Essays*. The present essay was read at the morning session; in the afternoon Professor Lionel Trilling read his fine essay "Our Hawthorne."

mocking infamy and ridicule, might then be invested with almost as stern a dignity as the punishment of death itself." Hawthorne then goes on to enrich the whole matter by some remarks about the female Bostonians of the 1640s that throw a fascinatingly ambiguous light, in advance, over Dimmesdale's appeal.

As he looks at the females pushing and crowding around the scaffold and watches them "wedging their not insubstantial persons . . . into the throng," as he runs his eyes over their "broad shoulders and well-developed busts" and listens to the startling "boldness and rotundity" of their speech, Hawthorne is led to conclude that: "Morally, as well as materially, there was a coarser fibre in those wives and maidens of old English birth and breeding, than in their fair descendants, separated from them by a series of six or seven generations." For Hawthorne, at least in this novel, the nature of woman is susceptible to historical definition. These seventeenth-century New England women, like everything else in the book, are identified within a long process of physical and moral transformation. Hawthorne traces the process backwards half a century and across the waters to sixteenth-century England and the age of "man-like Elizabeth"—an epoch of "beef and ale . . . [and] a moral diet not a whit more refined;" and forward through the years to Hawthorne's time, noticing how "every successive mother has transmitted to her child a fainter bloom, a more delicate and briefer beauty, and a slighter physical frame, if not a character of less force and solidity."

The passage reveals the characteristic narrative tactic of *The Scarlet Letter,* even though the tactical aim reveals itself more slowly. The temper of the Puritan men during the period of the novel's action is, like the nature of the women, established by the tracing out of a historical process, and one which again stretches back to the Elizabethan age, forward into the later generations of Puritans, and on into the nineteenth century. Hawthorne (in chapter xxi) pauses in his account of the holiday games to insist that "the great, honest face of the people smiled grimly, perhaps but widely too." For they were, he reminds us, "not born to an inheritance of Puritan gloom. They were native Englishmen, whose fathers had lived in the sunny richness of the Elizabethan epoch." They were men, in fact, who by 1645 were only "in the first stages of joyless deportment;" it was not they but their "immediate posterity, the generation next to the early emigrants, [who] wore the blackest shade of Puritanism, and so darkened the national visage with it, that all the subsequent years have not sufficed to clear it up."

What Hawthorne is doing by means of this recurring dialectic of historical epochs is to create the terms—the very sources of meaning—of the drama he is engaged in describing; and the achievement is a remarkable one. Hawthorne knew, better than any writer of his time, that existence for the Puritan "was completely dramatic, every minute was charged with meaning."[2] In his own words, the Puritans tended to speak of human existence as simply a state of "trial and warfare"—the scene of the great war between God and the devil; a scene overwhelmed by allegory. It was just this quality of Puritan life that made it so attractive a subject for a novelist of Hawthorne's dramatic persuasion. But the crucial point is this: that the meaning with which every minute of the action in *The Scarlet Letter* is charged is never quite the meaning assigned to it by the characters involved, nor could it be. For surrounding the meanings so confidently attributed to events and relationships by the magistrates and the clergymen, the matrons and the maidens, is the creative play of Hawthorne's historical imagination. This is, so to speak, the charging force of the novel; and this it is that invests what I take to be the supreme moment in the story, the swift exchange between Dimmesdale and Hester in the forest, with something like a revolutionary significance.

Between the opening scene and that encounter, much had been happening and much a-building; one of the many things Hawthorne taught James was to let narrative power accumulate at a fairly measured pace, so as to give maximum resonance to those otherwise slender moments when the entire drama is asked to change course and, in doing so, to yield up its central meaning. Among the several developments in *The Scarlet Letter,* we may mention the two most obvious ones. There is, on the one hand, the long patient effort of Chillingworth to drag Dimmesdale out of his psychological hiding place and onto a private scaffold, a place of moral exposure, of Chillingworth's own making. And on the other, there has been the strange career of Hester's interior musings. The exchange in the forest is the created compound of these two developments—and of Hawthorne's handling of them.

2. Perry Miller and Thomas H. Johnson, *The Puritans* (New York, 1938), p. 60.

In her lonely cottage by the sea, Hester has come into touch with the array of new ideas that, as Hawthorne says, were stirring the minds of Europe and toppling the systems of "ancient prejudice" ("wherewith," he characteristically adds, "was linked much of ancient principle"). But she is able to do so because, in her tragic freedom, she is gifted with the mode of imagination that informs the entire narrative—the historical imagination—and she is the only person in the book to be so gifted. Hawthorne permits Hester to share a little in his liberated perspective: she alone envisages the possibility of significant historical change, and she alone is allowed thereby to escape some real distance from the allegorized world of fixed and changeless meanings and conditions and relationships which all other figures in the book inhabit. As Hester reflects upon "the whole race of womanhood," she arrives at the vision of social and sexual revolution to which, Hawthorne implies, women in her position are always liable.

> As a first step, the whole system of society is to be torn down, and built up anew. Then, the very nature of the opposite sex, or its long hereditary habit, which has become like nature, is to be essentially modified, before woman can be allowed to assume what seems a fair and suitable position. Finally, all other difficulties being obviated, woman cannot take advantage of these preliminary reforms, until she herself have undergone a still mightier change.

The consequence of all this—as Hester, at the book's end, is still telling the unhappy women to whom she ministers—would be to "establish the whole relation between man and woman on a surer ground of mutual happiness." But until it is revealed to her by Dimmesdale, Hester does not truly perceive the ground of that ground.

Hawthorne reminds us how appalling Hester's speculations would have seemed to the Puritan authorities: "as perilous as demons." He reminds us, too, how genuinely dangerous, how gravely unsettling, such speculations can be for the person who entertains them: they can quite literally, he suggests, draw one on toward madness. But what Hawthorne most deeply distrusts is not Hester's revolutionary dream, but the essentially intellectual source and nature of it. It is too much a product of the head; and "a woman," Hawthorne declares, "never overcame these problems by any exercise of thought." The remark is by no means condescending, for *The Scarlet Letter* is animated by the belief that these problems can be overcome, or at least that the overcoming of them should be among the supreme goals of human effort. Hawthorne so far believes that a woman will lead the way, if anyone will, that he grants the woman Hester the unique privilege of entering into his own historical perspective. But his dominant conviction is that the solution must come from the heart; that the problems will themselves vanish when, and only when, the heart "chance to come uppermost." And this, of course, is what does happen during the meeting in the forest.

There, for a brief and perhaps illusory moment, the relationship between Dimmesdale and Hester, between the man and the woman, stands upon that surer ground of mutual happiness that Hester has dreamed of. One even conjectures that for a few seconds the scarlet letter betokens those words—"angel" and "apostle"—with which Hester hoped to associate herself as the destined prophetess of the new revelation. Such religious titles and allusions are, in any event, not out of place. For what comes flickering into view, what the whole course of the novel has been preparing for, and what terrifies Dimmesdale when he catches a glimpse of it, is something much more far-reaching than social reform. It is, indeed, a religious revolution. "May God forgive us both!" Dimmesdale says sadly. And then:

> "We are not, Hester, the worst sinners in the world. There is one worse than even the polluted priest! That old man's revenge has been blacker than sin. He has violated, in cold blood, the sanctity of a human heart. Thou and I, Hester, never did so!"
>
> "Never, never," whispered she. "What we did had a consecration of its own. We felt it so! We said so to each other! Hast thou forgotten it?"
>
> "Hush, Hester!" said Arthur Dimmesdale, rising from the ground. "No; I have not forgotten."

In context, the implication is almost breath-taking. It is just because neither of them had violated the sanctity of the other's heart that what they had done—their entire relationship—had had a consecration of its own. Dimmesdale's words release Hester's extraordinary contention and give all her wandering meditations a sudden coherence. It is from the implications of Hester's answer that Dimmesdale shies back in a kind of horror, for he is equipped to appreciate the enormity of them. He had been trained to pursue his priestly calling among a people for whom "religion and law were almost identical, and in whose character both were . . . thoroughly interfused." But latent in his attribution of sanctity to the human heart, and still more, in the suggestion it leads to, that of the sanctification of lawless love, is the seed of a new sacramental order; and one that, from the Puritan standpoint, is altogether blasphemous. No wonder that Dimmesdale rises to his feet, cuts short the exchange, and commands Hester to hush. It is a moment characteristic of Hawthorne —the short glimpse and the speedy covering over of the world-disturbing truth—and Hester hushes. But she does not relinquish her vision, nor will she for the rest of her fictional life.

She takes no steps to bring that new order into being, except for her humane ministrations to the forlorn who come to her door. But Hawthorne tells us that, had matters been otherwise, Hester "might have come down to us in history hand in hand with Anne Hutchinson"—"sainted Anne Hutchinson," as he has called her earlier—"as the foundress of a religious sect." It is the very substance of that projected and unrealized religion that is gradually created by the novel's historical dialectics; and Hester's limited eligibility to lead it can be measured by the limited but real degree of her participation in those dialectics. It would be a religion founded on the doctrine of the inviolable sanctity of the individual human heart; and one in which the human relation—above all the relation between man and woman—itself shaped by allegiance to that doctrine (by the mutual reverence of heart for heart), would become the vessel of the sacred, the domain of the consecrated. It would have provided a sacramental basis for a genuine community, of the kind envisaged, for example, by Henry James the elder in *Society the Redeemed Form of Man*. Indeed, it is tempting to look beyond Hawthorne across a dozen decades, to notice how, from the two Henry Jameses onward, writer after writer has reflected the same curious but persistent brand of religious humanism—and usually in an escape from traditional religious institutions and dogmas, and in despite of the world's irreverent practices. But no writer ever succeeded in making this epochal possibility as compelling as did Hawthorne: for no American writer possessed the vision, both historical and transcendent, to set the new possibility amid and against the stiffening vigor, the hard historical actuality, of the older order. In the clarity of his perception and in his unsentimental compassion, Hawthorne was able, as well, to do honor to both the old and the new, while seeing each as an absolute challenge to the other. If Hester had become the destined prophetess, she "might, and not improbably would, have suffered death from the stern tribunals of the period, for attempting to undermine the foundations of the Puritan establishment." Within the world of *The Scarlet Letter,* the establishment triumphs; but within the novel as a novel, its foundations are constantly and quietly undermined by a play of perspectives to which only Hester is privy; and the fusion of religion and law is giving way to a new conception of sanctity.

II

About *The House of the Seven Gables,* there is for present purposes less that needs to be said; but we can begin by remarking that its narrative method to some extent reverses that of *The Scarlet Letter,* and that the Hawthornian formula emerges here from a different direction. In *The Scarlet Letter,* an action set in the past completes its meaning under the pressure of a shifting later-day perspective; in *The Seven Gables,* events occurring in the present—or anyhow in "an epoch not very remote from the present day"—draw much of their force from the shifting pressure of a long past, through a series of what seem about to be fated re-enactments and turn out to be reversals. *The Scarlet Letter* projects forward, beyond the consciousness of its characters, from the 1640s to Hawthorne's own time; *The Seven Gables* reaches backward from Hawthorne's time almost to the age of *The Scarlet Letter,* touching upon happenings that took place in or around 1670 (Hawthorne's arithmetic is casual), 1707, 1820, and 1850. In *The Scarlet Letter,* Hawthorne, observing the robust physiques of the Puritan matrons, glances ahead to the fainter bloom and briefer beauty of their descendants. In *The Seven Gables,* almost everything is described as diminished or decaying, and contrasted with the heartier qualities of earlier times. Even Jaffrey Pyncheon, for all his wicked strength, carries in his face the marks of a physiological decline:

> The Judge's face had lost the ruddy English hue that showed its warmth through all the duskiness of the Colonel's weather-beaten cheek, and had taken a sallow shade, the established complexion of his countrymen.

The brother and sister are dreary relics: Hepzibah is a "far-descended and time-stricken virgin," and Clifford, until the book's climax, is no more than an elderly wreck of what had been a beautiful and brilliant young man. Their habitation, the molder-ing house with its garden-plot "so unctuous with two hundred years of vegetable decay," and its "ugly luxuriance of gigantic weeds" is dismally appropriate, an objective correlative for their weedy spirits. It is within such an atmosphere that Hawthorne's historical imagination—working with no less agility than before, but, as it were, reversing its direction—once again brings into dramatic play the principle of the heart's sanctity.

The principle is no doubt less central here than in *The Scarlet Letter:* ideas in general are less central in *The Seven Gables* than in its much more dramatic predecessor. But it does make its important appearance, and it is, as formerly (though less tightly), related to a cluster of "new ideas." Given the time-laden atmo-sphere of the story, we may expect the new ideas in this case to be mainly ideas about newness itself: about getting rid of the past which, as the daguerrotypist Holgrave proclaims oratorically, "lies upon the Present like a giant's dead body," in every con-ceivable physical, psychological, social, legal, and religious form. Holgrave's rhetoric is, of course, excessive; it warrants the re-coiling comment of Phoebe about the ferocity of his hatred for everything old; and it is countered by the very figure of Clifford, by the infinite pathos of a man who really has gotten rid of the past, or been bereft of it. It is Holgrave's personal destiny, in the novel, to come to terms with the past, including his own genealogy. Nonetheless, Holgrave (and Hawthorne goes on to say as much) deserves our attention and that of his fellow characters; for more than anyone else in the novel Holgrave understands the necessary basis of any new system of life: a quality he himself possesses and which Hawthorne—in the milder and properly more modern but still religious idiom of *The Seven Gables*—describes as "the rare and high quality of reverence for another's individuality."

The phrase occurs (in chapter xiv) at a moment when Holgrave has very nearly mesmerized Phoebe by his histrionic reading of the story about Alice Pyncheon. The latter, one remembers, was herself completely mesmerized by one Matthew Maule, grandson of that Matthew Maule who had been executed for witchcraft upon the false testimony of Colonel Pyncheon; and who thus takes his family's revenge upon the wicked Colonel's granddaughter. Alice is held in thrall until Matthew's marriage, where-upon she wakes from her "enchanted sleep" and straightway dies —leaving Matthew "gnashing his teeth, as if he would have bitten his own heart in twain," not unlike Chillingworth on the occasion of Dimmesdale's death. This is the supreme instance, in *The Seven Gables,* of the violation of Hawthorne's first principle, a literally murderous invasion of another person's individuality: Maule "had taken a woman's delicate soul into his rude gripe, to play with—and she was dead!" Retelling that story almost a cen-tury and a half later, another Maule (who temporarily calls him-self Holgrave) comes to the verge of re-enacting that earlier sin and of casting a similarly fatal spell over the susceptible spirit of young Phoebe Pyncheon. "A veil was beginning to be muffled about her"—one thinks of the veilings and mesmerizings of *The Blithedale Romance*—"in which she could behold only him, and live only in his thoughts and emotions." Holgrave's gesture at this point not only liberates Phoebe's potentially enslaved self; it is a victory over his own dangerous and inherited power—and insofar a reversal and a rejection of the past.

> To a disposition like Holgrave's, at once speculative and active, there is no temptation so great as the opportunity of acquiring empire over the human spirit; nor any idea more seductive to a young man than to become the arbiter of a young girl's destiny. Let us, therefore,—whatever his defects of nature and education, and in spite of his scorn for creeds and institu-tions,—concede to the daguerrotypist the rare and high quality of reverence for another's individuality. Let us allow him in-tegrity, also, forever after to be confided in; since he forbade himself to twine that one link more which might have rendered his spell over Phoebe indissoluble.

And, with a gesture of his hand, he restores Phoebe to herself.

It is because he refuses to repeat his ancestor's blasphemous act and to make his spell over the girl indissoluble, that Holgrave becomes fitted for that highest kind of human relationship: a marriage, based not on human empire but on mutual reverence, a modest example, one supposes, of the right relation between man and woman prophesied by Hester Prynne. Holding back from the indissoluble spell, Holgrave makes possible the indis-soluble union, something that will have a consecration of its own.

Quite the opposite, needless to say, is the case with Jaffrey Pyncheon.

The Judge is totally bent on acquiring "empire over a human spirit"—a diabolic empire over the spirit of poor Clifford—and he acquires it by repeating the actions of his ancestor, by a combination of murder and false testimony. Those crimes were monstrous enough, but the final sacrilege, the very sin of the crimes as it were, is the utterly debilitating spell the Judge has cast and continues to exercise over Clifford: "That strong and ponderous man had been Clifford's nightmare. There was no free breath to be drawn within the sphere of so malevolent an influence." Clifford is released from his psychic imprisonment only by Jaffrey's death. Jaffrey, who had believed too much in the past, who believed that the past could endlessly repeat and re-enact itself and who even believed in the inherited tale of buried treasure: Jaffrey is himself destroyed by the past, by the inherited disease—"the physical predisposition in the Pyncheon race"—and he dies with the legendary blood on his lips. The Judge, as we may say, is defeated by the legend, as he ought to have been: for in the deepest sense, it was a heartless legend, and he is a heartless man. By his defeat and death, Clifford is released from the legend, enough at least to recover something of himself. Holgrave escapes further still from the confines of the legend, as Hester Prynne—in her thoughts and in her gentle advices to the wretched—had moved somewhat outside the confines of allegory. As a work of fiction, *The House of the Seven Gables* moves similarly away from the legendary and toward the more modern and realistic; and arrives at a form, the Romance, in which Hawthorne could present his steadiest belief about human nature and its relationships not as an ideal dimly visible in the far future, but as an immediate possibility among the modern realities.

III

> "Every one will, in his way—or in her way—plead the cause of the new truths. If you don't care for them, you won't go with us."
>
> "I tell you I haven't the least idea what they are! I have never yet encountered in the world any but old truths— as old as the sun and the moon. How can I know? But *do* take me; it's such a chance to see Boston."

The new truths to which, in the opening scene of *The Bostonians,* Olive Chancellor so passionately appeals and of which
her kinsman from Mississippi Basil Ransom, makes courteous
mock, are, like those of *The Scarlet Letter,* ideas bearing chiefly
upon the unhappy condition and possible future status of women.
There are times, indeed, in *The Bostonians* when Olive Chancellor
(though her surname more suitably if very faintly echoes that
of Chillingworth) markedly resembles Hester Prynne. Or, more
accurately, there are times when James is plainly drawing both
his rhetoric and his subject matter not from contemporary historical developments but—as literary artists tend to do—from
existing literature, and especially from *The Scarlet Letter.* "The
unhappiness of women! The voice of their silent suffering was
always in her ears, the ocean of tears that they had shed from the
beginning of time seemed to pour through her own eyes." That
is Olive, in James's articulation of her. "Women . . . —in the
continually recurring trials of wounded, wasted, wronged, mis-
placed, or erring and sinful passion,—or with the dreary burden
of a heart unyielded, because unvalued and unsought,—came to
Hester's cottage, demanding why they were so wretched, and
what the remedy." That, of course, is Hawthorne; and if Hester
has once "imagined that she herself might be the destined prophetess," so "it seemed to [Olive] at times that she had been born
to lead a crusade." It is, like the movement meditated by Hester,
to be a religious crusade: "This was the only sacred cause; this
was the great, the just revolution." And the nature and scope of
it, as they form themselves in Olive's overheated mind, resemble
those of the social upheaval Hester had pondered, with sacrificial
death once more the probable and even desirable outcome:

> It must sweep everything before it; it must exact from the
> other, the brutal, blood-stained, ravening race, the last particle
> of expiation! It would be the greatest change the world had
> seen; it would be a new era for the human family, and the
> names of those who had helped show the way and lead the
> squadrons would be the brightest in the tables of fame. They
> would be the names of women weak, insulted, persecuted,
> but devoted in every pulse of their being to the cause, and
> asking no better fate than to die for it.

In the near-hysteria of tone and the savagery of attitude toward the male race, the passage diverges markedly from the pas-

sage quoted earlier from *The Scarlet Letter*. It is, indeed, the meaningful differences between the two novels that I eventually want to stress—and that James himself, as I believe, wanted to stress; for James (to repeat my remark) seems to have counted upon our remembering Hawthorne and to have striven for his ultimate effects by means of a combined echo of and contrast with Hawthorne. But we should notice, meanwhile, that if *The Bostonians* shares with *The Scarlet Letter* an interest in revolutionary ideas about the condition of women, those ideas palpitate in *The Bostonians* within a general atmosphere of decline oddly similar to that of *The House of the Seven Gables*. In James's novel, as in Hawthorne's romance, almost every item participates in a pattern of diminution. The historical distance spanned in *The Bostonians* is nothing so large as that of *The Seven Gables:* it is at most the four score years of the saintly Fool, Miss Birdseye; and James's impressionistic and allusive evocation of even so short a stretch of history illustrates perfectly the remark of T. S. Eliot that Hawthorne's sense of the past "exercised itself in a grip on the past itself," but that "in James it is a sense of the sense." To which we should add, I think, that James had in particular a sense of Hawthorne's sense; and this made it possible for James to include in his own pattern of decay a much larger variety of elements than Hawthorne, and to cover a great deal more of the national landscape.

To begin with, the reformers who gather in Miss Birdseye's rooms appear aimless, bemused, rhetorically corrupted by comparison with "the heroic age of New England life," the age before the Civil War, an age "of plain living and high thinking, of pure ideals and earnest effort, of moral passion and noble experiment." And the social crusade, the marshaling of the feminist squadrons, sounds suddenly almost tawdry when James invokes "the simple emotion of the old fighting-time," the war itself, escorting us, with Basil Ransom and Verena Tarrant, into Harvard's Memorial Hall and remarking upon the "singularly noble and solemn effect" of the "temple" for the fallen soldiers, its symbolism of "duty and honor . . . sacrifice and example." But the conservative temper in *The Bostonians* is in no less sorry a state than the reformist: there is, on the one hand, the virtual medievalism of Ransom and, on the other, the mere muddled snobbishness of Adeline Luna, who, though she liked to think that the word "conservative" was "the motto inscribed upon her own silken banner" (the motto, in short, of her own crusade), limited her conservatism to prattle about the inferiority of republics and the bad manners of servants.

Places share in the general decay and are analogues of it. The entire Boston area is seen as disappearing into the spreading jungle of factories and engine shops. In James's famous and eloquent description of the western view from Olive's apartment on Charles Street, there is observed "something inexorable in the poverty of the scene," something

> shameful in the meanness of its details, which gave a collective impression of boards and tin and frozen earth, sheds and rotting piles, railwaylines striding flat across a thoroughfare of puddles, and tracks of the humbler, the universal horsecar, traversing obliquely this path of danger; loose fences, vacant lots, mounds of refuse, yards bestrewn with iron pipes, telegraph poles, and bare wooden backs of places.

(It is characteristic of Verena that she thinks this view lovely, just as at first she had secretly wished to emulate Adeline Luna rather than her sister Olive.) But if the northern landscape is thus being devoured by an industrial version of those ugly gigantic weeds that smothered the terrain in *The House of the Seven Gables,* the postwar South—"the poor, dear, desolate old South," as Ransom calls it—lies in utter ruin; and swift recollections of its former splendor sometimes flash through Ransom's consciousness and into ours, as a measure of its present desolation. Within the novel, in fact, and by a pattern of allusion more intricate than I can here suggest, the entire country is represented as having suffered some strange and terrible reversal of fortune (to borrow the phrase used about "the great drawing-room of Europe" in *The Wings of the Dove*). And this aspect is perhaps best summed up in the picture of the Cape Cod town of Marmion (i.e. Marion) which "was a good deal shrunken since the decline in the ship-building interest; it turned out a good many vessels every year, in the palmy days, before the war," but now Ransom gathers the impression "that it had had a larger life, seen better days." The larger life, the better days, stand everywhere behind the elements of the novel—persons, places, movements, ideals, interest—and testify to the present unhappy shrinkage.

In a much-quoted notebook entry for 1883, James wrote that—as his novel's main concern, and as "the most salient and peculiar point in [American] social life"—he had chosen "the decline in the sentiment of sex." That, certainly, is a major phenomenon in *The Bostonians,* and one which many of the other instances of "decline" explain and illuminate. But it is, I think, as much a symptom as a cause; and what the novel's action as well as its rhetoric more profoundly reveals is the decline of the religious sentiment—that is, of the specific religious sentiment to which, with and following Hawthorne, James was himself most profoundly committed. What is happening in this regard is indicated at a stroke, a single casual remark, almost an aside: when James reports that the Harvard library was "a diminished copy of the chapel at King's College," and that Verena Tarrant introduces Basil Ransom into it "with the air of a person familiar with the sanctified spot." These are lines that, in the theater idiom, James is quite willing to "throw away," and we miss nothing but a momentary pang of aesthetic pleasure and admiration if we fail to notice them. Nonetheless, in context, they fairly bristle with meaning.

We can best formulate that meaning by reference once again to *The Scarlet Letter*. There, Hawthorne set his action among a people—the Bostonians of the 1640s—for whom "religion and law were almost identical, and in whose character both were . . . thoroughly interfused." James set his own American novel among a people—the Bostonians of the 1870s—for whom *religion and ideology* were becoming almost identical, and in whose character both were already dangerously confused.[3] And both pairings are portrayed as the absolute enemy of the fundamental religious sentiment: the sense of the sanctity of the individual human heart. *That* is the sense that characterized "the heroic age of New England life"; that is the sense that has most fatally declined; and that is the sense which the novel seeks in its own subtle and dramatic manner to re-establish—though the characters in it do not.

Olive Chancellor, as we have seen, regards her feminist crusade as a sacred cause. Later in the story, she is made by James very tellingly to reflect that "without Verena's tender notes, her crusade would lack sweetness, what the Catholics call unction"; and with Verena, all during the winter of 187–, she looks forward across "the solemn vista of an effort so religious as never to be wanting

3. In his fine introduction to the Modern Library edition of *The Bostonians* (New York, 1956), Irving Howe makes a similar point within a somewhat different context.

in ecstasy." Basil Ransom—who in this regard as in others may be thought of as a deliberate inversion of Hawthorne's Holgrave —invests his own reactionary ideas, and especially his passionate antifeminist speeches, with no less ardent a religious quality; and though with much of what he says James would probably have agreed (in a quieter tone of voice), still Verena responds for James and for us when she is impressed "by the novelty of a man taking that sort of religious tone about such a cause." These are persons, Olive Chancellor and Basil Ransom, who really are violated by ideas, to draw again upon T. S. Eliot's inexhaustibly useful commentary and phrasing; who corrupt their feelings with ideas (the language is still Mr. Eliot's); who "produce the political idea, the emotional idea, evading sensation and thought"—and who make a religion out of the result. They are, in short, ideologues; and worse still, they are ideologues in action. They are not only violated by ideas, they use ideas to violate others; and in particular, of course, they violate, and fight to the death for the privilege of violating, the vulnerable individuality, the susceptible human heart, of Verena Tarrant.

The process need not be spelled out; to do so would be to rehearse most of the book's plot, for the plot turns exactly upon the effort and countereffort of Olive and Basil to possess themselves of Verena, and each in the name of Verena's perfect freedom and the holiness of the conflicting creeds. Two moments may stand for many. When Verena comes to live with Olive, the latter emphasizes the fact that the younger girl "should be as free as air, to go and come." But by that time, James informs us,

> Verena was completely under the charm. The idea of Olive's charm will perhaps make the reader smile; but I use the word not in its derived, but in its literal sense. The fine web of authority, of dependence, that her strenuous companion had woven about her, was now as dense as a suit of golden mail.

The literal sense of "charm" is, of course, a magic spell or incantation; and the suggestion of spells and webs carries us back instantly to the story of enchanted Alice Pyncheon in *The Seven Gables*. That masculine suit of mail, anyhow, retains its power, and its nature is reinforced by frequent allusions to actual or metaphoric cloakings and imprisonments: until, on an early spring afternoon in New York's Central Park, Basil Ransom casts his potent counterspell over the impressionable Verena. The sexual element is here all the more notable, since the ideas Basil expounds to her are, from her viewpoint, monstrous. The girl's reflections

> softly battled with each other as she listened, in the warm, still air, touched with the faraway hum of the immense city, to his deep, sweet, distinct voice, expressing monstrous opinions with exotic cadences and mild, familiar laughs, which, as he leaned toward her, almost tickled her cheek and ear. . . . there was a spell upon her as she listened.

As a dramatic construct—combining as it does the oratorical statement of social theory and of attitudes to history with a sort of psychological-cum-sexual hypnosis—the whole scene derives without much doubt from the long scene between Holgrave and Phoebe that extends from chapter xii through chapter xiv in *The Seven Gables.* The resemblance is worth emphasizing because in certain essential aspects James is carefully reversing Hawthorne, and the force of his accomplishment depends in no small part on our awareness of this. It is not only that all of Basil Ransom's eloquence goes toward getting rid of the present in the name of the past, rather than, as with Holgrave, the other way round. It is also that, Holgrave, for all his temptation to acquire "empire" over Phoebe's spirit, does have the high quality of reverence for her individuality, and releases the girl from her momentary enslavement. Ransom persists in his imperial design, to the end of the scene and the end of the novel.

That kind of reversal characterizes the relation consciously aimed at (as I am maintaining) and achieved between *The Bostonians* and the novels of Hawthorne. In the same way, the social revolution proposed by Olive Chancellor would in its consequences reverse those of the movement that Hester Prynne might have led. Hester's new sect would bring with it a relationship between man and woman grounded on mutual reverence; Olive apparently would like to see that relationship destroyed once and for all. The relationship Olive does establish in the novel (and even she perhaps comes to realize this) is a sort of paradigm of falsehood: it is sexually wrong, morally wrong, even politically wrong; and from the Hawthornian viewpoint of Henry James, it is religiously wrong. Its radical wrongness is one justification for Basil Ransom's ambiguous victory in the denouement; he is, after all, a man and a manly man. And beyond that—though Basil's crusade to "rescue" Verena from "ruin" is deeply suspect (there are too many examples in James's fiction of the lethally selfish nature of the rescuing impulse)—there is in Basil some faint occasional glimmer of the distinctive value of another person's individuality, or at least of Verena Tarrant's.

But "value" thus circumscribed is the strongest word we can use. There is no one in *The Bostonians* who, like Hester or Dimmesdale (for his moment of insight) or Holgrave, has and acts upon a clear sense of the heart's sanctity. The person who most nearly does is Miss Birdseye: she, as Verena exclaims, is "our heroine . . . our saint," exactly because she thinks only of others. There is evidence that James adjusted his attitude of Miss Birdseye as the novel progressed: in the early pages she is the victim of some of James's most brilliant comic writing; but from the second book onward she grows into truly heroic and saintly proportions, and in her final moments she is affectively larger than the life about her. But she *is* the ancient relic of an older epoch, the old heroic age; and in the book's most portentous scene, she does die. And that, of course, is James's point and the motive of his reversals: the antiquity and the death of the old selflessness, the old sanctity, the old sense of sanctity.

James, in *The Bostonians,* is exploiting Hawthorne to suggest a view opposite to Hawthorne about the fundamental *course* of human affairs, at least as those affairs were being conducted in America. James saw the American character moving away from, not toward, a belief in the sanctity of the human heart; away from, not toward, relationships consecrated by that belief. Where Hawthorne, in *The Scarlet Letter,* made tragic drama out of the possibility of religious legalism yielding to reverence for the individual, James in *The Bostonians,* in an equally impressive display of prophetic power, describes individual reverence yielding to a religion of ideology. The world in which that is happening is, as James makes almost appallingly clear, a world without sacrament, without any sort of sacramental sensibility: a world, from the point of view of the literary artist, unavailable to either allegory or legend, and fit primarily for satire and realism.

This is James in mid-career. During his major phase twenty years later, James for various reasons felt himself liberated in part from the clutch of the contemporary. He was then able to return to something like Hawthorne's tragically hopeful vision, and he would then adopt in consequence symbolic devices reminiscent of Hawthorne, along with a Hawthornesque atmosphere of the legendary and remote: precisely to suggest how a sacramental consciousness like that depicted in *The Scarlet Letter* could be quickened into being even within a world characterized by a lust for violation. But in *The Bostonians* James made his comment upon the American scene by casting a Hawthornian eye upon a non-Hawthornian world: by reassembling themes and motives and language from Hawthorne and by twisting and reversing them. It was James's comment as well upon American literature, upon what the novel in America had once done and could now do.

1961

HOLD ON HARD TO THE
HUCKLEBERRY BUSHES

The search for religious elements in literature, especially in
American literature, has become a phenomenon in recent years
that would have startled and bewildered Matthew Arnold, who
did not have this sort of thing in mind at all. An increasing
number of books address themselves to the subject, courses and
symposia are given over to it, and I believe a university department or two have been established to make the undertaking
permanent. Some of the work, like some of the workers, displays
a high degree of cultural relevance; but in general practice the
study of "religion and literature," as the phrase usually is, exhibits
several rather disturbing oddities, the first of which is implied by
the phrase itself. It is theologically correct but aesthetically
perilous: in a way which might ultimately damage the theology.
Absolutely speaking, as between religion and literature, religion
no doubt comes first; but in the actual study of a particular
literary text, it probably ought to follow, and follow naturally
and organically and without strain—for the sake of the religion
as well as the literature. Or so I shall try to suggest. We may
perhaps recall the remark made to Emerson by an old Boston
lady who, talking about the extreme religious sensibility of an
earlier generation, said about those pious folk that "they had to
hold on hard to the huckleberry bushes to hinder themselves
from being translated." Their instinct was as sound as their impulse was proper.

I

It was characteristic of Emerson to have quoted those words,
for he knew well enough that his own hold tended to slip from time

to time. He was articulately dedicated to the actual; he embraced, as he said, the common and explored the low and familiar, both in life and in literature. But the Over-Soul drew him like a magnet, and he was regularly prone to premature translation into the vast, unindividuated realm of the One. The atmosphere he found there was invariably sunny and smiling; and it is by stressing the sunshine and disregarding the translatability, that Randall Stewart, in *American Literature and Christian Doctrine,*[1] is able to condemn Emerson to the sixth circle, the place reserved for the burning tombs of the heresiarchs. "Emerson is the arch-heretic of American literature," says Professor Stewart, "and Emerson-ism [sic: a foreshortening rhetorically equivalent to the phrase Democrat Party] the greatest heresy. By no dint of sophistry can he be brought within the Christian fold. His doctrine is radically anti-Christian, and has done more than any other doctrine to undermine Christian belief in America." There is a kind of health in the hardness of Professor Stewart's saying. But I confess that it has for me a pointless irrelevance which it would not be easy to measure, though it may be important to define.

Professor Stewart's little book is amiably unambiguous in state-ment, and engagingly direct in style; it is sprinkled with nice personal reminiscences of a long and honorable academic life for which many of us have cause to be grateful. The book belongs, in its slender way, to the number of studies which have sought to examine the whole of American literature from a single organiz-ing viewpoint; and in this respect it follows a path opposite to the one followed by Frederick I. Carpenter in *American Literature and the Dream*[2]—a neglected work, in which Emerson appears as the high priest and dream purveyor rather than the arch heretic. But Professor Stewart's title is radically misleading, just as his method is revealingly—one is tempted to say, importantly and usefully—ill advised. By Christian doctrine, Professor Stewart means Protestant doctrine; by Protestant doctrine, he means American Puritan doctrine (in a manner that rather confirms than refutes the contention of the great Protestant historian of dogma, Adolph von Harnack, that there can be no such thing as Prot-estant dogma); by Puritan doctrine, Professor Stewart means very simply the doctrine of Original Sin; and by the doctrine of

1. Baton Rouge, La., 1958.
2. New York, 1955.

Original Sin, it is no longer clear what he means, since the matter
has grown too small to be visible. He seems to mean even less,
so far as one can make out, than T. E. Hulme meant thirty-five
years ago, when he said—in a sentence that has done as much
harm to the cause of cultural good sense as any that one can
rapidly remember—that "dogmas like that of Original Sin . . .
are the closest expression of the categories of the religious attitude." Separated from the rich theological framework within
which it historically evolved, the concept of Original Sin is not
much of a concept at all; it is more an image of unredeemably
depraved human nature shivering somewhere in the void. In any
case, this is the image that provides the single instrument by
which Professor Stewart gauges the value of American writers
from Edwards to the present. By the use of it, he denounces the
villains, those who seem unaware of Original Sin (Paine, Franklin,
Jefferson, Emerson, Whitman, Dreiser, Lewis), and salvages the
elect (Edwards, Hawthorne, Melville maybe, James, Eliot, Hemingway, Faulkner, Warren). But the writings of both heroes and
villains suffer a sort of total defeat. The latter are blown into
oblivion by the author's rumbling southern rhetoric; and the
former are blotted out behind an enormous O S, as Hester
Prynne's image was lost behind the gigantic A reflected in the
convex surface of the shining armor.

In Professor Stewart's case, the translation was effected before
the huckleberry bushes were ever taken hold of. The actualities
of the works in question—their actions, their words, their concrete embodiments, their sensuous images, their characters, their
incidents—seem to have evaporated before a single glance descended on them. This is the likely consequence of the doctrinal
approach to literature. If Professor Stewart had taken a more
generous view of Christian doctrine, he might have composed a
more interesting book; but I am not sure that it would have been
a more pointed and purposeful book, or that it would have done
better service to the field of literature or of religion; for the issue
of priority would still remain. This issue is whether one scrutinizes
literature for its univocal formulations of particular historical
doctrines one cherishes or whether one submits for a while to
the actual ingredients and the inner movement and growth of
a work to see what attitude and insight, including religious attitude
and insight, the work itself brings into being. Emerson continues
to be a valuable case. Proceeding from Emerson's words as he

uttered them, Newton Arvin—who is anything but a sophist, and is on the contrary one of America's most intelligent, tactful, and scholarly critics—has managed to bring Emerson some slight way "within the Christian fold."[3] Emerson, Mr. Arvin says, did after all have a knowledge of evil and an awareness of human sin; his famous cheerfulness was for the most part an achievement, a matter of discipline and hard intellectual choice. But Emerson could not convey his conceptions in the theological vocabulary available to him, because it was not comprehended within that vocabulary; and he was not in command of the vocabulary which could, in fact, convey it. He set it forth in tropes and figures, in shadings and insistences, in asides and repetitions of his own; and he emerged with a view of evil so profoundly different from that of his contemporaries that of sin itself he has seemed to have been simply and blissfully unconscious. For Emerson's sense of the problem was surprisingly similar to the older and more really traditional Christian attitude: the one that held firm from St. Augustine to the Reformation: the view of evil as non-being, as a privation, as a negation and an absence of good. Emerson normally preferred to talk about something rather than nothing, about being rather than non-being and affirmation rather than negation; he lacked the special taste and affection for evil of so many modern intellectuals. But (here I am pushing Mr. Arvin's argument beyond anything he would wish to claim for it) it might be salutary to reflect that, as regards the doctrine of sin, it is Hawthorne who was the heretic and Emerson who was working toward the restoration rather than the undermining of Christian belief in America.

Emerson did not knowingly aim at the restoration of anything: except of the soul's fresh and immediate perception of certain aspects of the universe, getting rid of the linguistic and institutional clutter in which those aspects had gone stale, and relating them anew to the instant of experience. "They only who build on Ideas, build for eternity. . . . The law is only a memorandum. We are superstitious, and esteem the statute somewhat: so much life as it has in the character of living men is its force." That is Emerson's authentic voice, or one of his authentic voices: the voice of a man disentangling the Idea from the historical record of it, and allowing it again to invigorate the present. But it is

3. "The House of Pain," *Hudson Review, 12* (1959), 37–53.

a suggestive and representative accident that, in pursuit of that aim, Emerson's metaphysical gaze lighted just occasionally and without historical awareness upon the essences of certain moral and religious doctrines that had been given their fullest elaboration in pre-Reformation Christian theology. It is this essential (or, may one say, essentializing) quality in Emerson that should dictate the method and scope of any significant religious inquiry into his writing; and it is this quality that relates him as an American of his time to his most talented contemporaries.

The same faculty for arriving by mistake at the very heart of some ancient doctrine, long since smothered by Calvinism, is observable in the two Henry Jameses, and to a greater or lesser extent in Hawthorne and Poe. The elder James, for example, wrestling in New York with the secret of Swedenborg, emerged with his own version of the Augustinian concept of the *felix culpa*, the notion that the fall of man was a happy and a fortunate event. Not a syllable of James consciously echoes either St. Augustine or the medieval *Exultet* which celebrated the fortunate fall; nor was his statement of the idea (Adam's fall was "an every way upwards step indeed, pregnant with beatific consequences") buttressed by the traditional theological scheme that lent some measure of logic to the paradox. But there he was, driven by his personal intellectual momentum and his private tropes, at the naked center of the old doctrine. Henry James, Jr., is a much more complex and awe-inspiring case, deserving lengthy analysis elsewhere. Here let us say only that either James is a cultural miracle, or else he had devoured (as seems distinctly improbable) almost all of Aristotle, St. Augustine, St. Thomas, St. Bonaventura, and Dante Alighieri. And as to Poe, his root idea, according to the persuasive essay by Allen Tate,[4] the one idea he did not merely "entertain" but which actually pushed and bedeviled him was the grand old heresy of attributing to human beings the intellect and imagination that God had reserved for the angels. It is a heresy, to be sure, but one form of it was indispensable to the scholastic thinking of the twelfth century, and in particular to St. Anselm, of whom Poe is unlikely to have heard. And so on.

The American Protestant analyst, if sufficiently limited in viewpoint, is apt to miss these strange appearances and theological throwbacks. He tends to go at the business wrong way round,

4. "The Angelic Imagination," in *The Man of Letters in the Modern World* (New York, 1955), pp. 113–31.

looking for unmistakable recurrences of key terms and neglecting the cumulative suggestive power of the terms or images or special private meanings of the individual writers; while the doctrine accidentally echoed or latent in the work inspected may not be a part of the American Protestant stock in trade. Hawthorne tried out *his* version of the fortunate fall by having Kenyon, the sculptor in *The Marble Faun,* broach it to conventionally Protestant Hilda; and "Oh, hush!" she tells him, shrinking away "with an expression of horror," saying that she could weep for him, she is shocked beyond words, his "creed" makes a mockery "of all religious sentiments . . . [and] moral law"—that is, the sentiments and the law drilled into her back in New England. Kenyon hushes.

II

I have probably not escaped, in the preceding few paragraphs, from seeming to honor in Emerson, Hawthorne, and the others their rediscovery of "pieties that are older and more solid than the Puritan ones"; but, much as I respect those older pieties, the pieties of age-old Catholic Christianity, that is not precisely what I am trying to do. It *is* what is attempted in *American Classics Reconsidered,* from which the last quotation above is taken. This book, edited by Harold C. Gardiner, S.J.,[5] brings together essays by ten Roman Catholic writers on the major American men of letters in the early and middle nineteenth century. It is by no means a work of systematic expropriation. The intellectual standards are Catholic ones, and the approach is explicitly theological; but there is a reasonably sustained effort to deal with the writers as writers and as Americans, and very little effort to scold or convert them. "Quite literally, I think," says Michael F. Moloney in a creditable essay on Thoreau, "[Thoreau] went out to Walden Pond to write a book. . . . He went . . . to strike a blow in defense of the poet's right to existence. . . . He must be evaluated primarily as a creative artist rather than as a thinker." Mr. Moloney does so evaluate him; yet it is a sign of a certain uneasiness, as of one who has muddled a little the right order of the goods, that Mr. Moloney's title is "Christian *malgré lui.*" The phrase luckily has almost nothing to do with the essay's content; for if it were Mr. Moloney's intention to Christianize Thoreau despite himself,

5. (New York, 1958).

it would be a serious misdirection of energy. A similar sense of strain is detectable, or seems to me to be, in most of the other essays; and I shall offer some hints about the possible reasons for it, by looking in some detail at the essay by Joseph Schwartz on Hawthorne.

The latter is not necessarily the best contribution to the book. Although the volume is almost inevitably uneven, the level of critical and scholarly accomplishment strikes me as pretty high. The treatments of Longfellow, Poe, Melville, and "the literary historians" are perfunctory, perhaps because the writers in question are perfunctory themselves, like Longfellow, or because they have been drained of blood, like Melville, by the interminable critical surgery of the past few decades. (I digress to wonder with a certain anxiety how long the relatively small store of American literature is going to survive the writing about it, and especially the writing about the whole of it. Our production has fallen badly behind our consumption, as Henry James foresaw seventy years ago when he told a summer school on "the novel" at Deerfield, Massachusetts, that "We already talk too much about the novel in proportion to the quantity of it having any importance that we produce.") But the long analysis by Robert C. Pollock of Emerson's "single vision," for example, is a work of genuine scholarly composition; it composes something (a view of reality), and it is about the effort to do so. Mr. Pollock makes good overt use of Charles Feidelson's brilliant *Symbolism and American Literature* to clarify Emerson's long struggle "to free men from the delusion of a split universe, which, as he knew, had reduced human life to a fragmented state." Perhaps Mr. Pollock presents Emerson as achieving too completely what Emerson only succeeded in aiming at, and when he says that Emerson "steadfastly refused to recognize any split between the higher and lower worlds," he may have chosen the wrong verbal. What Emerson refused was to accept a split that he did recognize; he remains, in fact, America's most knowing and moving portrayer of the failures of connection in human experience—of the appalling lack of context, in modern times, for action and for judgment.

In addition to the chapters on Emerson, Thoreau, and Hawthorne, several other items in *American Classics Reconsidered* are to be commended. They include Ernest Sandeen's sometimes awkwardly phrased but compassionate and suggestive examination of Whitman ("He must accept even the social and moral outcast because he is himself an outcast asserting his claim to be accepted"); Alvan S. Ryan's intelligent survey of Orestes Brownson and his dialectical involvement with New England idealism; Charles A. Brady's informed and even loving study of the life and writings of James Fenimore Cooper—in my opinion, the most valuable as well as readable essay in the book, rather unexpected considering not Mr. Brady but James Fenimore Cooper, and rising to a poetic evocation of Leather-Stocking as a godlike figure similar to Oberon and Herakles ("Hawkeye and Chingachgook . . . become twin numina, two great *genii loci,* two waiting presences, tutelary deities of the American continent, joining hands in amity over a coil of motives and cross-purposes, the Green Man and the Red Manitou");[6] and Father Gardiner's brief introductory chapter, which establishes the theological perspective and makes up for a debatable salute to Colin Wilson's *The Outsider* by citing the special relevance, for his volume, of Charles Feidelson's book.

Father Gardiner urges, in his introduction, that "modern criticism would do well to minimize somewhat its preoccupation with techniques and return to more theological approaches." With that advice, I am personally very largely in agreement, up to what is for me a crucial point. And it should be added, especially on the evidence of this volume, that *most* Catholic writers, unlike *some* Protestant writers, are aware that in the theological approach some account must be taken of God. There is an extraordinary contemporary intellectual reluctance to utter the name of God, or even to allude to God in any definite way at all: a phenomenon peculiarly notable in books and courses on religion and literature. This is a current characteristic of the highest significance, though it does not, I believe, mean that God is dead in the consciousness of the present time (the report of God's death has been very much exaggerated). It means something rather different, my main suggestion about which I shall shortly and belatedly come round to. But in much of the purportedly "religious writing" of the day, God is treated, if at all, in the

6. Like Henry Bamford Parkes, in an extremely valuable essay published in *Modern Writing* No. 3 (New York, 1956), Mr. Brady emphasizes the organic continuity between Leather-Stocking and the hard-eyed private detective of recent years, affirming the claims of morality in the midst of cross-purposes more frightful and treacherous than any Leather-Stocking knew of.

manner dramatized time and again by Graham Greene (who is, I am aware, a Catholic of sorts)—as a married man's mistress, someone who must never be mentioned openly, is only thought about with a far corner of the mind, and is met briefly and on occasion in dark and hidden places, for illicit reasons. God, in short, is associated primarily with the sometimes titillating modern sense of sin and guilt. Hence it is that the entire range of Christian doctrine can be narrowed down to a belief in Original Sin, and Emerson, who had a more sublime view of the universe and its creator, dismissed as a corruptive influence on young minds and one who made the better cause appear the better. Even certain American forms of Roman Catholicism, I am told, are not always free of this bleak reductive tendency. But Father Gardiner's volume of essays is. When Michael F. Moloney wants to distinguish between Thoreau's humanistic mysticism and that of an authentically Christian religious mystic, he says rightly and flatly, "Man is Thoreau's primary concern, not God"; and Father Gardiner's own list of the great issues that he regards as central to the theological approach includes "the indwelling of God in the soul" as well as "the nature of sin and responsibility and the role of free will in responsibility." It also includes "[God's] Providence and salvific will . . . detachment from created goods, the communion of saints . . . and the real and proper 'divinity of man.' "

Those terms (especially "salvific," which I had to look up, and which means "tending to save" and is listed as obsolete) are not ones that an outsider in the non-Wilsonian sense can feel very easy with. But that they partake of a comprehensive and unmistakably theological vocabulary is hardly open to doubt. What is open to doubt is not the value of a theological approach to literature, but the value of approaching this particular body of literature with any set of terms and doctrines that has been fully and finally elaborated, historically, once and for all. That is just the question perhaps unwittingly pushed into prominence by Joseph Schwartz, in his essay on Hawthorne: an essay in this case appropriately titled "God and Man in New England."

Mr. Schwartz begins with the proposition that "the history of literature has been an attempt to put such abstractions ["free will, the natural desire for God, fatalism, and providence"] into concrete statements for the benefit of mankind"; and hence that it is proper to seek out in Hawthorne his concept of "the moral and religious character of man." The crux of the problem may be right there. Mr. Schwartz's principle runs counter, of course, to the most influential critical convictions and prejudices of the past few decades, according to which literature does not "put abstractions into concrete statement," but, rather, generates a special kind of idea by the special processes of the creative imagination. The basis of those critical convictions has been the observation that modern literature, at least, can be shown to be doing just that: which has led to the suspicion that maybe the greatest literature in all ages has been up to the same poetic business. Hawthorne is an uncommonly tangled and contradictory case. From time to time, he most certainly did put abstractions into concrete form, and his notebooks let us watch him as he does so. But at other moments, he seems rather to have begun with a particular image or incident and to have allowed it to expand in his mind till it reached its maximum suggestiveness.[7] Similarly, while the conclusion of "The Artist of the Beautiful," published in 1844, declares that the symbol which makes beauty perceptible becomes at last of little value for the artist who has "possessed himself . . . of the reality," the conclusion of "The Antique Ring," published a year earlier, argues that the artist "can never separate the idea from the symbol in which it manifests itself." The two statements have different contexts, and they are not strict opposites in any case. But they illustrate the magnificent hedging of which Hawthorne was a master, and which was radically necessary under the cultural circumstances in which he found himself. The same thing shows up still more revealingly in his habit of dramatizing a humane resistance to the metaphysical and theological concepts he has at the same time splendidly acknowledged. So, at least, I read tales like "The Birthmark" and "Ethan Brand," neither of which would readily yield their full and echoing discordance to the critic who searches for the abstractions made concrete in them.

   Mr. Schwartz knows, at any rate, the right abstractions to look for: the conception of God and of God's relation to man. As he attempts to make these things visible, he (I think persuasively) disengages Hawthorne from the legend of an uninterruptedly

---

   7. Ronald Gray's little book on Kafka (Cambridge, 1958) traces in scrupulous detail an analogous development in the composition of *The Castle,* and manages thereby to demonstrate the relative unsoundness of the Christian or Jewish doctrinal attack on that novel.

Puritan ancestry. Militant orthodoxy seems to have vanished from
the Hawthorne family by the mid-eighteenth century; Nathaniel's
mother, who had exclusive charge of him from the time he was
four, was an unemphatic Unitarian; Hawthorne was never, on
the evidence, indoctrinated or proselytized; and when he arrived
at Bowdoin, he gravitated instinctively toward persons "of the
same noncommittal temperament." Mr. Schwartz draws the picture of a man with a strong religious impulse and an intense religious curiosity who yet had the opportunity of choosing the
forms in which his sense of religious experience might get itself
articulated and who disliked and distrusted all the forms available to a nineteenth-century New Englander—all the gradations
of orthodoxy and the varieties of "liberal Christianity." He then
makes too little of the form Hawthorne finally did choose for his
purposes: the form of the narrative art.

If he slights that eventuality, it is probably because the art of
narrative does not appear to Mr. Schwartz as one of the forms
accessible to the religious impulse. For a person to whom none
of the modes of Protestant Christianity in the nineteenth century
were satisfying, only one other religious mode—Mr. Schwartz
seems, not unnaturally, to assume—could be possible. He becomes explicit only at the moment when he relates Hawthorne's
account of Donatello's "way to the Lord" to a sermon by St.
Thomas Aquinas for "The Feast of Saint Martin," and expresses
"amaze[ment] at Hawthorne's knowledge of Catholicism as it affected a character drawn from that tradition." The religious pattern which Hawthorne is here found to be slowly fulfilling is the
pattern of traditional Catholicism. Central to that pattern and to
Hawthorne's fiction as studied by Mr. Schwartz is the image of a
God of love and of hope.

It is a useful counterbalance to the occasional description of
Hawthorne as presenting a hopelessly depraved human nature
cowering away beneath the imminent chastisement of a coldly
angry deity. And for about half of his essay, Mr. Schwartz holds
on pretty hard to Hawthorne's huckleberries, to the human and
artistic elements sensibly at work in the notebooks and some of
the earlier stories: but then the process of translation sets in, and
nothing further hinders it. The remainder of Hawthorne's writings, including *The Scarlet Letter* and *The Marble Faun,* are
translated out of their unique existence into the (for those writings)
deforming emphases of Catholic Christianity. An entire inter-

pretation of *The Scarlet Letter* rests on the theory that "Dimmesdale's fundamental weakness . . . is his failure to recognize that God is a God of love"—an excellent notion for a psychoanalytically trained confessor to try to inculcate into a real-life Dimmesdale, but not the one central to the realized stress and strain of the novel itself. And a bundle of quotations about "the promises of a blessed eternity" and "O beautiful world! O beneficent God!" leads Mr. Schwartz to identify Hilda, who sometimes does talk like that in *The Marble Faun,* as "winningly virtuous." Hilda comes at us in fact, from the fictional context she inhabits, as a girl so bloodlessly virtuous as to be well-nigh terrifying, and partly because of the way she talks. That Hawthorne, or a part of him, thought of Hilda as such is indicated by his references elsewhere to his belief that the words " 'genteel' and 'lady-like' are terrible ones," and to "the pure, modest, sensitive and shrinking woman of America—shrinking when no evil is intended, and sensitive like diseased flesh that thrills if you but point at it."

This is not to say merely that Hawthorne reveals more fertile contradictions in his work than Mr. Schwartz acknowledges; it is to say, rather, that the contradictions that give Hawthorne's work its particular mood and movement are not entirely translatable into traditional Christian terms—because they are moving away from rather than toward a demonstration of the relevance of those terms. Like Emerson, Hawthorne was largely free of the exact religious formulas of his own time (though he regarded them more closely, and always with a fascinated and creative skepticism). Hawthorne's gaze, too, in its curious range and freedom, rested betimes upon the essence of some central pre-Puritanical piety —an image of God, perhaps, a deep conviction about human responsibility. But those elements remained unrelated except in the quick of Hawthorne's imagination; they were unfortified by anything like a theology, much less a definitely Christian theology. There is no dramatic use (I do not say, no mention) in Hawthorne of the determining items in such a theology—no use whatever of the idea of an intermediary between man and God: of Mary, of the Holy Ghost, and, most crucial of all, of the figure and role of Jesus Christ. There is an important sense in which Hawthorne was not a Christian writer at all.

Hawthorne's view of religious experience is to be found only by following the actual evolution, in each work and from one work to the next, of his persistent images and patterns of relationship. I am not making one more pedantic defense of the absolute integrity of literature; I am trying rather to say something about American and modern literature and the forms of religious expression in our times. As regards Catholic *or* Protestant Christianity, as in his relation to any other major historical development, Hawthorne was neither an outsider nor an insider: he was an in-betweener. His writings and his habitual concerns and responses lie somewhere in between the Christian epoch and an epoch (our own) which, with due modifications, we have to call post-Christian; and Hawthorne's imaginative energies bent forward, not backward. The direction in which he was bending is made clearer by his logical successor, Henry James; for James is probably the representative or at least the introductory figure in the post-Christian epoch.

James was post-Christian in somewhat the way that Virgil seems to us pre-Christian—James could dimly remember about as much of the substance of Christianity as Virgil could dimly foresee. The two men stand at opposite ends of the most enormous cultural curve in Western history, and almost everything they wrote had to do with their sense of where they stood. Each was beautifully shaken by premonitions of some gigantic disaster and by opaque hopes of an eventual transformation scene in the affairs of the cosmos. James's fiction, R. P. Blackmur once remarked in a singularly tantalizing sentence, was his reaction to "the predicament of the sensitive mind during what may be called the interregnum between the effective dominance of the old Christian-classical ideal through old European institutions and the rise to rule of the succeeding ideal, whatever history comes to call it." To the phrase "sensitive mind" in Mr. Blackmur's remark, I should like to add "religious imagination"; for James was, I believe, a religious writer, and his fiction was increasingly caught up in the web of circumstances investing and indeed creating the relationship between man and God.

James never put it that way: he was American and modern. Both the human and the literary problem of the present epoch was summed up by Merton Densher in *The Wings of the Dove,* when, trying to make good his lie to Maude Massingham about having been on his way to church on Christmas morning, he asked himself miserably, "To what church was he going, to what church . . . *could* he go?" He went, finally, to the Oratory on Brompton Road, but we must not make too much of that decision, any more than Merton did. It was no more than a transient effort to find a traditional Christian form in which to acknowledge what Merton had long before realized was nothing less than a religious experience. That realization was compounded altogether of Merton's sense of Milly Theale and of the course and meaning of his relationship with *her*. It was this that was "too sacred to describe," just as it was the genuine sacredness of the relationship that James had spent some seven-hundred-odd pages in describing: or, rather, in creating. The creation is achieved while carefully avoiding any direct utterance of the name of God; we have instead the names of Milly Theale, Merton Densher, and the others. This is the point of a reverent witticism made by a friend of mine who, when asked whether he thought that Milly Theale is a Christ-figure, replied, "No, but perhaps Christ is a Milly-figure."

It was, in short, characteristic of James, as representative of the post-Christian epoch, to have conveyed his religious sense by intensifying the human drama to the moment where it gave off intimations of the sacred. And it was characteristic of him to have done so almost exclusively by the resources of the narrative art, generating the "vision" *within* the developing work of art, and with almost no help from and perhaps very little knowledge or recollection of the traditional Christian doctrines. (Hence, by the way, the strange and baffling quality—strange and baffling, at least, for those who probe them from a systematic theological viewpoint—of James's mainly self-begotten symbols.) It was toward the Jamesian position and method that Hawthorne and his contemporaries were heading in an earlier generation. Perry Miller was luminously right when he claimed, in his introduction to *The Transcendentalists,* that Emersonian transcendentalism was "a religious demonstration" in which, however, the persons concerned put their cause into the language of literature rather than of theology. But it must always be added that when that is done, as I have suggested elsewhere, something happens to the cause as well as to the language. There is a deep propriety in searching for religious elements in works of literature, since that is where they often appear with the greatest urgency in the modern epoch; but there is a certain impropriety and perhaps an irrelevance in searching for historically grounded doctrinal elements. Christianity itself may very likely *not* be a historical phenomenon, or at least not in any decisive manner a purely historical phenomenon. But its institutions and its vocabulary are historical phenomena, and they may in some instances become as unusable for our present religious purposes as Anglo-Saxon is to our linguistic ones. The analogy is intended to be reasonably precise, for in both cases some very important use yet remains. James is representative in this respect as well, for he is post-Christian in the sense of coming after and making scant dramatic use of the finished frames of doctrine: while various essences of Christianity continue to work in his prose and to color and flavor the forms he finds and the forms he creates in human experience.

1959

HENRY JAMES:
THE THEATER OF
CONSCIOUSNESS

Among the great artists in narrative, Henry James is the most persistently, even the most obstinately dramatic—though to say so will make restive a certain class of readers for whom he has never seemed anything of the kind. It is just the complaint of those who have tried to read him and failed, or who have been forced to read him and hated it, that virtually nothing *happens* in a novel by Henry James. As against, say, *The Charterhouse of Parma,* with its fund of passionate heroics, or *Nostromo,* with its series of desperate enterprises, a novel like *The Wings of the Dove* (it has been argued) appears long-windedly devoid of the sharply visualized incident, the daring gesture, the heartfelt outcry, the electrifying encounter—devoid of those "dramatic" moments that seize and compel a reader's imagination. But a contention of this sort, though by no means unreasonable or naïve, derives from an association of the dramatic with the overt, the sensational, the abrupt; with crises that intensify beyond endurance and then explode. There are explosive elements in James's fiction, and there is a good deal of (often surreptitious) passion; there are moments of sudden and extraordinary illumination, and there is perhaps a larger degree of sheer melodrama than one would like. These are aspects of James's essential dramatism, but the latter is not adequately defined in terms of them and even works, paradoxically, to reduce their traditional "dramatic" effect. James's dramatism was above all a principle of fictional form—but a principle rooted in a vision of human life.

James was a dramatist in fiction on the formal side because he sized up life as dramatic on the human and experiential side. He composed his best novels according to the principles of dramatic construction—almost, one sometimes feels, according to the principles of Aristotle's *Poetics*—because he believed it to be the purpose of fiction (as he once told a symposium on "the novel") to give an impression of life. And it was his impression that life—life truly lived, and not squandered or simply not attempted at all—revealed the shape, the rhythm, and the slow relentlessness of classical and especially of neoclassical drama. James's formula for the novel, "an impression of life," was almost his modern and American version of Aristotle's formula for tragedy, "the imitation of an action" (and, as it were, vice versa, since for Aristotle human life *was* a mode of action). But there was a difference, due to historical circumstances as well no doubt as to a limitation of personal experience and a lack of talent (that is, of the talent for plot-making). In any event, the most intense and accessible action for James was that of the aroused consciousness, as it expanded and came into focus through conflict with the consciousness of others. The ground of experience, in the Jamesian view, was the theater of consciousness, and the person most fully alive was the one who saw himself as a histrionic participant on that stage. The achievement of that special Jamesian kind of histrionic awareness and vitality is at the same time—so the discussions that follow try to suggest—an act of transcendence that partakes of the religious.

I: The Sense of Fair Play[1]

> Again the good lady [Mrs. Brigstock] looked hard at her young hostess. "I came, I believe, Fleda, just, you know, to plead with you."
> Fleda, with a bright face, hesitated a moment. "As if I were one of those bad women in a play?"
> The remark was disastrous.
>
> *The Spoils of Poynton,* chapter xv

Writing in the New York literary monthly, the *Galaxy,* in May 1877, Henry James—reporting from abroad—offered a small anecdote to explain his feeling that the London stage was in a

---

1. This brief discussion was written for an American Literature session in December 1960 at the Modern Language Association meeting. The subject of the session was the concept of beauty in the work of four American writers—the other writers being Dreiser, Pound, and Stevens.

poor way. His story had to do with an American visitor James had observed one day in a London grill-room and who, upon leaving, took with him innocently enough a copy of the bill of fare, no doubt as a memento for his wife. One of the English customers immediately rushed to the manager in a blaze of moral indignation to report the theft, and was overheard arguing, as James put it, "in the name of outraged morality.—'You know he oughtn't to have done that—it was very wrong in him to do it. . . . You know I ought to tell you—it was my duty to tell you —I couldn't *but* tell you.' . . . It is not easy," James continued, "to point out definitely the connection between this little episode . . . and the present condition of the English stage; but—it may have been whimsical—I thought I perceived a connection. These people are too highly moral to be histrionic, I said; they have too stern a sense of duty." It is not easy for me in turn to point out the connection between this passage and the topic to which we have been asked to address ourselves; but I think there is one, and I shall suggest that for Henry James the question of beauty was located somewhere amid that lively anecdotal dialectic of the moral and the histrionic.

The latter word indicates at once James's own reordering of the entire moral issue. In common with many of his contemporary men of letters, James was repelled by the static, declamatory moralism of the middle class. When he used the word "conscience," he normally meant the philistine conscience, and often presented it as a mode of self-satisfied treachery; while the phrase "good conscience" in his fiction could define a temperament that was positively lethal (as in the case of that man of good conscience, Lord Mark, in *The Wings of the Dove*). But James did not follow some of his English and continental peers in simply replacing the Victorian cult of morality with a *symboliste* cult of beauty. His view of things fused the moral *with* the beautiful; and the not unfamiliar form of moral beauty that resulted was given a peculiar vitality by what was, in James, an essentially histrionic imagination.

The process shows James hanging on to a family legacy, and at the same time crucially modifying it. In his autobiography, James recalled with immense pleasure the cheerful paradoxes of a father and a family all dedicated to the moral and all intensely opposed to the moralistic or priggish (just as he remembered "the particular crookedness of our being so extremely religious without having, as it were, anything in the least clarified or striking to show for it").

I can scarce sufficiently express how little [our family life] could have conduced to the formation of prigs [he wrote in *A Small Boy and Others*]. Our father's prime horror was of *them*—he only cared for virtue that was more or less ashamed of itself; and nothing could have been of a happier whimsicality than the mixture in him . . . of the strongest instinct for the human and the liveliest reaction from the literal. The literal played in our education as small a part as it perhaps ever played in any, and we wholesomely breathed inconsistency and ate and drank paradoxes . . . the moral of all of which was that we need never fear not to be good enough if we were only social enough: a splendid meaning indeed being attached to the latter term.

Thus we had ever the amusement, since I can really call it nothing less, of hearing morality, or moralism as it was more invidiously worded, made hay of in the very interest of character and conduct; these things suffering much, it seemed, by their association with conscience—that is, the *conscious* conscience—the very home of the literal, the haunt of so many pedantries.

To the word "moral," Henry James the elder thus opposed the word "social," "a splendid meaning indeed being attached to the latter term"; and to the notion of the self, he opposed his privately understood notion of humanity. The acquisition of selfhood, the birth of moral conscience, the formation of the ego—all this represented the capital sin in the father's universe: though it was a necessary and even a fortunate sin, a critical step in the individual psychic career beyond that mindless Adamic innocence in which the career took its start. But it was one of the father's ideas that the passage from innocence to conscience was an altogether self-ish affair; and to arrive at genuine human maturity there must occur a shattering of the ego, followed by a rejuvenation as a member of what he called "the divine-natural humanity," that being the elder James's phrase for the ideal socialism, the paradox of perfect individual integrity with perfect harmony, that he celebrated in 1879 under the telling title, *Society the Redeemed Form of Man*. In the doctrine of Henry James Senior, there was already a certain dramatic quality; he seemed to detect a plot in experience, a dramatic form of a tragic variety in the life that was really lived. The accomplishment of his younger son was to push and tighten the analogy; to implicate the moral in the social, but then to implicate both within the histrionic— so that the well-lived life had some of the formal beauty of the well-made play; and even the word "character"—as in the phrase "character and conduct"—carried with it something of the playwright's as well as the moralist's meaning.

The development of this attitude can, I think, be marked with sufficient clarity. Like his father, Henry James Junior had "the strongest instinct for the human." As a humanist, he was a strong moralist; but the human situation focused itself most sharply for anyone who regarded it as striving toward the conditions of art: that is, of an art-*work*. It is a clue to Merton Densher's potential for salvation in *The Wings of the Dove* that he can see himself as "but a sentence of a sort in the general text"; and the soundness of his moral aspiration is contained in his hope of avoiding the spiritual poverty of "reading the romance of his existence in a cheap edition." In the years following James's unhappy foray into the actual world of the English theater, during the nineties, the genre of art to which human experience was analogized tended increasingly to be the play rather than the novel. About her ailing young friend Milly Theale, Susan Stringham has the impression that she is not simply a princess, but "a princess in a conventional tragedy." And in *The Spoils of Poynton,* Fleda Vetch reaches a kind of peak of insight when she shocks Mrs. Brigstock by venturing that the older woman had come to plead with her about Owen Gereth "as if," Fleda says, "I were one of those bad women in a play."

It is a rich and cunning moment. The play both Fleda and Henry James had in mind was *La Dame aux Camélias* by Alexander Dumas the Younger: a play about which James had written at some length and with reverent memories of seeing Eleanora Duse as Marguerite, during the same year, 1896, that he completed and published *The Spoils of Poynton.* To Mrs. Brigstock, the allusion is unpardonably frivolous and downright immoral; in fact, however, the theatrical comparison is a main sign of Fleda's profoundly moral alertness. But Mrs. Brigstock is as insular as she is priggish: if she is too moral to be histrionic, she is also too British to appreciate the special histrionics of the French. The Jamesian analogy of human conduct with the conduct of persons on stage did not hold for any sort of play; he had in mind the play that grew out of the traditions of the French theater, and in particular the French neoclassic theater. What James admired in *La Dame aux Camélias* was "its combination of freshness and form, of the feeling of the springtime of life and the sense of the conditions of the theatre"—conditions James was emphatic in contending obtained almost exclusively in France. In such drama, James felt an ideal expression of life: which is to say that his father's ideal socialism, his redeemed form, became the son's ideal theater; to the extent that one sometimes imagines that God, for Henry James, was primarily the supreme dramatist—only to discover, in his story "The Birthplace" of 1903, that he voiced that very suggestion by converting William Shakespeare into at least a powerful local deity. In the ideal life, in any case, individual characters perform like persons in a French neoclassic drama: they are very distinctly *persons,* in gesture and speech, but they are engaged—and consciously engaged—in a single, binding social action; or, in stage language, in what is here called ensemble acting. The moral equivalent is of persons decidedly themselves who are yet thoroughly aware of the reality of others: are poised, so to speak, *toward* others. It is in this context that behavior is judged not so much as good or bad, but as beautiful or ugly; and James's tribute to Eleanora Duse—that for her, "the most beautiful thing is always the great thing"—could be applied to instances of actual or fictional behavior. There is thus a special twist and accent, even a kind of pun, in one of James's favorite phrases for defining any kind of honorable conduct: he liked to refer to it as "fair play."

It is in *The Spoils of Poynton* and specifically in the relation between Fleda Vetch and Mrs. Gereth, the widowed mistress of Poynton, that the Jamesian concept is most luminously rendered. The two women come together on the common ground of their love of beauty; or, more accurately, their revulsion from ugliness —from "the aesthetic misery of the big commodious house" of the Brigstocks at Waterbath. They are, as James says, spirits of the same family; and the narrative point of view in the early chapters makes no distinction between them. Throughout this section, indeed, the novel seems to promise us a familiar late

Victorian conflict between vulgarity and greed, supported by a crafty moralism, on the one hand (the Brigstock world), and an aesthetic devotion, on the other, that amounts nearly to the religion of beauty (the world of Poynton, where Mrs. Gereth says of its treasures that "They were our religion, they were our life!"). But what James calls his "little drama" unfolds in a manner absolutely characteristic of him; and that initial conflict suffers a radical change at the very moment it reaches its own climax—when the representative of Waterbath, Mona Brigstock, enters the world of Poynton to sit among its exquisite possessions like a bored tourist. On the instant, the movement shifts and deepens; for the spectacle of Mona so horrifies Mrs. Gereth that she bursts out with the suggestion that her son insure the safe-keeping of the precious spoils by marrying Fleda Vetch instead. The proposal reveals Mrs. Gereth as, suddenly, a representative far more terrible than Mona Brigstock of everything the James family meant by moralism—that is, of the conscious conscience, of lethally self-satisfied egotism—and precisely in her role as the high priestess of the cult of beauty. In her fanatical regard for her beautiful things, it is now Mrs. Gereth who assumes attributes formerly associated with the Brigstocks; and when Fleda, after her hostess's outburst, turns on her with a scorching, "How *could* you," Mrs. Gereth shows a face (as James observes) of "perfect blankness" that was "a sign of her serene conscience."

The conflict thereafter is between the two one-time spirits of the same family; and it is reflected exclusively in what James designates as Fleda's "intenser consciousness." Within that consciousness, the truth about Mrs. Gereth and the ultimate value of her kind of aesthetic devotion become fully recognized: especially when Mrs. Gereth intuits Fleda's secret—that she has fallen in love with Owen. Fleda then tells herself, apprehensively, that

There were things for which Mrs. Gereth's *flair* was not so happy as for bargains and "marks." It wouldn't be happy now as to the best action on the knowledge she had just gained. . . . There were ways in which she could sharply incommode a person, and not only with the best conscience in the world, but with a sort of brutality of good intentions. . . . She was nothing if not practical: almost the only thing she took account of in her young friend's soft secret was the excellent use she could make of it.

The language is exact, particularly in the seeming casualness of the repetition of the word "thing." Mrs. Gereth had, it is said elsewhere, "a maniacal disposition to thrust in everywhere the question of 'things' "; and when, as here, out of a perfect conscience which is just the symptom of her immense spiritual greed, she seeks to make use of other persons, she is treating human beings not as persons but, literally, as things.

If Fleda can appraise Mrs. Gereth so correctly, it is because of the nature of her own consciousness. She is the only one in the novel to possess that histrionic awareness that James so honored. When the parlormaid at Ricks comes flying out to announce the arrival there of Owen Gereth, "she became"—in Fleda's mind—"on the instant an actress in the drama." At this point, Fleda still assumes "that she herself was only a spectator," and she has the sense of looking "across the footlights at the exponent of the principal part." By the time, eight chapters later, that Mona Brigstock's mother calls to plead with her in London, Fleda has realized that she herself has had to take on the principal part, and she can even hint, lightly, at the content of the play they are engaged in. Such an awareness is the very basis of her moral sensibility; for, seeing all of the other persons as caught up, with her, in the central action of a carefully shaped play, she is peculiarly alive not only to her own desires but to the motivations and hopes and significance of each of the Brigstocks and the Gereths as well.

Her sense of the beautiful, as a consequence, is not less but far more refined than that of Mrs. Gereth, for it is always involved with the human and the histrionic. When she discovers at the little cottage at Ricks that Mrs. Gereth has transported there most of the Poynton treasures, she finds that they have lost their beauty for her. Surveying them, Fleda "was impressed anew with her friend's genius for composition . . . [but] there was no joy for her" in the spectacle. "She couldn't care for such things when they came to her in such ways; there was a wrong about them all that turned them to ugliness." The beauty of the *things* had been destroyed by Mrs. Gereth's violation of a higher beauty: the principle of fair play, of beautiful conduct between human individuals. That is what Fleda requires of Owen, even after they have confessed their love to one another: that he play fair with Mona, that he give her a final chance. Mona, of course, seizes that chance greedily; and Fleda's secret hopes disappear in the ultimate holocaust of the Poynton estate. Her very loyalty to her principle is her practical undoing; at the end she is totally and irrevocably alone; but she has, at least, been constant and faithful to the Jamesian vision of beauty in action.

1960

II: *The Wings of the Dove*

There is no small talk, there are scarcely any manners. . . . Well in the very front of the scene lunges with extraordinary length of arm the Ego against the Ego, and rocks in a rigor of passion the soul against the soul.

Henry James on *John Gabriel Borkman* (1897)

James's uncommonly spirited remark about *John Gabriel Borkman* gives us our best working hypothesis for *The Wings of the Dove*. Almost everything James said about Ibsen can be applied, with a little stretching or reduction, to himself—even though, when he wrote Gosse in the first enthusiasm for the Norwegian that "you must tell me more about I.," he added, "That is not in this case female-American for *me.*" But in a sense it was; it always was; and as his feeling for Ibsen deepened, James began to admire in the plays the very quality that distinguishes his own later novels—the ability to arrive "for all his meagerness at intensity." The achievement of *The Wings of the Dove* (or the one, at any rate, I want here to consider) was the product of intensity; and it was something for which the only word that will do is "religious," and that word will not do very well. For the religious experience to which the adventure rises is very meagerly supported; it cannot depend upon creed or doctrine, upon church or institution; it is a matter of mounting intensity, an affair— however artfully beclouded—of the passionate lunging of soul against soul, in an absence of small talk and a transcendence of manners. James held to the belief (historically exaggerated but prophetically sound) that, in the world he knew, there was little left for the artist to manipulate save the rocking and the lunging; and through them he regathered in his pages the forces of a recognizably traditional event of all but the highest order.

In one of his prefaces, James would define experience itself in social terms, as the apprehension and measure of the self in its social being. But in 1902, when he was composing *The Wings of the Dove,* he had been smitten by a characteristic American uncertainty over the actual possibility of that kind of experience. Milly Theale has hardly settled in London before it is hinted to her that, for all her desire to become "involved," there may be precious little to become coherently involved *with*. Were there even (Lord Mark, that man of good conscience, raises the question) such things as social sets any longer? "[W]as there any thing but the senseless shifting tumble, like that of some great greasy sea in mid-Channel, of an overwhelming melted mixture?"[2] A good many weeks and books later, the hint is confirmed by poor Merton Densher when he contemplates the Venetian pavements "greasy now with the salt spray." In the context of his disturbing drama, Venice is an image of a declining, perhaps even a shattered culture: "the whole place, in its huge elegance, the grace of its conception and the beauty of its detail, was more than ever like a great drawing-room, the drawing-room of Europe, profaned and bewildered by some reverse of fortune" (chapter XXX). *The Wings of the Dove* is about senselessness and collapse, about both dissociation and confusion; and it is a triumph over them. It shows what can be done—or what James could do—to give value and meaning to experience when those qualities were no longer discoverable in social terms. And what James could do, in the face of profanation and bewilderment and out of the observed battle of the spirit, was to recover something like a sacramental sensibility. This is what happens within the texture of the novel; and this is what happens, in the story, to Merton Densher.

At the same time, James's imagination, like that of his father, was two-edged. It was, as he said, an imagination of disaster; but there was also the dim imagining of what, in describing his father's most vigorous expectation, he called "a transformation scene in human affairs." There might be emerging, James felt, a different society altogether from the one visibly declining in Europe and the one struggling to be born in America. Associations between and among the members of both societies "have created"—he argued, in the preface to *Lady Barberina*—"a new

2. (New York, Scribner's, 1902), chapter VII. Subsequent references to this edition—identical in pagination to the Modern Library edition—are cited in the text. In the New York Edition, James revised the above passage to read: ". . . was there anything but the groping and pawing, that of the vague billows of some great greasy sea in mid-Channel, of masses of bewildered people trying to 'get' they didn't know what or where?"

scale of relations . . . a state of things from which *emphasized* internationalism has either quite dropped or is well on its way to drop." And so the subject of *The Wings of the Dove* and *The Golden Bowl* could in each case (James continued) "have been perfectly expressed had *all* the persons concerned been only American or only English or only Roman or whatever." This points toward a different and a more delectable kind of melting and mixing. It too is hinted at in *The Wings,* and leads similarly to a perception religious in its peculiar energy: when Milly, in the most ardently alert moment of her life, feels "the elements melt[ing] together," feels at Matcham that "Once more things melted together—the beauty and the history and the facility and the splendid midsummer glow: it was a sort of magnificent maximum, the pink dawn of an apotheosis" (chapter XI). And she knows, confronting the Bronzino painting, that she will never again be better than this.

It should be said that the social and cultural ties had in fact not slackened as much by 1902, the distinctive natures of persons and things not become as mixed and melted—to an end either sanctified or profaned—as James appeared to believe. His account is essentially prophetic. It is more accurate as a picture of our immediate condition, after the great drawing rooms of Europe and America have been more radically bewildered by a couple of wars and an assortment of betrayals and misalliances, and following our stumbling, ill-conceived, but not ill-motivated efforts to stage some sort of transformation scene. Both processes have become accelerated; and now our vague hopes for an apotheosis alternate with the dull conviction that the great greasy sea is upon us. This is a major reason why we can detect and honor James's bold achievement, and why it is an almost poignantly appropriate moment to do so—to honor this bequest as an earnest of what can yet be accomplished in the melting season.

As to the source of James's prophetic power, I hazard the following—a personal variation on a pretty old tune. When he left America and settled in Europe, he departed from a culture which had, or thought it had, to build afresh, from the ground up, with new tools and new blueprints, constructing new kinds of relationships with new names. It could give James little to travel with, and he brought with him nothing but the inexhaustible fertility of a uniquely creative consciousness. The culture he then inhabited was slowly loosening at the joints; his consciousness was sufficient to make him aware of the loosening, but not enough to get really in touch with what still held firm. In Europe, he celebrated the artistic availability of the famous list of items lacking to the American scene; but because he was so American, or rather because he was so incorrigibly a native of the James family, the items presented to his inspection only their surfaces. What lay beneath— all the crowded history that had gone into them and that Hawthorne responded to so warmly—remained invisible; but the surfaces suited James very well, for by genius and by the "sensuous education" foisted on him and William by their father, he was an insatiate devourer of surfaces. It is recorded that, to the consternation of his elders, he could recall in detail the surface of a monument he could only have seen (in Paris) when he was less than two years old; it is not recorded that he ever knew to any depth what the monument stood for. His early fiction gleamed with its bright notations of the outsides of things—surfaces humanized into manners—but when he worked his way inward, he could discover only what his fertile consciousness had put there— the rocking of the souls, the lunging of the egos. And that was quite enough; he saw so small an amount of what was present that he could powerfully envisage what might be in the future; his blindness was the very instrument of his vision.

The Wings of the Dove recapitulates its author's career by working its way through and beyond surfaces to the collision of psyches, and through the achieved intensity thereof to a fleeting glimpse (the most, after all, we humans are ever vouchsafed) of the divine. The plot, or "letter," of the novel is conventional enough, especially as sketched in James's notebooks: the wicked scheming of youth, and its fatal effect upon a radiant, consumptive, and enormously rich young woman whose whole desire is to live, out of the very warmth of her affection for the schemers. It was when the plot was elaborated in the novel and the effect of the scheming began to work both ways that it took on its remarkable substance, its relentless momentum. It acquired, first of all, a series of suggestive surfaces—the most striking of which is the assortment of homes and houses, the variety of drawing rooms which represent the great drawing room of Europe. The vast act of profanation is reflected in the arc along which those surfaces may be plotted. It ascends from "the vulgar little room" of Lionel Croy, with its shabby sofa, sallow prints and soiled centerpiece; to the dreary residence of Marian Condrip in "comfortless Chelsea"; to Lancaster Gate; to Matcham (the high point, the scene of creative melting and the dawn of apotheosis); to the Palazzo Leporelli; to Merton Densher's "shabby but friendly" faded old rooms (here the descent is marked) in Venice; to Marian Condrip's once again; and finally comes to rest on a note of total dissociation in Merton's dim London lodgings. As the tale moves from setting to setting, we witness one of the supreme instances in modern fiction of what Kenneth Burke calls "the act-scene relation," the tactic whereby settings are made to explain and comment on the actions that occur in them.

It is not merely that the dark and dismal vulgarity of Lionel Croy's room and the Chelsea household help us to sympathize with Kate's hard aspiration to go (as her aunt puts it) "high, high up—high up and in the light" (chapter IV), and to understand her enjoyment of the "high retreat" in which she is installed at Lancaster Gate. It is also that inanimate things bespeak, in this novel, the forces that invade them—forces which are human and other than human—and they do so by their own mute dialectic, by the contrasting messages they seem to issue to the minds that observe them. To Kate, a person to whom "material things spoke," Lancaster Gate spoke all of charms and pleasures; but to Merton, for whom "it was the language of the house itself that spoke," it hinted of something "ugly—operatively, ominously . . . cruel." The division between the lovers will not be clearly sensed by them until the encounter in Venice and not acknowledged until two months after the following Christmas; but it is foreshadowed at once in the difference between their responses to the power of surfaces.

The moral pressure of material things and the ambiguity of their language are so important in *The Wings of the Dove* that Lord Mark, though as tenaciously obtuse as ever, may have been only superficially wrong when he misunderstood the murmured plea of Milly Theale in Book Seventh. "Ah, not to go down— never, never to go down!" (chapter XXV) she had strangely sighed, gazing from the high window of the Palazzo Leporelli; and Lord Mark thought she meant descending the tremendous old staircase to the courtyard and the canal. Milly referred to a decline into unconsciousness, into death; but her visitor unwittingly grasped the way such an action is rendered or resisted in the fiction he inhabits: going down, in his meaning, would insure not going down in hers. Milly's inability any longer to go down the staircase is as suggestive as Merton's inability (during most of the ninth book) to go up into her presence. The quality of moral beauty personified by Milly Theale exists only in the high places; it may walk briefly in Regent's Park, but the atmosphere there is fatally thick; it is truly at home on an Alpine plateau or in the upper story of a great palazzo. There only it can live, and, given the conditions of actual morality, it can only die there, felt by but above the reach of a Merton Densher.[3] Milly cannot go down; and Kate Croy can do nothing else. The distance of her fall is measured by the descent from her high retreat in Lancaster Gate to the obscurity of the rooms where we last indistinctly see her; and it is due to a tough but faulty judgment of what might constitute a worthy and acceptable height—to her "dire accessibility to pleasure" from material things and from the kind of loftiness Mrs. Lowder planned for her.

But surfaces in *The Wings of the Dove* are   as has perhaps been indicated—so deeply penetrated by consciousness that little tangible or palpable remains of them. That is why we can say about *The Wings* what James said about *John Gabriel Borkman:* that there are, in fact, scarcely any manners, in the formal sense, as there is certainly no small talk at all. There are manners enough to conceal for a while the horror of the action; their function is to keep the action furtive, to subdue, as it were, the shout of appalled recognition to a soft murmur; but they tend to yield rather early in the game to the impact of the lunging Egos. And what, in their place, is gradually begotten by the drama is best illustrated (I suggest) by the novel's evolving definition of marriage—of marriage and its calamitous relation to money. Marriage means so little when the novel opens that it can mean almost everything before it closes; and here again we notice the singular value of James's view of the contemporary cultural condition— his curious remoteness from the historical actuality of institutions. A comparison with Jane Austen is useful. Marriage was the key event and the constant goal in the characteristic Austen novel: it could be assumed as a known thing, permanent in its nature, before the novel began; and nothing that happened during the narrative could or did affect its significance. In the world of Jane Austen, marriage may no longer have been what it once primarily

---

3. The phrasing here is itself a tacit acknowledgment of R. P. Blackmur's essay, "The Loose and Baggy Monsters of Henry James," in *The Lion and the Honeycomb* (New York, 1955), pp. 268–88.

was—a sacrament—but it was still an honorable estate; it was altogether à la mode. By the end of the century, James suspected (and, as usual, he was historically wrong but prophetically right) that marriage as such meant little or nothing; what it *could* mean would be produced in each instance by the conflict of consciousness. That conflict is so intense in *The Wings of the Dove* that marriage, which starts with considerably less meaning than it had for Jane Austen, ends up with very much more. It is enabled to recover not so much its honorable as its sacramental character; it is made vulnerable to blasphemy.

Kate Croy and Merton Densher are in love when the story opens; they become engaged; they wish to marry. For Merton, with his as yet uncreated conscience, there is no great mystery about marriage; he is simply impatient over the delay. But Kate has a more complex sense of the matter, owing to her family experience of it and the vigorous but still undefined ambition that experience had stimulated in her. Marriage had been a suffering for her mother, and connected with something horrid and unknown; Mrs. Croy had had to learn that her husband was "a terrible husband not to live with." And as to her sister Marian and the snuffling dejection to which marriage had reduced her— "If that was what marriage necessarily did to you, Kate Croy would have questioned marriage" (chapter II). With her severe inherited actuality, Kate contemplates marriage within the dangerous drama of poverty and wealth, power and freedom, habits of conduct and the energies of relationships; and she sets herself to mastering the dangers for the future well-being of Merton and herself. Marriage becomes a source of friction between the lovers as it is pushed thus into the midst of Kate's tough-minded strategy —which, upon the entrance of Mrs. Lowder, doubles into a pair of hostile strategies—and it enlarges steadily in significance till it appears the crucial event, the determining condition of life and value.

But it is still further enlarged, and now beyond the limits of ordinary human measure, with the arrival of Mildred Theale. For at this point the two strategies of Kate and her aunt no longer touch merely each other—touch, that is, robust and worldly people; they touch a fragile and fatal image of moral beauty; they touch a princess, a seraph, a dove, an image doomed to destruction and doomed to destroy: little Miss Theale from New York, the fatality in the lives of everyone. All the lunging, all the maneuvering, all the meditation and the talk over nearly six hundred pages—the exploratory discourses of Kate and Merton, the gossipy planning of Maude and Susan, the delicate fencing between Sir Luke and Milly, the more guarded conversations between the latter and each of the lovers, and the inward ponderings of them all—work to produce and invest the epiphanic moment in Book Eighth when Merton understands that he is being urged toward sacrilege. The quotation follows, but the force of it is not in its language, but in the dialectical movement that leads toward it. Kate's fully evolved plan emerges at last, as she talks with Merton at the party in the Palazzo Leporelli; but she requires of him that he name it: "If you want things named, you must name them."

> He had quite, within the minute, been turning names over; and there was only one, which at last stared at him there dreadful, that properly fitted. "Since she's to die I'm to marry her?"

Kate is brave enough to repeat his words. He continues, puzzling it out, in a deepening sense of the prodigious. "So that when her death has taken place I shall in the natural course have money?"

> It was before him enough now, and he had nothing more to ask; he had only to turn, on the spot, considerably cold with the thought that all along—to his stupidity, his timidity—it had been, it had been only what she meant. Now that he was in possession, moreover, she couldn't forbear, strangely enough, to pronounce the words she had not pronounced: they broke through her controlled and colourless voice as if she should be ashamed, to the very end, to have flinched. "You'll in the natural course have money. We shall in the natural course be free."
> "Oh, oh, oh!" Densher softly murmured. (chapter XI)

That soft murmur is James's subdued, still partly ironic, even very slightly playful version of tragic terror—the acknowledged awareness of the source of Kate's energy. It marks the closest approach possible in James to a religious experience: except for the silence, a response too deep even for the softest of murmurs, with which both Merton and Kate greet the smile thrown at them from across the room, a few moments later, by Milly Theale. It had already been observed, from Susan Stringham's point of view, that Milly's smile was a public event; the smile she now suddenly flashes at the two lovers who are conspiring to betray and destroy her, transcends even that. If inanimate things are the elements by which James renders what Dante called the tropological or moral meaning of his story; and if the historical or allegorical dimension is revealed in what the conflict of consciousness can do to revitalize institutions historically drained of importance; then Milly's smile, like that of Beatrice, gives a piercing glimpse of the anagoge. To Merton—in his excruciatingly heightened state, dazzled by Milly's pearls (to which Kate had insistently drawn his attention), beside himself with desire for Kate and quavering on the edge of some abyss—it expresses the quintessential quality of everything that harried and excited him, the very core of all mystery:

> . . . they watched a minute in concert. Milly, from the other side, happened at the moment to notice them, and she sent across toward them in response all the candour of her smile, the lustre of her pearls, the value of her life, the essence of her wealth. (chapter XI)

It is Merton's sense of "the reality she put into their plan" that later breeds in him his "consecrated idea"—of renouncing the money—that in fact consecrates the idea that gets bred and that he takes reverently into the Oratory on Christmas morning and then down to the house in Chelsea. He sees himself now as "a young man, far off yet dimly conscious of something immense and holding himself, not to lose it, painfully together. . . . Something had happened to him too beautiful and too sacred to describe" (chapter XXXIV). It was indeed indescribable in the language available, or seemingly available, to a novelist writing in English in 1902: it was the terrible and totally unprepared-for fragmentary vision of grace. *That* was something Merton Densher could not begin to express coherently. It could be expressed only in the manner James did express it—by dialectic made flesh, by the dramatized struggle of unenlightened but illuminating passion.[4]

1957

4. It was only after delivering the above paper that I succeeded at last in finding Dorothea Krook's essay on *The Wings of the Dove*. I warmly recommend this essay—as well as Miss Krook's study of *The Golden Bowl* —to all students of James and indeed of modern fiction. My agreement with her is so substantial that some of my remarks seem now to be as it were anticipatory echoes.

sents something done earlier and more resolutely by Henry James, and later and more suggestively by Scott Fitzgerald. Certainly, a clear line (perhaps the clearest line of development in the history of the novel in America) connects Mrs. Wharton with the other two writers just mentioned. All three are artistic historians of manners, particularly of the widening breach between manners—the palpable externals of behavior—and a significant morality, Mrs. Wharton's major accomplishment in this mode being *The Age of Innocence* (1920). Elsewhere, however, the focus of her imaginative energy results in a very different kind of book, distinctly un-Jamesian and indeed closer in nature to American novels since the second World War. At such a moment, her narrative form approaches the picaresque—the episodic ramblings of the morally ambiguous personality through an unstable and discordant world—and in this mode Mrs. Wharton's masterpiece is *The Custom of the Country* (1913), the career of Undine Spragg, literature's most indomitable female rogue since Becky Sharp. It is the unique and almost accidental achievement of *The House of Mirth* to have successfully combined both modes into a genre that Mrs. Wharton can be said to have made her own.

I have no name for this genre except that of its ablest practitioner, Edith Wharton herself. But I have no doubt that it was invented, or stumbled upon, during the apprentice years, to convey her sense of life; her sense of what was happening, historically, to the conditions of the social and moral and psychological life. And I have no doubt that the combination described is the very source of the remarkable and enduring features of *The House of Mirth:* the mysterious appeal of its often vexatious heroine, its odd but engrossing changes of narrative pace, its mixture of the vivid and the crepuscular, its dramatized realization of the fateful consequences for *both* matter and spirit when they are divorced from one another, and, above all, its steady command of our moral and emotional sympathy. To justify those claims and to identify the fictional genre of *The House of Mirth,* we may begin by reminding ourselves who Edith Wharton was.

I

She was the former Miss Edith Newbold ("Pussy") Jones, and, as a friend remarked, she was a true daughter of New York City, having been born there on January 24, 1862, of a well-established and reasonably prosperous upper-middle-class family.[1] She was also or, rather, she became, as someone else remarked in a different rhetorical vein, "a self-made man." In her adult years, the two sides of her nature—the feminine side begotten by the conventions of the older New York and the masculine side begotten by personal ambition—engaged in just the sort of internal quarrel that, as Yeats has famously pointed out, can lead to poetry; for example, in Mrs. Wharton's case, to the poetry of *The Custom of the Country,* where the two sides appraise each other as the handsome and notably unfeminine Miss Spragg moves like a tornado among the debilitated daughters and sons of New York City. Later, of course, Mrs. Wharton fell unhappily to quarreling with others, in the way that Yeats equally observed led only to rhetoric: to her increasingly frequent lectures to twentieth-century America on its gross cultural deficiencies. The daughter of New York was in the ascendancy at times like that; but during much of Edith Wharton's life, and starting early, the self-made side was a deep necessity.

There is good, apparently incontrovertible evidence that she believed herself to be illegitimate: the daughter of New York only in part and via her mother; the offspring, paternally speaking, not of that heavy nonentity Mr. Jones, but of some man of distinguished intellectual and artistic qualities, someone who had spawned her and vanished—leaving her to develop those inherited qualities by her own energies, as it were self-creatively.[2] This may well have been only the restless romanticizing of a young girl whose talents found no outlet within the milieu in which she was reared. The fact remains (and reappears as a

1. Her mother had been a Miss Rhinelander, of the solid Dutch stock that is regularly honored and smiled at in Mrs. Wharton's fiction; and she was a descendant of Ebenezer Stevens, a veteran of the Revolution and later a successful merchant. Edith's father, George Frederic Jones, had a less socially illustrious but no less firmly respectable background; he was an independently wealthy and thoroughly conventional gentleman.

2. Mrs. Wharton's papers, some of which may possibly shed light on the question of her origins, are locked up in Yale University Library and will not be available until 1968. One unsubstantial rumor has it that Mrs. Wharton once searched in England for traces of her father. Meanwhile, it is perhaps worth noting that, although illegitimacy is an occasional theme in her fiction—a minor one in *The Age of Innocence,* and a central one in the novella *The Old Maid* (1924)—there is no example in her writing, so far as I know, of that grand archetypal theme of the search of the child for the father.

fertile tension in her work) that Mrs. Wharton while still Miss Jones did feel that way about her own milieu: in it, as the saying goes, but not altogether of it; obscurely illegitimate, in such a manner as to make her at once, in her private estimation, secretly dubious *and* secretly superior. The New York "high" society of the 1870s and '80s comprised a world that she belonged to and did not belong to or want to belong to. She could assert its importance with all the excess and the uncertainty that betoken the perfect snob, but she could also see its dullness, its obstinate defenses against reality; she could feel in her throat its oppressive and sterilizing effect, and she could feel herself feeling it. New York society was a kind of home, and it was a kind of trap, or cage. "She was everything that was right and proper," observed a visitor to the Jones family, "but the young hawk looked out of her eyes."

The right and proper young lady, at the age of twenty-three, made a suitable marriage with Edward Robbins Wharton of Philadelphia and Boston, a gentleman of considerable private means and no literary interests. The young hawk chafed under the bondage of charming banality, fell sick, took to travel and, later, to writing; and even as the marriage was crumbling (because of various calamities, ending in Mr. Wharton's incurable mental illness), she formed a relationship of an as yet undefined intimacy with one Walter Van Rennsalaer Berry.[3] Berry was an international lawyer, an American residing in Paris, a lifelong bachelor and an austere amateur—something more than a dilettante—of the arts. It was his shadowy distinction that Marcel Proust regarded him as "a Greek of the Golden Age," found his face "beautiful . . . to look upon," and dedicated to him a volume called *Pastiches et Mélanges*. Berry was not popular among Mrs. Wharton's friends. But for more than thirty years he was a valuable literary counselor, giving her the most sustained encouragement and the most searching advice she was to receive from anyone. He seems indeed (though the evidence is not quite clear) to be the first to have sensed a crucial portion of the untamed in Edith Wharton's imagination, and to have urged her not to hold that element too firmly in check—not to cage the young hawk too absolutely in her writing.

3. Thus, a psychologist might conceivably argue, replacing one sort of "father-figure" for another—the false one for the secretly true one.

Her first publications had been as right and proper as any publications could be, from the disapproving point of view of her parents. In 1878, when she was sixteen, there had been *Verses,* courteously supported (and influenced) by Longfellow and printed privately in Newport. Almost twenty years later, after the marriage and a series of illnesses and the recourse to writing as therapy, she collaborated with the architect Ogden Codman on a book called *The Decoration of Houses* (1897). At that same moment, Louis Sullivan, as he was to report later in his autobiography, was contemplating with despair the near-fatal setback to a native American architecture in the triumph of the European and the eclectic, and of Stanford White, at the 1893 Chicago Fair. Mrs. Wharton, however, wholeheartedly joined Stanford White in an expressed reverence for "the best models"—"models . . . found in buildings erected in Italy after the beginning of the sixteenth century, and in other European countries after the full assimilation of the Italian influence." It is hard not to feel that the phrase "best models" is a variant of the phrase "best people," and that her perfectly genuine and richly informed admiration for Renaissance villas and gardens came in part from the application of social snobbery to the aesthetic question: a right and proper attitude. Still, as we shall see, Mrs. Wharton had a developing sense of what we might call the *drama* of houses, a creative insight that went far beyond snobbery and would serve her imaginative purposes well—beginning, as its very title implies, with her first significant novel.

The same addiction to Italy and its historic culture led, after three volumes of shorter fiction between 1899 and 1901, to her first *published* novel, *The Valley of Decision* in 1902. This was a tediously long narrative about the Italian *sette cento,* in which an eloquently described background smothers, even while it partly atones for, an inert foreground plot of love, renunciation, and inexorable propriety. There followed another set of short stories and another novella; and then two more forays into the Italian scene. The latter—*Italian Villas and their Gardens* (1904) and *Italian Backgrounds* (1905)—are still quite readable, and they confirm Mrs. Wharton's eminence in that minor but often fascinating if loosely defined genre, "travel literature." Few American writers have tried their hand at this genre, and fewer still with the knowledge and ability of Edith Wharton. But now, in 1905, she seems to have begun meditating the comment Henry James made to a correspondent about *The Valley of Decision:* "The little lady . . . *must* be tethered in native pastures." James had already become her friend, her mentor, and her gossip; his advice had to be listened to. She set to work on a novel located in her own contemporary New York; and within six months she was able to offer *The House of Mirth* for serialization in *Scribner's Magazine.*

II

It had not always been called *The House of Mirth.* Mrs. Wharton experimented with two other titles before settling on that now familiar phrase, and the shifts involved provide some clues both to the content and to the eventual emphasis and the unusual form of the novel. The manuscript title was *A Moment's Ornament.* This was changed in typescript to *The Year of the Rose*—until that phrase in turn was struck out by hand and replaced with *The House of Mirth.* The two earlier titles share the same connotation: namely, of something beautiful and yet evanescent; and the emphasis in each case is, of course, upon the heroine, on Lily Bart herself and the final period of her blooming and fading. Lily, moreover, is associated alternately in those phrases with something artificial (an ornament) and something natural (a rose); but, while there is a running opposition throughout Book I between the natural and the artificial, the common defect of the two original titles lies in the fact that Lily characteristically possesses a degree of *both* qualities. The third title transfers attention from the heroine to the world—or one of the worlds—in which she seeks her fortune; and suggests at once the reason why (given her divided nature, her attraction to the spiritual as well as the mirthful) she is pathetically destined to fail.

Mrs. Wharton's ultimate choice was typical and revealing. In her published titles, she customarily focused upon a context for action, rather than on the human actors concerned or the meaningful shape of the drama to be enacted. Her books speak to us initially of a valley, a house, a milieu, a time, a city, a river (*The Valley of Decision, The House of Mirth, The Custom of the Country, The Age of Innocence, Old New York, Hudson River Bracketed*)—with a quality or function added on as generally indicative of just that kind of context. *Ethan Frome* is an exception and it is Jamesian; for Henry James, by contrast, habitually pointed to his chief characters (*Roderick Hudson, Daisy Miller*) or to the dramatic or symbolic function of his characters (*The American, The Ambassadors, The Wings of the Dove*). This does not mean that Edith Wharton was uninterested in characters and action, or inept in the handling of them; and it certainly does not mean that her novels were no more than fictionalized additions to her informative discourses on Italy and interior decoration. What it means is that Mrs. Wharton's view of motive and of causality in human affairs was rather different from that of James. The latter's dramas were driven by a deadly but mainly human and individual dialectic; for while James felt that society, almost by definition, was the very arena of experience, nonetheless he did not see society as a thing apart. In his view, life itself, the significant life, consisted (to borrow his comment on Ibsen) in the lunging of ego against ego, of soul against soul—no matter how socially located the lunging might be. There are instances of just such lunging throughout Edith Wharton's fiction, but there is, one feels, usually a third party to the contest. Her characters tend to be affected not only by each other but also by pressures in the atmosphere; by the more general and pervasive temptations and taboos, by the inexplicable conventions and the vague ex- pectancies of the social setting in this place or that time. No doubt there is in this novelistic perspective of Mrs. Wharton a trace of what literary historians sometimes call "naturalism"—the per- spective according to which environment (metaphysical as well as physical) is the major force that determines human activities. But the parallel should in no way be insisted upon, since, as Mrs. Wharton describes it, the environment—society—is itself an extract of human attitudes; and the warmth of human possibil- ity rather than the dry coldness of impersonal force is always her main subject.[4]

The so-called James aspect of Edith Wharton is worth pursuing for a moment: partly to examine further the composition and revision of *The House of Mirth;* but chiefly to insist that this aspect was largely a superficial one, a matter literally of occasional sur- face items. Mrs. Wharton's work kept veering, so to speak, back toward James's, even to touch it tangentially from time to time;

4. For an extended and thoroughly cogent discussion of Edith Wharton and "naturalism," see Blake Nevius, *Edith Wharton: A Study of her Fiction* (Berkeley and Los Angeles, 1953). I have occasion to cite this excellent study below.

but there was never any real degree of duplication of substance. *The House of Mirth,* for example, may seem to incorporate some of the essential stuff of *The Wings of the Dove* (1902), but one useful and negative way to define the former would be to show that in fact it does not. Both are stories of marital intrigue, and in both the plot turns on the ill-fated effort of an impoverished young woman—Kate Croy, Lily Bart—to combine marriage, material prosperity, and personal satisfaction. The two heroines are comparably poised between instances of well-being (in the form of shrewd and wealthy patronesses) and of the dingy dreariness of unrelieved poverty (warnings incarnate in their own families—sister Marian Condrip, cousin Gerty Farish). Both narratives conclude in the complete and final separation of the women from the men they love. But all of that belongs to the mechanics of staging; the structure and stress, the very theory of life at work in the two novels, are radically different. We are left with a misleading accumulation of echoes by Mrs. Wharton of Henry James: echoes of plot details, of allusion, of names, of phrasing.

"The continued cry that I am an echo of Mr. James," Edith Wharton wrote her editor in the year before *The House of Mirth* was published, "makes me feel rather helpless"; and she added that James's "books of the last ten years I can't read, much as I delight in the man." The remark is disingenuous or muddled (as Mrs. Wharton's observations on writing often tended to be). The plain fact is that she *had* read the later James; and the evidence is exactly in the number of surface echoes. An utterly unimportant character in *The House of Mirth* is given a name—Kate Corby —that is almost an anagram, or a misspelling, of Kate Croy. The Veronese painting that is invoked at the Venetian dinner party in *The Wings of the Dove* and the reference to which is arguably the key to the entire "meaning" of that novel is presented as a *tableau vivant* by guests of the upstart Welly Brys in an easily forgettable scene (I, 12) in *The House of Mirth.* The wording of Densher's appalled realization of Kate Croy's extraordinary plan, at that same party—"It was before him enough now, and he had nothing more to ask"—passes through Lawrence Selden's mind (II, 3) as he contemplates Lily Bart on the French Riviera: "It was before him again in its completeness, the choice in which she was content to rest."

Similarly, in the final sentence of *The House of Mirth,* the verbal description of Selden, kneeling beside Lily Bart's dead body and "draining their last moment to its lees," derives most probably from the language of the terrible denouement of James's "The Beast in the Jungle" (1901), when John Marcher, standing beside the grave that contains the corpse of May Bartram, "emptied the cup to the lees." The derivation of the one common-place phrase from the other is confirmed when the famous remainder of James's sentence—"he had been the man of his time, *the* man, to whom nothing on earth was to have happened"—turns up in pale but recognizable shape in *The Age of Innocence* at the moment when Newland Archer sees himself as "a man to whom nothing was ever to happen." Wisps of substance no doubt stick to these verbal borrowings and get carried over from James into Mrs. Wharton; but they remain primarily verbal borrowings. What we eventually make of these similarities, in short, is simply this—that Mrs. Wharton took from James something of his verse, but little of his poetry.

James's poetry resided to a considerable extent *in* his words, often in his much-meditated proper names. The juxtaposition of May Bartram and John Marcher in "The Beast in the Jungle" is patently intended at once to enlarge and to focus the import of the tale by implicating the individual characters in a perennial contrast of seasons (May and March) which is at the same time the fundamental contrast of life and death. The name of Christopher Newman in *The American* is almost too bluntly suggestive; more engaging implications flow from the name of Isabel Archer. But the names Edith Wharton seems to have evolved from those just cited—names like Lily Bart and Newland Archer—are, by comparison, no more than satisfactory sounds. The manuscript of *The House of Mirth* shows that, while Mrs. Wharton fiddled end-lessly with the names of her characters, the changes she made do not bring with them any sizable amount of new meaning. Selden, Lily Bart, Judy Trenor, and Gerty Farish appear originally in Mrs. Wharton's longhand as Hensley, Juliet Hurst, Georgie Druce, and Nelly Varick, respectively; and Miss Juliet Hurst was modified briefly into Miss Lily Hurst before becoming once and for all Miss Lily Bart. But what the novel is trying to say is scarcely affected by those changes—the impotence of the relation between Selden and Lily Bart would be no less poignant if the persons concerned were called Hensley and Juliet Hurst. What has been achieved by the substitutions is a faint but definite gain of tonal propriety, of auditory relevance. The combination in Mrs. Wharton's heroine of gentleness and toughness is better conveyed by joining Lily to Bart than by joining Juliet to Hurst; and the sporadic vitality and congenital slackness of her lover is better suggested by Selden—probably because it sounds like "seldom" —than by Hensley. Further than this it would be difficult to go. For, again to cite the manuscript, Mrs. Wharton's countless emendations of words and phrases rarely aim at broadening the range of implication or at packing the expression symbolically, in the manner of James. They serve rather for rhetorical and dramatic tightening, for an increase in visual clarity, for pushing ever closer to accuracy of psychological and historical detail, and sometimes for a more ladylike decorum.

If Mrs. Wharton borrowed little of James's poetry, it was because her own poetry rarely got into her language. It resided elsewhere. For one thing, it was (especially in *The House of Mirth* and *The Age of Innocence*) the poetry of the hidden life, the poetry of silence and the unspoken word. "And in the silence there passed between them the word which made all clear." That final clause in *The House of Mirth* fittingly and ironically concludes a tale in which the necessary word is habitually withheld until it is too late. It is a tale, moreover, in which the heroine, Lily Bart, often withholds the necessary word from her own consciousness. "Her mind shrank from the glare of thought as instinctively as eyes contract in a blaze of light" (II, 13). The poetry of such a tale must attempt, paradoxically, to suggest the dramatically unrealized, must seek the effect of psychological reticence and encourage the reader to supply the sense of panic or illusory hope or sheer protracted suffering that Lily Bart will not give voice to, either to others or to herself. (In this respect, Lily Bart's fit of the horrors in chapters 13 and 14 of Book I, when she feels pursued by some Furies out of Euripides, is a rhetorical flaw, the less persuasive the more it is outspoken.) But, in addition to vibrating thus faintly beneath unexpressed or only partly expressed emotional reactions, the poetry of *The House of Mirth* resides also and no less obliquely in the description of a house, a hillside, a teashop, a waterfront. The drama that is artfully unrealized in the human encounters can be detected working itself out in the intricate play of "contexts." This brings us back to Mrs. Wharton's grasp of what I have called the drama of houses, or more simply the drama of place. It brings us back, in fact, to the implications of the title of *The House of Mirth.*

III

That title is only the most conspicuous example in the novel of Mrs. Wharton's method of identifying persons—individuals, family clans, entire social groups—in terms of place. Two other examples may stand for many. The Gryce clan (into which Lily Bart schemes for a while to marry) is summed up at a stroke in the image of their home on Madison Avenue (I, 2)—"an appalling house, all brown stone without and black walnut within, with the Gryce library in a fire-proof annex that looked like a mausoleum." Subtler and more precise is the description of Lily's aunt, Mrs. Peniston: first by reference to the "glacial neatness" of her drawing room, which is evidently a correlative of the meticulous but frosty-hearted nature of the lady in question; and then in the comparison between Mrs. Peniston's secretively vigilant mind to "one of those little mirrors which her Dutch ancestors were accustomed to affix to their upper windows, so that from the depths of an impenetrable domesticity they might see what was happening in the street." Figures of that sort—though there are not many so brilliantly effective—build into a pattern which gives the book its structure and reveals the action that the structure is devised to carry.

As the examples just quoted may suggest, the action involves a portion of social history—of Mrs. Wharton's personal notion about the history of American society in the late nineteenth and early twentieth centuries. Social history of this kind provides the largest though the least clearly visible of the contexts from which characters and events draw their meaning; and we should consider it before closing in at last on the particular fortunes of Miss Lily Bart. In *The Custom of the Country,* Edith Wharton gives us her own explicit and eloquent summary of the matter. The passage is worth quoting, since it is Mrs. Wharton's most expert use of houses as representative of persons. It is an extended architectural image of an entire society in transition, in a sort of quiet convulsion, one segment disappearing and another emerging into prominence—and in a way that, in *The House of Mirth,* remains half-concealed from the book's view, though it is already happening and deeply affects the lives of Lily Bart and the others.

In the passage that follows, Ralph Marvell, the gentle and cultivated young man who is to be the second husband of Undine Spragg and who will destroy himself because of what she does to his life, is returning one evening to the Marvell home on Washington Square (I, v). He

> looked up at the symmetrical old red house-front, with its frugal marble ornament, as he might have looked into a familiar human face.
>
> "They're right,—after all, in some ways they're right," he murmured, slipping his key into the door.
>
> "They" were his mother and old Mr. Urban Dagonet, both, from Ralph's earliest memories, so closely identified with the old house in Washington Square that they might have passed for its inner consciousness as it might have stood for their outward form; and the question as to which the house now seemed to affirm their intrinsic rightness was that of the social disintegration expressed by widely-different architectural physiognomies at the other end of Fifth Avenue.
>
> As Ralph pushed the bolts behind him, and passed into the hall, with its dark mahogany doors and the quiet "Dutch interior" effect of its black and white marble paving, he said to himself that what Popple [a fashion-loving portrait-painter] called society was just like the houses it lived in: a muddle of misapplied ornament over a thin steel shell of utility. The steel shell was built up in Wall Street, the social trimmings were hastily added in Fifth Avenue; and the union between them was as monstrous and factitious, as unlike the gradual homogeneous growth which flowers into what other countries know as society, as that between the Blois gargoyles on Peter Van Degen's roof and the skeleton walls supporting them. . . .
>
> Ralph sometimes called his mother and grandfather the Aborigines, and likened them to those vanishing denizens of the American continent doomed to rapid extinction with the advance of the invading race. He was fond of describing Washington Square as the "Reservation," and of prophesying that before long its inhabitants would be exhibited at ethnological shows, pathetically engaged in the exercise of their primitive industries.
>
> Small, cautious, middle-class, had been the ideals of aboriginal New York; but it suddenly struck the young man that

they were singularly coherent and respectable as contrasted with the chaos of indiscriminate appetites which made up the modern tendencies.[5]

The whole of the above repays the closest scrutiny. There is nothing so good in *The House of Mirth,* no moment in that novel (or any other) where Mrs. Wharton's imaginative view of social and moral history is so firmly controlled and so justly balanced, no image in which the history is so richly bodied forth in an organic interplay of buildings and psyches. Nor could there be. By 1913, when Mrs. Wharton was writing *The Custom of the Country,* the process whereby "the chaos of indiscriminate appetites" was overwhelming the "coherent and respectable" ideals of old New York had become unmistakable. By 1920 and *The Age of Innocence* (and more skimpily in the four novellas of 1924, *Old New York*), Mrs. Wharton could portray those small and cautious virtues at the time of their flowering, with a sure sense both of their coherence and their perilous limitations, and with a settled conviction as to how and when the "chaos" set in and of the destructive course it had run. But in 1905, the issues were not so clear, the elements not yet sorted out; the moral and social landscape was heaving confusedly, but the source of the disturbance was not yet altogether evident. For Edith Wharton, this situation posed a challenge, and she triumphed over it. For Lily Bart, it posed a dilemma, and she succumbed.

The triumph is reflected in a novelistic structure which at first glance seems to have been badly fumbled. Between Books I and II of *The House of Mirth* there is what looks like an awkward imbalance, a yoking of two parts that are nearly incompatible in focus and narrative method. Book I adheres to a relatively "closed" situation; in a more or less traditional manner, it explores the interlocking intrigues of a single social set (the Trenor set at Bellomont and in New York City); it covers a short space of time (early September to the following January); and it is shaped distinctly enough by the rhythm, the faint flaring and uncertain flickering, of the love relation between Selden and Lily Bart. Book II is much more open, meandering, and episodic. It covers a long and unhappily drawn-out year (from April to April). It moves without any obvious design from one house or place to

5. Edith Wharton, *The Custom of the Country* (New York, 1913), pp. 72–74. Copyright, 1913, by Charles Scribner's Sons.

another—from the Dorsets' yacht on the Riviera to Mattie Gomer's estate on Long Island and then west to Alaska; to Carry Fisher's little house in Tuxedo; to the Emporium Hotel and the swank overheated suite of Mrs. Norma Hatch; to the depressing workshop of Mme. Regina's millinery establishment; to a narrow room with "blotched wall-paper and shabby paint" in a New York boardinghouse; to the bed where Lily Bart quietly dies of an overdose of sleeping medicine. Book I has its affinities with the fictional genre of which Henry James was the master; and in its compressed and circumscribed locale, "themes"—especially the theme of freedom and imprisonment—are made to palpitate in a notably Jamesian manner. Book II has affinities rather with the wandering, groping, uncentered, and downward-spiraling novels characteristic of American writing in the past decade; and amid all that loose and blurry movement, we do not easily find any mode of continuity, thematic or otherwise. Between them, however, the two parts form a curious but successful unit; they comprise the genre which, I have suggested, Mrs. Wharton virtually invented—to convey her sense of what was happening, historically, to the conditions of the only life that interested her.

What was happening was that the house of mirth—here represented by the Trenors and their playfellows—was *giving way* to those other "houses," those other and still more appetitive and treacherous social clusters represented, in Book II, by the Dorsets, the Gomers, the Hatches, and so on. The whole moral history of modern New York (to adopt a phrase of Henry James) is in the progression or descent from Bellomont to the Emporium Hotel. The selfish and mirthful world of the Trenors, having no moral coherence, cannot help dissolving into the meretricious jumble we encounter in Book II, when the chaos that was half-hidden beneath the spurious modishness of Bellomont becomes fully experienced. Examining Bellomont, we can see why. It is made up of people like the thoughtless if not ill-intentioned Judy Trenor, the perennial hostess who "knew no more personal emotion than that of hatred for the woman who presumed to give bigger dinners . . . than herself"; her husband Gus Trenor, red and massive, with his heavy eyes, his rumbles of coarse emotion, his perfect blend of financial and erotic acquisitiveness; Percy Gryce, the millionaire collector of Americana, whose arrested development is marked by the "settled look of dulness" that regularly creeps over his blankly candid features; Bertha

Dorset, petite, malicious, morally irresponsible; and others— Kate Corby, Ned Silverton, Lady Cressida Raith, and the like —dimmer in outline and no more discriminating in ethical aware- ness. This is the "crowded world of pleasure" that passes for society in New York, 1905; and it has quite elbowed aside what Mrs. Wharton would call the cautious and middle-class ideals of the older New York. Of the latter, indeed, there is hardly any sign whatever in *The House of Mirth,* except in the frozen forms of the Peniston household, and, in a way to be examined, in the bafflingly exhausted form of Lawrence Selden. The absence of that old order is a main cause of Lily Bart's dilemma, though she never quite realizes the fact.

Strictly speaking, of course, we encounter the deteriorating jumble in Book II only as Lily Bart, victimized by and expelled from the Trenor society (after Gus Trenor's attempted rape and gross falsifications), forms her brief and increasingly tenuous associations with the Dorsets and Gomers and Hatches. The Trenor group may be imagined as continuing its round of point- less pleasure, and Bertha Dorset her lies and infidelities; but what Mrs. Wharton has done is to compress her chapter of social history into a period of nineteen months by passing her heroine through a succession of "houses," each one a sort of degradation of the one before. At the same time, however, *The House of Mirth* does belong to Lily Bart; it is her story that engages us, her history that we want to follow. The deterioration sketched for us, and reflected in the novel's structure, is primarily a decline in Lily Bart's "position," in fact in her very hold on life. Mme. Regina's hat shop (in II, 10) is no doubt an ultimate and naked instance of the dehumanized commercialism that is the root of the social disintegration writ large in the novel. Walking back to her rooming house (II, 10), Lily Bart seems to herself to be walking "through the degradation of a New York street in the last stages of decline from fashion to commerce." There is the whole social history in a nutshell. But it is also a last stage in the declining career of a particular young woman. What gives *artistic* coherence to Mrs. Wharton's narrative image of spreading moral incoherence—what protects the novel against what literary critics call "the fallacy of imitative form" (whereby a disorderly society is described by a disorderly book)—is the fictional logic in the account of Lily's last year on earth. Within the general disarray, there is a clearly traced process of narrowing, as Lily's destiny almost literally closes in on he.; as she moves from the spacious grounds at Rhinebeck to the more restricted domain at Roslyn to the oppressive suite in the hotel to a single room in a boardinghouse to the narrow bed in which she dies.

IV

Lily Bart is one of the authentic creations of American fiction. She is by turns admirable, touching, exasperating, forlorn, sturdy, woefully self-deceptive, imprudent, finely proud, intuitive—and, for one reader at least, not much less than humanly adorable. She is not a tragic heroine. She does not have a truly fatal flaw, only a dangerous weakness: an inability to resist a certain kind of temptation. The temptation is not erotic; Lily Bart is not vulnerable (as are some of her associates) on the sexual side. She can imply a promise of exquisite intimacy; the gesture by which she leans forward to light her cigarette from the tip of Selden's has more real suggestiveness (and I do not mean symbolism) than a dozen pages of anatomical espionage from popular fiction. But Lily Bart is a creature, not of sexual passion but of a physical passion of a different order. She is, let us say, a nymphomaniac of material comfort; *that* is what she is helpless to resist. Her entire being in this respect is characterized by her attitude toward the notion of marrying Rosedale—that "plump rosy man of the blond Jewish type," whose "smart London clothes fit[ted] him like upholstery," and who somewhat surprisingly is permitted by Edith Wharton to manifest qualities ("a certain gross kindliness," "a rather helpless fidelity of sentiment") that distinguish him favorably from his gentile social superiors. Lily cannot quite bring herself to like him, or anyhow to like him enough; and as she contemplates married life with him (II, 6), "she did not indeed let her imagination range beyond the day of plighting; after that everything faded into a haze of material well-being, in which the personality of her benefactor remained mercifully vague." Into that same haze of material well-being, Lily's sexual reactions regularly tend to fade.

The career of Lily Bart (the action of *The House of Mirth*) is, as I have said, determined by the interplay of the character outlined above and the social scene in which she is required to make her moves. But the game is really lost in advance. For the only society in which Lily might have found the combination she sought—the older New York society, where decency did blend with an adequate material ease—was not observable on her horizon. It had been superseded by the house of mirth; and what was left of it had retreated into "the republic of the spirit." Entrance into the house of mirth had to be paid for by marriage to someone like the intolerable Percy Gryce; and, although Lily attributes her failure to establish a footing there to her own "unsteadiness of purpose" (II, 7), it was due in fact to a habit of discrimination that all her self-delusion cannot overcome. Edith Wharton's private feeling of belonging and not belonging to the social order that flourished in the 1870s and '80s was greatly exacerbated in Lily Bart's contradictory attitude—her urge toward and repugnance to—the Trenor society of a generation later. At every turn she undercut or slid away from her material opportunities, always regarding her refusal to make the final compromise as a failure of nerve. But the only alternative she is ever made conscious of (apart from the curiously compassionate proposals of Rosedale) is Lawrence Selden and his spiritual republic.

Lily Bart's journey is punctuated by the shifts in her relation to Selden. Each of the two books begins as Selden and Miss Bart are drawing toward one another, and each ends in separation. Through the house party at Bellomont and the New Year's gathering at the Brys in Book I, their intimacy and understanding grow to the point where Selden is about to ask Lily to marry him. Lily, while assuring herself that she will not of course accept him, is half-ready to hear him out—until the affair is blasted by the dreadful contretemps with Gus Trenor. In Book II, Selden is again caught up in Lily Bart's troubles and again rises to that point of animation where he is determined to propose to her. But while he is on his way to her shabby room, Lily takes an excessive dose of sleeping drops, and just before he arrives, she sinks through unconsciousness to death—a manipulation of timing and incident by Mrs. Wharton that would seem tediously contrived and melodramatic were not the mode of Lily's death the almost inevitable culmination of her sagging career.[6] The relation between Selden and Lily Bart thus gives the novel that "he loves me, he loves me not" pattern in terms of which *The Age*

6. A careful look at the final pages of II, 13 will convince the reader that Lily Bart's death was not an act of deliberate suicide. As to the danger of an overdose, against which she had been warned, "She did not, in truth, consider the question very closely," Mrs. Wharton writes; "the phys-

of Innocence is so much more smoothly constructed, and which, in the latter novel, is announced in the very opening scene by the song from *Faust* (*"M'ama, non mi ama"*) the main characters gather to hear in the old Opera House.

What Lawrence Selden has to offer but never quite nerves himself to offer is companionship in "the republic of the spirit." Here, as against the house of mirth, the keynote is freedom: "freedom from everything," as Selden explains in the book's most moving, indeed its most passionate encounter (I, 6); "from money, from poverty, from ease and anxiety, from all the material accidents." It is a freedom, in short, from all the *external* pressures that limit or deflect the exercise of moral choice. The notion of so exclusive, so sparsely inhabited, and so morally elevated a society has provided one of the great and recurring themes in American fiction; and its appearance in *The House of Mirth* links Edith Wharton unexpectedly with Cooper, Hawthorne, Melville, and Mark Twain—each of whom dramatized his own ideal community, conceived in opposition to actual society and to which never more than two or three were eligible to belong.[7] But Lawrence Selden, as Mrs. Wharton's most illuminating critic has remarked, "is the least attractive ambassador of his 'republic of the spirit,' and Mrs. Wharton knows this as well as her readers."[8] If this is so—and the description may be a bit exaggerated—it is not only because Mrs. Wharton's view of the male sex, and her usual narrative strategy as well, led her time and again to depict her masculine figures as all too unmasculine, as intelligent but ineffectual (Selden, George Darrow in *The Reef,* Ralph Marvell, Newland Archer). It is also, and I think more importantly though relatedly, because Mrs. Wharton knew something else, an insight she shared with Henry James (who dramatized it, for example in *The Spoils of Ponyton*), but one that readers of both novelists have often failed to understand.

---

ical craving for sleep was her only sustained sensation." There was, of course, an element of the self-defeating in her nature, and by this time she was psychologically worn out. The reader may, if he wishes, impute to her a fatigued but quite buried desire for death.

7. This theme is the subject of a recent book by Mr. A. N. Kaul, *The American Vision: Actual and Ideal Society in Nineteenth Century Fiction* (New Haven, 1963).

8. Nevius, p. 59.

Edith Wharton knew that in the fatal modern dislocation between manners and morals, between actual conduct and ethical principle, as the former become crude, the latter become bloodless. This is not a matter of allegory; it is a matter of fact. Selden is dimmer, dryer, harder to discern than, say, Rosedale, with his vigorous vulgarity, because that kind of psychological fade-out is (Mrs. Wharton saw) what is likely to happen to a man who achieves the freedom arrived at by Selden—freedom not only from material anxiety, but almost freedom from the material world itself, from the flesh and blood of the actual. In *The Age of Innocence,* the unfortunate split in question would be explicitly named, as a division between "the actual" and "the real." But while we have long been accustomed to accounts of the terrible effect upon the actual of its divorce from the real (or ideal), we hear less often about the opposite—how the real goes dry and sterile when dissociated from the actual. There is a portion of anxiety, or shall we say of moral alertness, that goes with the condition of being human; and to break free of that is to break away from humanity itself. The point about the republic of the spirit is not (or not only) that Lily Bart is too impurely devoted to material things to get into it, but that it is too airless for anyone with blood in his veins to survive in it.

This great divorce is the "malice of fortune" which Lily Bart vaguely invokes, along with her own infirmity of purpose, as the cause of her failures. It is a historical malice, a calamity brought about by historical developments within the social and moral order; and Lily's infirmity is in good part due to her bemused awareness that neither alternative that the times can offer will satisfy. She wilfully spoils her chances for marrying into the house of mirth; but she distrusts the republic of the spirit. She has no place to go.

1962

THE CURRENT OF
CONRAD'S *VICTORY*

The opening sentences of *Victory* introduce us half-playfully to a number of "close relations," the surprising similarities between seeming contrasts—coal and diamonds, the practical and the mystical, the diffused and the concentrated, an island and a mountain. All of them have their literal and thematic importance in the story, which describes a profound conflict rooted in opposition and likeness, and which has to do with coal, diamonds, and an island; but the first effect of such dialectical teasing is the imparted sense of enlargement and creativity, of some idea or insight being made to grow. The last sentences of *Victory,* and especially its last word, are something else again:

> "And then, your Excellency [says good Captain Davidson], I went away. There was nothing to be done there."
>
> "Clearly," assented the Excellency.
>
> Davidson, thoughtful, seemed to weigh the matter in his mind, and then murmured with placid sadness:
>
> "Nothing!"

Between that initial sense of conceptual growth, with its cautious jocularity, and the thoughtful sadness of the closing negation there lies the truth of *Victory,* and its reality.

Victory is, in fact, a novel intimately concerned with questions of truth and reality, as it is with lies and illusion. Those big considerations force themselves on the imagination of the characters, and hence upon that of the reader; for it is that kind of novel, the kind Conrad normally attempted to write. In his preface to *The Nigger of the Narcissus,* Conrad defined art as the effort to render the highest justice "to the visible universe, by bringing to light the truth, manifold and one, underlying its every aspect." That creative ambition found an exact analogue in the experience narrated in *The Nigger of the Narcissus* itself, in the story's movement from the emphasized darkness of the ship's nighttime departure to the sunlit morning that greets its arrival in the English channel—after a voyage featured by the crew's effort to bring to light the truth and reality incarnate in the dying dark man, James Wait. And measured by Conrad's own standard, *Victory* achieves the conditions of art; for the manifold *and* unitary truth of things is just what Conrad succeeds in making real and visible, and what the persons of his island drama are most vitally concerned with. How the process is managed in this particular instance is the subject of present examination. But we have first to take a hard pull on our intellectual reins.

I

Revisiting *Victory* today, one cannot help being struck by its "existentialist" qualities—by how much it shares the intellectual preoccupations and postures notable in continental literature during recent decades. Here, for instance, is an elaborated image of human isolation: the isolation not only of man from man, but even more of man from his metaphysical environment—Axel Heyst, the rootless drifter, who has settled alone upon a singularly remote little island, near an abandoned coal mine, there to meditate in silence his late father's reflections upon "the universal nothingness" and "the unknown force of negation." Here, too, is the familiar counterattack upon metaphysical isolation, the unsteady impulse toward human fellowship—those compassionate gestures toward Morrison and the girl called Lena which belie Heyst's habitual detachment and are the source of his misfortunes and maybe of his redemption. Here is the articulated obsession with the feeling of existence and of nonexistence, as clues both to character and action. "If you were to stop thinking of me, I shouldn't be in the world at all," Lena says to Heyst; and, "I am he who is——" announces plain Mr. Jones, in a breath-taking moment which, in context, has an overpowering propriety. Here are modes of nihilism yielding to modes of self-annihilation, in the oddly similar catastrophes of both hero and villain. Here, in short, is a tale of violence that oscillates richly between the fundamental mysteries of being and nothing. Conrad, we are inclined to say, is the still insufficiently acknowledged grandfather of the most recent literary generation.

To say so is not necessarily to praise Conrad; and it is more likely, indeed, to impose upon him a false identity. *Victory* is not—and it cannot be discussed as—a novel of ideas, for example, in the manner of Malraux's *The Walnut Trees of the Altenburg.* Nor is it a calculated work of metaphysical revolt, like Camus' *The Plague.* Conrad did of course display attitudes, and he had a stiff little set of convictions. But E. M. Forster has rightly, if unsympathetically, made the point that Conrad had no "creed" —no coherent order of intellectual principles—and no more than other novelists writing on English soil did Conrad possess that occasional French and German talent for making the war of thought itself exciting. He wanted to exploit the power of words, as he said, in order "to make you hear, to make you feel—before all to make you *see*"; and the end of each of his best novels was simply its own composition. He did not believe with Malraux that art is "a rectification of the universe, a way of escaping from the human condition"; and he would scarcely have understood Camus' parallel and derivative contention that "the novel is born simultaneously with the spirit of rebellion and expresses, on the aesthetic plane, the same ambition." *Victory* dramatizes basic aspects of truth and being; but as regards the human condition, its main aim is only to observe it in the way of art—with that idle but no less intense and sustained attention for which Conrad accurately thought he had a natural ability, and with which he recalled observing the living model for *Victory's* heroine.

The novel's final word—"Nothing!"—is, accordingly, less a cry of appalled metaphysical recognition than the quiet acknowledgment that the adventure is over and the art that described it has peacefully exhausted itself. It is in the mood less of Camus' Caligula than of Shakespeare's Hamlet: "The rest is silence." The drama is done, and everybody who had a significant part in it is dead. Lena is dead, accidentally shot by Mr. Jones. Heyst has died by fire; Jones has died by water; and both deliberately, as it seems. Ricardo has been killed by Jones's second try at him; and Pedro has been dispatched by Wang, the houseboy. "There are more dead in this affair," Davidson remarks to the Excellency, "than have been killed in many of the battles of the last Achin war." The bungalow and the other two houses are burned to ashes; the boat has drifted out to sea; a corpse lies rotting on the scorched earth. To close the account, only the word "nothing" needs to be uttered.

And yet. If there is no metaphysical vision or purpose at work in the novel, there can nevertheless be felt running through it something like a metaphysical tide. Or better, perhaps, one senses the active presence, the dangerous undertow, of a metaphysical current giving the story its energy and its direction. In the same way, if the tale is not plainly intended as an allegory, one feels in it nevertheless something like an allegorical swelling, as though everything were about to become bigger than itself. That very impression affects the nerves of the persons in the book. "I have a peculiar feeling about this," says Mr. Jones. "It's a different thing. It's a sort of test." In the long list of Conrad's writings, *Victory* also comes to us as a different thing and a sort of test. It is Conrad's test of the nature of fiction: in general, of the ability of drama to move toward allegory while retaining intact its dramatic form and essence; and in particular, of the ability of fiction to move toward drama while retaining its identity as fictional narrative. It is a test of the way truth and reality can become the subject matter of a novel which hangs on to its novelistic nature. And the result, in my judgment, is indicated by the last word Conrad actually did write in this book, as he tells us: the single word of the title.

Victory (1915) is itself the last of those works both Conrad and his critics have agreed to call major; and it ranked with *Nostromo* (1904) as Conrad's personal favorite. Conrad's appraisal of his writings was, I think, both sound and suggestive. He always had a special fondness for *The Nigger of the Narcissus* (1897), recognizing it for what it was, his first genuine artistic accomplishment; and his satisfaction with *The Secret Agent* (1907) was grounded correctly in his belief that he had succeeded, in that novel, in treating "a melodramatic subject ironically," as he wrote in the copy he gave his friend Richard Curle. But he disagreed with readers and critics who thought that *Lord Jim* (1900) was his best book; he felt the tale did not justify the great length of the novel, and suspected that he should have stuck to his original idea, which was to restrict the narrative to the pilgrim ship episode. The most he could say for *Under Western Eyes* (1910) was "rather good." We should probably speak more warmly, but the pain of composition clings to the pages of *Under Western Eyes;*

and the congealing of the action (for example, in Part III) is for long stretches greater than all the interpolated reflections on the art of fiction can overcome. About *Chance* (1913), in a manner not uncommon with authors, he began to talk deprecatingly the moment it became so huge a success. But he remained steadfast in his conviction that his two supreme efforts were the vast tale of the South American seaboard and the tight little story of Axel Heyst.

Surely he was right. *Nostromo* was, as Conrad knew, his largest canvas and his "most anxiously meditated work." It is also one of the greatest novels in English, with a greatness so complex and extensive that only belatedly and partially has it become appreciated. *Victory* is a triumph of a different kind, of a nearly opposite kind. Here Conrad has presented almost all the themes that interested him, but he has refracted those themes through the closely observed conduct of a tiny group of people in a tiny and absolutely isolated setting. *Nostromo* and *Victory* thus stand in a relation similar to the relation between *King Lear* and *Othello* (or perhaps like that between *The Possessed* and *Crime and Punishment*). Both *Nostromo* and *King Lear* comprehend more of the world and of human experience than the mind can comfortably contemplate; both are made up of a variety of parallel plots and involve several different groups of persons; in each we discover what Francis Fergusson calls "action by analogy," and the action so richly exposed in its multiplicity of modes reveals something not only about the individuals concerned but about the hidden drift of history, the secret and tragic movement of the universe. Both works engage the artist's most disturbing power —the prophetic power—which is of course not the ability to read the particular and immediate future, but the ability to read the future implicit in every grave and serious time, the future man is perennially prone to. In *Victory,* on the other hand, as in *Othello,* the action emerges directly from the peculiar temperaments of a few eccentric individuals. What happens, both artistically and psychologically, happens as a result of the impact of one unique personality upon another. This is not to deny any largeness to *Victory;* it is only to identify the source of the special largeness it does reveal. It is to say that the novel shows an allegorical swelling rather than an allegory, and that the creative force is less a pre-existent design the characters are re-enacting (for example, the myth of Eden, of the man and the woman in the garden and the invasion by the serpent) than the jarring effect of the human encounters.

The germ of *Nostromo* was an anecdote, the theft of a lighter-full of silver. But the germ of *Victory* seems to have been the remembered look of several unrelated persons glimpsed at sundry times and in sundry places. *Nostromo* houses characters enough for half a dozen novels; but it says something about Conrad's attitude toward them that he took most of their names from an old book of memoirs (G. F. Masterman's *Seven Eventful Years in Paraguay,* published in 1869) which gossiped about people called Carlos Gould, Monygham, Decoud, Fidanza, Barrios, and Mitchell (*sic*). Conrad's inventive power in *Nostromo,* I am suggesting, was mainly or at least primarily directed to the exposure of action through plot. In *Victory,* however, we remark a thinness, almost a casualness, of plot invention; for Conrad's attention here was directed initially toward people—toward the exposure of action through character. The distinction is exaggerated, and with luck we can make it collapse; but for the moment it can be helpful. It is intended, in any case, as a slight revision of the wonderfully fertile distinction offered by Jacques Maritain in *Creative Intuition in Art and Poetry*—the distinction between "the poetry of the novel" and "the poetry of the theater." The latter, Maritain argues, is essentially the poetry of the action; action comes first in the dramatic composition, and other elements —character, especially—are subordinated to and controlled by the shape of the action, which it is their chief function to illuminate. The poetry of the novel, Maritain continues, is the poetry of the agent, for the aim of fiction is not so much to present an action as to shed light upon the human heart. The incidents in a novel are accordingly selected in order to illuminate the peculiar and representative nature of individual human beings. M. Maritain's remarks and my respectful revision of them help explain the sense in which *Victory* is a test of the nature of fiction. For the "agents" of the book did come first in Conrad's planning and in his writing. But by his manipulation of his characters, Conrad brought into being an action virtually invulnerable in its design.

II

"Conrad was fond of discussing characters in *Victory,*" Curle reports; and in his author's note, Conrad discusses little else. He shares with us the memories that went into the making of the novel: a professional cardsharper he had seen once in the West Indies in 1875; the silent wide-eyed girl in a café orchestra in the South of France; the wandering Swedish gentleman who became "the physical and moral foundation of my Heyst." "It seems to me but natural," Conrad says, "that those three buried in the corner of my memory should suddenly get out into the light of the world." The reference was actually to the three bad men, Mr. Jones and Martin Ricardo and Pedro; but it applies equally to the three key figures in the story. They gathered together irresistibly in Conrad's imagination, just as they gather together for the culminating experience of each of their lives on Heyst's island. They are made known to us exactly through the process of gathering. And indeed the first and most obvious way to chart the unfolding scheme of the book is to point to the important moments in that process.

We meet Axel Heyst on the first page. We hear of Lena thirty-six pages later in Mrs. Schomberg's reluctant mutter to Davidson: "There was even one English girl." Mr. Jones makes his appearance fifty-five pages later yet: "a guest who arrived one fine morning by mail-boat . . . a wanderer, clearly, even as Heyst was." Conrad then devotes nearly seventy pages to acquainting us with the three desperadoes, and with the critical differences between them. But even before he begins that section, the gathering process has been at work in the meeting and the drawing together of Heyst and Lena, and their flight to the island refuge. The entire group of major characters (the Schombergs, of course, excluded) is not assembled in a single place until a little more than halfway through the book: when Wang interrupts the moment of deepest intimacy between Heyst and Lena to announce that a boat (containing, as we learn, Mr. Jones and his henchmen) is approaching the jetty. From that instant, the whole of the novel is caught up in the collision of personalities—in what Henry James (speaking about one of Ibsen's plays) called the lunging of ego against ego, the passionate rocking of soul against soul; every ego against every ego, in Conrad's masterful treatment of it, and every soul against every soul. From the instant the boat is sighted—or, more accurately, from the instant Heyst goes down to the jetty to stare in amazement at the spectacle of the three white men drifting in from nowhere, seemingly more dead than alive—Conrad's complex artistic purpose becomes clear and be-

gins to fulfill itself. The individual characters, explored individ-
ually or in small combinations, now meet and join in an adventure which becomes an action larger and more significant than
any of them. The novel, that is, begins to assume the defining
quality of drama.

Throughout the course of it, however, Conrad continues to
exploit the peculiar resources of the novel, for the traditional aims
of the novelist; but he does so, at the same time, as a way of
heightening and solidifying the dramatic design. In elaborating
the distinction I have mentioned, Jacques Maritain observes that
since the shape of the action is determining in a drama, con-
tingencies and coincidences and simple accidents have no place
there; but that these devices are proper to fiction, since they can
be exactly the occasion for some special insight into character.
During the latter half of *Victory,* the plot is heavily dependent
upon a series of "evitable" incidents, of which two may be cited
as typical: the theft of Heyst's gun by Wang and the shooting of
Lena by Mr. Jones. The latter is pure accident: Jones had intended
to kill Martin Ricardo. The former is a contingency: Wang might
have had a gun of his own, or Heyst another revolver hidden away
somewhere. Each incident is important to the plot as plotted, but
alternatives can easily be imagined, and neither incident seems
indispensable to the larger purpose. Yet both incidents serve to
shed light on the characters involved and are insofar novelistically
justified; and in the light they shed, a truth and a reality begin
to appear, as elements toward which an action is steadily in
motion.

These incidents, in short, are literally accidental, but they are
symbolically inevitable and dramatically appropriate. The theft
of the gun tells us a good deal about the curiously hidden nature
of the houseboy, his swift and agile selfishness with its portion
of quiet cruelty; and it reinforces the sense pervading the world
of the book, that in it the distance between men is nearly absolute.
At the same time, by rendering Heyst physically defenseless, it
provides an "objective correlative" for his more fundamental
defenselessness, that of a man of thought like himself in the hour
of necessary action. The time spent in puzzling and worrying over
the absence of the gun is time artistically well spent. The death of
Lena has a still higher degree of propriety. Mr. Jones's bullet,
though aimed at Ricardo, only grazed Ricardo's temple before
burying itself in Lena's heart, just "under the swelling breast of

dazzling and sacred whiteness"—the accident is compounded by the terrible chance that the bullet should strike her exactly there. Yet we need little instruction from the Freudians to perceive that the accident probably masked an act of deepest deliberation. Toward Ricardo, Mr. Jones felt only fury mixed with a lively sense of danger; but toward Lena, toward any woman, he felt the much more destructive emotion of radical disgust. The shooting of Lena is one of the last and most meaningful of the gestures by which we take the full measure of plain Mr. Jones—the evil ascetic, the satanic figure whose satanism springs from a loathing of woman and a horror of sex. (Graham Greene, who has written a short essay called "Plain Mr. Jones," and who is indebted to Conrad on many counts, has provided a comparable image in Pinkie Brown, the inflamed ascetic of *Brighton Rock*.) And in the mode of her death, we have the final revelation and indeed the vindication of Lena's character. Hers is the touching figure of the young woman of smudged virtue who prays she may lose everything for the sake of the man she loves (again, a figure we encounter in Graham Greene). She has drawn upon herself the death that threatened Axel Heyst. To do so is not only a part of her character; it is a part of her plan.

Each of the main figures in *Victory* has his or her private plan; and in this respect, *Victory* too, like *Nostromo,* has a number of plots—as many as the number of central characters; the plot in each case being what happens at last to the individual plan. As each plan is lit up for us, so much more of the action comes into view. In human terms, the separate plans are catastrophically irreconcilable, and in their difference they provide the "manifold" truth—to use Conrad's word—that the novel brings to light. But artistically, they form a living pattern of parallels and contrasts, and so provide the unitary truth Conrad equally envisaged.

Each of these secret programs of conduct is rooted in the mystery of one or two absolute characteristics. Schomberg's malice, for example, is an absolute trait of character, as unmotivated as the malice of Iago. Like Iago's hatred of Othello, Schomberg's hatred of Axel Heyst can pretend to a specific reason: Heyst's snatching away of the girl, which led to the funny Faulknerian madhouse involving Schomberg and the orchestra leader Zangiacomo, over which Conrad used to laugh reminiscently. But the hatred existed already, existed even before the episode, which Schomberg so evilly misrepresented, of Heyst and poor

Morrison. Schomberg's private plot, rooted in his malice, is the business of his so-called revenge upon Heyst, along with the business of diverting the outlaws from his own hotel to the safe distance of Heyst's island. In its vicious way, it is successful, but not because it has anything to do with the facts about Heyst and Lena. Schomberg's plot is strictly his own creation; it is not nourished to any real extent by external circumstances. The same is true of his malignancy. It is a key factor in releasing the terrible events of the book; but it is not developed by outside pressures, it is *revealed* by them. Thus it is with the determining features of the other people in *Victory*. For here, as is customary in Conrad's work, the characters do not grow; they only grow more visible. That is the precise effect of their mutual impact.

Mr. Jones is perhaps the most fascinating instance in the novel of the motion toward visibility, if only because it is the most paradoxical. What becomes fully and finally visible about him is a kind of absence, a nothingness. His plan is the least reconcilable of all the plans, and hence the most irreducible symptom of the "manifold" aspect of *Victory:* because Mr. Jones's plan opposes not only the substance of all the others but the very terms of their existence. Ricardo, we remember, has his own particular reasons—reasons he cannot disclose to Mr. Jones—for urging the invasion of Heyst's island; and no doubt some dumb dream of conquest occupies the primitive skull of Pedro. But the mission of Mr. Jones undercuts all that. It has to do with the condition of his being, which is, as it were, a mockery of being itself. Heyst reports to Lena on his conversation with Jones:

> " 'I suppose you would like to know who I am?' " he asked me.
> "I told him I would leave it to him, in a tone which, between gentlemen, could have left no doubt in his mind. He raised himself on his elbow—he was lying down on the campbed—and said:
> " 'I am he who is———.' "

"No use asking me what he meant, Lena," Heyst adds. "I don't know." What Jones meant was probably a theatrical blasphemy. In very similar words, according to the Old Testament, God announced his name and his nature to his chosen people: "I am," or "I am that I am." Jones, of course, is not god-like, and especially not god-like in the sense of representing the source of being itself. He is devil-like—his character bulges in the direction of the devil (he is not *the* devil, any more than *Victory* is an allegory); and exactly because he represents the source of non-being.

The association with Satan gratifies Mr. Jones immensely. He describes, in an echo from the Book of Job, his habit of "coming and going up and down the earth"; and Heyst replies that he has "heard that sort of story about someone else before." Jones at once gives Heyst a ghastly grin, claiming that "I have neither more nor less determination" than "the gentleman you are thinking of." But the nature and end of his determination emerge from a later allusion to the devil. Jones speculates for Heyst's benefit that a man living alone, as Heyst had been living, would "take care to conceal [his] property so well that the devil himself——." Heyst interrupts with a murmured "Certainly."

> Again, with his left hand, Mr. Jones mopped his frontal bone, his stalk-like neck, his razor jaws, his fleshless chin. Again, his voice faltered and his aspect became still more gruesomely malevolent, as of a wicked and pitiless corpse.

Those last four words summarize the character of Mr. Jones and point to his unswerving purpose: he is not only deathly, he is the cause that death is in others. To Schomberg, too, Jones had seemed "to imply some sort of menace from beyond the grave"; and in Heyst's first view of him, Jones is "sitting up [in the boat], silent, rigid and very much like a corpse." At the outset of their duel, Jones seems to exert a greater force of sheer existence than Heyst; for Heyst, as he confesses mournfully in language highly reminiscent of one of Hawthorne's isolated men, has lived too long among shadows. But Heyst's determining quality has only been lying dormant; he is like the indolent volcano, to which he is lightly compared on the second page of the book; he is moving—though moving too late and too slowly—toward existence and reality. Jones's characteristic movement is all in the other direction.

The force in Jones is all negative, though not the less emphatic for being so. That is why he hates and fears women, for they are fertility incarnate and the literal source of life. Jones's particular and personal plot is not really to seize Heyst's alleged treasures, but to inflict his deathiness upon others. He comes as an envoy of death, disguised as an envoy of the living: of death not in the sense of murder, but in the sense of a fundamental hostility to existence. He is the champion of the anti-real, and he arrives at just the moment when Heyst, because of the presence and love of Lena, is feeling "a greater sense of reality than he had ever known in his life." Jones's plan, too, is superficially successful: everyone he has brushed against on the island is dead. Jones is dead also; but he has not been killed, he has simply shrunk, collapsed, disintegrated. He has reached the limit of his true condition. And what is visible of him at the end is exactly the outward sign of that condition. "The water's very clear there," Davidson tells the Excellency; "and I could see him huddled up on the bottom between two piles, like a heap of bones in a blue silk bag, with only the head and feet sticking out."

Mr. Jones's most astute enemy in the book is not Heyst but the girl Lena, though Jones and Lena never in fact confront one another. But Lena is the one person able to understand not only the threat represented by the invaders, but the very threat of the threat; and she understands it so well that, as things develop, she can formulate her own plot and purpose to herself with exactness —to "capture death—savage, sudden, irresponsible death, prowling round the man who possessed her." Lena stands for a possibility of life. Yet, curiously enough, her role as the actual source of Heyst's sense of being is rendered less visible—rendered, that is, with less apparent success—than are the deadly negations of Mr. Jones. Lena is the one member of the cast who remains in partial darkness. Many critics have remarked upon this, and some have gone on to say that Conrad rarely had much luck with his women. But his achievement elsewhere is not always unimpressive: Winnie Verloc, in *The Secret Agent,* seems to me one of the most compelling females in modern literature; and one has little difficulty making out the attractive features of Emily Gould and Flora de Barral, in *Nostromo* and *Chance* respectively. It may even be that a kind of haziness, a fragility of substance was intended in the portrayal of Lena. She *is* like that, and the frailty of her being determines the nature of her plot. For her aim is precisely to win for herself a greater measure of reality by forcing upon the man she loves a greater recognition of her. She lives in his acknowledgment of her: "If you were to stop thinking about me I shouldn't be in the world at all. . . . I can only be what you think I am." This is a trifle unfortunate, since Heyst, the only human being who could have seen Lena, can never manage to see quite enough. Richard Curle observes nicely about Lena that she is "the supreme example of a 'one-man' woman, so supreme that even the reader is kept out of the secret." Heyst peers at her in the half-light, and we peer over his shoulder, dimly discerning a creature of considerable but only guessed-at bodily appeal and intense but only partially communicated spiritual desire.

Her desire is stated plainly enough for us, as it takes form after Ricardo's attempt to rape her. From that moment onward, "all her energy was concentrated on the struggle she wanted to take upon herself, in a great exaltation of love and self-sacrifice." And we know enough about her history to find that exaltation plausible. We have heard of her mother's desertion of her father, of her father's career as a small-time musician and of his removal to a home for incurables; we have heard of her bleak childhood and adolescence, her blurred unhappy life with a traveling orchestra; we can easily imagine what Heyst's compassion must have meant to her. "I am not what they call a good girl," she has said; and through Heyst's impression of her, we are struck by her mixture of misery and audacity. She alone fully understands that it is Schomberg who has put the outlaws on Heyst's trail, and she can comprehend the hotel keeper's motiveless motive. Lena's plot, accordingly, is the most coherent of all the plots, and the most important. It is also the most private, since it requires of her that she lie both to the man she hates and the man she loves. She is altogether successful, at least as successful as Schomberg or Mr. Jones. She does disarm Ricardo, literally and psychologically; the dagger she takes from him is indeed "the spoil of vanquished death" and "the symbol of her victory." By dividing Ricardo from Jones, she creates a situation in which, as the demonically brilliant Jones instantly realizes, Ricardo must be killed; and through a chain reaction, she is responsible also for the death of Pedro and Jones himself. All this we know, understand, and can rehearse. But Conrad has nonetheless not finally managed to fulfill his ambition with respect to Lena. He has not made us see Lena completely. Between her and ourselves, there falls a shadow. It is, of course, the shadow of Axel Heyst.

III

If the victory is Lena's—if her end, as Conrad insisted, is triumphant—the major defeat recorded in the novel is that of Heyst. His is the ultimate failure, and for the reason he gives in almost the last words we hear him speak: "Ah, Davidson, woe to the man whose heart has not learned while young to hope, to love—and to put its trust in life." But that very statement demonstrates that Heyst, by acknowledging his failure and perceiving its cause, has in the literary manner of speaking been saved. He is, at the last, completely in touch with truth. And, similarly, if Heyst's personal plan—which is not only to rid the island of its invaders and to protect Lena, but also to join with Lena in an experience of full reality—if that plan is the least successful plan in the book, Heyst is nonetheless the true and steady center of the novel from its beginning to its end. So central is Heyst within the rich composition of *Victory* that neither his character nor his conduct may be clearly seen apart from that composition. They are identified only through a series of analogies and contrasts, and as the vital center of the book's design.

As analysis moves to the figure of Axel Heyst, it moves of necessity from the Many to the One—from the many separated individuals with their irreconcilable differences of purpose to a pattern of action in which they seem to echo and reflect and repeat one another. It is the felt flow of the Many into the One that accounts for the feeling one has of a strong metaphysical current running deep through the novel, of very real human beings and events gathering together in a way that suggests an allegory of universal proportions. Let it be emphasized again that we have to do with a process, not with an imposition. And as it develops, we begin to detect parallels between contrasting and inimical elements, continuities between divisions—and by the power of the book's current, more radical contrasts between newly observed parallels. At the center is Axel Heyst, whose entire being—*artistically,* within the actual pages of the book—is created by the play of likeness and difference.

We must, accordingly, approach Heyst by way of those relationships—which is to reconsider some of the persons already inspected, but to consider them now not in their enormous differences, but in their unexpected similarities: an undertaking the first page of *Victory* (with its references to the similarities between coal and diamonds, an island and a mountain) has warned us would be the key to the novel's meaning. Between Lena and Ricardo, for example, between the mystically devoted young woman and the thickheaded roughneck who plunges headlong through the blue serge curtain to assault her, an unexpected likeness is uncovered. It is a fatality in Ricardo's crude imagination that he should exaggerate it. "You and I are made to understand each other," he mumbles, after a stupor of surprise and admiration at the vigor of Lena's resistance. "Born alike, bred alike, I guess. You are not tame. Same here! You have been chucked out into this rotten world of 'ypocrites. Same here!" Because of his conviction of their likeness, Ricardo trusts Lena more simply and unquestioningly than Heyst trusts her; Ricardo trusts what there is in Lena of his own animal and prehensile nature, and he dies of that trust, as Heyst dies of mistrust. But within disastrous limits, Ricardo is right—he and Lena do have a good deal in common. "Perhaps because of the similarity of their miserable origin in the dregs of mankind," Lena realizes, "she had understood Ricardo perfectly." Even her physical strength and tenacity match his: "You have fingers like steel! Jiminy! You have muscles like a giant." That is scarcely the pathetic child seen through Heyst's impression of her, the child suffering helplessly the venomous pinchings of Mrs. Zangiacomo; and the ferocity of her response to Ricardo's attempted rape correctly suggests a ready perception, based on experience, of that kind of jungle behavior. It also suggests the strength in Lena which has been brought to the surface since the Zangiacomo days: brought to the surface and focused as a powerful instrument, through the effect upon her of Heyst.

An important ingredient in her strength is a talent for lying, exercised for the sake of truth. Ricardo is quite justified in attributing to Lena a duplicity equal to his own; he knows that both of them have had to become skilled in duplicity as the one indispensable resource in the world's hypocritical "game of grab." "Give the chuck to all this blamed 'ypocrisy," urges Ricardo. Lena seems to agree, and she embarks deceptively upon a plot to deceive Heyst—"her gentleman," as Ricardo calls him—which notably parallels Ricardo's systematic deception of *his* gentleman, Mr. Jones. It seems to Ricardo natural that Lena should lie to the man who has befriended her; such is the norm of behavior in the world he inhabits—that is, the world of *Victory*. It is what people do to each other in that world: witness Mrs. Schomberg's trickery of her own gentleman, her fat braggart of a husband. The cluster of duplicities has, up to a point, a common element, for each aims initially at the salvation of the man deceived. Mrs. Schomberg, when she helps frustrate her husband's plans (his "insane and odious passion") by helping Lena to escape, imagines she is keeping Schomberg out of serious trouble and preserving their wretched marriage. Ricardo's organization of the invasion of Heyst's island is a contrivance to rescue his chief from the habitual state of sloth into which Jones had fallen. To do so, Ricardo must cunningly keep silent about the presence on the island of a young woman; since, were Jones to hear about it, he would instantly abandon the adventure. Only later does Ricardo's helpful deceit deepen into betrayal. And as to Lena, "she was not ashamed of her duplicity," because "nothing stood between the enchanted dream of her existence and a cruel catastrophe but her duplicity." She will deceive every one, and she will especially deceive Heyst; she will wear the mask of infidelity to save the life of the man toward whom her fidelity is the very assurance of her existence.

The relationship between Lena and Ricardo thus illuminates one of the major themes of the novel—the theme of truth-telling, and the significance of truth-telling, as a value, in the scheme of human behavior. By the same token, Lena and Ricardo illuminate the character of Axel Heyst; for it is almost a weakness in Heyst that—at the opposite extreme from Mr. Jones and his self-association with the Father of Lies—he has an absolute regard for truth. He is so obsessed with truth that he becomes literally disempowered when confronted with lies; and he is so inflexible toward truth that only lies can save him. Even more than the theft of his gun, as it seems, it is the lies Schomberg has spread about Heyst's treatment of Morrison that, when they belatedly reach Heyst's ears, succeed finally in rendering him defenseless by provoking in him the emotion of paralyzing disgust. His only defense thereafter is the multiple duplicity of Lena.

It is not inappropriate that such should be the case, for between Morrison and Lena, too, there is a revealing similarity. Lena shares with Ricardo a certain seamy background and a certain practical toughness; but with Morrison, the unfortunate master of the trading brig *Capricorn,* she has shared the magnanimity of Axel Heyst. The story of Morrison is a sort of rehearsal for the story of Lena; for, like Lena, Morrison is not only the object, he is in a sense the victim of Heyst's compassion. Morrison is miraculously rescued by Heyst in a way that, as events work out, both leads to and makes plausible the rescue, not long after, of Lena; and the consequence in both cases is a fresh involvement, a chance for life, that results in fact in their death. Both look upon Heyst as a kind of god, especially because to both of them Heyst's conduct appears purely gratuitous, like the undeserved and disinterested mercy of God. It is not merely pity; Heyst's father had advised him to "cultivate that form of contempt which is called pity," but the salvaging of Morrison and the benevolent theft of Lena are due to no such calculated attitude. They reflect rather a temperament which, as we are told, was incapable of scorning any decent emotion—a temperament so fine and rare as to seem literally godlike to the bedeviled of the book's world. When Heyst offers Morrison the money to save the latter's boat, Morrison gazes at him as though "he expected Heyst's usual white suit of the tropics to change into a shining garment down to his toes . . . and didn't want to miss a single detail of the transformation." In the procedure typical of *Victory,* a reaction which will later become serious, complex, and tragic is presented in the early pages in simple and partly comic tonalities. Lena's reaction to Heyst's rescue of her is less extravagant and open-mouthed; but it partakes of a still deeper awe and of a genuinely self-sacrificial reverence.

In the same way, it is Morrison who first strikes the note, in his droll and touching way, which will develop into a theme close to the tragic heart of the book. Morrison wonders in panic if Heyst is joking about the money. Heyst asks austerely what he means, and Morrison is abashed.

"Forgive me, Heyst. You must have been sent by God in answer to my prayer. But I have been nearly off my chump for three days with worry; and it suddenly struck me: 'What if it's the Devil who has sent him?' "

"I have no connection with the supernatural," said Heyst graciously, moving on. "Nobody sent me. I just happened along."

"I know better," contradicted Morrison.

That moment has its louder and more serious echo a couple of hundred pages later, when Heyst catches sight of Jones and his henchmen approaching the jetty. He stares at them in disbelief: "[He] had never been so much astonished in his life."

The civilisation of the tropics could have nothing to do with it. It was more like those myths, current in Polynesia, of amaz-

ing strangers, who arrive at an island, gods or demons, bringing
good or evil to the innocence of the inhabitants—gifts of unknown things, words never heard before.

"Gods or demons, bringing good or evil"—those ambiguous
phrases greet the first glimpse Heyst and Jones have of each
other; and they frame and give shape to the most telling of the
patterns of similarity and contrast that *Victory* has to offer—the
one that says most about Heyst himself, and the one that best
reveals the drama of which he is the protagonist. Between Heyst
and Jones, the differences are of radical dimensions. Heyst is a
bringer of good (though the recipients of his gifts suffer evil by
consequence). Jones is a bringer of evil (though his gift is the
occasion of greatest good for Lena, and her victory). Heyst has
some godlike element in his nature; but the insinuation makes him
highly uncomfortable. Jones has a kind of private understanding
with the Devil, and that insinuation never fails to excite him. But
between Axel Heyst and plain Mr. Jones, there is a vibrant flow of
analogies, a movement back and forth like electrical currents.

A likeness is registered at the instant Jones first turns up in
the novel; a guest at Schomberg's hotel arriving from Celebes,
"but generally, Schomberg understood, from up China Sea way;
a wanderer clearly, even as Heyst was." Both men are drifters by
profession ("I'll drift," Heyst had decided as a young man); both
have occupied themselves for many years by "coming and going
up and down the earth." Both men are gentlemen, in the conventional meaning of the word and within the book's definition as
pronounced by Martin Ricardo: "That's another thing you can
tell a gentleman by, his freakishness. A gentleman ain't account-
able to nobody, any more than a tramp on the roads." Heyst invokes a comparable notion: "I, Axel Heyst, the most detached of
creatures in this earthly captivity, the veriest tramp on this earth."
As gentlemen and as tramps, both Jones and Heyst are products
of highly civilized society who have chosen the career of the
rootless outsider. Both are wellborn, perhaps aristocratic; they
are elegant, sophisticated, mannerly; both have an excessive vein
of fastidiousness, a too easily outraged austerity. And both are
outcasts who in different ways are outside the law: Heyst by being
in some manner beyond and above it, Jones by being several
degrees beneath it. With one of his ghastly grins, during their first
interview, Mr. Jones confesses to Heyst that the latter was not

the man he had expected to meet. For he sees or thinks he sees, startlingly, *son semblable, son frère.*

Jones misjudges Heyst just as Ricardo misjudges Lena, and with the same limited warrant. "We pursue the same ends," Jones remarks; and he argues that his presence on the island is neither more nor less "morally reprehensible" than Heyst's. Jones assumes that, like himself, Heyst is simply a gentlemanly scoundrel, sharing with him the impulse common to gifted men—the criminal impulse. About this mistake there is something as ridiculous as it is fatal; but Jones has intuited a fragment of the truth. Heyst does share with Jones a basic indifference to the habitual practices of society and to its moral verdicts. He appraises the world in terms nearly identical to those of Jones: "The world's a mad dog," Heyst tells Davidson. "It will bite you if you give it a chance." These two lean and handsome gentlemen, these radical drifters, have an extraordinary amount in common, and Jones's contention is justified—"Ah, Mr. Heyst . . . you and I have much more in common than you think." Jones and Heyst reflect each other with a sort of perfection, the way an object is reflected in a mirror. Each is the other seen wrong way round.

That is why they are dramatically indispensable one to the other—the visibility of each is dependent upon the presence of the other. They come from opposite ends of the universe, and they meet where opposites are made to meet: in a work of art. The strength of each often appears as an extension of the other's weakness and vice versa; which is one reason why the conflict between them, as it assumes its form, seems to extend endlessly, to enlarge almost beyond the reach of human reckoning. It brushes the edge of allegory and touches briefly on the outskirts of myth—one of "those myths, current in Polynesia, of amazing strangers . . . gods or demons." But the drama hangs on to its human vitality and its immediacy and continues to draw its force from the peculiar nature of the two men involved—the man of intellectual sensibility with an inadequate but incipient trust in life and the man of occasional action with a strenuous but insufficiently examined faith in the power of death. Mr. Jones's tendency to sloth, which leaves him spread motionless over three chairs for hours at a time, is reflected in Heyst's long periods of meditation on the hostility of thought to action, while he lounges on the verandah and smokes his cheroot. But Jones's condition has the terrible and explosive power of an ancient sin; and Heyst's skepticism is marred by a vein of tenderness. If Heyst had mistrusted life more completely, he would perhaps have been a better match for Jones from the outset. As it is, the novel catches him at the moment when mistrust is giving way to an urge toward reality and communion.

He had long since, so he tells Jones during their last conversation, divorced himself from the love of life; but then he adds, with painful accuracy, "not sufficiently perhaps." So he acts and reacts without "distinctness." His conception of the world, taken from his father, had for too many years been of something "not worth touching, and perhaps not substantial enough to grasp." The experience of Lena was beginning to put substance into the world; but Heyst can neither participate fully in that experience nor resist it, for he has absorbed either too much or too little of his father's doctrine that "the consolation of love" is the cruelest of all the stratagems of life. He can still insist that "he who forms a tie is lost," but his actual feeling is that he is about to find himself, that Lena is giving him "a greater sense of his own reality than he had ever known in his life."

Greater: but still inadequate to fit him for the challenge that arises. For that challenge is exactly the embodiment of the challenge his father had honorably faced. "With what strange serenity, mingled with terrors," Heyst thinks about his father, "had that man considered the universal nothingness! He had plunged into it headlong, perhaps to render death, the answer that faced one at every inquiry, more supportable." It is only four pages later that Wang arrives to announce the approach of a strange boat. And Mr. Jones, the corpse-like figure at the tiller of the boat, is himself the harbinger and representative of that "universal nothingness." He is the body of that death "that faced one at every inquiry." Trapped between a waning skepticism and an undernourished sense of reality, Heyst cannot emulate his father; cannot make the plunge or launch the assault. All he can do, at the end, is to take death upon himself, purgatorially, by fire.

But if Heyst is unable to plunge, Jones (like Ricardo on his lower level) plunges too incautiously. The sinister mission he engages on is unsupported by the necessary amount of cold intelligence—of just that kind of intelligence that Heyst possesses supremely. Heyst begins finally to exercise it at Jones's expense during their climactic interview, after Heyst has learned the reason for the invasion of the island—Schomberg's preposterous falsehood about treasures hidden on it. At this instant, a reversal is effected, and Heyst takes command of their relationship; it is his strength now which becomes visible because of the revelation of Jones's weakness. "You seem a morbid, senseless sort of bandit," Heyst says with weary contempt. "There were never in the world two more deluded bandits—never! . . . Fooled by a silly rascally innkeeper," he goes on remorselessly. "Talked over like a pair of children with a promise of sweets." It is the logical weakness of Jones's asserted belief in universal fraudulence that it must contain in itself an element of the fraudulent. If he had been wholly convinced of the depravity of all the inhabitants of a wholly vicious world, Jones would have trusted less in the strength of his authority—his graveyard power—over Martin Ricardo; and he would not have overlooked the possibility of mere vulgar vindictiveness in Schomberg. He leapt too swiftly from sloth into action, in a way that, in retrospect, invests one of Heyst's casual pronouncements, made early in the book, with prophetic implications: "Action is the devil."

Heyst and Jones need each other for artistic visibility; but both of them need Lena, as she needs them, to make clear the full shape of the drama they have begotten between them, when the current of the novel carries them (this is one's impression) into a dimension beyond the dimension occupied by all the other persons in the book. The action disclosed by the effect of those three upon each other is the gradual location of that dimension, of the very domain of reality and truth. The domain lies somewhere between the dialectical stirrings of the book's first page and the observation of nothingness on its last—somewhere, as it turns out, between the intellectualism of Heyst and the deathiness of Jones. Between the two kinds of failure, Lena's victory is squeezed out in a way that is a victory both for her and for the novel in which she has her being. As against Jones, Lena has dedicated herself to the actual cause of living; and as against Heyst, she has seized with fingers of steel upon the immediate and necessary facts of behavior. Her practicality (again the book's first page is recalled) derives from a mystical exaltation that transcends the particular situation and attains to universal value while remaining sharply and intently focused upon the single figure of Axel Heyst. Lena's accomplishment reflects the accomplishment of the novel. *Victory* is, in a sense, a reproach to the fascination with death of so much modern fiction. But even more, perhaps, it is an admonition about the tendency of both fiction and criticism to intellectualize the art—to lose the drama in the allegory—or to deform the art—to lose the novel in the drama. The form of *Victory* grows dramatic, and it gives forth intimations of allegory. But it remains faithful to its own nature, for it never makes the mistake of Mr. Jones—it never fails to take account of the variable and highly unpredictable character of individual human beings.

1959

MALRAUX AND HIS CRITICS

"Malraux is interested in painting," Maurice Blanchot remarked in 1950, "but we know that he is also interested in man." What is beguiling about the remark is not only its deceptive simplicity—in an essay not otherwise notable for simplicity—but the ordering of its key terms. Blanchot to be sure, was engaged at the moment in appraising Malraux's interest in painting as reflected by *The Psychology of Art;* even so, his formulation was, and I think, remains essentially correct, especially when he continued: "To save one through the other—[Malraux] was unable to resist this great temptation."

Not many readers were as quick to grasp the point: the intimate relation between Malraux's supposedly new concern with the total world of art forms and his abiding concern with the condition and the destiny of man. Writing in 1957, Armand Hoog remembered "the outburst of surprise . . . and bafflement that accompanied the publication, in 1948, of the *Musée Imaginaire,"* the first part of *The Psychology of Art.* "More than one critic," Hoog said, "marveled, however admiringly, that such an excellent novelist should turn into an art historian." No novelist of his generation had been more closely associated, in the vague consciousness of the reading public, with the raw violence of contemporary events. Malraux had dramatized the 1926 uprising in Canton (*The Conquerors,* 1928[1]), his own penetration of the Siamese jungle with something of the tribal warfare going on there (*The Royal Way,* 1930), another and larger phase of the Chinese revolution (*Man's Fate,* 1933), aspects of brutality and enslavement in Nazi Germany (*Days of Wrath,* 1935), the Spanish Civil War (*Man's Hope,*

1. Dates are those of the first French edition.

1937), and most recently a poison-gas attack on the German-Russian front in World War I, preceded by a glance at the Young Turk revolutionary movement before that war and framed by memoirs of World War II (*The Walnut Trees of the Altenburg,* 1943). No writer, not even Hemingway, could seem less likely to the unknowing to devote himself to researches into Sumerian or Gothic art.

But the surprise occasioned by Malraux's art studies was due of course, as Hoog says, to an inattentive reading of the novels just mentioned, and to popular ignorance of Malraux's several interrelated careers. It is now clear that there is an astonishing unity to everything Malraux has written; one is inclined to add "everything he has done," since his first significant book, a sort of epistolary novel bearing the Spengler-echoing title *The Temptation of the West* in 1926. A main element of that unity has been a persistent preoccupation with art: with works of art and the cultures they comprise and express; and with the role of art in a generally "absurd" universe. It was Malraux who, in *The Temptation of the West,* introduced the word "absurd" into the modern philosophical vocabulary: in a contention that to the eye of modern man the universe appeared fatally bereft of meaning because of the loss of compelling and explanatory religious belief and, with it, the collapse of any direction-giving concept of man; because of the successive "deaths" of the idea of God and the idea of man. Most of Malraux's novels have been symbolic assaults upon history, in an endeavor to wrest from history a persuasive definition of human nature and a dependable guide and measure of human conduct; while in his life, Malraux has been committed to intensive action and to what Picon calls "the myth of the great individual" as sources, perhaps of insight but certainly of compensation. But he has also and ever more strenuously been committed to the great art-work as performing, more satisfactorily yet, these same functions. If Malraux evidently still believes in the efficacy of the master, he believes even more in the saving power of the masterpiece.

The play of these terms—man, the absurd, action, history, and art—has been constant in Malraux's writing from the beginning. But before criticism could arrive at them, it had to get beyond a prior misapprehension—namely, that Malraux was primarily a chronicler of contemporary revolutions, a skillful journalist of the political and economic upheavals peculiar to his age.

I

Leon Trotsky posed the issue in 1931 when he said about *The Conquerors:* "The book is called a novel. What in fact we have before us is a fictionalized chronicle of the Chinese revolution during its first period, the Canton period."[2] Trotsky, as we know, had an uncommonly quick perception of literature; he was among the first, a couple of years later, to detect the achievement of Ignazio Silone's *Fontamara*—in which, he said, revolutionary passion was raised to the level of art. He felt that *The Conquerors* was itself a work of considerable art and made some acute and generous observations about its beauty of narrative. But he felt that the author's revolutionary passion was flawed; that Malraux's effort to give a faithful portrait of insurrectionist China had been (in Trotsky's word) corrupted, both by an "excess of individualism" and by "aesthetic caprice." Even in retrospect, the charge (which Trotsky supported with considerable and pressing detail) is not without substance and pertains to a wider problem: for there has always been a sort of murky imbalance between Malraux's political affinities (the presumptive ones in his novels and the actual ones—communist and then Gaullist—in his life) and his stated or implied beliefs about literature. Nonetheless, Malraux had reason to say, in answer, that his book was not intended and should not be judged as a fictionalized chronicle, and that, in effect, it was just the individualism and the aesthetics that made it a novel.[3] As to the former, the book's stress was placed "on the relationship between individual and collective action, not on collective action alone." As to the latter, Malraux made the crucial remark that the novel was dominated not by considerations of doctrinal loyalty and historical inclusiveness, but by the vision, the way of looking at things—in Malraux's French, by *"l'optique"* —proper to the novel as an art-form. The entire critical "problem" of Malraux—the "Malraux case," as some French commentators have called it—lies, implicit but bristling, in this early exchange.

2. "La Révolution Etranglée," *Nouvelle Revue Française, 211* (1931). Most of the critical essays discussed here can be found in the paperbound volume of Twentieth Century Views *Malraux,* ed. R. W. B. Lewis (Englewood Cliffs, N.J., 1964).
3. "Réponse à Trotsky," *Nouvelle Revue Française, 211* (1931).

Still, when *The Conquerors* was followed by a more full-scale narrative of the Chinese revolution, the betrayal and defeat of the communist effort to seize Shanghai in *Man's Fate,* and that by an account (manifestly first-hand in part) of the Spanish Loyalist rebellion in *Man's Hope,* it became generally agreed that Malraux, even more than Silone or Koestler, was *the* novelistic historian of the great social agitations of the century. However original he might be as a craftsman, his subject, it was agreed, was the specific contemporary battle between socialism and capitalism —"the central struggle of modern times," according to Haakon Chevalier in his introduction to his own English translation of *Man's Fate,* "the struggle of a dying order with the forces within it that are molding a new world." That opinion, too, now strikes us as limited rather than misguided: and limited exactly in its failure to see Malraux's passionate hostility to limitations. For Malraux's heroes, as Joseph Frank has observed, "were never simply engaged in a battle against a particular social or economic injustice; they were always somehow struggling against the limitations of life itself and the humiliation of destiny."[4] The socialist revolts loomed, in Malraux's view, as instances, urgently important in themselves, of a much grander revolt; and he took them as occasions for depicting in fiction the revolt of man against his spiritually and intellectually hemmed-in condition. This was why Malraux's writing had so immense an impact during the thirties upon the rebellious spirits of so many different countries with their so different modes and objects and strategies of revolt, and why he was able to enlist a far-flung loyalty that has persisted with a sometimes unsubdued fierceness.

Malraux's main characters really are protagonists: that is, etymologically, primary combatants. What they do about the human condition is to take arms against its historical embodiments; and they will go to the ends of the earth to seek them out. The point has been noticed more than once: Garine, son of a Swiss father and a Russian mother, comes in *The Conquerors* to southern China; Perken, in *The Royal Way,* literally as well as psychologically *heimatlos* (his native state, Schleswig-Holstein, has been annexed by Denmark), probes uncharted areas of Siam on a crusade against death; in *Man's Fate* and *Man's Hope,* persons from many nations foregather in Shanghai and Madrid, as they

4. *The Widening Gyre* (New Brunswick, N.J., 1963), p. 106.

did in actual fact, at the moment of supreme historical crisis; the Alsatian Vincent Berger, in *The Walnut Trees of the Altenburg,* pursues a mirage of Ottoman nationalism through central Asia. Berger's mission is a failure: the holy war he believes in is not to be kindled; but the others find and take part in the (losing) battle of their deepest desire. In short—and the commonplace is worth repeating, since it applies more unequivocally to Malraux than to any other modern novelist—Malraux's heroes make their test of life in those places and times where human experience is most intensified, where indeed it has become most decisively embattled. It is on a succession of darkling plains, where ignorant armies clash by night, that Malraux's characters attempt to find an explanation of man's essential nature, a justification of his condition, a glimpse of his destiny, a reason for his being.

But as they do so, we move with Malraux into perplexities which, if not wholly philosophical in nature, are at least sources of logical anxiety. Time and again, Malraux has implied that it is in *action* that the strong-willed individual may hope to find not only assuagement but revelation. Victor Brombert reminds us that many of Malraux's key personages are intellectuals— former university professors and the like—but intellectuals who for the most part have lost faith in the values of ideas as such and who have come to distrust the pure exercise of mind.[5] They have therefore abandoned the contemplative or the teaching life and have turned to some arena of explicit action—usually by attaching themselves to a revolutionary cause where the cause is undergoing trial by warfare—in search of some truth more vital than the truth of ideas. It is a belligerent version of the perennial pragmatic strategy. Chiaramonte remarks that Malraux "pushed to its extreme consequences the modern pragmatic impulse which tends to see in the world of action the only reality, and, what is more, to reject any proposition which cannot be directly translated into a force, an act, or series of acts." The word "modern" in that admirable sentence might well be replaced by the phrase "ancient and traditional," for it has always been the hallmark of the pragmatist that he sees "in the world of action the only reality." Customarily, moreover, the pragmatic temper not only rejects propositions that cannot be translated into actions; it also

5. "Malraux: Passion and Intellect," in *The Intellectual Hero* (Philadelphia, 1961), pp. 165 ff.

dispenses with any branch of thought and despises any activity of mind that is not involved with—cannot be tested by—human experience. So it is that *history*—that is, precisely, "the world of action"—history in both its first and second intentions, as a series of actual events and as the record of events: history, in the usual pragmatic scheme, takes the place of metaphysics and of any independent theory of knowledge. The tumult of history becomes the one accessible context of truth and value; and inspecting it, the pragmatist has often been able to disclose some developing and meaningful shape, some gratifying or alarming design of things past and passing and to come. His chart of that design is the pragmatist's account of reality. The very troubling question about Malraux and for Malraux is whether he has ever managed to suggest in his fiction any such disclosure.

But Malraux is or has been a novelist, a person dedicated (as he told Trotsky) to *l'optique* of fiction rather than that of history or philosophy. The literary issue here is at least as complex as the philosophical one, and goes far beyond the confines of this essay. It has to do with that level of a work of literature—that is, of any work that aspires to such a level—on which the literal incidents and characters, the actual clashes and conversations, can be seen enacting an allegory of some large and generalized historical process: a process in which an entire social order may be caught up, or even a whole world; and a process which may or may not be "true" in the perspective of a scientific historian as it fixes on the historical period where the process is allegedly unfolding. Conrad's *Nostromo*—to stay simply with the modern novel (and apart, that is, from the tradition of epic poetry) —is a splendid example; and so of course is Dostoevsky's *The Possessed.*

In *Nostromo,* the various convulsions that rend and then reshape the little South American republic of Costaguana, the assortment of plots and purposes, the interaction of a host of ambitions and devotions: all this secretes an appalling myth of modern economic, political, moral, and even religious history. It is the history, most generally, of the devious and yet absolute conquest by "material interests" of the spirit and energy of modern man; more particularly, of the process by which material interests, trusted and supported as a source of order and justice in a repressive and unstable backward society, bring in their own brand of intolerable injustice and repression and thus assure further upheavals in the future.[6] One looks in vain for anything like so powerful if so grim a pattern in *The Conquerors* or *Man's Fate* or *Man's Hope,* or in the three taken together. Nor can one make out in those novels the tremendous and still more emphatic kind of historical pattern (the inevitable spawning of nihilism by liberalism in mid-nineteenth-century Russia) set forth in *The Possessed.* Nor, at an opposite extreme of fictional stress, do we find the sort of far-away but sizable implications about social and moral history that exist somewhere in the depths of James's *The Golden Bowl.*

Malraux's dilemma, if dilemma it be, is caused in part by the very subject—contemporary historical violence—which he has been brave enough to deal with. When, as in *Man's Fate,* he remains faithful to the historical outcome of the struggle, he concludes with a disaster which is not, *within the novel,* invested with any particular significance. But when, as in *Man's Hope,* he shapes historical fact to his fictional purposes (by concluding with the Loyalist victory at Guadalajara), he suggests an outcome and a meaning other than those history was already bleakly providing. Chiaramonte, who makes this latter point, relates it to what he describes as Malraux's evasion of "the implications of tragedy";[7] but I am not so sure. The case of *Man's Hope* is problematic; but it may well be that in most of his novels, Malraux, far from evading the implications of tragedy, was resolutely facing up to something more terrible yet—to the absence of tragedy as a discernible and determining form at work in modern historical experience. Needless to say, one great way to find and to make evident an illuminating design within the confusions of history is to subject the course of the events in question to the organizing power of the tragic imagination. Herman Melville did exactly that when he confronted the turbulence of the American Civil War in his loosely epic volume of war poems, *Battle-Pieces.* Most of those poems were written while the war was still in progress; but looking back both at the war and the poems after the pacifica-

---

6. In *Politics and the Novel* (New York, 1957), Irving Howe credits *Nostromo* not only with dramatic significance but with historical accuracy and even prescience. It verifies, says Mr. Howe—"in the limited way a novel can verify anything"—"Leon Trotsky's theory of the 'permanent revolution' "; and, on the level of actual history, it describes in advance what would be "a basic pattern of Latin American politics."

7. "Malraux and the Demons of Action," *Partisan Review* (1948).

tion, Melville (in a prose supplement) could draw upon Aristotle's definition of tragedy in the *Poetics* to define the war as a "great historic tragedy" which he prayed had not "been enacted without instructing our whole beloved country through terror and pity." But Malraux has not felt or envisaged the civil wars he has participated in as genuine tragic actions: not, at least, on any scale beyond that of a few driven and defeated individuals.

The importance, indeed the artistic and spiritual "value," of those individual destinies should not be minimized. It is true, as several critics have noticed, that there are no truly evil figures in Malraux's novels: no persons who either are evil through some private wayward impulse or who represent the force of some evil principle in the universe. But it is not true, as Claude-Edmonde Magny would have us believe, that Malraux has never created a character who "changes and really grows."[8] Malraux does not concentrate his narrative on the change and growth of an individual psyche with the patience, say, of a Flaubert or a Proust. Change, in Malraux's fiction, is a regular phenomenon, but it occurs spasmodically, with earthquake speed and shock, and almost always during moments of greatest intensity. Ch'en in *Man's Fate* has grown into an altogether different phase of being before the novel is ten pages old; Vincent Berger's very soul turns over in the midst of the apocalypse on the plains of Russia. And, in fact, all those persons whom Frohock has called "Neophytes"[9] (the narrator of *The Conquerors,* Claude Vannec in *The Royal Way,* Kassner in *Days of Wrath,* and so on) change and grow to a greater or lesser degree, and in fits and lurches; and the mark of their development is the acquisition of insight. It is an insight, customarily, into the solitary, mortal, spiritually blinded and fundamentally helpless condition of individual man; and with it, a conviction about the supreme value of human companionship, "virile fraternity." This is one of the great themes of contemporary fiction, and no writer has handled it more efficiently (and influentially) than Malraux. But these insights do not arise, so to speak, as the lesson of history: for example, as its tragic import. They are much rather the individual human response to history's failure to deliver any lesson at all.

That failure is acknowledged with devastating rhetoric in the

8. "Malraux le fascinateur," *Esprit, 149* (1948).
9. *André Malraux and the Tragic Imagination* (Stanford, 1952), pp. 142 ff.

extraordinary debate that occupies the center of Malraux's last novel, *The Walnut Trees of the Altenburg*. Here Malraux's entire personal and fictional endeavor, the whole "action" of his life and his novels over two decades, is recapitulated in terms of intellectual discourse: when the question of the definable nature of man is posed as a question about the continuity and coherence of the *history* of man. The debate seems at least, via the somber climactic speech of the anthropologist Möllberg, to set the seal on incoherence as the only fact, as it were the truthless truth, discoverable in history. One might still turn to human fraternity as a form of consolation, on the edge of this abyss of meaning. But had no other truth been seized from the plunge into action, the long encounter with history?

II

In one perspective, the answer has to be in the negative. Insofar as it aimed at anything more than sheer nervy excitement, the pragmatic impulse had been defeated along with the revolutionary causes in which it had variously exerted itself. Contemporary history had proven to be as shapeless and discordant as the vast history of human cultures so bleakly examined by Möllberg; from neither could those passionately sought-after explanations be extracted. But if Malraux's pragmatic strategy had failed, what we might call his Romantic strategy had been faring a good deal better; and in another perspective, the perspective of art, a very different and decidedly affirmative answer had long since begun to issue. Malraux had learned—the hard way, as the saying goes —and had shown his characters learning that, in E. M. Forster's phrase, human history "is really a series of *dis*orders"; but he had also learned with Forster that "[Art] is the one orderly product which our muddling race has produced." Perhaps he had always known this. It is implicit in a part of his reply to Trotsky; and it is even more implicit in his developing style. For, as Geoffrey Hartman remarks, from *Man's Fate* onward "the style itself intimates the author's freedom from the law to which his world remains subject, so that if the idea of Man remains inseparable from the idea of tragedy"—or, as I would prefer to say, of incoherence and absurdity, seen perhaps as tragic fatalities—"the idea of the artist pairs with the idea of freedom."[10]

10. *Malraux* (New York, 1960), p. 55.

About this contention, however, there has been a significant disagreement: significant because it bears upon the nature and degree of Malraux's own artistic achievement, and on the relation between it and the absurdities he has confronted in his subject matter. Mme. Magny, for example, before registering her deep disapproval of what she takes to be Malraux's message, warmly and brilliantly praises Malraux's style, and exactly on the grounds that (far from being "free" of the world it treats) it is a splendidly contrived equivalent of its own setting—that the syntactical dis jointedness, the jerky cadences, the rapid transitions, and the startling juxtapositions in Malraux's novels serve as a precise enactment of the discordant realities they describe. Malraux's best novels, this critic says without any detectable trace of irony, are "beautiful, disconnected and truly *decomposed.*" Mme. Magny, in short, endorses Malraux's effort to commit what American criticism sometimes calls the fallacy of imitative form: the fallacy of trying to render a decomposed world by a decomposed book.[11] Gaetan Picon appears to agree with Mme. Magny; he tells us that "Of all the novels, *Man's Hope* is the one that vibrates most with discordant voices (and perhaps for that reason it is the greatest)." But Picon is satisfied that one can locate the source of harmony in Malraux's novels—in a virile fraternity, as we might say, of ideas and attitudes. Although Malraux "never stops dramatizing inimical truths," and though his is unmistakably "a universe of debate," nonetheless "all those enemies are brothers," because all of them "unite in the one who animates their dialogues," in the creative consciousness and the narrative voice of André Malraux.[12]

In this view (which approximates Hartman's), what provides wholeness and harmony in Malraux's writings is not so much the arrangement of the incidents or the patterns of characters and relations between characters, and even less the control and shaping power of some dominant idea.[13] It is rather a style, a presence,

11. "The fallacy of imitative form"—a critical concept to which I referred in the essay on Edith Wharton—was best and perhaps first formulated by Yvor Winters in *Primitivism and Decadence* (Denver, 1937), mainly in the essay called "The Morality of Poetry."

12. *Malraux par lui-même* (Paris, 1953), p. 38.

13. "Malraux has little esteem for ideas. He would tend to say that they serve to obstruct or to betray the moment of decision, and to be mere adornments to those sham dialogues between beings or groups who have nothing to say to each other"—Emmanuel Mounier, *L'Espoir des Déses-*

what Henry James would call a tone: some quality of artistic expression, however we name it, that works against and away from the images of chaos and defeat that the novels otherwise contain. Such, certainly, has been Malraux's increasingly dedicated purpose. "The way to express the unusual, the terrible, the inhuman," he has said, talking about Goya, "is not to represent carefully an actual or imaginary spectacle but to invent a script capable of representing these things without being forced to submit to their elements." Nor was this any casual matter. For Malraux, everything—his own literary achievement, his view of the human condition and of the possibility of human freedom—hang on the capacity of inventing that "script." This is, finally, the grand "truth" that emerges from the debate at Altenburg.

The Walnut Trees of the Altenburg is probably the best place to test any claim one would wish to make about Malraux as a novelist. For my part, I can only hope that Malraux's reputation will not stand or fall on *Man's Hope,* which, despite some uncommonly fine individual episodes, strikes me as a showy and ultimately a rather tiresome performance, and one in which the style is held captive by the subject; though the reader (who will have his own opinion anyway) is invited to consider the high estimates cogently argued elsewhere. *Man's Fate* has, of course, been Malraux's most widely admired novel, and it is no doubt his major contribution to the history of literature in his generation; beyond that, and beginning with its original title (*La Condition Humaine*), it is so impressive and enduring a challenge to its own content that it is likely to endure long after that revolutionary content has ceased to agitate the mind of readers. But the work of Malraux's which best fulfills the requirements of art—in Malraux's terms or anyone else's—seems to me to be *The Walnut Trees.*

The accomplishment of *The Walnut Trees* is the more astonishing, since it consists of only the first third of a novel called *La Lutte avec L'Ange,* the remainder (which Malraux may yet rewrite) being destroyed by the German Gestapo during the war. (Another mystery, as Frank says, is that the book "should still

---

pérés (Paris, 1953). It is a challenging statement, partly true and partly defensible, but eventually misleading. Victor Brombert, who quotes the first of the two sentences, offers a subtle and necessary corrective of the argument.

no longer possible for anyone to suppose, as some of the novel's first readers did, that when Möllberg asserts the utter discontinuity between human cultures he speaks for Malraux: or, anyhow, that he is the whole voice of Malraux; for, like the other characters, Möllberg is a part of Malraux and one way of looking at the history Malraux had lived through. But a much larger part of Malraux is bespoken in the midst of the Altenburg debate in the quiet voice of Vincent Berger, saying what Malraux had tried to say to Trotsky before he had himself quite grasped the principle:

> To me, our art seems to be a rectification of the world, a means of escaping from man's estate. The chief confusion, I think, is due to our belief—and in the theories propounded of Greek tragedy, it's strikingly clear—that representing fatality is the same as submitting to it. But it's not, it's almost to dominate it. The mere fact of being able to represent it, conceive it, release it from real fate, from the merciless divine scale, reduces it to the human scale. Fundamentally, our art is a humanization of the world.

What Berger says (and what, later, Malraux would say in reference to Goya) is precisely what the novel illustrates and enacts. The real answer to the despair of Möllberg lies in the novel he inhabits: in the movement and texture, the composition and tone of *The Walnut Trees* itself. The novel is the final confirmation of its own stated conviction.

III

In the light of that conviction, Malraux's subsequent and voluminous art studies are so little surprising as to be altogether inevitable. *The Psychology of Art* and *The Voices of Silence* are vast discursive demonstrations of the theory about the relation between art and man's estate of which *The Walnut Trees* was the great fictional presentation. This is what, for us, lends a strangely moving accent to Maurice Blanchot's discussion of Malraux's

---

to the 1948 Gallimard edition that Berger's "appeal to happiness is here simply a psychological reaction"; as it were, a phase in Malraux's fictional characterization of the man.

"museum" as standing for "the end of history."[17] The American reader will notice in Blanchot's expert account certain parallels between Malraux's views and those espoused in Anglo-American critical theory, parallels that help clarify the idea of art as escaping from history. There is, for example, something like T. S. Eliot's notion about the literary tradition, and the way every new masterpiece subtly reorders the body of past literature. More striking yet is the parallel with Northrop Frye's *Anatomy of Criticism* and its concept (spelled out more emphatically than it had been by Eliot) of the self-contained nature of literature, the sense in which the *literary*—or, more broadly in Malraux, the artistic—element of the art-work exists outside of time, and belongs to the timeless trans-historical order of art itself. But it is not easy to find any sort of parallel to the sheer passion (reflected in Blanchot) with which Malraux has proclaimed and elaborated these principles. It is the passion born from the encounters with history—those of Malraux's life and those of his fiction—and its form is the passionate conviction that, while history has to be reckoned with, has to be entered and participated in and investigated, it also has to be transcended; for when all is said and done, the truth is not in it. The knowledge provided by the "museum," says Blanchot, "is historical, it is the knowledge of histories, and of a series of histories that we accept"; but "at the same time, it is not historical, it does not concern itself with the objective truth of history . . . and this is the knowledge we accept and even prefer." We prefer it, according to Malraux, because the knowledge discoverable in the timeless, trans-historical world of art forms (the museum without walls) is a definition of man as free, heroic, creative, and purposeful. Art restores the definition that had been questioned and shattered by history: restores it and gives it an unassailable permanence. "To save one through the other—[Malraux] was unable to resist this great temptation."

1964

17. "La Musée, l'Art, et le Temps," *Critique, 43* (1950) and *44* (1951).

DAYS OF WRATH AND LAUGHTER

And I am a red arrow on this graph
Of Revelations.
ROBERT LOWELL, "WHERE THE RAINBOW ENDS"

"What's that about the Apocalypse?"
UNIDENTIFIED VOICE IN HERMAN MELVILLE'S
The Confidence-Man

"Our American literature and spiritual history," Emerson observed something over a century ago, "are, we must confess, in
the optative mood." Today, in the 1950s and '60s, we have
equally to confess that those elements—especially in fiction—
have entered much rather into a resoundingly apocalyptic mood.
Several traditions converge here, and we shall need to make a
good many distinctions as we go along; but we can begin with
the narrowest and gloomiest meaning of apocalypse—namely,
the foreboding of some total catastrophe or cosmic wreckage. In
part, this has been a natural response to the second World War
and the invention of the atomic bomb, to the quite literal threat
of planetary destruction. But only in part. For the bomb, when
it has been mentioned at all in our imaginative literature, has
usually been taken as a symptom and an instrument: the inevitable
product of the diseased energies of mankind, and the physical
force that can bring about that grand conflagration which, morally
speaking, mankind has long been striving to deserve. (So it has
been at comparable earlier moments of world history: the Reformation doomsters, for example, once regarded the menacing
Turkish hordes, the atom-bomb incarnate of that age, with the
same mixture of horror and satisfaction.) The current imagery of
disaster, moreover, carries forward directly from the apocalyptic
peerings of the earlier or prewar and prebomb generation, not to
mention that of several still earlier generations. What has been
added in recent years, and again especially in fiction, is a pervasive sense of the preposterous: of the end of the world not only
as imminent and titanic, but also as absurd.

The addition may be all important. It testifies, anyhow, to the healthful influence of Nathanael West; for it was West, following hard on Melville and Mark Twain, who established for contemporary American writing the vision of the ludicrous catastrophe, and who searched out and bodied forth some of its human sources. A complex apocalyptic vision ran through all of West's short novels; but it reached its climax, of course, in the last book he lived to write. *The Day of the Locust* (1939) borrowed its title and much of its conviction about the course of human events from the seminal Book of Apocalypse, or Revelations, in the New Testament: "And the fifth angel sounded . . . . And there came out of the smoke locusts upon the earth: and unto them was given power . . . . and their faces were as the faces of men." But West's hate-filled and mindless locusts appear finally, to the creative eye of their observer, as a mob of "screwballs," carrying baseball bats and torches through the streets of California, dancing amid the fires they have lit to burn down Los Angeles and implicitly the whole of America, chanting their allegiance to an unnamed "super-promiser," their maniacal leader. It has been by exploiting a perspective of just that kind that novelists as variously gifted as Ralph Ellison and John Barth and Joseph Heller and Thomas Pynchon have made the day of doom the great saturnalia of our time—a *dies irae* converted into a *dies irae risusque*. For our literature and our spiritual history are in fact caught between the wrath and the laughter; and our survival, in many meanings of the word, may hang upon the outcome.

I

The apocalyptic mood, in this or any other generation, has by no means been limited to fiction; though fiction seems at present its most appropriate habitat, and though elsewhere the tone has been less regularly relieved by the partially healing sense of the comic. Forty years ago Hart Crane (himself, as I shall say, the possessor of a very different mode of apocalyptic imagination) could contend in an excellent formula that the fashionable poetry of the day was the poetry of "humor and the Dance of Death." But by "humor" Crane meant chiefly the ironic Laforguian wit that T. S. Eliot had been making available for English poetry. It was this that permeated Eliot's death-dancing in *The Waste*

Land, and that would color Eliot's more purely apocalyptic pronouncement of a couple of years later that

> *This is the way the world ends*
> *Not with a bang but a whimper.*

Crane might also have meant the steely amusement with which Robert Frost (in 1924) had meditated two further alternative theories about the world's end:

> *Some say the world will end in fire,*
> *Some say in ice.*
> *From what I've tasted of desire*
> *I hold with those who favor fire,*

and so on. Eliot foresaw the human spirit fading out in mere animal mouthings; Frost looked instead for a final choice between lethal lust and lethal malice. But let me pause to suggest that Frost's little poem is a sort of poker-faced gloss on traditional apocalyptic theorizing—as set forth with grave precision, for example, by R. H. Charles in his definitive study of the matter, *Eschatology:*[1]

> According to science, there are two possible endings of the earth. Either it will perish slowly through cold . . . or the earth will suddenly be destroyed catastrophically, by the impact of some other heavenly body, or by the outburst of its own internal fires. While science of necessity can only predict two possible endings of the world, apocalyptic declared that the end of the present order of things will be catastrophic.

Apocalyptic writing, like Frost, has always held with those who favor the quick holocaust rather than the gradual freeze.

Even the wry detachment of "Fire and Ice," however, is missing from Frost's later piece of eschatology, "Once by the Pacific," where the catastrophe occurs in a new way—or, rather, in the oldest way, by a flood like the flood with which God destroyed the wicked according to the Book of Genesis. The voice in this poem is conversational, but the wrath is uncontaminated by laughter; the waves crashing in upon the Pacific coast seem to

---

1. (London, 1899; paperback New York, 1963.)

the onlooking poet to presage the extinction of a humanity whose own bestial rages will bring down the annihilating anger of God and the reversal of his world-creating *fiat lux:*

It looked as if a night of dark intent
Was coming, and not only a night, an age.
Someone had better be prepared for rage.
There would be more than ocean-water broken
Before God's last Put out the Light *was spoken.*

And in the characteristic early poetry of Robert Lowell, the most eminent American poet in the generation after Eliot and Frost, both irony and wryness get swallowed up in sheer apocalyptic fury —a fury that takes charge of the rhetoric to the point of becoming not only emotional substance but a sometimes exceedingly effective poetic strategy.

Recently, though still watchful of the cruelties and folly of society at large, Lowell's poetry has centered upon the personal fatality: the "skunk hour" of the private self ("I myself am hell;/ nobody's here— / only skunks . . . ."). But his first volume, though in its turn kindled by autobiographical passion, envisaged the entire human landscape as spiritually blasted and desiccated—

Is there no way to cast my hook
Out of this dynamited brook?

It was, in the medieval formula Lowell adapted for his title, a "land of unlikeness"; and the poems explored the skunk hour of a world in which the human soul, having forfeited the god-resembling image in which it was formed, had for that reason also lost its likeness to itself, to its specifically human essence. Lowell was dealing with something like a theory of history, and looking at what seemed to him the present consequences of an American and especially a New England culture that had combined a driving piety with a ruthless acquisitiveness. The most hideous of these consequences, in Lowell's view, was the second World War (or anyhow, America's conduct of that war); and his apocalyptic vigor reached its own peak of grandeur in the poems that were wrenched out of him in the mid-1940s, and published in *Lord Weary's Castle,* when his ferocious pacifism was challenged past endurance by the greedy belligerence of the time. Poem after poem expressed a highly intensified vision of finality—

This is the end of the whaleroad and the whale
Who spewed Nantucket bones on the thrashed swell
And stirred the troubled waters to whirlpools
To send the Pequod packing off to hell:
This is the end of them, three-quarters fools . . .

The vortex of death thus realized in the heaving rhythms and flailing language of "The Quaker Graveyard at Nantucket" is the ultimate consequences of the warlike, indeed the murderous, materialism of modern man; and Lowell, drawing upon Melville's *Moby-Dick,* finds his most terrible representation of modern man in the old Quaker whale hunters—those allegedly peaceable, loving, and God-serving people who were nonetheless, as Melville had put it, "the most sanguinary of all sailors and whale-hunters . . . fighting Quakers . . . Quakers with a vengeance." Out of its own bloodthirsty folly, the Pequod (the modern world, or at least modern America) launches its assault upon what turns out to be the godhead itself, and is smashed and utterly destroyed and packed off to hell.

These poems of the mid-1940s echo with the continuing dry thunder of a Last Judgment. In both "Where the Rainbow Ends" and "As a Plane Tree by the Water," Lowell contemplates his representative city of Boston on the fateful day amid echoes of the Book of Revelations, the fiery indicator of which Lowell (in the first of the two poems) declares himself to be:

> *the scythers, Time and Death,*
> *Helmed locusts, move upon the tree of breath;*
>
> . . .
>
> *I saw my city in the Scales, the pans*
> *Of judgment rising and descending. Piles*
> *Of dead leaves char the air—*
> *And I am a red arrow on this graph*
> *Of Revelations.*

The day of wrath—or the hour or season, according to the figure —is everywhere visible and audible; and even a private domestic drama like Lowell's "Between the Porch and the Altar" reaches its self-lacerating climax when

> *the Day*
> *Breaks with lightning on the man of clay,*
> Dies amara valde.

The famous Latin hymn there quoted (*"Dies Irae"*) continues, one may remember, *"dum veneris judicare saeculum per ignem"*: "that day, great and bitter above all, when Thou shalt come to judge the world by fire." American writers in the modern epoch can almost be distinguished by their individual notions, or imagery, first of the causes and then of the nature of the catastrophe that many of them have agreed is very nearly upon us. In "The Fire Next Time" (1963), the essay by which James Baldwin—as accomplished an essayist as Lowell is a poet—summoned expository prose onto the field of apocalyptic vision, it is American inhumanity rooted in racial terror and racial hatred that will bestir the ultimate wrath. As to the form of the latter, Baldwin also holds with those who favor fire; his epigraph, from a Negro slave hymn, is emphatic on the choice:

> *God gave Noah the rainbow sign,*
> *No more water, the fire next time!*

Upon this thoroughly traditional view of the last things, a commentary has been supplied far in advance by Jonathan Edwards in *A History of the Work of Redemption* (lectures written in 1739):

> And if the wickedness of the old world, when men began to multiply on the earth, called for the destruction of the world by a deluge of waters, this wickedness will as much call for its destruction by a deluge of fire.

"No more water, the fire next time!" Like Edwards, the anonymous Negro hymn-writer (who probably got the idea from touring evangelists) was speaking about the actual and physical obliteration of this world because of human sinfulness, while he will hide himself for his salvation in the Rock of Ages. But in the context of Baldwin's essay and of current events, the marvelously resonant, even springy little couplet announces a secular and symbolic though not less dreadful development. Against a technological background that poses, as Baldwin puts it, "the threat of universal extinction" and so "changes totally and forever the nature of reality and brings into devastating question the true meaning of man's history," Baldwin sees in the hate-ridden American foreground the quickening possibility that Negroes can "precipitate chaos and ring down the curtain on the American dream."

If they do so, Baldwin believes, there will occur a tremendous act of vengeance for the white man's suicidal refusal to transcend his whiteness and achieve his manhood—a manhood he shares with the black man, whose transcendence of his own color the white man must not arrogantly allow or condescendingly encourage, but must wholesouledly acknowledge here and now. But the act of vengeance will not at all be a purely Negro adventure. It will be an act of and by history; it will express as it were the wrath of history itself, a terrible secular equivalent to the wrath of God. It will be "a vengeance that does not really depend upon, and cannot really be executed by, any person or organization, and that cannot be prevented by any police force or army." This is why, in closing, Baldwin calls it "cosmic vengeance," something forced into being by uncontrollable disturbances within the human cosmos, an "outburst [to quote R. H. Charles again] of its own internal fires." Baldwin's apocalyptic diagnosis is selective; but the continuing facts of life in America have not yet done very much to belie it.

The difference between Baldwin's most aggressive essayistic predecessors—H. L. Mencken, for example—and Baldwin himself is parallel to the difference between the Eliot of *The Waste Land* and the Lowell of *Lord Weary's Castle*. It is akin to the difference—the distinction is an ancient one and hard to hang on to—between the prophetic and the apocalyptic; between the demand for moral rehabilitation, accompanied by warnings and animated by the belief that they can be listened to in time, and the expressed feeling that it is very likely too late to prevent the coming holocaust (that is, total destruction by fire; from the Greek words for "whole"—*holos*—and "burnt"—*kauston*). The rhetorical postures have much in common, but the difference should be suggested; in part because it is also the difference between the mood of the 1920s and the much darker mood of the period beginning in the 1940s. It is made palpable in the very cadences of poem and essay. Like Lowell's, Baldwin's argument is exalted by a rhetorical fervor that sweeps through and beyond the actualities that have aroused it. Irony and humor would be mainly out of key here. Only occasionally, indeed, and much less often than in his earlier volumes of essays, is *The Fire Next Time* lit up by that extraordinary change of expression, that sudden and electrifying smile of utter and yet oddly delighted incredulity, that have characterized Baldwin's writings and his public *persona* in the past. The result, it seems to me, is a foreshortening of reality. "Reality" is more and more a major term for Baldwin, and one which he uses both to threaten and persuade. But a true view of reality in our time depends, I think, not only upon an unflinching confrontation of horror, but also upon the measuring and accommodating power of laughter—that is, of what Hawthorne called "the tragic power of laughter." That power, anyhow, has been affectively absent from Baldwin's recent declarations, as well as from his fiction and his dramatic work.

Even literary criticism has of late proved vulnerable to the apocalyptic impulse, no doubt infected by constant exposure to the same in poetry, fiction, and the essay. The very titles of some recent books of criticism by some of our most notable and "younger" critics indicate the shared concern. Irving Howe, invoking a phrase from Leon Trotsky—*A World More Attractive* (1963)—reminds us of another of the basic distinctions to be elaborated upon later: the secular apocalyptic tradition which, descending through the imaginative responses to the American and French Revolutions and catching fire again with the Russian upheaval, has focused less upon the grand conflict than upon the millennium it will usher in; with only the bad old world coming to its predestined end, and the incomparably more attractive new society being realized once and for all. The theme is in fact muted in Mr. Howe's luminous and muscular essays, but it lies just beneath his conviction about the crucial "relationship between politics and literature, action and reflection." Stanley Edgar Hyman, for his own collection of essays over the years, borrows a portion of the most famous apocalyptic passage in English literature, the exchange between Kent and Edgar gazing at the dead body of Cordelia and at her grief-stunned father in the final moments of *King Lear:*

> *Is this the promis'd end?*
> *Or image of that horror?*

But to judge from the emphases in *The Promised End* (1964), Mr. Hyman has in mind, as he quotes the phrase, not so much the age-old notion of the ultimate earthly catastrophe to which it overtly refers as the tragic vision of human life which that dramatic moment is bringing to full and final disclosure, and upon which Mr. Hyman discourses with much learned vivacity.[2] Leslie Fiedler is closer to the queer temper of postwar writing, which indeed he examines in some detail, in the title and content of his book-length essay *Waiting for the End* (1964).

Mr. Fiedler's title comes neither from the Book of Revelations nor a Negro hymn, neither from Trotsky nor Shakespeare, but from a rambunctious ballad by William Empson:

> *Shall we go all wild, boys, waste and make them lend,*
> *Playing at the child, boys, waiting for the end?*
> *It has all been filed, boys, history has a trend,*
> *Each of us enisled, boys, waiting for the end.*

The end Mr. Fiedler is awaiting and describing is the end of civilization, at least as he has known it: the end of the modern novel and the modern poem; the end of those ("three-quarters fools," one can almost hear Mr. Fiedler saying), the novelists and the poets, who have occupied the literary scene since the age of Faulkner and Stevens. Mr. Fiedler sees modern culture ending as the creative imagination is defeated at every turn: by a failure of nerve and a decline of sheer talent; by the rise to literary authority of minority spokesmen who promptly lose or shed or are robbed of the minority characteristics (Jewish and Negro, mainly) that had empowered them; by a situation in which the entire reading public, perhaps the entire middle class, has become avant-garde or anyhow so welcomes the avant-garde as to smother it to death; by a moral and philosophical anarchy which deprives the writer not only of a subject but even of an enemy. *Waiting for the End,* in its racier and cheerfully irresponsible way, is composed in the spirit of Pope's *Dunciad;* and, like Pope in the closing lines of that matchless apocalyptic satire, Mr. Fiedler traces the process whereby

> Art *after* Art *goes out, and all is Night.*

Mr. Fiedler, too, arrives at his American version of Pope's conclusion:

> *Lo! thy dread Empire, CHAOS! is restored;*
> *Light dies before thy uncreating word.*

2. Mr. Hyman has since intimated that his title has a much more private and personal, and half-humorous, connotation.

But this is to say that Mr. Fiedler does not fully believe his own message of disaster; and in fact the poem by Empson from which he takes his title (it is called "Just a Smack at Auden") is a parody of the apocalyptic imagination rather than a statement of it. Like some of his novelistic contemporaries, Mr. Fiedler aspires, by mingling the catastrophic with the comic, to help avert the worst possibilities of the former.

We return to the narrative arts. The movies made a start at providing a visual image of apocalypse in such vaguely science-fiction films and solemn artifices as *On the Beach.*[3] But with *Dr. Strangelove* (1963), the medium came at one stride into the area not only of the truly catastrophic imagination—the planet earth really is being blown to smithereens at the fadeout—but also of the comical catastrophe. The end of the world in *Dr. Strangelove*—as envisaged by Terry Southern and his collaborators on the film-script—is due to bumbling inefficiency, antic mischance, and a sort of hearty and yet total inhumanity,

3. The huge contribution of science fiction to modern apocalyptic literature would be very much worth investigating, but it is beyond the scope of this essay and the competence of this writer. I suspect, though, that such an investigation would show that science fiction has often worked very squarely within the long apocalyptic tradition and has manipulated the great apocalyptic archetypes.

Let me name a few personal favorites which can also stand as superior examples of countless similar treatments of the great theme. In *When Worlds Collide* (1929), not only is the end of this world accomplished in one of the familiar ways—"the earth" (to quote again from R. H. Charles) is "destroyed catastrophically by the impact of some other heavenly body." The saving human remnant, more importantly, is transferred (by spaceship) to another planet, in an engagingly literalistic version of the Old Testament notion—which I discuss in the next section—of the righteous being carried off from the annihilated earth to the heavenly kingdom of God. In Sax Rohmer's *The Day the World Ended* (1929), a story fairly teeming with recognizable apocalyptic imagery, the world is in fact saved at the last instant; but before that happens, the would-be agent of destruction, a Satanic dwarf named Anubis, offers a rousing indictment of mankind as fatally corrupted and unsalvageable, even as the pornographic quality of his dominion (a castle in the Black Forest) suggests that *his* is in fact the final apostasy. In A. Conan Doyle's recently republished *The Poison Belt* (1913), the emphasis is upon the actual catastrophic process; and we can identify the latter as one of those enormous periodic disasters envisioned in Revelations as a portent of the final horror—perhaps, for Doyle in retrospect, as a symbolic portent of the World War which erupted a year after the original publication.

plus of course the instrument of annihilation, the super-bomb itself. There is a rough political allegory in the film; but as more than one reviewer has observed (Miss Midge Decter in *Commentary,* especially), the allegory is thin and lopsided. The villains are exclusively of the fascist variety; and the depth and breadth and complexity of the destructive mentality in America today are scarcely hinted at. Both the humor and the human nature in the film are, as a result, markedly narrowed in range. But *Dr. Strangelove* is an adventurous piece of work, and one full of well-compounded fright and fun. It is also a film that comes closer than any yet made to the fictional achievement of Nathanael West, and Terry Southern's glimpse of an America conniving with mindless intensity at its own annihilation at least approximates West's vision of the absurd debacle toward which the country is hurrying.

But much of the superior power of West's diagnosis and of the shape he gave it came from his sense—in part his knowledge, in much larger part his creative intuition—of the long and contradictory Judaeo-Christian apocalyptic tradition. We need to rehearse that tradition at this stage, at whatever risk of gross oversimplification. For the accomplishments both of West and of those contemporary novelists who follow him can best be measured in terms of it; and those terms, however much in fashion, need to be a little straightened out.

II

The concept of apocalypse—a word which basically means no more than a revelation or uncovering from the Greek word for such an act[4]—may be thought of as a branch of eschatology: a word which, in turn, means the knowledge or doctrine of the last things, of what is ultimately in store for man, nature, the world, the universe (from the Greek *eschatos,* furthest or uttermost). At some time in the later but still pre-Christian period of Judaism, the dominant theory of the last things turned from what is called the prophetic to what would eventually be known as the apocalyptic. It began, that is, to point forward to cataclysms so enormous that they would utterly destroy the earthly world and lead to the

---

4. *Apokalupsis.* The root, verb, *kalupto,* means to cover or conceal; and the dictionary reminds us that it was the function of the nymph Calypso (in the English spelling) to conceal Odysseus on his way home from Troy.

Day of Judgment for all mankind, and to the establishment of a Kingdom of Heaven inhabited purely by the saints and the angels. In the earlier or prophetic period, the eschatological imagination had concerned itself with the earthly destinies of men and nations, and upon the morality or immorality that would determine them; even at its most somber, it had remained convinced that men could return to righteous ways and could thus in part control their earthly fate; and at its most hopeful, it had anticipated a permanent Messianic Kingdom on this earth. But around 100 B.C., according to R. H. Charles, "the earth had come to be regarded as wholly unfit for this kingdom," and it then began to be taught "that the Messianic Kingdom was to be merely of temporary duration, and that the goal of the righteous was to be—not this temporary kingdom or millennium—but heaven itself." Along with this radically pessimistic view of the moral salvageability of the earth, there arose the necessary and corollary notion of the catastrophe—usually a cosmic conflagration—which would put an end to the world, while the saintly remnant was transferred to the eternal kingdom above.[5]

"It was," Charles argues, "from the apocalyptic side of Judaism that Christianity was born." The statement is probably true, but it is misleading. The Christian vision of history is undoubtedly apocalyptic: if we can grant that latter term a high degree of dialectical flexibility. But Charles tended to identify apocalypse with catastrophe, and hence with an uncompromisingly glum view of the moral and spiritual potentialities of mankind. Given that identification, I should prefer to say that a certain great phase of Christianity was born out of Judaean apocalyptics—and I am tempted to call it "the Lutheran phase," as against the Thomistic

---

5. Among the studies which have been particularly indispensable for the summary report in this section, and which I do not always cite even while drawing from them are: R. H. Charles, *Eschatalogy* (London, 1899; paperback New York, 1963); Martin Buber, "Prophecy, Apocalyptic, and the Historical Hour," in *Pointing the Way* (New York, 1957; paperback New York, 1963); Austin Farrer, *A Rebirth of Images* (London, 1949; paperback New York, 1964); Ernest Tuveson, *Millennium and Utopia* (Berkeley, 1949; paperback New York, 1964); M. H. Abrams, "English Romanticism: the Spirit of the Age," in *Romanticism Reconsidered*, edited by Northrop Frye (English Institute Essays, New York, 1963); Perry Miller, title essay and the essay called "The End of the World" in *Errand into the Wilderness* (Cambridge, 1956); James P. Martin, *The Last Judgment* (i.e. in Protestant theology; Grand Rapids, 1963).

phase, for example, or even the Augustinian; using quotation marks to indicate a strain as old as Christianity and one which seems to be in the ascendancy today, and on not unreasonable grounds. The apocalyptic side of Judaism, at any rate, was what found expression in the Old Testament books of Ezekiel, Daniel, and Zechariah. And the earliest of the Christian writings in which (to borrow a phrase from Austin Farrer) those older apocalyptic images were given "rebirth" include the Gospel of Saint Mark, the Second Epistle of Saint Peter, and supremely of course the Book of Revelations by St. John the Divine of Patmos. The latter is the enduring treasury of apocalyptic elements, allusions, archetypes. It is here that we encounter the seven blasting trumpets, the seven seals, the seven vials of wrath; here are the seven candlesticks and the figure whose hair is "white like wool"; here are the four horsemen of the apocalypse and the locusts with faces like men and the beast that rises out of the sea; here is the symbolic number 666, here the battle of Armageddon; here are the Whore of Babylon and Gog and Magog; and here the vision of "a new heaven and a new earth" and of "the holy city, the new Jersusalem, coming down from God out of heaven, prepared as a bride adorned for her husband."

It is in Revelations, too, that we make out—dimly, as through an enchanted glass—the most crowded and extensive of the Christian visionary accounts of history. Such is the complexity of St. John's imagination, however, that "history" is an imprecise word: better, perhaps, a revelation of spiritual reality which sometimes takes the form of an actual historical process, of future events narrated in sequence, and sometimes invokes events to come as pure metaphor; the constant subject being the universe as designed by God. The account touches more or less seriatim upon a succession of "moments," some of which we may select and number for our present purposes: (1) periodic natural disturbances, earthquakes and the like; (2) the advent and the turbulent reign of the Antichrist or the false Christ or false prophet (sometimes called the period of the Great Tribulation); (3) the second coming of Christ and (4) the resultant cosmic warfare (Armageddon) that brings in (5) the millennium—that is, from the Latin, the period of one thousand years, the epoch of the Messianic Kingdom upon earth; thereafter, (6) the gradual degeneration of human and physical nature, the last and worst apostasy (or falling away from God), featured by (7) the second and briefer "loosening of Satan"; (8) an ultimate catastrophe, the end of the world by fire; (9) the Last Judgment; and (10) the appearance of the new heaven and earth.

These have always been among the major ingredients of apocalyptics in all ages, but only in Revelations, if there, do all the elements appear; and only there, if ever, do they appear in the order just indicated. There has been as much controversial wrestling with the meanings of Revelations over the centuries as there have been shifts and rearrangements of the elements by other and later apocalyptic writers. On the one hand, for example, it seems now generally believed that phrases like "a new heaven and a new earth" and "coming down" are primarily spatial metaphors; that "a new heaven" is not God's heaven, but the visible heavens— taken metaphorically, however, as part of a radically transformed spiritual condition; while God's heaven, the divine kingdom, continues as traditionally to be the eventual domain of the blessed —but, again, as the name of a spiritual estate, wherever the blessed might be simplemindedly thought to reside in physical fact. On the other hand, both before and after Revelations, from version to version of the apocalyptic "story," this or that element is omitted; or two elements are fused into one—especially the Great Tribulation and the second visitation of Satan; the moment or moments, the figure or figures, given stress differ crucially.

The author of the Book of Revelations, for example, saw the earthly millennium in the far future, and was not, one gathers, very much interested in it; though the sense of the universal triumph on the far side of the millennium, and after the worst apostasy, pervades his verses. The prophecy of Christ, as recorded in the thirteenth chapter of Saint Mark, concerned itself mainly with the long period of persecution, and with the activities of "false Christs and false prophets" who "shall rise, and shall show signs and wonders, to seduce, if it were possible, the elect"; and only in four short verses does this voice foretell the time of total darkness over the earth, the second coming of Christ, and (skipping the millennium altogether and all subsequent plot complexities) his drawing together all the elect "from the uttermost part of the earth to the uttermost part of heaven." The African-born convert Lactantius, writing in the latter part of the third Christian century, was eloquent about the massive variety of evil in the age about to come, but he was no less eloquent about the earthly paradise which would succeed it—when "the rocky mountains shall drop with honey . . . [and] those things shall come to pass which the poets spoke of as being done in the reign of Saturn." (The poet whom Lactantius must have had chiefly in mind was Virgil, with his description—in *Aeneid* VIII.319 ff.—of the descent of Saturn from heavenly Olympus, and his union of the belligerent Italian tribes into a single nation: "the period called in legend the Golden Age." Throughout Western literature, it has often been rather the *Aeneid* than the Bible, or sometimes the *Aeneid* combined with the Bible, which has supplied the poetic imagination with its apocalyptic patterns and tropes.)

Lactantius marks the end of the first great wave of apocalyptic writing. The second wave coincided with the Protestant Reformation; and here the emphasis is almost entirely upon the irreversible dark finality. It is indeed from sixteenth-century apocalyptics that the modern connotation of the word "apocalypse" as the revelation of imminent catastrophic horror most obviously derives; and when Martin Buber in an indispensable essay says that "the mature apocalyptic . . . no longer knows an historical future in the real sense," and that in its view "the end of all history is near," his words apply less to St. John of Patmos than, say, to Martin Luther. It was Luther, in a preface to Revelations in 1545 and out of his profound and infectious mistrust of mankind's capacity to do anything whatever in the way of self-regeneration, laid it down that the millennium foreseen in Revelations was by his (Luther's) epoch already far in the past. It had simply been the first thousand years of Christianity. The real reign of Antichrist, which for Luther followed rather than preceded the millennium, began with the rise to power of the Papacy at Rome in the eleventh century; and now, five centuries later, the world trembled on the brink of the all-engulfing catastrophe. John Foxe, whose apocalyptic scheme in *Actes and Monuments* (1596) is probably the closest among Reformation writings to that of Revelations, calculated all these matters with hardheaded arithmetical precision. The first age of Satan, Foxe argued, had run to the end of the third century; the Christian millennium that followed that time of tribulation (and which apparently did not need a second coming of Christ to initiate it) lasted until about 1300 A.D. The world thereupon entered, as Revelations had said it would, into a second and more frightful reign of Antichrist, and this, as of the moment of writing, was nearing its climax: holocaust and the last judgment were in the offing. For though the author of Revelations, according to Foxe's arguable interpretation, had predicted a series of Antichrists, he had made it clear that "the head and principall Antichrist" would not appear until "the later end of the world, at what time there shall be such tribulation, as neuer was seene before: whereby," Foxe concluded with gloomy satisfaction, "is meant (no doubt) the Turke"—the Turk, that is, as the scourge or, perhaps even more dreadfully, as the secret agent of the Papal Antichrist. And so it went, with each writer eager to claim the worst of visits by the worst of Satans for his own particular generation.

What is common to all these visions is a fundamental rhythmic alternation of tribulation and triumph, of disaster and felicity: whether the rhythm occurs once, as in St. Mark, or whether it is a sort of habitual universal sistole and diastole, as in Revelations and perhaps John Foxe. But on the whole, and not surprisingly, the apocalyptic writers of the Bible and the early Christian centuries saw just about everything happening in the future—or they were more disposed to employ a futuristic metaphor—and they tended to hang on more hopefully to a conviction about a season of earthly happiness as well as an unending heavenly glory in the far distance. The Reformation commentators saw just about everything happening in the past or in the present time; they were fascinated by inventories of the symptoms of worldwide apostasy and less committed imaginatively to the possibilities of the heavenly world to be. This is a main part of what I mean by "the Lutheran phase" of Christianity as it has regularly announced itself apocalyptically. And it is just this sense of the historical moment and this emphasis that some of the contemporary novelists I shall belatedly get round to share with the Reformation writers: time present in the contemporary American novel is precisely the moment of the last loosening of Satan.

So convinced were speculators in the sixteenth and early seventeenth centuries about the very real approach of the day of doom that they rather enjoyed making estimates of its exact date. Henry Bullinger (a Swiss writer whose sermons were published in London in 1573) drew upon the numerology of Revelations, and by adding 666 to 1000 came up with the year 1666 as the time of the world's termination. But as these *anni horribiles* came and went, and the world wagged on, the apocalyptic emphasis gradually underwent another fundamental change. There is neither space nor occasion here to explore the effect upon apocalyptics of the developing theory of history as cyclical (whereby world history, instead of arriving at its explosive end, simply returns to the beginning of the cycle) or the theory of unbroken human progress (which eliminates catastrophe completely). I move on to the end of the eighteenth century, when, for large historical reasons, the apocalyptic stress rested (briefly) upon the element of millennial triumph—and led to the next-to-last important phase of the apocalyptic imagination for the purposes of this discussion.

The causes mentioned were primarily the successful outcome of the American Revolution and, much more importantly, what seemed at first to be the successful outcome of the French Revolution. For a range of English writers in the 1790s, those Revolutions *were* the titanic upheavals foretold in Scripture—the cosmic war announced in Revelations—and the new social orders begotten by them were the long anticipated millennium, at which point history—in the sense of further basic change—could have a stop. For the English imagination of the decade, in short, the word "apocalypse" meant not a vision of horror but of dazzling splendor, not of catastrophe but of the epochal and triumphant social transformation that catastrophe led to.

The English Romantic spirit, M. H. Abrams has recently and brilliantly argued, was essentially revolutionary; but its rhetorical expression was biblical—it "looked upon contemporary politics through the perspective of Biblical prophecy," and it tended to describe human progress in terms that were "Messianic, millennial, and apocalyptic." One notices the transforming effect upon the term "apocalyptic" there (as against, say, the Reformation usages of the concept) of the associated adjectives "Messianic" and "millennial." For with early English Romanticism, we arrive at what Martin Buber has aptly called an "inverted apocalyptic," "an optimistic modern apocalyptic" (of which, according to Buber, "the chief example . . . is Marx's view of the future"). It is this that Wordsworth announced, in a passage quoted by Mr. Abrams from *The Excursion,* a characteristic mingling of Virgilian and biblical millennialism:

> *I sang Saturnian rule*
> *Returned,—a progeny of golden years*
> *Permitted to descend and bless mankind.*
> *—With promises the Hebrew scriptures teem.*

And it is this that Blake enacted in *The Four Zoas* (1797), an epic fragment which, as Mr. Abrams remarks, "explodes into the most spectacular and sustained apocalyptic set-piece since the Book of Revelations."⁶ But as it does so, what *The Four Zoas* celebrates is not the cosmic explosion itself but what had been exploded into being: the grand new world, the permanent good and just human society. Such was the apocalyptic idiom of the age: "Hey for the New Jerusalem! The Millennium!" This cry, of one Thomas Holcroft, was the age's echoing motto.

The Romantic apocalyptic was indeed optimistic, and—considering the apocalyptic tradition generally—it was "inverted." It was also altogether secular and humanistic; it manifested, in Buber's phrase, an "immanent dialectic"; it surveyed forces working entirely within human history, and the triumph it saluted was not that of saints and angels in the heavenly kingdom but of men and women in the earthly here-and-now. It is in part a tribute to the vigor of Romantic rhetoric that these happy connotations of "apocalypse" have survived long after the faith that begot them had died. For, in fact, the Romantic enthusiasm scarcely lasted through the decade of its origin. Historical developments in France proved all too rapidly to be a source of the bitterest disillusionment. What the Romantic imagination thereupon turned to was what Mr. Abrams (it is his most valuable insight) defines as "apocalypses of imagination." The expression of apocalyptic confidence, that is, while still conveyed in biblical and especially in Revelations imagery, tended to refer less and less to the current actualities of social change and more and more to an achievement of the poetic imagination—to events occurring not in France but in poetry. The millennial hope remained, Mr. Abrams says,

> but the hope has been shifted from the history of mankind to the mind of the single individual, from militant external action to the imaginative act; and the marriage between the Lamb and the New Jerusalem has been converted into a marriage between subject and object, mind and nature, which creates a new world out of the old world of sense.

6. In *Blake's Apocalypse* (New York, 1963), Harold Bloom has made this aspect of Blake's poetry the center of his massive and definitive study, concentrating attention where he believes it should at long last *be* concentrated—on those late epics which are sometimes called "prophetic books," but which Mr. Bloom contends are more accurately called apocalyptic.

The issue of that wedding (in the Romantic view) may some day and somehow and astonishingly enough *be* an actual and historical millennium, through the very force of the poetic vision upon history, through its capacity to alter the consciousness of mankind: whereby, in the extraordinary closing lines of *Prometheus Unbound,* "hope" is seen by Shelley as creating "from its own wreck the thing it contemplates." It is, we should observe in passing and further to clarify the point, from this second and major phase of Romantic apocalyptics that, in the American twentieth century, Hart Crane unmistakably emerges. *The Bridge* (1930) is the very type of the apocalypse of imagination: a poem written out of a deepening despair over the conditions of life in America, but a poem which, while in no way seeking to falsify or sentimentalize the grim observable facts, aims nonetheless at establishing a new relation between the human consciousness *and* that life; and by so doing, but only by so doing, to assist a little in the conversion of the age of iron into the age of gold.

III

Hart Crane, however, stands virtually alone among twentieth-century American poets in perpetuating the mood of apocalyptic *hope,* even though his hope rests, as I have just said, upon faith in the power of poetry rather than faith in the goodly impulses of men or the benevolent dispositions of history. Crane indeed had few companions in mood in the whole history of American literature; Poe, I will suggest, was the closest of his predecessors; for while the millennial temper has been notable and noisy in America, it has not often found expression in imaginative writing —and it is of course toward imaginative rather than discursive or speculative writing that I have been gradually shifting.

Before completing that shift, we may remember that the notion of New England as the scene of the New Jerusalem was widespread during the first years after the Massachusetts settlements. Such men as John Cotton and Thomas Goodwin, in commentaries on Revelations (both sets compiled in 1639), predicted the start of the millennium in the very near future: Cotton dating the grand event as early as 1655, Goodwin more cautiously putting it around 1700.[7] There was some dispute as to whether Christ would

7. For this and related information, I am grateful to *The Puritan Apocalypse,* an unpublished Yale doctoral dissertation (1964) by Joy Bourne

personally initiate the splendid age and inhabit the earth during it or whether he would appear only at the end. But there was considerable agreement in those hopeful decades with the quaintly worded announcement of John Eliot, the apostle to the Indians, that "In these times the Prophesies of *Antichrist* his downfall are accomplishing," and with the heady declaration of Richard Mather that the time was coming, and soon to be, "when all Kings shall fall down unto [Christ], and all Nations do him service . . . [as] plentifully foretold and promised in the Holy Scriptures." Such a sentiment could be voiced as late as 1697 by that most attractive of Puritans, Samuel Sewall in *Phaenomena Quaedam Apocalyptica,* or in its English title *The New Heaven upon the New Earth.*[8] Secular versions of the thesis continued to inform what might be called liberal American thought in the eighteenth and nineteenth centuries—for example, the histories of George Bancroft, with their (essentially Virgilian) image of America as the triumphant culmination of world history, and the proclamations of those settlers of frontier communities who attempted, as H. Richard Niebuhr has indicated in the title of his fine study, to establish *The Kingdom of God in America.*

Nonetheless, the major apocalyptic tradition in this country— and the one which has stimulated the literary imagination proper —dates rather from the later seventeenth century, when the felt failure of the New England mission produced a stream of "doomsday sermons," all of them envisioning the cosmic wrath by which God would punish an apostate people. It was then, in the second and third generations of Puritans, that, as Hawthorne would observe, the characteristic darkness of the Puritan visage set in, and the Puritan temper lost its capacity for laughter. It was then that the "Jeremiad"—a prophetic discourse, in the Old Testament sense of prophecy, combining lament and exhortation addressed to the backsliders—gave way to a more genuinely apocalyptic rhetoric, intoning the multiple agonies and the fractional beatitudes of the Day of Judgment.

"The Day of Trouble is Near," Increase Mather asserted dire-

Gilsdorf. Mrs. Gilsdorf underscores the effect upon early New England apocalyptic thinking of the guarded optimism of John Calvin about the spiritual progress of man in history, as against the severe Lutheran position.

8. Whittier included bits of Sewall's work, including the celebration of Plum Island, in his poem "The Prophecy of Samuel Sewall."

fully in the 1670s, quite reversing the cheerful claim of his father, Richard. A decade before, Michael Wigglesworth of Malden, had given an elaborate account of the awesome moment in *The Day of Doom* (1662), after mourning over New England's spiritual and moral decline in a poetic Jeremiad (published in the same year) called *God's Controversy with New England.* The former lengthy, oddly sweet-natured, and enormously popular piece of apocalyptic doggerel begins its disclosures on a serene and lovely night, when "wallowing in all kind of sin/ Vile wretches lay secure." At midnight precisely the catastrophe occurs. There "brake forth a light/ Which turn'd the night to day,/ And speedily an hideous cry/ Did all the world dismay." Violent upheavals follow, mountains catch fire, hills are set a-swaying, the earth is "rent and torn" by quakes, and the Son of God appears with his train to judge both the quick and the dead. The sheep, those invited to sit on Christ's right hand, are glanced at for a few stanzas; but the goats, those summoned to the left, take a good deal longer to sort out. Similarly with the act of judgment: the righteous are assigned their thrones with a certain briskness; but Christ cross-examines, crushes in argument, and sentences the multitude of sinners for something over one hundred and sixty stanzas. In the course of them, Wigglesworth provides an anatomy of impiety, a softly bouncing survey of humanity in its last and worst apostasy and of the infinite variety of the wickedness of the whole "sinful crew," as Christ calls them:

> *Adulterers and Whoremongers*
> *Were there, with all unchast:*
> *There Covetous, and Ravenous,*
> *That Riches get too fast:*
>
> *Who us'd vile ways themselves to raise*
> *t'Estates and worldly wealth,*
> *Oppression by, or Knavery,*
> *By force, or fraud, or stealth—*

and so on. After the immense task of unmasking, Christ commands the actual punishments to proceed, while Wigglesworth, shuddering delicately, averts his eyes—"Who can tell the plagues of Hell,/ And torments exquisite?" Only in a brief epilogue are the saints, those reborn into eternal life, again remembered: "O blessed state of the Renate!/ O wondrous happiness."

While Wigglesworth, in the guise of envisioning the post-catastrophic judgment, was thus exploring the worldly lapses that justify catastrophe, larger apocalyptic patterns still aroused interest elsewhere, mainly through the influence of speculative apocalyptic histories imported from abroad. We notice, among these latter, familiar and long-standing differences of opinion—as to whether, for example, there would or would not be a millennium or period of righteousness and earthly happiness between the present age and the ultimate apostasy which would lead to the ultimate disaster; and if so, whether those future good times should or should not be dwelt upon. It remained, as usual, for Jonathan Edwards to give the culture of the new world its major statement on the entire subject—in *A History of the Work of Redemption* (written in 1739, published in America in 1786).

The *History* is a sort of updated *City of God*—a long narrative of the Christian past from the Creation and the Fall through the career of Christ and on to the Protestant Reformation—combined with the visionary pronouncements of Revelations. In the latter or eschatological portion of the work, Edwards argued that there would, at some moment in the future, begin a one-thousand-year period in which the world would be ruled by Christ and which, Edwards hints once or twice, might just possibly arrive sooner than one might think. But toward the close of it, the world would once more revolt or fall away from Christ; and this time to such a degree that Christ would declare the Day of Judgment and the planet would be destroyed by fire. (I have already quoted Edwards' conviction, recently seconded by James Baldwin, that next time the world would be annihilated not by flood waters but by fire.) This whole portion of Edwards' history has been described by Perry Miller, among others, as "simple, old-fashioned chiliasm": "chiliasm" being a word one uses when one is tired of the word "millennialism," of which, denotatively, it is an exact synonym (chiliasm coming from the Greek for one thousand—*kilias*—rather than from the Latin), though as used by historians the words have acquired somewhat different connotations. The word in any case is not quite accurate: for though Edwards' interest does divide between the rule of Christ and the catastrophe to follow, it is the disaster that rather engages his mind and imagination. In a sprightly essay of 1951, however, written in the wake of the atomic explosions and called "The End of the World," Miller suggested that Edwards' visual description of the cosmic explosion might after all be the most important part of his eschatology, and that it might indeed contain a large and unsettling amount of sheer realism—that Edwards had given a literal image of the way the world really would end, along with the sound of its bang.

To this, I think, we can add a quality of moral and metaphorical realism. In our later generation, Edwards, as he draws upon the conventional machinery of the apocalyptic tradition, can perhaps be seen describing realistically enough the perennial degenerative tendencies of human nature, and providing metaphors—in the form of world-consuming holocausts and the like—that can gauge their enormity. To some extent, this seems to be precisely what St. John the Divine had been doing—that is, composing a poem, not a tract, and poem crowded not with believed-in facts but with revelatory images and symbols. And this is just what Edwards' American successors have done, and it is why we find them not so much among the theologians but among the novelists and poets, among those who have recognized and realized the truth of the imaginative life. We find those novelists and poets deploying scattered remnants of the apocalyptic vocabulary for their own humanistic and creative purposes, and so recurrently as to encourage us to deal with them in the same vocabulary for our critical purposes (on the assumption that *for* those purposes the apocalyptic language may be as serviceable, say, as the Freudian or the existentialist or the sociological). What has happened on the creative side, I venture, and beginning in America with Edgar Allan Poe, is another "rebirth of images," another reanimating of those great and ancient archetypes by which Western man has periodically explained to himself the full range of his condition, and the most spectacular of his expectations or terrors.

IV

Poe, perhaps surprisingly, seemed on one occasion to be the most thoroughly conventional of the apocalyptic visionaries among nineteenth-century American writers. In a curious little dialogue-in-heaven called "The Conversation of Eiros and Charmion" (December 1839), Poe gave an account of the end of the world not only charged with quotations from Revelations, but told from the vantage point of the superterrestrial realm to which the blessed have already been transferred. What happened back on earth, the shadowy male figure Eiros tells his shadowy female companion Charmion, was "the entire fulfillment, in all their minute and terrible details, of the fiery and horror-inspiring denunciations of the prophecies of the Holy Book." It was also, we might observe, in exact accord with the later theorizing statement of R. H. Charles: another planet approaches the earth and shuts off its supply of nitrogen, whereupon the earth is destroyed by an outburst of its own fires.

> Then, there came a shouting and pervading sound, as if from the mouth itself of HIM; while the whole incumbent mass of ether in which we existed, burst at once into a species of intense flame, for whose surpassing brilliancy and all-fervid heat even the angels in the high Heaven of pure knowledge have no name. Thus ended all.

The conversation occurs in the domain of Aidenn (as it is spelled), a place full of "joys and wonders" and pervaded by "the majesty of all things": Poe's aesthetic version of the biblical heavenly kingdom.

But Poe turns out, as always, to be a very special case. His imagination was persistently apocalyptical in both the terrible and the hopeful sense. It was drawn regularly to the imagery of utter catastrophe—to the wiping out of a whole community, as in "The Masque of the Red Death" ("and Darkness and Decay and the Red Death held illimitable dominion over all"), or of a family and its mansion and estate, as in "The Fall of the House of Usher." But both the frequent catastrophes and the occasional glimpse of post-catastrophic otherworldly bliss belong to what Richard Wilbur has eloquently identified as Poe's "myth of the poet."[9] In this highly original version of a most central Romantic theme, what is being symbolically destroyed in tale after tale is the power of earthly beauty and the grip of worldly life; and what is being sometimes realized is the recovered vision of perfect beauty once enjoyed in childhood but lost in maturity. "The Conversation of Eiros and Charmion" is in this perspective a beatific sequel to "The Fall of the House of Usher" (of which it was in literal fact a sequel, the two stories following one another

9. Wilbur's interpretation of Poe is available in his preface to the Dell Laurel volume of Poe's poetry (New York, 1959) and his introduction to the Poe section in *Major Writers of America* (New York, 1962).

in *Burton's Magazine* in September and December 1839). Poe's essential design—vision; the disappearance of vision; the struggle to recapture it—is the obvious American ancestor of Hart Crane's epical design in *The Bridge*. But it would take us much too far afield, however fascinating the detour, to pursue Poe's special contribution to American apocalyptics. In our own now narrowing context, the key American figure of the past century was Herman Melville, and the key book was *The Confidence-Man*.

Much of Melville's best writing is animated by a sort of apocalyptic intuition; and indeed "apocalyptic" is a more precise adjective for Melville's imagination than the more usual ones, "mythic" or "metaphysical." Like every other element in this highly dynamic vision, however, the apocalyptic element was constantly in motion, constantly modifying or reversing itself. In *Moby-Dick* (which cites the Book of Revelations on several occasions), the focus is on catastrophe: the catastrophic end of the *Pequod,* seen as a microcosm of America or even the modern world ("the world's a ship on its passage out"); the disastrous result of the human effort to transcend human limits and to penetrate and destroy the divine or at least nonhuman power secreted in the heart of reality. But this mad, majestic enterprise is set alongside quite different apocalyptic motifs: for example, the doomsday tract called "The Latter Day Coming; or No Time to Lose," which the hypocritical Captain Bildad presses on Queequeg, or the apocalyptic screechings of the self-styled prophet Gabriel, who, at secret meetings of the Neskyeuna Shakers, used to "descend from heaven by the way of a trap-door, announcing the speedy opening of the seventh vial" (the last of the vials of destruction) "which he carried in his vest-pocket." Gabriel is simply a humbug prophet; but Captain Ahab is that incomparably grander traditional figure, the False Prophet or False Christ: with something in him of Satan, especially Milton's Satan ("There was an infinity of firmest fortitude, a determinate, unsurrenderable wilfulness" in his glance), but also something of Christ the King ("moody stricken Ahab stood before them with a crucifixion in his face; in all the nameless regal overbearing dignity of some mighty woe"). In the apocalyptic pattern of *Moby-Dick,* Ahab is the Antichrist, misleading mankind to the point of bringing down upon it the annihilating wrath of God; but in the book's supple play of perspectives, he is also of course the Antichrist as a noble, heroic, and tragic figure.

The characteristically radical ambiguity of Melville's apocalyptic outlook is perhaps even better displayed in "The Conflict of Convictions," the main opening poem of *Battle-Pieces* (1866), Melville's volume of poems about the Civil War. Here, with somber allusions to Satan and Raphael and the eternal battle between good and evil, Melville posed the ultimate alternatives—the fundamental dialectic, as it were, of the entire apocalyptic tradition. Out of the violent intranational upheaval, during which the very "gulfs their slimed foundations bare," there might emerge the millennium: "the final empire and the happier world." Or, on the contrary, the nation might—spiritually speaking—be catastrophically destroyed; become utterly dominated by power without grace, whereat "the Founders' dream shall flee,"

And death be busy with all who strive—
Death, with silent negative.

As the war moved forward, Melville seems to have felt that the iron age was a more probable outcome than the happier world; and, like the English Romantics observing the defeat of their millennial hopes in France, Melville concluded *Battle-Pieces* with an "apocalypse of imagination": a poem called "America" which provides a vision, true rather for the poem than in the fact, of an America reborn out of the agony, possessed of a "hope grown wise. . . . Law on her brow and empire *in her eyes*"[10] (italics added).

But Melville's most searching statement about the fatal direction in which America was heading was contained in his pre-Civil War novel, *The Confidence-Man* (1857), an extraordinary work that ranks second only to *Moby-Dick* among his writings. With it, I come at last to the peculiar modern American strain of the savagely comical apocalypse; for if *Moby-Dick* is in a sense the American culmination of the older apocalyptic tradition, *The Confidence-Man* stands at the start of a distinctive new genre, its first and still its most remarkable example.

The Confidence-Man is a narrative image of the American world at the moment of its last apostasy. In the course of describ-

10. Melville himself felt the analogy between his own forebodings and the English Romantic reaction to the developments of the French Revolution. In a footnote to *Battle-Pieces,* he compared the dismay aroused in America by the events of 1860–61 to the impact upon "kindred natures" of "the eclipse which came over the promise of the first French Revolution."

ing a day-long journey aboard a Mississippi river steamer wryly called the *Fidèle,* the novel gives a relentless series of examples, each more formidable than Wigglesworth's, of (to borrow some of Wigglesworth's categories) the covetous and the ravenous, of oppression and knavery, of force and fraud and stealth. At the outset, there appears briefly a seemingly Christ-like figure, a nameless and gentle person whose head and hair, in one of Melville's favorite quotations from Revelations, are "white like wool"; but, whoever he is, he is derided, reviled, and dismissed. Thereafter, under the auspices of the metaphoric Confidence Man himself, the narrative dramatizes and forces into prominence those qualities of greed, hypocrisy, ignorance, moral timidity, and ice-cold heartlessness through which the American society, a world that had once promised to become the millennial heaven-on-earth and still claimed to be just that was in fact steadily turning into a hell-on-earth, as though to fulfill the bleak prediction of Jonathan Edwards. These are the conditions which invite the catastrophe: an event, one is intended to suspect, which will take place only a second or two after the book's closing sentence. The final scene is awe-inspiring. In a darkening ship's cabin, a conversation between the title figure and a nearly senile old man is interrupted three times by shouted phrases from some person hidden in one of the bunks—three exclamations which, within the darkly ritualistic atmosphere of the scene, come like three blasts of the apocalyptic trumpets. First, when one speaker makes a reference to the Gospel, or "good news": "Too good to be true." Then, when Ecclesiasticus is quoted about the wiles of the devil: "Who's that describing the confidence-man?" And finally, after the word "apocrypha" has been invoked: "What's that about the Apocalypse?" Not long afterward, the Confidence Man extinguishes the cabin's last lamp (an object decorated with what appear to be symbols borrowed from Revelations) and leads his befuddled companion out into the total darkness. It is just on the stroke of midnight, and surely some revelation is at hand.

If this often disconcertingly realistic fable is, as I am contending, the pivotal text in the history of apocalyptic literature in America, it is because, while drawing heavily upon the familiar elements, it is also the first to exploit what would be the chief features of so much of the imaginative apocalyptic writing that followed. It is a conventional inspection of humanity during the last loosening of Satan: but its perspective is profoundly and almost shatteringly comic. The sinners are made to seem as ridiculous as they are unredeemable; and Melville's rhetorical strategy, which is flawlessly executed throughout (and which comprises one of the great rhetorical inventions of modern writing), is by action or meditation and by a slow grave maneuvering of language to strip each of the *Fidèle's* passengers of his pretensions, layer by layer, until each is revealed in all his naked absurdity. And while the novel explores "the later end of the world," in John Foxe's phrase, and introduces what Foxe had called "the head and principall Antichrist," the Antichrist in question—that is, of course, the Confidence Man himself—is the first and largest of an expanding list of Satanic comedians. His most conspicuous talent, geared to a world bereft of any kind of intellectual or moral stability, is a talent for metamorphosis: he is the master of change and the changing, a very king of chaos; before the novel is through, he has appeared in eight thoroughly different roles and personalities and garb. His genius, moreover, is a genius for satire, rooted in a profound understanding of the folly and depravity of mankind; and in a world where the basic terms (such as "confidence" and "man") have come to mean their opposites or to mean nothing, he is a master of satiric deception and exposure. In nature he is a fabulous comic analogue to Ahab—a demonic angel and an angelic devil who incarnates the preposterous contradictions of that humanity which he is blandly escorting to its doom. His descendants are many.

The first of them, perhaps, is the young man named Satan in Mark Twain's *The Mysterious Stranger*. This amicable and terrifying character, who seems to be a nephew of the original Satan, is—like Melville's hero—an inveterate comedian; though, characteristically with Mark Twain, a comedian of a rather boyish and prankster type. With this story, which was only published posthumously in 1916, Twain carried into the twentieth century the American genre of the comical apocalypse; and in it, Twain brought to their finality fictional themes and attitudes toward the human race that had been growing steadily blacker in his imagination from *Huckleberry Finn* through *The Gilded Age* and *Pudd'nhead Wilson* to "The Man That Corrupted Hadleyburg" (1900). The mood of *The Mysterious Stranger* is that of ultimate chill; during a long wintry season in the late sixteenth century, the citizens of the Austrian village of Eseldorf (Donkeytown) display in incident after incident an icy inhumanity that is total and incorrigible. The cool indifference with which young Satan perpetrates some miraculous atrocities of his own simply expresses a moral nihilism which the villagers, including the adolescent narrator and his companions, hypocritically deny even while acting in accord with it. Mark Twain ends his parable with a peculiarly inventive sort of metaphysical or even ontological catastrophe: not the reported end of the world in ice or fire, but the revelation that the world, the very universe, does not even exist and never has. *"Nothing* exists," Satan informs the narrator Theodor at the moment of his disappearance; "all is a dream. God—man—the world—the sun, the moon, the wilderness of stars—a dream, all a dream; they have no existence. *Nothing exists save empty space and you."*

Beyond that uncovering of absolute nothingness, the apocalyptic imagination can hardly venture. But Satan also knows what Mark Twain knew, and what this devastating *Nunc Dimittis* has been constantly exemplifying—the implicit first principle of modern American apocalyptics: namely, as Satan puts it, that our human race has only

> one really effective weapon—laughter. Power, money, persuasion, supplication, persecution—these can lift at a colossal humbug—push it a little—weaken it a little, century by century. But only laughter can blow it to rags and atoms at a blast.

Satan's metaphor, as apt as it is unexpected, helps to identify the imaginative aim of a series of novels which, over the past two and a half decades, have explored a thickening American chaos, an America hovering ever more perilously on the day of doom. For while attempting to do full justice to the conditions perceived, these novels have a further apocalyptic purpose—to reveal the essential fraudulence within the horror, to uncover the ridiculous within the catastrophic; in the hope, at least, of letting in a little light.

V

We might well begin with Faulkner's *The Hamlet* (1940), where the unmistakable figure of Satan unloosed is named Flem Snopes, where the victory of the Antichrist over the novel's world is virtually complete, and where laughter is indeed a major instrument for coping with the awfulness. But this antipastoral master

piece has such a variety of fictional tones and narrative modes
that an effective analysis of it would pull us off course. We will
do better to begin with Nathanael West's *The Day of the Locust,*
and its hardminded comic portrait of the imminent destruction
of America by a holocaust of hate. The Satanic character in
West's novel, the harnesser of all that hatred, goes in fact unnamed; but we know that he will be an even greater scoundrel,
making even wilder promises, than the lesser demagogues we
have seen throughout the book serving the bitter frustrations
of the aging California citizenry. He will be a successor as well
to West's earlier Antichrists, the editor Shrike in *Miss Lonelyhearts* (1933) and Shagpoke Whipple in *A Cool Million* (1934).
The realm of the California super-promiser, however, seems larger
than that of Shrike and Shagpoke; for if there is not, unarguably,
an increase in West's imaginative power from *Miss Lonelyhearts*
to *The Day of the Locust,* there is an observable increase in the
range of the horror always comically explored.

The world of *Miss Lonelyhearts* is an airlessly tight little island
—Manhattan Island, in fact, plus a short stretch of countryside;
a world so narrowed, in a novella so compressed, that its rhythms
and tensions (which themselves are eschatological in nature and
have to do with the last things) are well-nigh uncontainable. The
novella moves unfalteringly between nightmare and actuality, its
tone between horror and jesting; which is West's exemplary way
of apprehending *our* world as under the dominion of a contemporary Antichrist. The human condition thus apprehended is characterized by a sort of absolute dis-order, by a dislocation
observable pre-eminently in the relations of love, in almost every
heterosexual and homosexual variety; but also a dislocation in
man's other crucial relations—his relation to things, to words,
to the rituals of life, to his own perennial aspirations. Human
life, as depicted in *Miss Lonelyhearts,* has become a grotesque
parody of itself; and the name of the book's Antichrist, Shrike,
has the merit not only of meaning a toothbeaked bird of prey,
but also of being as it were a parody of the name Christ, or
Christ almost spelled backward. It is Shrike who rules over and
preys upon an urban scene composed of the heartless, the violent,
and the wretched. And it is Shrike who pits himself against the
would-be imitator of Christ, the hapless columnist we know only
by his pen name Miss Lonelyhearts, and whom Shrike torments
in particular by spoken parodies of the Eucharist—that holy

communion after which Miss Lonelyhearts so yearns. The central image of the novella, indeed, is a parody of the Gospel encounter between Christ and the Devil—in this case between a man, on the one hand, whose soul is sickened by a human misery he cannot assuage; and, on the other, the spokesman of an ice-cold and yet witty and intellectually brilliant inhumanity. In speech after speech, Shrike tempts and taunts Miss Lonelyhearts with vistas of grandeur, channels of escape, resources of compensation; until he drives the columnist to attempting the final absurd miracle. In a ludicrously ill-timed and feverish effort to embrace and hence to redeem by love at least one individual human victim— a crippled homosexual named Pete Doyle—Miss Lonelyhearts is accidentally shot and killed; and in the abrasively ironic eschatology of this novella, the field is left to the further machinations of the Antichrist. But Shrike, consummate satirist though he be, is at the same time an object of satire—that is, of West's satire— and the field of his triumph is no more than a frozen chaos.

The enlargement of setting in *A Cool Million* is suggested by this: that Miss Lonelyhearts is shot (in an obscure rooming house) not even by a man but, as though in its supreme revolt, by a thing, by the freakish explosion of a gun wrapped in a newspaper; while Lemuel Pitkin, whose gradual "dismantling" is half of the theme of *A Cool Million,* is shot by a hired assassin, "Operative 6348XM," during a huge political rally staged in New York by the National Revolutionary Party. The satire in *A Cool Million* is cruder and broader than in *Miss Lonelyhearts;* and West is not himself implicated in that which he satirizes, as he had been earlier. Still, while *A Cool Million* plays comical havoc with the Horatio Alger tradition and the American daydream of the easy surge upward to fame and fortune, it is also this country's most vigorous narrative vision of the political apocalypse—far more penetrating, for example, than the rather hastily contrived image which appeared the following year in Sinclair Lewis' *It Can't Happen Here.* The devil as the editor Shrike is succeeded in *A Cool Million* by the devil as national political Fuehrer: by Shagpoke Whipple, a more ambitious and amiable and even more completely fraudulent figure than his predecessor. The "mantling" of Shagpoke, former President and future dictator of the United States, is the other half of the book's theme; his loudmouthed and evidently interminable reign is just beginning as the story ends. On the national holiday commemorating young Lemuel's assassi-

nation, Whipple spells out his triumphant program to shouting
thousands at a Fifth Avenue parade:

The National Revolutionary Party [has] triumphed, and by
that triumph this country was delivered from sophistication,
Marxism and International Capitalism. Through the National
Revolution its people were purged of alien diseases and America became again America.

This is a fine example of what Richard Hofstadter has defined
as the paranoid style in American politics: a style historically
based, as Mr. Hofstadter points out, on a most intensive apocalyptic outlook—a belief in some evil worldwide conspiracy,
an identification of a wild conglomeration of elements as agencies
of the Antichrist (communism, eastern capitalism, intellectual
sophistication, and so on), a conviction of approaching disaster
unless counteraction is swiftly taken.[11] West's complex achievement in *A Cool Million* is to satirize this apocalyptic temper in
such a way as to show that it is itself the source of the potential
catastrophe. But Mr. Hofstadter was talking primarily not about
the political debaucheries of the 1930s, the actual scene of *A Cool
Million,* but about the presidential campaign of 1964; and it is
because that phenomenon is still so close to us that one finds it
harder to laugh at Shagpoke's speech or at Shagpoke than it used
to be. Yet, even as we are once again astonished at the capacity
of life to follow slavishly in the wake of art, and as our admiration
for West's prophetic power deepens into downright awe, we also
become aware that the perspective in *A Cool Million* is exactly
right. For in West's perspective of rough-hewn satire, the squalid
reality of American fascism—the absurdities that pervade its
spurious nostalgia and its venomous racism, its radical ignorance
and contradictory assortment of fears—gets utterly exposed. What
passes among the brutalized citizenry as the New Jerusalem is
revealed to be a catastrophic vulgarity. And the very real menace,
even as it is uncovered and defined, is in part overcome (insofar
as a work of art can ever overcome anything) through the restoration of sanity by laughter.

But *The Day of the Locust,* as I have already said, is West's
supreme Book of Revelations. This beautifully composed novel
makes dreadfully and hilariously evident in the superb dance of

11. *Harper's Magazine,* November, 1964.

its elements a threat beyond that of *A Cool Million:* a threat to the very roots of life in America, a threat as it were to the human nature of American humanity. It is a threat incarnate in a certain mass of people—bored, frustrated, vindictive, and moribund— who have come to California impelled by a dream of their own obscene millennium, by a sterile lust for some experience of violence that might exhilarate and revivify. They are disappointed —"nothing [could] ever be violent enough to make taut their slack minds and bodies"—and with a devouring sense of having been betrayed, they await the summons to provide out of themselves the violence denied. The summons begins to be audible in the animal roaring of a mob rioting outside a Hollywood theater as the novel ends.

Against that tremendous force of hatred—and for West, since love is the sign of spiritual grace, hatred, its polar opposite, is the defining quality of apostasy and damnation—West poses the allied powers of art and comedy. His hero is a young painter named Tod Hackett, presently employed as a set designer in Hollywood; a tougher-spirited Miss Lonelyhearts and a more self-protective Lemuel Pitkin. It is Tod who takes to studying the dead ferocity of the invaders, seeking them out in odd nooks and corners of the city, driven by a profound fascination with their "awful anarchic power" and determined to represent them on canvas. He finds them gathered, more than anywhere else, in the temples and churches, the lunatic-fringe cults of California; for one of the most terrible of the truths and prophecies disclosed in *The Day of the Locust* is the organic connection in America between radical religiosity, an extreme Protestantism gone finally insane, and the organized impulse of hatred and destruction.

> As [Tod] watched these people writhe on the hard seats of their churches, he thought of how well Alessandro Magnasco would dramatize the contrast between their drained-out feeble bodies and their wild disordered minds. He would not satirize them as Hogarth and Daumier might, nor would he pity them. He would paint their fury with respect, appreciating its awful, anarchic power, and aware that they had it in them to destroy civilization.

Nathanael West does not precisely satirize them either; despite its carefully wrought poetic intensity, *The Day of the Locust* stays closer to a palpable historical reality than his other fictions. The tone and movement of the novel are comic, nonetheless, and both are suited to a world in which, due to the utter instability of its outward forms, everything is on the verge of giving way.

The scene upon which the locusts descend is a scene made up of masqueraders and impostors; of movie actors dressed up as French and British generals and of ordinary citizens dressed up as Tyrolean hunters. Even plants and natural phenomena are fictitious: cactus plants are made of rubber and cork; a hill on a movie set, as it collapses, spills the nails and rips the canvas of which it is composed. A world so grotesquely insubstantial is ripe for conquest; and yet within its atmosphere, the wrath to come can be contemplated with just that drunken and hazily amused equanimity that Tod Hackett expresses when, lying on his back in a clump of wild mustard, he thinks about the invasion of California by "the cream of America's madmen" and feels certain that "the milk from which it had been skimmed was just as rich in violence. The Angelenos would be first, but their comrades all over the country would follow. There would be civil war." That antic Armageddon, however, takes place not quite in the actual rioting and lynching and sexual assaults of the final scene; but, rather, in an interpretive work of art, in the painting (and it is to be a great painting, West clearly wants us to believe) Tod Hackett is meticulously projecting on the last page, even as he is being mauled and half-crushed by the frenzied mob.

Thus superimposed in thought above the actual disorders, the painting—it will be called "The Burning of Los Angeles"—will eventually explain and comment upon the apocalypse it describes by the patterned juxtaposition of its elements. It will show a "mob carrying baseball bats and torches" down a long hill street, a mob that includes "the cultists of all sorts" whom Tod had been observing—"all those poor devils who can only be stirred by the promise of miracles, and then only to violence." Now, "no longer bored, they sang and danced joyously in the red light of the flames," following the leader who "had made the necessary promise"; "they were marching behind his banner in a great united front of screwballs and screwboxes to purify the land." Elsewhere on the canvas, various postures suggest various responses to that savage absurd Puritanism: a girl running naked in smiling mindless panic; a man named Claude turning to thumb his nose; Tod himself pausing to throw stones at the mob like a small boy. Nose thumbing and stone throwing are commendable

acts of derision; but Tod's major response is of course his painting, just as West's major response is the novel that contains it.
And both painting and novel fulfill their purpose by portraying
these maddened humans, whirling forward in their orgiastic dance,
as devils who are yet poor devils, seized by a fury of hatred which
is as silly as it is explosive.

Ralph Ellison's *Invisible Man* (1952) likewise ends with a riot,
the last and largest of several in the novel, and with a riot
similarly charged, in the account of it, with apocalyptic comedy;
though this time the scene is Harlem rather than Hollywood.
And the world as experienced in *Invisible Man* is again a world
spoiling for catastrophe: a world rank with duplicity and violence,
infested by cheats, liars, betrayers, and impostors, all caught up
in a continuing and somehow wonderfully exuberant masquerade.
In the novel's climactic stage, moreover, the world again reveals
itself as altogether bereft of stabilizing shape or form: a world
without boundaries, as the narrator dazedly realizes, "a vast
seething hot world of fluidity." Within such a world, the fluid man
is king; and his name here is Rinehart—Bliss Proteus Rinehart,
in fact. Rinehart is the very paradigm of Protean frauds, the
culmination of a long sequence of frauds of lesser or greater accomplishments strewn through the novel, from a Negro college
president in the south to a white political organizer in the north.
And with Rinehart, the "master of chaos" as the narrator calls
him and the man of "multiple personalities," we return—Ellison
has been the first to acknowledge it—to Melville's figure of the
metamorphic Confidence Man. After the narrator, groping his way
behind tinted glasses through the dim embattled streets of Harlem,
has been constantly accosted by mistake as Rinehart, he is able
to list some of the rascal's varied activities: "Rine the runner
and Rine the gambler and Rine the briber and Rine the lover and
Rinehart the Reverend." He is, in short, the Harlem Negro as
super-promiser; and a false priest and prophet in literal fact, a
"spiritual technologist" who holds forth at the Holy Way Station,
where he makes visible the invisible and unfolds the new apocalypse—"the NEW REVELATION of the OLD TIME RE-
LIGION." Nothing looser or more elusive can be imagined than
this slippery Satan, whom, indeed, we never actually encounter.
But his shadowy presence is the unmistakable sign of the traditional loosening of Satan, or, in the modern idiom, of all hell
breaking loose: it is almost immediately "after Rinehart appears

in my novel," Ellison has remarked, "that the riot breaks out in Harlem."[12]

It is the destiny of the book's nameless hero, as he wanders and stumbles and plunges across the scene, to discover chaos as the determining condition of life; and to become aware, belatedly, that the chaos is deliberate and planned. The rioting in Harlem has been carefully managed and directed by a political organization known as the Brotherhood; just as the battle royal the narrator had been forced to engage in as a schoolboy had been supervised by the leading white citizens of his home town; or as the free-for-all that erupts in a paint factory is artfully stimulated by unionists and management spies, and the sexual traps the unsuspecting young man falls into encouraged by complaisant husbands. The chaos is total and ubiquitous. It represents the considered program, as it were, of the agents of Antichrist for drawing the world onward to the great catastrophe—with the manifest intention of seizing power in the post-catastrophic wreckage. For Ellison has elevated his political theme, the familiar authoritarian strategy of making disaster serve the ends of conquest, into universal apocalyptic significance. In the same way, he has in the book's climax converted the original or "real-life" setting (the Harlem street wars of 1943, which Ellison covered for a metropolitan newspaper) into that nightmare country which Martin Buber finds the definitive scene of apocalyptic fiction, when "the actual historical-biographical situation of the speaker [or writer] is deliberately replaced by an alien scene taken over as analogous to his own."[13] And, finally, Ellison has heightened

12. *Shadow and Act* (New York, 1964), p. 181. Ellison has much to say in this volume about Rinehart and the tradition of the trickster-god, though he is skeptical about the critical category of the "archetype." So far as I can discover, Ellison added Rinehart's middle name, Proteus, retrospectively; in the novel, he is given only a middle initial P. Bliss is also the first name of the main character in Ellison's second novel, which at one time, I believe, was to be devoted to Rinehart or somebody resembling him. Ellison, by the way, seems not to have read *The Confidence-Man* before writing *Invisible Man;* the similarity he himself points out is due to an affinity of imagination with Melville.

13. One further result of Ellison's heightening and, as it were, ritualizing of the 1943 riot scenes is that his battle image has become prophetic of all later Harlem disorders: for example, the disorders that broke out in the summer of 1964, in which one could observe the same emotional sources, the same kind of triggering incident, and the same rhythm of events as those depicted in *Invisible Man.*

the racial theme into a representation of the condition of man as such; the plight of the Negro in the novel—his confused readiness to be recruited by all and sundry, his psychological invisibility—provides a perspective on the plight of every man under the modern circumstances.

Against all that, Ellison, like West, offers the counterforce of art, especially the power—the shaping power, the power to give form and hence explanatory meaning to experience—of comic narrative. The narrator fails to achieve visibility and vision through the normal channels of education or a job of work or sex or political action; and he fails in particular to achieve those things through his long and fiercely dedicated participation in what he took to be the struggle to make life more tolerable for his fellow Negroes. But his true resource, as it turns out, is storytelling. He becomes himself a master of chaos, of his own experienced chaos, by going underground and lingering there to draw his breath in pain and tell his story. But for all the very considerable pain, there is also the permeating comic awareness: which is to say that *Invisible Man* is in some sort an expanded narrative equivalent of that musical mode known as the blues, at least in Ellison's definition. "The Blues," he has written,

> is an impulse to keep the painful details and episodes of a brutal experience alive in one's aching consciousness, to finger its jagged grain, and to transcend it, not by the consolation of philosophy but by squeezing from it a near-tragic, near-comic lyricism. . . . [It is the] chronicle of personal catastrophe expressed lyrically.

Add the phrase "or even universal" to the word "personal," and we have a fairly exact summary account of this uncommonly distinguished novel, and a strong clue to its form.

In *The Sot-Weed Factor* (1960), John Barth's robustious novel about various fantastic forewarnings of the apocalypse in late seventeenth-century Maryland, the artistic dimension has become paramount, and in such a way as to offer an explanation, even a defense, of the prevalence of its genre—the genre of apocalyptic comedy—in our twentieth-century time. In essence, *The Sot-Weed Factor* (which is an archaic phrase meaning "Tobacco Merchant") is a portrait of the artist as an exacerbated and scandalously ill-treated young Colonial American. The portrait, it is important to know, is historically based, and *The Sot-Weed Factor* is among many other things a prodigiously learned historical novel. It gives us the life and times of a genuine historical figure, Ebenezer Cook or Cooke (1680 to 1730 or thereabouts), who was probably born in the New World, most likely spent some years in England and then (as he does in the novel) returned to America, where he really did write a satirical poem called *The Sot-Weed Factor,* which was published in London in 1708.[14] It is a rowdy poem of some seven hundred lines, emulating the manner and metrics of Butler's *Hudibras* and relating the astonishing (and, one assumes, imaginary) adventures of the author during a brief visit to Maryland, where he is persistently robbed and cheated, and alternately terrified and disgusted. Barth's Ebenezer Cooke suffers the same mishaps, along with a great many more of his own; he encounters the same people—white men and Indians, slatterns and doxies—and listens to the same reminiscences. Toward the end of the second part of the novel, we watch young Cooke convert these experiences into the same brisk, embittered satire.

Barth's modernistic device of multiple mirroring—a novel about a young man writing a poem about a young man and so on —goes even further than usual. For Barth himself is a Marylander to the core; all his fiction to date has been set in his own home county, almost his own backyard; and in his own *Sot-Weed Factor,* he enacts his major celebration of the region by supplying it with a hectic and racy myth of its seventeenth-century origins. The fictional myth is on an incomparably larger scale and more widely ranging and crowded than the original poem. It encompasses scores of events and persons, major and minor, historical and contrived; probably Barth alone knows how close is the resemblance between the "real-life" characters and his treatment of them, especially as they all tend to become participants in a farcical pornographic dance, which is the image of history that emerges in the novel. But it is Barth, anyhow, who has the more decisively earned the title "Poet and Laureate of Maryland" that

14. Cooke, in fact and in Barth's novel, was also the author of *Sotweed Redivivus* (1730), of a burlesque "History of Colonel Nathaniel Bacon's Rebellion" and of elegies on Nicholas Lowe (an important shadowy figure in the novel) and William Lock. The original *Sot-Weed Factor* is most easily available in the paperbound *Colonial American Writing,* edited by Roy Harvey Pearce (New York, 1950).

is granted his less talented predecessor. It is within this sometimes dizzyingly self-reflective context that we make out the great and thoroughly contemporary concern of *The Sot-Weed Factor:* which is a certain familiar kind of world, and the relation to it of the creative imagination.

On one level, it is the exhaustively evoked world of seventeenth-century England and America; but, on another, it is our immediate world as we have been taught by Barth and his peers to recognize it. The book's rhetoric is an echo and parody of the diction of Ebenezer Cooke's generation; Leslie Fiedler has remarked upon "the insouciance with which [the novel] moves in and out of its counterfeits of seventeenth century diction," and calls the book "a joyous series of raids on half-forgotten resources of the language, largely obscene."[15] But in content, in perspective, and in fictional method, *The Sot-Weed Factor* is as modern as can be; and if, as everyone who has mentioned it has inevitably and correctly said, it is Rabelaisian and Swiftian, it is also Melvillian, Joycian, Proustian, Faulknerian—and Westian. Barth can find the occasional apocalyptic cliché of the actual poem (where it is a device of comical exaggeration) handy to his purpose: for example, Cooke's statement that on the Maryland scene

> *all Things were in such Confusion,*
> *I thought the World at its Conclusion.*

But usually the condition of ultimate chaos is conveyed in the contemporary idiom, after it has been soaked in neoclassic cadences. There is no "pointed order to the world," Ebenezer's tutor, Burlingame, tells him; and continues in the curious blank verse he sometimes affects: "In fact you see a Heraclitean flux; whether 'tis we who shift and alter and dissolve; or you whose lens changes color, field and form; or both together. The upshot is the same." We are, in short, back in the "vast seething hot world of fluidity" that Ellison's narrator came to identify; and, like West's California, Barth's Maryland is, in Burlingame's phrase, "a happy climate for imposture." It is "a motley, mindless world," Burlingame adds; and Man is no more than "Chance's fool . . . a mayfly flitting down the winds of Chaos." The modes of chaos—the sources of the catastrophe apprehended—are

15. *On Contemporary Literature,* edited by Richard Kostalentz (New York, 1964), pp. 241–42.

erotic and political, usually both: in Maryland, the world seems transformed into one vast brothel and opium den, under the command of a "grand high whoremaster"; elsewhere it is rather a political stew, a "pot of faction and sedition" that boils and boils again, until, as someone exclaims, it must be "about to explode."

Barth's fictive seventeenth-century setting permits him to draw upon the traditional apocalyptic vocabulary more and with a greater propriety than most of his contemporaries. The word "apocalypse" is on everyone's lips, especially as the violently opposed political forces seem about to settle their struggle for power by meeting head-on in a Maryland Armageddon. Lord Baltimore identifies his arch-enemy John Coode as a "very Antichrist" and a "false priest," and portrays Maryland under Coode's control as a country dominated by Satan unbound. But we recognize again the modern imagination when Henry Burlingame, speaking of both Baltimore and John Coode, says to Ebenezer:

> It may be they are all that rumor swears: devils and demigods, whichever's which; or it may be they're simply clotpolls like ourselves, that have been legend'd out of reasonable dimension; or it may be they're naught but the rumors and tales themselves.

"Devils and demigods, whichever's which." The metaphysical and even theological doubt thus chattily and sardonically expressed is what the novel has been busy bringing all-powerfully into play. In no novel since *The Confidence-Man* has doubt of such universal proportions been disclosed as man's proper and necessary state of mind, the one intellectual fruit of his experience. Similarly and consequently, in no American novel since *The Confidence-Man*—not often in any work of literature since the *Odyssey*—has a supreme talent for metamorphosis been so much the distinguishing mark of a major character.

In *The Sot-Weed Factor,* it is Henry Burlingame who, as the man always ready at need, demonstrates his readiness by an ability to take on every variety of role and personality, according to the shifting dramatic situation. He exploits the special skill of Odysseus to the ends of Telemachus, for his private mission is to establish his identity by determining his true Burlingame ancestry —a search that leads him, among other things, to dig up and examine the lurid secret chronicles of Captain John Smith and his epochal defloration of the Indian Princess, Pocahantas. En route, Burlingame validates the theory spelled out in deeply serious mockery in Barth's superb earlier novel *End of the Road* (1958), which, with its apocalyptic title and closely woven content, relates to *The Sot-Weed Factor* as *Miss Lonelyhearts* does to *The Day of the Locust*. The theory voiced by a mountebank of genius in *End of the Road* is based on "good existentialist premises," and it holds not only that human existence precedes human essence and thus that man is free to choose his own essence, but that he is also free to change his essence at will. He can assign himself whatever role he pleases, depending upon the circumstances. "This kind of role-assigning," says the mountebank, "is myth-making, and when it's done consciously or unconsciously for the purpose of aggrandizing or protecting your ego . . . it becomes Mythotherapy." Burlingame, master mythotherapist in search of an ego, assigns himself the masks and personae of an engaging and learned young tutor to Ebenezer and his twin sister Anna; of a mysterious and influential old gentleman named Colonel Peter Sayer; of Tim Mitchell, the son of a plantation owner and a youth of singularly original and imaginative perversities; of Lord Baltimore in London and John Coode in the New World; of friend and foe, Catholic and Protestant, white man and Indian, sexual giant and sexual incompetent. In a world characterized and convulsed, like all great fictional worlds, by the two supreme forces of love and war, Burlingame's supreme mask is that of the erotic warrior. And his penultimate act—before he begets a child by Anna and disappears—is to deploy a monstrous erection to avert a battle that would have been a much bloodier and much more terrible version of the riots that suggested how the world might end in the novels of West and Ellison.

The metamorphoses of Burlingame are matched by the metamorphoses of the poem which Ebenezer Cooke comes to America to write; and it is in this dimension of the book that *The Sot-Weed Factor* contributes its exceedingly impressive statement about the creative or visionary possibilities in our time. As originally conceived, Cooke's poem was to have been an optimistic modern apocalypse, an epic celebration of the millennium arrived at in Maryland, modeled on the *Aeneid* and called the *Marylandiad*. But after attending to the shocking disclosures of Lord Baltimore (actually, as it develops, of Burlingame disguised as Lord Baltimore, uttering a farrago of truths and inventions) about the wild disorders and double-dealings in the new world, Ebenezer decides, gasping, that Maryland "were fitter for a Jeremiad! Ne'er have I encountered such a string of plots, cabals and machinations in life or literature." Baltimore-Burlingame, however, dissuades him from the prophetic mood, and urges him to "put [Maryland's] history out of mind," to look beyond the disgraceful actualities in order to sing a visionary Maryland of moral and natural perfection. to attempt, as we should say, something like an apocalypse of imagination. This indeed is what Ebenezer makes a start on during the first months of his journeys: for example, describing the *Poseidon,* the ship that brings him to America as

A noble Ship, from Deck to Peaks,
Akin to those that Homer's Greeks
Sail'd east to Troy in Days of Yore—

though in fact, as Burlingame points out sourly, "Thou'rt sailing west . . . and the *Poseidon* is a rat's nest." But an uninterrupted experience of indignity, humiliation, and colossal vice causes Ebenezer to abandon altogether even this reconceived *Marylandiad.* "Will I sing these lies? Here's naught but scoundrels and perverts, hovels and brothels, corruption and poltroonery." It is then that he settles upon what he knows to be the only appropriate literary mode for the world he lives in: the mode of apocalyptic satire. *The Sot-Weed Factor* that he eventually composes (and which includes and expands upon the historical original) begins with a ship "freighted with fools," and a voyage of "dreadful pain"; proceeds to a "shore where no good sense is found," and to the grotesque episodes and careening duplicity in which he had himself got involved; and ends with the poet's mighty curse summoning God to visit unredeemable Maryland with the final catastrophe; "May Wrath Divine then lay these Regions wast/ Where no Man's faithful, nor a Woman chast!"

Millennial epic, Jeremiad, visionary image, apocalyptic satire: the progression is clear, and it is exemplary. Ebenezer Cooke and his poem pass through the stages that any aspiring American writer might well pass through, in our appalling and preposterous times: to discover at the end that his available subject matter is "scoundrels and perverts . . . corruption and poltroonery"; his "world" unbounded and chaotic; and his creative weapon a laughter that both scorns and illumines. *The Sot-Weed Factor* is, after all, a portrait of the artist as a mid-century American.[16]

VI

The world-pervading warfare that is at least postponed in *The Sot-Weed Factor* has become the fixed condition of life in Joseph Heller's *Catch-22* (1961). Heller's novel is set in an American airforce base off the Italian coast during what is purported to be World War II. But in fact the novel carries us once again onto that "alien scene" identified by Buber as the locale of the fictional apocalypse: something dimly reminiscent of an historical locale by virtue of being a parodic distortion thereof. Heller's is a world of absolute entrapment, of permanent apocalypse and built-in catastrophe; a world in which the human situation is coextensive with total war. In it, the endlessly recurring representative act is the act of killing, and the defining emotion is the emotion of murderous hatred. "You haven't got a chance, kid," the book's hero, a navigator named Yossarian, tells his fellow airman Clevinger, "They hate Jews."

"But I'm not Jewish," answered Clevinger.

"It will make no difference," Yossarian promised, and Yossarian was right. "They're after everybody."

Clevinger recoiled from their hatred as though from a blinding light.

"They" are all those persons in the high commands of all the armed forces, most of them nameless and faceless, who have decreed for reasons unknown and unknowable that killing is the one and constant business of men. It is *they* who, from the standpoint of Yossarian's astounded and outraged egotism, have decided to kill *him*. And it is precisely as *they* that Satan makes his enigmatic appearance in this novel; for one of his masks, in the modern world and the contemporary American novel, is just that

---

16. In his admirable and insufficiently known study *Catastrophe and Imagination* (London, 1958), John McCormick argues that the reality confronted in both English and American fiction for most of this century has been catastrophic in nature; and that the major aim—in Mr. McCormick's view, the major accomplishment—of this fiction has been to find new narrative resources for taking hold of catastrophe. *The Sot-Weed Factor,* had it appeared in time, would have provided Mr. McCormick with a paradigm for his thesis.

of a faceless, impersonal, plural anonymity. The action of *Catch-22*, such as it is, consists in Yossarian's gradual discovery of the world's secret cabal, and his emphatic signing off, in flight at the book's end in the direction of Sweden, the only war-free (or, more simply, the only free) country that conceivably remains on the face of the earth.

In the perpetual and lunatic Armageddon of *Catch-22*, all values and standards are inverted, and opposites exchange place. Heller's main comic technique, which he tends to overwork, is similarly that of instantaneous reversal ("Appleby was a fair-haired boy from Iowa who believed in God, Motherhood and the American way of life . . . and everybody who knew him liked him. 'I hate that son of a bitch,' Yossarian growled."). The comedy in the novel contains, indeed, a good deal of unabsorbed zaniness, like the funny names (Scheisskopf, A. Fortiori, and so on) that abound like funny hats at some boring gala; but as the atmosphere tightens, even the horseplay is revealed as the symptom of a genuine desperation, a stay against hysteria. Survival, in a world that has gone coldly insane, is predicated upon a talent for clowning; *Catch-22* is also, in this regard, at once an addition to and an explanation of the genre to which it belongs. And as the clowning goes forward, one becomes conscious of a deeper comedy swelling into a deeper horror. Violence, as in *Miss Lonelyhearts*, is sudden and casual: an airman, capering naked on a beach, is literally cut in two when a plane piloted by a close friend swoops too low; in Rome, an ugly Italian chambermaid is raped by another airman and thrown out of the window and killed—when the police arrive, they (*they*) ignore the murderer and arrest Yossarian for being in Rome without a pass. It is during Yossarian's subsequent night-walk through Rome that the novel's apocalyptic vision, almost drained of its laughter, becomes the spectacle of greed, lust, and cynicism and of a human misery that, in his helplessness, simply infuriates Yossarian, as it had Miss Lonelyhearts. But at the heart of the horror there throbs the universe's enigmatic and immensely cruel joke: the cosmic catch, the given steel trap in human affairs—"Catch-22," or the principle, as an old Italian woman puts it, that *they* "have a right to do anything we can't stop them from doing." It is in defiance of the universe that Yossarian makes his hurried undignified farewell to arms and takes off for Sweden; but where madness rules, desertion is the act of honor.

Toward the end of Thomas Pynchon's *V.* (1963), the novel's semihero Stencil also departs in haste for Sweden. But Stencil wants desperately to believe that he is pursuing rather than running away; that he is simply continuing his life-long quest for a phantom female of many names and appearances, now rumored to be in Scandinavia. Stencil's decision betokens his refusal to accept the hideously circumstantial report of the death of the woman V., during an air raid on Malta during the second World War—if only because the manner and occasion of the death carry a symbolism too horrible for Stencil to accept. The symbolism has to do with nothing less than the settled meaning of modern history and the final end of Western man; and to accept it would be to acknowledge that the catastrophe had already happened. *V.* is a novel of enormous if unsteady imaginative power, and a work that often blazes with poetic and intellectual energy. More than any novel of its generation, *V.* faces up to the full political, technological, and war-making fury of the modern age; and in thus being a novel quite literally *about* history and possibly about the termination of human history, it also presents the purest, most savage, and at moments the funniest of the apocalyptic visions that pervade postwar writing.

Pynchon's historico-fictional onslaught takes two forms, and the relation between them is another illumination of the resources of the contemporary novel and the reason for their being invoked. On the one hand, there is the current human condition, represented by a bunch of New York misfits known as "the whole sick crew," a phrase Pynchon perhaps adapted and ironically modernized from Michael Wigglesworth's "You sinful crew," those Christ was dispatching to hell in the poem. The sickly New Yorkers are a conglomeration of drunks and renegade artists and sterile orgiasts and race-conscious nymphomaniacs and mindless do-nothings—components of a familiar but more than usually repellent world, a world on the far side of apostasy and already doomed and judged; though amid its vicious shadows the novel's other semihero, a "schlemihl" named Benny Profane (with one or two others), tries clumsily to keep alive some fragment of human decency. And, on the other hand, there is the figure and career of V. as Stencil and the reader reconstruct them: V., whom Stencil's father, formerly a member of the British Foreign Office, had known to his peril, and whose name across the decades and in many countries seems to be anything beginning with the letter

V—Victoria, Veronica, Vera, and whatever else. These two dimensions overlap: Stencil consorts with those crew members who can contribute biographical data on V., and Benny Profane accompanies Stencil to Malta on the last recorded stage of the quest-journey. But they are two distinct modes of narrative: the pictorial and the inquisitive; the representational and the dramatic. And they relate expertly as effect and cause, as present and past, as situation and diagnosis—as the given damned condition and its historic, even mythic, origins. The lady V. and her career enact in far-reaching historical terms the sickness with which the crew is afflicted; and while V.'s "awful anarchic power" (to borrow from *The Day of the Locust*) is treated with increasing respect and awe, the domain of the sickly is the object of a sort of nauseated laughter.

V. seems to have been born around 1880; but she enters the pages of history and the novel as Victoria Wren, late of Yorkshire, during the Fashoda crisis in Cairo in 1899—that is, as she approaches her majority, as the Middle East hovers on the brink of disaster, and as the twentieth century is about to begin. Cairo, where she seduces one Goodfellow of the Foreign Office, is the scene of the first of what young Herbert Stencil calls her "young, crude Mata Hari acts"; she goes on at once to perform a similar erotico-political role with the elder Stencil in Florence. More mature, refined, and dangerous intrigues follow in various places: "until 1913," Stencil reports, "when she knew she'd done all she could and so took out time for love." The amorous interlude, a peculiarly decadent Lesbian affair with a dancer named Melanie L'Heuremaudit, takes place in Paris; the next year, it is guessed, she went to Malta where she spent the years of the first World War; Herbert's father, Sidney, unluckily discovers her on the island just after the armistice. During the 1920s she showed up as an imperial agent named Vera Meroving in German South Africa; and it seems likely that she resided in Germany itself during the Hitler '30s (though there are also obscure reports of conspiratorial activities in Spain and Asia). In any event, she was back in Malta for the second World War—"Paris for love, Malta for war," observes young Stencil. And she was probably though not certainly killed in Malta in one of the worst of its almost daily air raids. Whether or no, war was her natural environment; and the "etiology of war" (the causal explanation) was, Stencil believes, the etiology of V., while "riot," he adds, "is her atmosphere." But what she represents is something even worse than war: it is "something monstrous" that "had been building" throughout her career.

Conspiracy, perversion, war, riot, and something more monstrous altogether: V. is of course the dark lady of the apocalypse, the Whore of Babylon. In the novel, she is associated with innumerable other V-formations (Venus, Venezuela, the Maltese town of Valletta, and a nightmare never-land named Vheissu; her name V. also seems to be an ideogram of female genitality). But we recognize her at once as the fateful female successor to Melville's Confidence Man and Mark Twain's Satan, to West's super-promiser, Ellison's Rinehart, and Barth's Burlingame; the promised end and climax of an extraordinary fictional species. She is Satan himself in the guise of the Whore of Babylon, let loose upon an apostate world to hurry, enlarge, and direct the great catastrophe; and to embody and symbolize it in her own being, her own very body. Young Stencil sees her as the contriver of "the ultimate plot that has no name." Wherever she walks, there are apocalyptic tremors; and even the name of the girl she takes as her mistress on the eve of the first war means, in English, the accursed hour. But it is the nature of the cosmic curse that for long escapes definition. The elder Stencil will not believe it to have been the horrors of World War I. "Ten million dead," he cries to a friend in Malta in 1919; "Gas. Passchendale. Let that now be a very large figure . . . but dear Lord, not the Nameless Horror, the sudden prodigy sprung on the world unaware." Soon thereafter, Stencil is destroyed by (apparently) the black arts of V., who is living on the island as Veronica Manganese, a friend of D'Annunzio and Mussolini; and the prodigy he apprehends is in fact already coming into view. For the real horror is neither war nor riot nor totalitarian terror. It is that something more monstrous—it is the progress, in young Stencil's formula, "towards inanimateness."

As she magnifies into the demonic spirit and presiding goddess of modern history—as the force which historical humanity has let loose upon itself—V. becomes equally the supreme mistress of metamorphosis, and assumes that multiplicity of roles which her great traditional function calls for. She seems at the end to be truly more than human; and, like her predecessors over the ages, her ultimate role is that of the False Prophet—on Malta in the second war and during her last days, she is known as "the

Bad Priest." But her major and continuing metamorphosis is something else again. It is the process whereby a human being slowly turns herself into an inanimate thing. Early on, out of some chilling caprice, she had acquired a foot of gold and an eye of glass, and had worn a watch imbedded in the flesh of her arm. The children who ransack her broken (but still breathing) body amid the rubble on Malta discover that both her feet are made of precious metal, and that, in addition to a wig and false teeth, she secretes a star sapphire in her navel. Young Stencil, day-dreaming in 1956 and persuading himself that V. is still alive, imagines the outcome of this grotesque process in a vision that is at once absurd (scientific double-talk) and unspeakable:

> Skin radiant with the bloom of some new plastic; both eyes glass but now containing photoelectric cells. . . . Solenoid relays would be her ganglia, servo-actuators move her flawless nylon limbs. . . . A complex system of pressure transducers located in a marvelous vagina of polyethylene; the variable arms of their Wheatstone bridges all leading to a single silver cable which fed pleasure-voltages direct to the correct register of the digital machine in her skull.

Such is the end of the human world, and the obliteration of whatever is animate in humanity. Pynchon's theme—that is, to put it oversimply, the mechanization of man—is of course a familiar one, and one that began to be formulated in the early nineteenth century with the first awareness of the effect of science and technology upon the human spirit. In English-language fiction, the great predecessor of *V.* in this regard is no less obviously Lawrence's *Women in Love,* which was written during the first World War but not published until 1920. And Gudrun Brangwen, the dark Satanic goddess of that novel and a young woman whom Lawrence describes as "a new Daphne, turning not into a tree but a machine," is the detectable predecessor of V. herself. Lawrence's apocalyptic vision in *Women in Love*—his vision of worldwide disaster—is close to absolute. It includes the passing fancy of a planet swept clean of humanity and given over to animal and plant life. England, where Lawrence introduces his own sick crew as the denizens of a London café, is compared to an aged parent suffering from an incurable disease; and indeed actual as well as spiritual death (and including the long-drawn-out death of an incurably sick aged parent) invades almost every nook and cranny of the novel. But, above all, Lawrence perceives and expresses with a passion and eloquence a good deal more powerful even than Pynchon's the dreadful paradoxical coupling of mechanization and chaos—as in the famous account of the "strict, terrible, inhuman" reorganization of the coal mines by Gerald Crich, which is clearly the image of a universal development:

> It was the first step in undoing, the first great phase of chaos, the substitution of the mechanical principle for the organic.... It was pure organic distintegration and pure mechanical organization. This is the first and finest state of chaos.

Lawrence understood, too, and strained to make palpable in narrative a major symptom of the fatal modern illness, the identical symptom observed by Pynchon: a limitless and immeasurably depraved and yet willed and intellectualized and so hideously deflected eroticism; a "voluptuousness," as Lawrence puts it, that "was like that of machinery, cold and iron." Again as in *V.*, Lawrence's characters sometimes speculate about the apocalypse—they may even, like Gudrun and her new lover Loerke, "laugh out some mocking dream of the destruction of the world by a ridiculous catastrophe of man's own invention"—without any consciousness that the catastrophe has already happened; that disaster has already struck almost all of mankind. Only Birkin and Ursula, those lonesome spokesmen for the inverted or hopeful apocalypse, escape, fleeing together toward, as it were, their own "Sweden"—fleeing into "nowhere," in Birkin's phrase; for "nowhere" is the name and the location of heaven in the dying world of *Women in Love*.

But Pynchon, though he is far less assured an artist (at this stage anyhow) than Lawrence, has taken one or two steps beyond *Women in Love* in his diagnosis and his narrative tone. On the one hand, Pynchon's apocalyptic theme—and the comparisons with Lawrence help finally to make this clear—is not exactly the mechanization of man after all. It is rather the deliberate and systematic *reicization* of mankind: the transformation of persons not so much into machines as into sheer motionless *things*. That process is somehow more blood-chilling yet; but Pynchon handles it in the contemporary American manner with tigrish comedy. We recognize once more the example of Nathanael West: not only his image of the revolt of things in *Miss Lonelyhearts,* but also his sardonic narration of the dismantling of poor Lemuel Pitkin, who in the course of events had to replace various parts of himself—his teeth, an eye, a thumb, his scalp, and one leg—with artificial members, each of which was then knocked off or out each afternoon in a vaudeville act in which he was made to engage.[17] Pynchon goes beyond West too, in a vision not of the reicization by others of victimized innocence, but of all humanity by its own suicidal efforts—following the lead of its Satanic representative. The encroachment of the thing becomes, in this novel's world, the major historical motif: whether as a supplanting of the human, like the mechanical dancing figures introduced by the Germans into prewar Paris (in one of the book's moments of transparent political allegory); or as a process of conversion, like the "nose of ivory . . . check-bone of silver and . . . paraffin and celluloid chin" with which a wounded airman, V.'s sometime lover Evan Godolphin, seeks to repair his shattered visage. And it is of course in the postwar America (our America) of the whole sick crew that the act of de-animation is most evident.

The associates of Benny Profane show themselves willing if unconscious servants of the novel's Antichrist by their cheapened versions of V.'s characteristic indulgences—in their sordid malicious intriguing and their disconsolate alcoholic promiscuity. But with V. as paradigm, we can discern the more fundamental deterioration that is everywhere taking place: when, for example, a girl named Esther undergoes an operation to acquire an artificial gentile nose and, her mind caught in a confusion of surgery and sex, dreams of changing other parts of her anatomy; when a whole episode turns on the effort to steal a set of false teeth; and, most explicitly, during Benny's tour of duty as night watchman for Anthro-research Associates. His job is to guard two plastic mannikins named SHOCK and SHROUD, utterly synthetic and horribly lifelike creations of the researchers; and of an evening, he holds imaginary converse with one of them:

> "What do you mean, we'll all be like you and SHOCK someday? You mean dead?"

17. Poe provided the earliest American version of this motif, in a joking anecdote called "The Man who was Used Up," wherein the elegant General Smith is found to be composed of a cork leg, false teeth and shoulders and chest, a wig, a glass eye, and a mechanical palate.

Am I dead? If I am then that's what I mean.
"If you aren't then what are you?"
Nearly what you are. None of you have very far to go.
"I don't understand."
So I see. But you're not alone. That's a comfort isn't it?

Months later, in Malta, it seems likely that Benny does at last understand: namely, that the human impulse to transmute live flesh into metal or plastic and the scientific urge to construct mechanical men are only the outward signs of the slow deliberate and perhaps inexorable petrefaction of the human spirit that is the ultimately discoverable fact of modern history. This is the unhappy crew's real sickness unto death; and it is no doubt with this ghastly revelation in his mind that Benny, in our last glimpse of him, dashes off into "the abruptly absolute night," toward the island's cliff edge and the Mediterranean beneath.

Contemporary American fiction, or the vein of it which I have been mining, seems determined to draw us on toward that cliff edge, or to watch with a sort of bitter contemptuous laugh as we draw ourselves on—only to leave us there, swaying ambiguously, just before the sound of midnight. *Is* this the promised end? It is not the end of American fictional apocalyptics, anyhow, or even of the comical apocalypse; fiction in this manner continues to outrun the critical absorption of it. James Purdy, who had offered intimations of the end of the world in the brilliant murk of "63: Dream Palace" and *Malcolm,* has now given us a full-toned apocalyptic blast in an uproarious if sometimes uncontrolled satire on American urban life in *Cabot Wright Begins.* And there are the much more exacerbated and compulsive visions, conveyed by a desperate harrying of the resources of fiction, of William Burroughs and Hubert Selby (especially in the section of Selby's *Last Exit to Brooklyn,* appropriately called "Land's End"), each of whom seems to represent in his own way a new and spreading mood of furious hopelessness. But, at the same time, one detects symptoms of an impatient counterimpulse, a restive disclaimer of the apocalyptic temper. "Safe, comfortable people playing at crisis, alienation, apocalypse and desperation, make me sick," says the letter-writing hero of Saul Bellow's *Herzog.* "We must get it out of our head that this is a doomed time, that we are waiting for the end, and the rest of it. . . . We love apocalypses too much, and crisis ethics and florid extremism with all its thrilling language. Excuse me, no," Herzog concludes. "I've had all the monstrosity I want."

Such remarks are refreshing; one does sometimes feel the way Satan himself was said to feel some years ago in the jauntily ironic ballad by John Crowe Ransom, "Armageddon": "The immortal Adversary shook his head: . . . . 'These Armageddons weary me much,' he said." But in a sense these are just the attitudes implicit in the fiction I have been primarily concerned with. West, Ellison, and the others have without a doubt kept us well informed about everything that is cruel, deadly, inhuman, hate-filled, disruptive, congealing, and in general chaotic and destructive on our modern American scene. The apprehension of immense catastrophe is close to the heart of their imagination. But at the heart itself is a humane perspective rooted not quite in hope but in a hope about hope. The sense of the comic is at once the symptom and the executive agency of that root sensibility. For if there is a large portion of bitterness in the laughter, and if laughter sometimes seems the only response still possible in a radically graceless world, it has served nonetheless to define, to measure and assess the horror, to reveal its sources and make visible its shape. To do this is to reassert the human. These apocalyptic visions indeed are offered as weapons for averting the catastrophe.

1964

INDEX